THE RUNNING OF RICHARD NIXON

by Leonard Lurie

THE KING MAKERS
THE RUNNING OF RICHARD NIXON

LEONARD LURIE

THE RUNNING OF RICHARD NIXON

COWARD, McCANN & GEOGHEGAN, INC.
 NEW YORK

Grateful acknowledgment is hereby made to the authors and publishers for
permission to quote from the following copyrighted works:

From *Witness,* by Whittaker Chambers. Copyright © 1952 by Whittaker
Chambers. Reprinted by permission of Random House, Inc.

From *Six Crises,* by Richard M. Nixon, copyright © 1962 by Richard M.
Nixon. Reprinted by permission of Doubleday & Company, Inc.

For my Mother, Anna,
who has led a hard, honest, loving life.
She is a beauty
and the happiness of her later years brings me joy.

Acknowledgments

To my darling wife, Doris, who reads with perception and criticizes with a gentle logic that found its way into every part of this book.

To Theron Raines, my agent and friend, who wanted this book written, and whose encyclopedic mind and sound judgment helped make it possible.

To Patricia B. Soliman, my editor, whose suggestions on *The King Makers* and this book were invaluable.

And to Edward M. Allen, indexer par excellence, whose output of fifty to seventy-five books a year since 1929 has placed myself and many of my colleagues in his debt.

With gratitude,
Leonard Lurie

June, 1972

. . . a fast track. Any person tends to vegetate unless he is moving on a fast track.

—Richard M. Nixon

. . . a chronic campaigner.

—Lyndon B. Johnson

Contents

I recoil at the prospect of Mr. Nixon as custodian of this nation's future.

—Adlai E. Stevenson

THE RUNNING

OF

RICHARD

NIXON

I.

Poor Richard

"I've often wished," Hannah Nixon said after her son had been Vice President for eight years, "that Richard and his brothers had not been burdened with the hardships they had to endure as boys; they should have had more fun."

The Yorba Linda world into which Richard Milhous Nixon was born on January 9, 1913 was not a world of fun. It was a world of duty, hardship, marginal existence, religious bigotry, where the presence of death was always felt, in short, the world as it largely is, and as it is never supposed to be in Southern California.

The landscape around the Nixon house was bleak. Dick's father had built the small frame structure himself. He had selected a site on a knoll above a deep irrigation ditch. Beyond the ditch were the tracks of the Santa Fe. Freight trains rumbled by at all hours of the day, shaking the jerry-built house and making a restful night's sleep impossible. The young Nixon, knowing that joy was not a resident of Yorba Linda, often let his eyes follow the gleaming tracks into the distance, and dreamt of someday riding them to a happier place. "The train whistle," he said, "was the sweetest music I ever heard."

He was the second of five sons. They were named Harold, Richard (after "the Lion-hearted"), Donald, Arthur and Edward, as though offsprings of some English king.

Nixon's ancestors were almost exclusively Irish. His mother came from a line of Milhous Irish Quakers which went back in America to Thomas Milhous, who, penniless and in desperate need of a new start, settled in Chester County, Pennsylvania, in 1729. A relatively rare bird in Catholic Ireland, Quaker Milhous found William Penn's colony a more promising, but ultimately equally unrewarding milieu.

15

Frank Nixon, Dick's father, came from a family which had been in America almost as long as the Milhouses. Edward Nixon, of Scotch-Irish ancestry, migrated in 1753 and settled in Delaware. He was a Methodist, as were most of the future generations of Nixons, and interpreted the Bible with fundamentalist vigor.

The Milhouses and Nixons, although here much longer than most American families, accomplished little with their long head start. They were universally illiterate or semi-literate, almost always dirt farmers, invariably poor and undistinguished. Two of Edward Nixon's sons fought in the Revolution, one of them crossed the Delaware that cold night with Washington. But aside from qualifying Julie and Tricia for membership in the Daughters of the American Revolution, their exploits added little spark to the oncoming generations of Nixons.

Frank Nixon was born in 1879. His mother, Sarah Ann Wadsworth Nixon, died of tuberculosis in Ohio when he was seven. His formal education ended in the fourth grade when he dropped out to become a farmhand. From all accounts he was a man of exceptionally strong opinions, a black Irish temper—and a notorious rolling stone.

Extroverted and argumentative, he wandered the country from Ohio to Colorado and back before getting to California, earning his bread at whatever job happened to present itself. He was Jack glass worker, potter, house painter, potato farmer, sheep rancher, telephone lineman, motorman, oil field roustabout, carpenter, labor agitator, and master of none. But he was always ready to tell anyone within hearing distance, including his intimidated sons, exactly how to do everything.

Hannah Milhous Nixon was an even stronger, more forceful person. One of nine children, she settled with her family in the newly founded hamlet of Whittier, a dozen miles east of Los Angeles, in 1897. The few hundred residents were all Quakers. The town had the feeling of a religious commune, where everyone was expected to work hard and make something of himself.

When Frank rolled into Whittier there was no reason for him to feel that he had finally found a settling place. The outlines of the town had barely taken shape. There was a Quaker meetinghouse and a population of meditative, serious men and women in whom he could not possibly see his own boisterous self reflected.

Hannah Milhous changed all that. They met on February 15, 1908 and were married four months later. Frank was then thirty and unable to muster a gathering of relatives for his own wedding ceremony; he was thought by all to be a poor match for Hannah. However, Hannah's mother, who lived to be ninety-six and shared the reigning influence in the family with Hannah until her death, saw the marriage as any mother of nine would. Her ordinary-looking daughter had at least found a healthy man.

Frank and Hannah moved north to the San Joaquin Valley, but after a brief struggle to find their footing moved back to Southern California, to Yorba Linda, which was 18 miles east of Whittier. Since Frank knew more about farming than anything else, he bought that barren hillside and planted a lemon orchard.

"We hoped to coax a living from the lemon grove," Hannah Nixon said in a *Good Housekeeping* article years later. But things went as badly as they usually did for Frank.

On two occasions Richard came close to losing his life in Yorba Linda. When he was three he fell from a horse and buggy being driven by his mother. She was holding baby Donald on her lap and Richard squirmed away from the neighbor-girl who was looking after him. As he fell to the road the metal-rimmed buggy wheel grazed his scalp. During the desperate 25-mile drive to the hospital, he bled from a gash which stretched from his forehead to his neck. The doctor told Hannah that they had arrived barely in time to save him. The scar remains, hidden by the careful parting of his hair.

The following year he almost succumbed to pneumonia, in those days frequently fatal. After the buggy accident he was susceptible to motion sickness, which was most acute in automobiles, and after the pneumonia he was often prey to severe illnesses.

Finally at the end of their rope, after years of exhausting and frustrating effort, the family returned to Whittier, where Hannah's mother could exercise her stabilizing influence. "After we had moved," Hannah commented morosely, "oil was found under the lemon grove—oil that would have made us millionaires if we had remained—but while we were there, the lemon grove only kept us poor."

This was a period of general prosperity just before World War I, but the Nixons were living from hand to mouth. "Many days I had nothing to serve but cornmeal. I'd bring it to the table and exclaim, 'See what we have tonight—wonderful cornmeal!' And they would gobble it up as if it were the most delectable of dishes."

Back in Whittier Frank managed the down payment on a ramshackle gas station out by a crossroad where there was no competition for miles. It was 1922 and Dick was ten. Frank had been married for fourteen years and was still living at a subsistence level. The station proved to be his first lucky business move. Although he never became more than modestly successful, the family was relatively secure from this moment on.

Slowly Frank and Hannah managed to build up the business. Milk was stocked in a refrigerator near the gas pumps. When that worked out, additional grocery items were offered for sale. Frank enlarged the grocery line by buying the old Quaker meetinghouse across the road, which was being replaced, California-style, with something a few years newer, and moving it next to the gas station. It now became the "Nixon Market." The family lived at the back of the store.

Dick described his father as "cantankerous." But he saw his mother in a different light. "My mother is the complete opposite. My mother is the gentlest, most considerate woman. She never turned a tramp away from the door. That was one of the things she and my dad used to argue about. My father thought they ought to be made to work before helping them out."

Hannah was often described as a quiet, helpful woman. She was a devout Quaker, who used the soft *thee* and *thou* when speaking to her mother and sisters, though those terms of archaic endearment were not used in her own home. Nixon's associate and biographer Ralph de Toledano, whose admiration for her son was only somewhat dimmed by the years, described Hannah bluntly in an interview with me in October, 1971. "She was tough."

In *One Man Alone* he said it with more restraint. "In her slight and gentle way Hannah Nixon was a woman of iron, annealed in a Quaker sense of duty."

In 1960 Hannah suggested that the differences between Frank and herself might not have always made life easy. "My husband himself had talents as a debater and used to turn our store into a kind of club, where he debated the customers on political issues while I tried to soothe them, so they would continue buying from us." Hannah had a well-developed business sense. She might have been expected to say that she tried Quaker-fashion to soothe everyone's temper because she abhorred violence. Instead, she concerned herself with the practical side of the question.

The relationship between Hannah and her second son was marked by her austerity and reserve. "I always called him Richard [although she learned to call her grandchild Richie] and he always called me Mother."

Richard seemed to suffer from the sense of being ignored that many second sons experience. Not only did he have an older brother, but he had three younger ones. He invented ruses to keep from being lost in the crowd. Although a successful student, he insisted on having his mother around when her workday was over and he was at his books.

"As a youngster, Richard seemed to need me more than my four other sons did," Hannah remarked candidly. "As a schoolboy, he used to like to have me sit with him when he studied. . . . But it wasn't that Richard needed my help with his work. Rather, it was that he just liked to have me around."

Nixon commented years later that his A average in high school Latin was attributable to her help. Apparently time had dimmed his recollection of the type of help he sought from her.

His intense dependence on her is powerfully illustrated in a strangely perverse story he wrote when he was ten. In a flight of fantasy that suggests a well-developed secret world in which a troubled youngster sought comfort, Richard framed his story as a letter to his mother. He pictured himself as a dog.

> My Dear Master,
> The two boys that you left me with are very bad to me. Their dog, Jim, is very old and he will never talk or play with me.
> One Saturday the boys went hunting. Jim and myself went with them. While going through the woods one of the boys triped [sic] and fell on me. I lost my temper and bit him. He kiked [sic] me in the side and we started on. While we were walking I saw a black round thing in a tree. I hit it with my paw. A swarm of black thing [sic] came out of it. I felt a pain all over. I started to run and as both of my eys [sic] were swelled shut I fell into a pond. When I got home I was very sore. I wish you would come home right now.
>   Your good dog
>   Richard

University of California professor psycho-historian Michael Rogin, who discussed this letter in the November, 1971, issue of *Transaction* magazine, chose to analyze it in terms of anal symbolism. What stands out more clearly, though, is Richard's portrait of himself as poorly treated by others, as abused, as short-tempered and given to striking back, and then as being punished unjustly. The final, most poignant note in the letter, the note at which Richard had taken deadly aim in his self-pitying story, was his plaintive plea, "I wish you would come home right now." Although always in the house, Hannah was apparently too remote, too busy with her large family and the daily struggle to be at home for him.

Making his role as second son even more difficult was the illness of two of his brothers. In 1925 his youngest brother, Arthur, who was seven, became ill with what has been described as tubercular meningitis. Harold, Richard and Donald were sent to stay with Frank's sister in nearby Fullerton. In less than two weeks Arthur was dead.

"I can still see Richard when he came back," Hannah said, recalling that terrible moment. "He slipped into a big chair and sat staring into space, silent and dry-eyed in the undemonstrative way in which, because of his choked, deep feeling, he was always to face tragedy."

Whatever thoughts were passing through Richard's mind, he never saw fit to expose them to his mother. From earliest youth he revealed as little of himself as possible.

Although only thirteen and already hard working beyond his years, Richard seemed, in Hannah's eyes, clearly changed by this tragedy. "I think it was Arthur's passing that first stirred within Richard a determination to help make up for our loss by making us very proud of him. Now his need to succeed became even stronger."

His effort to excel in everything and win the approval of his parents became obsessive. He had always done his share of chores in the store. However, at sixteen he was put in charge of the fruit and vegetable counter. Brother Donald described his routine: "He had to get up at three or four in the morning, and drive the truck into LA to market. Then, when he brought the load back, he dumped the vegetables in a big tub out back, and washed them off." This was followed by the setting up of the display, a process which his mother says he did with great care and pride.

He then put in a full day at school, returned home to work in the store, and finally, according to Donald, "Dick used to go up into the bell tower [of the converted church-store] which was the store's office, to study by himself at night. . . . Many's the time the delivery men who came before dawn would find him with his light still on, after studying all night." Donald helped with the meat and Harold did his share, but neither did as much as Richard. The demon that drove him was unique even in this industrious family.

Just when Richard should have been receiving accolades from his parents for his strenuous efforts, fate stepped in to cheat him. Harold contracted tuberculosis, and so became the center of his parents' thoughts. By the time Richard was eighteen, Harold's illness was so severe that Hannah told him to put plans for applying to Harvard out of his mind. She explained, "We needed Richard at home."

However, Harold, she was told, would do better in Arizona. In that day of primitive understanding of tuberculosis, climate was mistakenly thought to be a cure. Not that the climate in Whittier was bad. The sun shone practically every day. But at a crucial moment like this there must be no quibbling. If Arizona was going to provide the slightest advantage for Harold, then the trip must be made.

However, Frank was reluctant to go and Hannah had practical reservations about his leaving. He had rolled far enough in his life. Now past fifty, he had finally established a surviving business. Was he to abandon it? The question must have seemed especially grotesque in the early 1930's with the Depression deepening daily.

After months of agonizing Hannah packed some baggage and took Harold to Tucson. The impact on Richard was devastating. Despite everything he had done to be an obedient and deserving son, he had been deserted by his mother and for what may have seemed to a second son the worst possible reason. His older brother, who except for coughing spells seemed perfectly normal, was going off alone with his mother. Once again Harold—always first, always older and wiser, always taller, always listened to more at- tentively—was usurping his mother's affection.

Hannah stayed in Tucson for two years. She earned some money to support Harold by nursing other tubercular patients in her apartment. Back in Whittier the already puritan family routine degenerated into a Spartan regimen. For Richard life became a series of repetitious flash cards, work and study, interspersed with a few hours of reluctantly taken sleep. Without his mother, the drabness of the bell tower and the apartment behind the store became crushing. Mealtime, which had been a family ritual marked by Bible reading and Hannah's ascetic benevolence, became an ordeal pervaded by Frank's unrelieved gloom. He was already suffering from the bleeding ulcers that eventually led to his death. The three of them ate out of cans and there was no Hannah around to tell them how delicious it was.

As soon as school was over, Richard left his father and Donald and headed for Tucson, despite their reluctance. If anything, he was needed more than ever in the store, as Hannah's tactful management was sorely missed. Without Richard, Frank's existence during those two summers became a trial.

In Tucson Richard strove to please. He got a part-time job at Prescott's Slippery Gulch Rodeo. This was his first serious venture into commerce outside the family circle and the compromises began immediately. He became a barker for the Wheel of Fortune, his task to lure the suckers into the tent where the gambling concessionaire maintained a slick fleecing operation.

In his time off, Richard devoted himself completely to Hannah and Harold, bustling around on errands for them in the punishing heat of the Tucson summers.

After two years of isolation from her family Hannah returned to Whittier. Harold insisted. He was lonely in Tucson. The financial drain of maintaining two households and paying doctor bills had left them close to bankruptcy. Years later Nixon wrote a letter to British journalist Peregrine Worsthorne explaining his attitude toward government aid to the needy and illustrating his convictions with reference to this terrible period in his life.

During the Depression, he pointed out, he could not accept the New Deal philosophy "due to a strong streak of individualism which probably was more than anything else rooted in my family background. . . . We had drilled into us the idea that we should if at all possible take care of ourselves and not expect others to take care of us."

He told of Worsthorne of Harold's five-year "catastrophic illness" which financially destroyed the family. Their doctor advised them to put Harold in a county tuberculosis hospital "not only so that he could get more adequate care but in order to relieve us of the financial burden."

With a note of pride Nixon wrote that his parents "adamantly refused." They were "almost fierce in their adherence to what is now deprecatingly referred to as puritan ethics," and considered it "wrong from a moral standpoint" to accept help from the government.

Although his parents were convinced Harold would receive "more adequate care" at the county hospital, their pride would not allow him that chance. They would work harder, they would shatter the family, they would deprive themselves of everything but they would never have the sense of guilt that would have burdened them if they had accepted help from Franklin Roosevelt.

Back in Whittier Richard made every attempt to show how hard he was trying to save his brother, but, under the circumstances, nothing could help. Hannah described the moment in a strangely detached tone:

> One morning, after we had returned to Whittier, Harold asked Richard to drive him to town to buy me a birthday present. Harold chose an electric mixer. Richard took Harold home, then went to his college classes. When he got there, however, he was told that he was wanted at home. When he got back to the house, we had to tell him Harold had died suddenly and unexpectedly.
>
> Hearing the shocking news, Richard, who was twenty, behaved very much the same way he had behaved when Arthur had died eight years before. He sank into a deep, impenetrable silence. From that time on, it seemed that Richard was trying to be *three* sons in one, striving even harder than before to make up to his father and me for our loss. With the death of Harold his determination to make us proud of him seemed greatly intensified. Unconsciously, too, I think that Richard may have felt a kind of guilt that Harold and Arthur were dead and that he was alive.

Hannah was universally thought to be a completely honest woman. When she clearly saw Richard's sense of guilt, she could not restrain her impulse to speak of it. There were obviously some things more important to her than her son's peace of mind, and one of them apparently was her own commitment always to be truthful. It is such qualities that make it difficult to live with saints.

II.

The Starting Gun

Richard Nixon recalled he was "dressed in hand-me-downs mostly in grammar school." However he always treated his brothers' legacies with meticulous care. Even as a young boy he determined to appear correctly dressed in public, his tie always neatly squared under his chin. It was not a sense of style that alerted him at such an early age to the importance of clothing. Rather, he seemed resolved to conform perfectly to the image of the good student popular at that time. Hannah remarked, "My sister used to help me with the ironing when I was working both at home and in the family grocery store. But she served notice: 'Give me anything to iron but Richard's shirts. He's too fussy.'"

Along with the fussiness went an insatiable desire to achieve. Nixon explains this by referring to his father: "He was a very competitive man. He always instilled this competitive feeling in all of us—I guess I acquired my competitive instinct from him. He was a fighter. He loved to argue with anybody about anything. . . . He very much wanted me to win."

And the drive to succeed was all-pervasive in Richard's family. In part it was very much a phenomenon of the time. Andrew Carnegie, John D. Rockefeller and Teddy Roosevelt were the epitome of the successful men, men who had surmounted early handicaps to become leaders by sheer power of will and ceaseless effort.

"We all worked like hell—we had to. There was a drive to succeed, to survive almost." It is revealing to see Nixon so clearly combine the ideas of survival and success.

"My mother and father instilled in us the desire to get going, to be good not just at one single thing but at everything. . . . We had a disciplined family—we always had to clean up our plates at a meal. My father was a real disciplinarian."

23

Frank was quick with his fists, the strap, the rattan or anything else within reach when it came to punishing his sons for some breach of his codes. However, Richard was never able to recall a single instance in which his father had ever had reason to discipline him: "Dad was very strict and expected to be obeyed under all circumstances. If he wanted something he wanted it at once. He had a hot temper, and I learned early that the only way to deal with him was to abide by the rules he laid down. Otherwise, I would probably have felt the touch of a ruler or strap as my brothers did."

The picture Nixon painted of his youth was almost unrelievedly grim. "We never had any vacations. . . . I never went hunting or fishing or anything like that—there wasn't time." It was not lack of money that kept him from these common boyhood pleasures—it was time. With so many things to do, and so little time, the first thing to be sacrificed was the frivolity of pleasure. Occasional family gatherings became tense confrontations where Richard's account-keeping mind did not allow him to relax. "He was also reticent when it came to such social affairs as picnics," his mother recalled. "He used to say that people took home, from among the leftovers, more food than they brought with them in the first place."

It may not have been polite for Richard to notice such things, but his mother seemed at least as indiscreet in her willingness to expose her son's ungenerous reaction and his more intimate worries to public view. "He used to be very fastidious," she confided, when describing his preparation for the daily bus trip to high school. "Each morning he would take great pains in brushing his teeth, was careful to gargle, and asked me to smell his breath to make sure he would not offend anyone on the bus."

This same preoccupation with success showed itself as soon as he entered school. During all the years he spent in elementary school he was never late. His teachers uniformly described him as "hard working" and "serious." At an early age he had already become interested in developing the facility which was to enable him to rise in the world. "I remember my first debate in fifth grade at school. The subject was 'Resolved, that it is better to own your own home than to rent.' I was on the renting side.'' His father's propensity for debating anyone who came into the store, despite the possibility that a paying customer might be alienated, impressed Richard with the importance of verbal facility. His father encouraged him to sharpen his forensic skills. In this first debate, "Father sat down and did a lot of figuring and proved that it was more economical to rent than to own—he very much wanted me to win." Nixon recalled, "It was a sort of tradition in our family that whatever you did you had to do as well as you could."

However, there were certain things that were impossible for Richard to do well. He was poorly coordinated, and athletic achievement was out of the question. This did not prevent him from trying, though. But since grim determination could take a boy with two left feet only so far down the field toward the goal line, how much more reasonable to play to one's strength. If your feet could not run smoothly, but your tongue could, then the wise course was to stand still and keep your mouth moving.

There was a torment in this advice, for Richard Nixon not only found physical coordination difficult, he found speaking painful. His mother, once again pulled no punches: "Richard, as a boy, was not much for social chatter—or any other kind of talk. He was so tight-lipped, as a matter of fact, that he could always be trusted with a secret."

He needed privacy and avoided conversation. In Yorba Linda the boys shared a large room. However, when they moved to Whittier and more space was available Harold, Donald and Arthur shared a room, while Richard asked for and was given a small room of his own. But even the sanctuary of his own room was not enough. More often he sought the solitude of the bell tower, where visitors were even less likely to find their way.

Brother Donald also remembers his close-mouthed ways. "Dick was always a deep thinker. Some people thought he was aloof or stuck-up because he walked right past them in the street without seeing them. He got totally wrapped up in his thoughts. . . . At family picnics, he would always go off by himself. . . . Even now, he likes to ride in the car with friends or members of his family, because we know he doesn't want to waste time talking. He can't stand small talk."

Every description of the young Nixon agrees on one point. He was "painfully shy." Classmates in high school and college concur: "He was personally somewhat shy." "Basically aloof . . . very careful to keep people from getting too close to him." "He was not what you would call a real friendly guy." "He tended somewhat to shyness."

How strange it was for a young man who was so reserved to make up his mind to excel in public speaking, and a particularly combative type of public speaking—debating—at that. It was not that he could simply deliver a speech he had carefully memorized. It was necessary for him to make his points and then defend his position in an impromptu, pressured situation, where a slip of the tongue could bring instant disgrace. To make matters worse, his father insisted on attending his son's every formal high school and college debate. Mrs. Nixon said, "I can still see my husband driving Richard and his forensic manager to tournaments. Sitting in the audience, Mr. Nixon would hang on Richard's every word." Imagine Dick struggling to clinch an argument while Frank sat conspicuously in view, always involved, always telegraphing his every reaction to a point made or missed with exaggerated gestures of pleasure or disgust. No wonder Dick quickly developed the ability to talk his way out of any situation. His high school debating coach, Mrs. Norman Vincent, recalled she felt "disturbed" at his facility, for "He had this ability to kind of slide round an argument instead of meeting it head on, and he could take any side of a debate."

In 1928 he represented the West Coast high schools in the National Oratorial Contest. But he knew his limits. He constantly cautioned his brothers against getting into debates with their father, and personally insisted on avoiding arguments with the champ. It must have been a point of occasional secret vexation for him to realize that no matter how good he was, he could never be the best.

When Richard graduated from high school he was at the top of his class— an intellectual by Whittier's undemanding standards. And when he went to college he stayed in the same small pond. He chose Whittier College, just down the road. Whittier was a minimal challenge, drawing its approximately 400 students exclusively from the area's Quakers. Many a successful bank manager and car salesman has graduated from Whittier, but few philosophers. Richard was admitted on a partial scholarship provided by a fund left by Hannah's father, Franklin, a prosperous fruit farmer. Intent on looking after his own, Franklin had left instructions that his bequest was to be used only for scholarships "for my children and their descendants."

Richard's aloofness persisted into college. Although many admired his persistence and respected his determination to succeed, there is no one from his Whittier days who has come forward to say he considered Richard Nixon his friend. He seems to have gone through his adolescence without establishing a single meaningful relationship. A classmate wrote about him years later: "Dick was not universally popular in college because he was not what you would call a real friendly guy and, as most scholars, he had little time for activities which result in popularity. Many students felt Dick was above them in thinking and that probably he didn't care to associate with them. . . . Dick lived somewhat abnormally. He studied a great deal and worked in the store. It wasn't uncommon for him to work himself ill."

At Whittier he majored in history, in preparation for law school. He joined the debating team and quickly became its captain. Proudly he brought home his debating trophies and medals to present to his mother, who kept them in the top drawer of her bureau.

For athletic ability he substituted energy. "I was a lousy football player," he admitted in later years. "But I remember Chief Newman, our football coach, saying 'there's one thing about Nixon, he plays every scrimmage as though the championship were at stake.' That's the competitive characteristic—I suppose it goes back to my dad."

He made the freshman team because eleven men were needed and only eleven applied. For the next four years, perpetually on the squad against which the first team scrimmaged, Nixon served as an animated tackling dummy. His coach was one of the few people in his life who was not overwhelmed by Richard's capacity for hard work. "Weeks would go by and he wouldn't even play a minute, but he'd hardly ever miss practice, and he worked hard. He was wonderful for morale, because he'd sit there and cheer the rest of the guys, and tell them how well they'd played. To sit on a bench for four years isn't easy."

Another teammate remembered his getting into a game every once in a while, after the contest was either so thoroughly forfeit or so safely wrapped up that it did not make any difference *what* he did. Invariably, the teammate said, when Nixon was on the field he knew a "five-yard penalty was coming up. Richard had such determination to win that he would rush ahead before the play started, oblivious to the quarterback's signals. I knew he'd be offside just about every play."

Off the field, he remained distant and apart, and there is no trace of any of that tremendous energy being expended on casual flirtation or romance. His mother recalled, "Richard was not much of a mixer in college, either. He never had any special buddy, and on what dates he had during his college years he talked not of romance but about such things as what might have happened to the world if Persia had conquered the Greeks or what might have happened if Plato had never lived."

His lack of success with girls—he was, after all, a Big Man on Campus—is as startling as his success as a campus politician. He campaigned hard, without a touch of winsomeness, and was annointed senior class president. (One classmate said, "I would put him down as the man least likely to succeed in politics.") But despite the cachet of dating the class president, no status-seeking coed appeared to share his passion for Cyrus the Great. A classmate recalled she "thought Dick Nixon was too stuck-up." Another said, "There was always about him an intensity of purpose, a tremendous drive which was perhaps in itself what made him seem brusque, almost brash. He was not generally liked by the girls whom I knew best, one of whom detested his admitted cockiness."

Girls are not one of the publicly acknowledged interests of monks, and the Richard Nixon of Whittier days, dour, withdrawn, silent for long periods of time, utterly devoted to his books, resembled nothing more than an unfrocked monk too dazzled by the variety of the outside world to venture beyond the monastery walls.

The Whittier college yearbook for 1934 reinforced the image of an isolated, strangely remote figure. "Although political dictators managed to cause as much trouble as possible, Dick Nixon came through the melee unscathed with the title of student body president." Accompanying this rather cryptic comment was a cartoon showing a group of seniors lounging informally, talking and laughing. The artist placed Nixon at the very center of his drawing, but while the rest are clearly enjoying themselves, Richard stands alone, neatly dressed, completely devoid of emotion—solemnly dominating the group, but not a part of it.

His drama coach, Dr. Albert Upton, remembered Richard once playing a lonely old innkeeper. At one point he had to appear alone on stage, weeping. "I told him, 'Dick, if you just concentrate real hard on getting a big lump in your throat, I think you can cry real tears.' He did, too—buckets of tears."

He must have welcomed the opportunity to play that cathartic role, for there were buckets of tears in the young Nixon.

III.

Richard the Apostate

Dick Nixon took his religion seriously. There was no alternative for a child of Hannah desperate for her approval. His great-grandmother and great-great grandmother had been itinerant preachers for the Society of Friends, and all family meals began with prayers and Bible verses. Hannah's mother, Almira Milhous, a matriarchal figure of awesome dimensions, addressed Dick as "thee" and left a well-marked trail of religiosity during her frequent visits.

"We used to go to church four times a day on Sunday," Nixon recalled. "Sunday school, then church, then Christian Education, then church in the evening." Wednesday nights were also reserved for churchgoing. This routine continued through college. Hannah remarked, "Whittier College was under the control of the Quakers. He used to go to church three times on Sunday and once at midweek."

When he was admitted to Duke Law School, now close to twenty-two and no longer under direct family scrutiny, he continued to attend the Raleigh North Carolina Quaker church, although not with predictable regularity. In short, until his mid-twenties Richard Nixon was the very model of the well-brought-up God-fearing Christian. His mother persisted in her hope that he might decide to become a Quaker preacher. "She wanted me to become a missionary in Central America," Nixon revealed, and if he had not won a full scholarship to Duke, he might possibly have bent to his mother's will. While in Whittier he played the church organ and taught Sunday school. He did not drink, swear or smoke and never danced.

It was unrealistic of Richard's mother and grandmother to think he would follow the old-time religion with the same vigor they exhibited. His mother's brand of Indiana-based Quakerism lost its hold on him during the period when she went off to Arizona with Harold. This abandonment by her brought him closer to his father. Frank had been brought up in a "Bible-pounding" Methodist family, and had the questionable loyalty toward his wife's religion of any convert. Richard testified to this revisionist streak in his father in an article he wrote for Billy Graham's magazine *Decision* in November, 1962.

> I remember vividly the day just after I entered high school, when my father took me and my two brothers to Los Angeles to attend the great revival meetings being held there by the Chicago evangelist, Dr. Paul Rader.

Frank the Apostate was leading his sons down the same path. Nixon made the point that his mother was unaware of what was going on. This fundamentalist meeting, remembered more than thirty years later, was a turning point in Richard's religious life. Although always secretive about his religious beliefs, he unexpectedly admitted:

> We [his father and brothers] joined hundreds of others that night in making our personal commitments to Christ and Christian service.

From this point on Nixon's religion was hybrid. He was now a Quaker-Fundamentalist, more anxious, in later life, to follow Billy Graham than George Fox.

His change of stance is clear in his support of the move to eliminate compulsory Sunday chapel attendance at Whittier. A practical young man, he quickly realized that with the shortage of time available in the work week it was illogical to spend hours each week silently meditating truths which were self-evident, to which he had committed himself in the presence of Donald, Edward and his father. And so, as Hannah noticed, but was unable to explain, "Thinking compulsory chapel was wrong, he helped bring about a change in the regulations." Beyond a doubt he had rationalizations for his position that "slipped round" the central facts smoothly enough so that his mother came to accept this breach in her faith as a higher form of moral understanding. One can almost hear Richard stoutly maintaining that truly devout men could speak to God in any setting. Score a solid point for Dr. Rader.

Taken by itself, this sign of apostasy could be written off as insignificant—a token rebellion in a life otherwise oppressively conformist. However, in retrospect, it appears to have been one of the early omens of a new attitude toward God which represented a sharp break with his mother's family.

The one thing that is apparent about this split is that Richard never wanted it. He never deliberately rejected Quaker ideals. He simply sloughed them off, one at a time, as the need arose.

For example, having lost the election as class president in high school by a hair, Richard seemed unwilling to risk that possibility in college. As the time for senior elections drew near there seemed to be only one issue that captured the interest of the student electors. They wanted to be able to dance at school socials. The administration, recognizing temptation in one of its more masterful disguises, determined to draw the line.

Despite Richard's personal distaste for dancing and his conviction that it led to carnal abuse, he adopted dance reform as his issue. His slogan was "A Dance a Month" if he was elected president. Young people were going to dance, he maintained. Since this was inevitable, wouldn't it be wiser to have them dance on campus under proper Christian supervision, rather than forcing them to frequent those downtown dives where those who entered checked their religion with their hats.

The Whittier yearbook, rhapsodizing over his enlightened administration, pointed out the shrewdness of his approach: "On a platform advocating a new deal for those who enjoy the social niceties, he stormed to his position."

Nixon was one of twenty-two students admitted to the newly created Duke University Law School in 1934. The Duke tobacco family, anxious to improve its image, was distributing full scholarships to any top-man-in-the-class from out of state who was willing to spend three years in Durham. Hannah and Frank supplied him with thirty-five dollars a month. Making another major compromise with his principles, he supplemented his income by accepting thirty-five cents an hour from F.D.R.'s National Youth Administration for doing law library research. Great need called for great compromise.

Even with this government dole he was forced to live in a ramshackle farmhouse a mile from the campus, which he shared with three other students. They were so poor that they were unable to afford electric lights or running water. The four slept in two double beds, their only source of heat a potbellied stove, which they loaded with newspapers on chilly Carolina nights.

Although he continued to show a willingness to bend, now downing an occasional beer despite his Quaker pledge, Nixon was essentially the somber, diligent loner he had always been. Although his classmates elected him president of their tiny graduating class, they apparently felt no closer to him than had any of the students who had put him in office in Whittier. They nicknamed him "Gloomy Gus."

One of his roommates drew a depressing sketch: "Nixon usually got up one or two hours before the rest of us, anywhere from 5:00 to 6:00 o'clock. We out-voted him on the matter of the stove, so that he couldn't light the fire, which meant that he got up in the chill and damp of the dawn, dressed in the dark or semi-dark without the benefit of any heat, and left for school in order to get in an hour or two of study before school started. . . ."

Another classmate said, "My impression was that Richard Nixon was not an exceptionally brilliant student, however he was outstanding because of his ability to do prodigious amounts of work. . . . He was a man of such high ambition and a man capable of pursuing his ambition with such intensity that I . . . believe he would and could do whatever was necessary to attain the goal he had set for himself."

There seemed to be no improvement in his social life. Richard never went to any of the numerous campus parties, and another law student recalled, "I never heard of him having a date with a girl the whole time he was in law school. . . . My original impression of him in law school—basically aloof, very sure of himself, and very careful to keep people from getting too close to him."

Still another classmate, who undoubtedly voted for him, observed: "He did not encourage comradeship. My impression is that he was a very studious individual—almost fearfully so. I can see him sitting in the law library hunched over a book, seldom even looking up. He never smiled to my knowledge, and wore a very solemn expression."

Again and again the same theme. "On Saturday nights and Sundays when most of the law students were doing a little celebrating or out courting some of the girls, Dick was usually in the library studying. He certainly gave no indication of being interested in women or in wasting his time socializing."

Despite his interest in campus politics, however, Nixon never expressed any desire to pursue a political career after graduation. His concern seemed to be with business law. He wrote an article that appeared in the Duke *Journal of Law and Contemporary Problems,* entitled "The Changing Rule of Liability in Automobile Litigation." He seemed to be equipping himself to become an ambulance chaser.

June, 1937 was a bad time to graduate. Franklin Roosevelt, thinking that the economy was headed up and wanting to redeem his 1932 pledge to balance the budget, cut back severely on government pump-priming expenditures. He underestimated the effect government spending was having on economic recovery. The result was that as Richard emerged from the sheltered halls of Duke, the country was slipping back into a period of greater unemployment and uncertainty.

At this pivotal juncture in his life, when he was in the process of laying out his career, his determination was to set himself up as far away from Whittier as possible. Washington was fine, New York equally attractive, but if an opening had appeared in Kalamazoo there is every indication he would have made a strenuous effort to land it. So loath was he to practice law in California that he made no plans to take the state's bar examination.

He applied immediately for a job with the FBI. Later he explained, "The FBI looked very good to a young lawyer that year." While he waited for J. Edgar Hoover to make up his mind, he went to New York. With his usual tenacity he made the rounds of the most prestigious firms. He was rejected by Donovan, Leisure, Newton, and Lombard, one of the giants in corporate law, and John Foster Dulles' firm, gilt-edged Sullivan and Cromwell, among others. Finally after desperately and unsuccessfully trying to get some response from the FBI (which was giving him serious consideration), he reluctantly returned to Whittier.

Realist that he was, once convinced that dreams of Wall Street gold were fantasies, he headed home, where he knew *some* gold, if of a lower grade, could be found. He immediately buried himself in stacks of California law books and supplemented his reading with a cram course, leaving, Nixon-style, as little to chance as possible. On November 9, 1937, he was among the 46 per cent of the successful applicants sworn in before the California Supreme Court.

Having cleared this major obstacle, he made directly for that Dickensian-named law firm in his home town, Wingert and Bewley. Evelyn Dorn, who was his first secretary and took care of Hannah Nixon's correspondence until her death, spoke of her former boss in 1968:

> He came in to see Mr. Bewley and I knew, after one glance, I had just met a very serious young man. His grandfather had known Mr. Bewley's grandfather back in Indiana.
> The first thing he did was to go to work on the library books, putting them in order. His law experience was mainly probating and oil lease contracts. He would sleep on the couch in the office some nights; after awhile he opened a branch in La Habra—it was just a desk in a real estate office. He was living above a garage in Fullerton.
> I used to come into the office in the morning and work around my desk for fifteen or twenty minutes before he looked up and said, "Oh, good morning, Evelyn." He doesn't let anything interrupt his concentration.

He was now firmly intent on financial success, and was willing to venture away from his law practice into a processing industry in order to achieve it. He conceived of an ingenious new way to merchandise orange juice. It would be frozen and shipped to dealers all over the country. Evelyn Dorn, who was working for Donald in 1968, still suffered as she thought of their failure. "We all worked so hard on Citra-Frost, his idea for a frozen orange juice company. It was a great idea, as other attempts later proved, but we couldn't find the right container. We were freezing it in plastic bags, which didn't hold up. The failure of Citra-Frost was a great disappointment to him."

Still, he was a young man, barely twenty-five. His failure as an entrepreneur convinced him to devote all his energies to the law. Richard Nixon was as suited to corporate law as Louis Armstrong was to the trumpet. But he was a rather specialized personality—a lawyer who would have been content searching out obscure precedents and accumulating voluminous briefs which would be noted for their compendious triviality. During that first year with Mr. Bewley's grandson, though, he found himself dealing instead with an aspect of the law that caused him endless distress. He was assigned a number of divorce cases.

Years later when talking about it to Stewart Alsop it was clear he had not yet gotten over the trauma:

"I remember when I'd just started law practice, I had a divorce case to handle, and this good-looking girl, beautiful, really, began talking to me about her intimate marriage problems."

"And you were embarrassed?"

"Embarrassed? I turned fifteen colors of the rainbow. I suppose I came from a family too unmodern, really. Any kind of personal confession is embarrassing to me generally. I can discuss the issues, general subjects. . . . But any letting down my hair, I find embarrassing."

Experience in the world outside the Whittier monastery tends to be embarrassing. True, the torments of sibling rivalry were over, the long silences of the bell tower no longer had to be endured, and a cantankerous, hot-tempered father who expected to be obeyed under all circumstances had lost his direct dominion, but the ghosts of such a martyrdom have a way of racking their victim long after they should have been laid to rest.

By the end of his first year, he was made a partner and the new name of the firm became the absolutely Gothic, Wingert, Bewley and Nixon. From his rear desk in the La Habra real estate office he took on the minuscule responsibilities of Town Attorney. Quickly he became the Assistant City Attorney (under Bewley) and police prosecutor in Whittier. His duties were simple but satisfying to a man of his temperament. If the cafe sold too much booze to its sinful customers Dick would call out the police force (it was barely large enough to handle a problem of this magnitude) and the rummies would be collared as they attempted to stagger away down side alleys. If the violation was flagrant, the lion-hearted Assistant City Attorney would obtain a court order with the proper number of seals and ribbons, and close the place.

RICHARD THE APOSTATE   35

There is enough work in such affairs to fill up a lifetime. Had Richard been forty-five or fifty, such employment with its undeniable contributions to the orderly functioning of the community might have contented him. But he had too much energy to sit smug for any length of time behind the desk at the rear of the store.

He became a member of the Whittier 20-30 Club, a kind of Junior Chamber of Commerce, where the younger set served out their apprenticeship while waiting to be inducted into the varsity team. He registered for the first time on June 5, 1938 and became a member of the Republican Party of Los Angeles county. Other honors came his way. He was elected to the Whittier College Board of Trustees at twenty-six, its youngest member ever.

However, his prolonged bachelorhood was becoming a matter for comment. Successful lawyers had wives. Never one to let a perceived disadvantage go uncorrected, Nixon almost appears to have set out deliberately to marry. Jack Drown, whose service in this instance won him the unique distinction of being one of Nixon's long-time acquaintances, told Dick of "a gorgeous redhead" who was active in the Whittier Women's Club drama group. Richard immediately went for a tryout at the playhouse and got a date with Pat Ryan. Then, on their first night out together, after knowing her for only a few hours, he proposed. "I thought he was nuts or something," Pat confessed years later. "I guess I just looked at him. I couldn't imagine anyone saying anything like that so suddenly."

Pat had had a hard life, more difficult in most respects than Richard's. Her father was a miner in Ely, Nevada, when she was born. Economic conditions were so bad that they migrated to California when she was two. Her mother died when she was twelve. Her father five years later. She experienced all the deprivations commonly visited on orphans and, to survive, she developed a will of iron and a tough protective, coolly competent veneer. She worked her way through USC, partly with the money she earned as a Hollywood extra. When Dick met her, she was teaching typing and shorthand at Whittier High School.

A girl with this stern background was hardly likely to view such an unexpected proposal without suspicion. She turned him down out of hand, apparently as nonplussed by him as the other girls who had crossed his path.

Richard was not completely open with his mother about his attitude toward Pat. Hannah had to guess at the nature of their relationship, and the outward signs posted by these two extremely private people were often misleading. "Writers like to say that Richard fell in love with Pat at first sight," Hannah commented almost testily. "That wasn't so. They met, they liked each other, and when they got to know each other, they fell in love."

But things do not seem to have proceeded at the even pace Hannah recalled. Pat repeatedly said that, despite Richard's now dogged pursuit, she continued to go out on dates with other men. She described his behavior during this period as "dutiful," but there also seemed to have been an element of strangeness in it. "He would drive me to meet other beaux and wait around to take me home."

Pat's reluctance to accept him might have stemmed in part from the fact that she was more than a year older than he. The romance wandered on without any sign Pat would cease her search for someone with superior qualities. Hannah professed to understand her son's motives. "I know what Richard saw in Pat. She was pretty and intelligent, and they both liked the theater and outdoor life. And perhaps, too, there was an even more subtle reason for them to be drawn to each other. For, far from being two kids on a lark, they both were self-sufficient and very determined people whose lives had been molded in a serious case by early exposure to tragedy. Pat's parents died when she was very young, and Richard had lost his two brothers."

Whatever the reason, shortly after her twenty-eighth birthday, Pat finally said yes. They were married on June 21, 1940. Pat, brought up as a Methodist, agreed to pledge her vows before a Quaker minister. The ceremony took place, however, not in the simple Whittier Quaker Church, with its silent prayer, but in the neon-lit, brightly-painted, Hollywood renaissance, sham elegance of the Mission Inn in Riverside, California. This was another retreat from Quaker traditions, this time brought on by no greater pressure than personal preference.

They rented an apartment in Whittier. Pat continued to teach and Richard continued to order out the police force when the occasion called for it. And although his knowledge of the subject had increased substantially, there was no indication he was any more comfortable when confronted with a client determined to discuss the more graphic details of her marital malaise.

Pearl Harbor changed the direction of Nixon's life as it did for most young men his age. However, unlike most, Richard could have lived through World War II with no great change in his life style. He was, after all, officially a Quaker and entitled to exemption from military service. Had he chosen to remain at home there would have been an absolute minimum of social pressure put on him.

Instead he used the war as an opportunity to make what he saw as that long-overdue break with Whittier. He and Pat hurried to Washington, leaving their California responsibilities without a backward glance. On January 9, scarcely a month after "the day that will live in infamy," Richard went to work for the Office of Price Administration.

Although some hide-bound traditionalist might have felt he was already violating Quaker principles by contributing to the war effort, Richard was presumably not upset by the thought of such criticism. He had evidently trekked eastward hoping to make his way in the flux of wartime Washington. Clearly he had no intention of giving up his deferred status. He could have done that in California. By early spring, however, he had grown tired of devoting his time to issuing routine tire rationing orders and applied for a naval commission.

This dramatic personal decision had been heralded by previous signs of apostasy which no one bothered to notice at the time. However, its significance could not be denied. Nixon was violating the fundamental tenet of the Quaker faith. He was committing himself to wage war, possibly to kill. It must have been difficult for him in the privacy of his nights during the summer of 1942 as he examined what he had done. It was possible to be a good Quaker American and not bear arms. It was difficult to be a good American Quaker and swear to kill your country's enemies.

IV.

Deal Me One off the Top, Dick

Just before Lieutenant (j.g.) Richard Nixon left for boot camp at Quonset, Rhode Island, his mother recalled, he told his younger brother, Edward, "Now *you* take good care of your mother." Despite his slip from grace, he was still a good son.

When he arrived in Quonset on September 2, he was lean and eager to please his martinet drill masters, who he may have secretly been comforted to discover "expected to be obeyed under all circumstances." For Richard Nixon was, now just short of his thirtieth birthday, the personification of the nice young man. He did not drink, smoke, or swear, and he was considerate of elderly women.

He was stationed at Ottumwa, Iowa, for six months until May, 1943, when he was reassigned to the South Pacific Air Transport Command. It was not a combat outfit; Air Transport's duties were custodial. It took soldiers and material from America and transported them to the staging areas. But the pilots and crews who flew the DC-3's and C-47's were men of substantial bravery. In effect, they often flew into forward combat zones without adequate armor or fire power to guarantee their successful return.

Nixon was only peripherally associated with these heroes. Although part of the Air Transport outfit, he rarely saw the inside of a plane. Although a navy lieutenant, he seldom felt the movement of a ship's deck under his feet. One of his former mates has described him as "a glorified Seabee." It was Nixon's duty to take his crew onto an island after the fighting was over and clear out a landing strip in the jungle. For a period of fourteen months, he did this on Bougainville, Vella Lavella and Green Island. Those were fourteen pivotal months in Richard Nixon's life. He began them chaste and finished them wised-up, hooked-in and turned-on. He was over thirty at this point. It had been a late adolescence.

39

Dick learned to curse with the best of them. At crucial moments in his life, when pressure mounted or he wanted something done, he reached back to his Green Island days for the proper word of command. Hannah later recalled that when he came back from the service "he cursed like a sailor." In 1959, Dick's friend Earl Mazo wrote, "He can swear like a sailor, but does it only among friends, mostly when it becomes necessary to open a safety valve on pent-up frustrations and anger." Dick's swearing is a genuine reflection of his tough, quarrelsome, contentious nature.

There was another dramatic shift in values during his South Pacific days. He became a gambler: a calculating, relentless, incessant cardsharp. To his fellow officers he was known as "Nick." Once landing strips were built, there was only occasional minor maintenance work to keep Nick's mind off the mosquitoes. Gambling was a natural outlet. However, he brought a joyless intensity to his gambling that was strictly his own. He mastered it with the same thoroughness he had applied to the intricacies of rules on torts.

He sought out the poker experts, the men with a theory and style of their own, and he picked their brains. One fellow officer named Stewart described him, "I had a theory for playing draw poker. Nick liked what I said. . . . We played two-handed poker without money for four or five days, until he had learned the various plays. Soon his playing became tops." Most servicemen considered poker a pleasant way to pass a few hours. They learned the basic rules that gave them the confidence to put their money in the middle of the table and draw to an inside straight, but they were really intuition betters, in the game for the thrill of guessing right.

This was not Nick's style. Games were not played for fun. Being beaten up on a football field with little chance of retaliation could be fun only for the most confirmed masochist. One had to *get* something out of such a painful experience, be it a reputation for courage and persistence that would advance his political ambitions, or satisfaction for his puritanical determination not to admit that some things were beyond him.

Poker was, consequently, a particularly attractive venture for Lieutenant Nixon. Where fun was not a legitimate objective, the acquisition of money was, and not since his Prescott's Slippery Gulch Rodeo days had Nixon had so large an audience of bored, restless and heavy-pocketed suckers.

He built a little shack on Green Island which passed for a Melanesian last frontier casino. It included a jerry-built bar constructed under his supervision and dispensing liquor which he managed to requisition. There officers rotated back from the distant front for a brief rest—combat men loaded with back pay and no place to spend it—would find Nick waiting. The poker games on Green Island were for high stakes. There were sometimes more than a thousand dollars in the pot.

Nixon played a cautious, calculating game. He never took chances unless the odds were strictly in his favor, and then he pushed his advantage mercilessly. One veteran of the Green Island games recalled, "He never lost, but he was never a big winner. He always played it close to the belt. He always seemed to end up a game somewhere between thirty and sixty dollars ahead."

Lester Wroble, a Chicago businessman who was interviewed by William Costello for his 1960 book *The Facts About Nixon*, said Nixon would play poker for hours, his face like a rock and "a hundred Navy officers will tell you that Nix never lost a cent at poker."

By the time his tour of duty was up, Nixon had accumulated over $10,000. Those were ten thousand pre-inflation dollars and they were loaded with the type of clout that could make many things possible for the son of poor Quaker parents.

But what had he done to earn this stake? He had violated the teachings of his youth and the practices of his young manhood. Yet, it is exactly his family background which finally seems to explain Richard Nixon's plastic morality. He was harnessed and broken to the concept of hard work to achieve recognition. Taken in a reasonable fashion, such a training produces moral men. Tuned to a slightly finer intensity, training of this sort distorts judgment and leads to the eruption of excesses that were first witnessed on Green Island.

V.

Tricky Dick

With me, the way I work is different. It's a matter of being in the right place at the right time. . . . Now I don't mean I'm above seeking office, or the maneuvers and machinations involved. And I'm always willing to take a chance. . . . Maybe it's that old poker-playing instinct.
                                                                    —Richard Nixon

Nixon was rotated back to the Alameda Naval Air Station in California toward the end of the war. After reclassification he was shipped to Washington for legal training in termination of Navy contracts. It was a dream assignment, since his work took him to New York, Philadelphia and Baltimore. It was as though he was starting all over again. The war had given many men a second chance, and the peripatetic Nixon had an opportunity to survey the Eastern Establishment corporate law field once again. This was where he wanted to work. This was where the big pots were.

As in the case of many small town boys, he was fascinated by New York. It was an incredible city, the only one of its kind in the country. Everything happened there. One day in 1945, while he was looking out the thirtieth floor window of 50 Church Street, where he was assigned to the Bureau of Aeronautics office, he caught sight of General Dwight David Eisenhower. The Supreme Commander of Allied Forces in Europe was being given a triumphal march through the canyons of lower Manhattan.

"My only glimpse of him was in that characteristic gesture of his—you know—where he had his hands up, and I could see that he was smiling." A view from such a peak was not available in Whittier.

However, as Nixon observed, our destinies are often decided by the accident of being in the right place at the right time. And for him, at that time, the right place was not New York. Neither was it with the now improbably titled Wingert, Bewley, Knoop and Nixon, in which he was still a partner, if only on paper.

43

While he was struggling to save some money for Harry Truman's new Administration, his fate was being decided by a group of strangers three thousand miles away.

The Twelfth Congressional District of California embraced Nixon's home town and large parts of Los Angeles County. It had been predominantly Republican before the Roosevelt landslides. During the previous five elections, however, the voters of the Twelfth had sent Democrat Horace Jeremiah Voorhis to Congress with increasing majorities.

Jerry Voorhis was an extremely likable son of a rich family, who had a sentimental attitude toward poor people which reflected itself in his desire to help everyone less fortunate than himself. During the 1936 campaign he had supported socialist candidate and consumer advocate Upton Sinclair, whose unsuccessful campaign for the governorship was based on the miscalculation that with almost everyone in the state poor to the point of desperation, he could not possibly lose.

While Nixon was investigating the mysteries of stud poker, Voorhis was winning friends all over the Twelfth. He was described by one of Nixon's supporters: "Strongly entrenched even among Republicans, he seemed to be a permanent fixture. His tenure had given him a national reputation, he was well liked by his fellow Congressmen and popular with the press. He was, moreover, conscientious and hard-working—tending to the mail from his constituents and handling their problems with dispatch."

Voorhis was not just another glad-handing political extrovert. In his soft-spoken, sincere, steady way he had become one of the more substantial members of Congress. About the time that Nixon was peering down on Ike, with no premonition he was looking at his savior and his tormentor, the hard-nosed Washington press corps was voting Voorhis "the best Congressman west of the Mississippi."

The leaders of the Republican party in the California Twelfth, which is to say the bankers, the insurance executives and the unclassified rich of all occupations, were upset almost beyond comprehension by Voorhis. He seemed to symbolize for them all the do-gooder impulses they so rigorously suppressed in themselves and which they so vigorously despised in the turncoat rich, such as F.D.R.

In an effort to make things more difficult for Voorhis they had managed to gerrymander the district so that two strongly Democratic towns were made some other Republican's headache. This was a sign they were serious, but it was no measure of the depth of their despair as they approached their task.

Ignoring the paper-tiger regular Republican organization in the district, they set up the *Committee of One Hundred.* Since there were no doctrinaire problems separating them, their energies could be concentrated on eradicating Voorhis. Aside from his popularity, they faced one enormous problem. They had no candidate.

They made an attempt to interest Walter Dexter, former president of Whittier College and then California Superintendent of Education. However, Dexter wanted to be guaranteed that in the likely event he would lose, the movers-and-shakers of the committee would provide a job for him with pay and prestige equal to the one he now possessed.

The committee was now forced to radical extremes. They submitted a classified ad to twenty-six newspapers in the district. Being men of means, their ad was not in agate print on one of the back pages. It appeared in August, 1945, over a year before the 1946 election, and read in part:

> WANTED: Congressman candidate with no previous political experience to defeat a man who has represented the district in the House for ten years. Any young man resident of district, preferably a veteran, fair education . . . may apply for the job. Applicants will be reviewed by 100 interested citizens. . . .

Without a doubt, this was the most innovative approach to selecting a candidate for Congress since, as the story goes, Andrew Jackson proposed to run any random monkey available in the Washington zoo against Henry Clay.

The response was poor. Only eight Angelenos considered it an attractive offer. They included a small-town mayor, who apparently thought any direction from where he was at was up, a smog expert who, having failed to solve the major problem in his field, now felt it was time to move on to another, and an outspoken segregationist, who surmised he might find some friends in this group.

The one hundred stalwarts were disheartened. A small group of them, led by Frank Jorgensen, a vice president of Metropolitan Life, gamely determined to continue their search privately. They recalled that Walter Dexter, as he had declined the honor, had pointed out a possible supernumerary. His name was Richard Nixon.

They were not impressed enough, however, to seek him out directly. Three committee sessions were held with prospective candidates before they reached out for him. Jorgenson and his subcommittee visited Hannah and Frank. They were delighted to hear that their son might have such an opportunity. However, they were unable to wipe out the lingering doubts of some as to whether he was really a Republican. After all, he had spoken in favor of Wendell Willkie in 1940, enough reason for suspicion.

It was decided that Herman Perry, a Whittier banker, would approach

Richard on this tender topic. He sent a telegram to Baltimore, to an address Hannah supplied. Nixon opened the telegram from Perry in complete innocence, and was puzzled at the request that he call immediately, collect. Perry was blunt. They were looking for a candidate to oppose Voorhis. "Are you a Republican and are you available?"

"I guess I'm a Republican," Nixon responded. "I voted for Dewey in 1944."

Perry told him he was sending three hundred dollars for plane fare and ended the conversation abruptly: "Fly out here right away!"

On September 29, Nixon appeared in the uniform of a lieutenant commander before the fourth session of the *Committee of One Hundred* at the William Penn Hotel in Whittier. He was given the same ten minutes that the smog expert and segregationist had to plead his case. He did an unexceptional job, his presentation consisting of debater clichés presented with the crisp, staccato delivery of a new brush salesman trying to sell his first customer. Seventy-seven members of the committee were present and heard him call for "a return to individual freedoms and all that private initiative can produce." He promised, if selected, to wage a "fighting, rocking, socking campaign."

The vote was fifty-five for him, twenty-two in favor of continuing the search.

There was something about Nixon that caused many of the committee members to hang back, even though their desire to find someone, almost anyone, was reaching the panic point. Despite the fact that he was almost thirty-three, he was transparently naïve. His nervous twitching and alternate displays of gloomy intensity and smiling desire to please telegraphed a lack of sophistication.

There seems every reason to believe Nixon was correct when he said he got this nomination because the stars were in their appointed places. Had he been in Whittier, perhaps the first candidate interviewed by the committee, American political history might well have taken a different turn. As it was, once he had proved his orthodoxy, the majority seemed to have been won over by the willingness of this veteran of the South Pacific campaigns to gamble on a loss. One of them summed it up simply: "He was the best of a bad lot."

On December 4, while still in the Navy, he announced he was accepting the committee's endorsement. Pat was pregnant with her first child, and there had been some minor debate about the wisdom of getting into a losing fight. Besides, they both liked Voorhis. Nixon said years later, "I suppose there was scarcely ever a man with higher ideals than Jerry Voorhis, or better motivated than Jerry Voorhis." They decided to set aside $5,000 of his $10,000 Green

Island winnings as an investment in his political career. Money won in one gamble was to be used in another.

How is it possible to explain his decision in the face of his known admiration of Voorhis? He has performed the service of explaining that decision in his own words.

> Voorhis looked impossible to defeat. He was intelligent, experienced, had a national reputation, and came from a well-known California family. Why did I take it? I'm a pessimist, but if I figure I've got a chance, I'll fight for it. And I thought this was as good a time as any to get into politics.

Although his Quaker ancestors might have been embarrassed at the ease with which he slipped around any ethical consideration, he was not going to let that chance go by.

He was released from active duty in January, 1946, and started campaigning immediately. The formal announcement of his candidacy came on February 12. It was his intention to exploit his veteran's status to the hilt. He was planning to campaign in uniform, and had brought back service pictures to use on his literature. However, his initial walking tours through the district convinced him that a lieutenant commander's uniform lost more votes than it won.

It is interesting to note that Nixon's start in politics was as unusual as his future career. Most politicians spend years in the clubhouse running errands, only partly slowed down by the weight of their dignified legal degrees. After making the requisite number of bows in the direction of the political boss, they are granted permission to negotiate the first low step on that slippery political staircase. By that time they are so deeply obliged to scores of benefactors-for-a-price that the short time remaining to them on earth is not long enough to allow them to pay their debts in full. Richard Nixon owed only a few minor debts to the conservative, business-oriented *Committee of One Hundred*, which was no doubt the main reason he concluded so ingenuously that one did not pursue political jobs, they simply dropped into your lap if you were in the right place at the right time.

The 1946 California primary was the delight of political buffs. Under the cross-filing system then in operation, it was not necessary to be a Democrat to run in the Democratic primary. Equal justice was meted out to Republicans. As a result, all serious candidates filed nominating petitions in the primaries of their opponents, hoping against hope that some miracle would bring victory. How pleasant it was for some who found success along this path to eliminate their opponents in the spring and find themselves majestically alone on the ballot on election day in November.

Most often this was not the case. A Democrat won in the Democratic primary and a Republican claimed his party's endorsement. However, it always gave psephologists an opportunity to gauge the relative strength of the major party candidates. By simply adding the primary votes each candidate had received on all party lines, one could predict the outcome in November.

In the 1946 primary Voorhis outpolled Nixon by over seven thousand votes. Considering the surgery that had been done on the district to eliminate two towns filled with Voorhis votes, this was considered a substantial victory for the Democrats.

Nixon took time out to see what he had been doing wrong. He also sought advice, and in so doing discovered the architect of his future success. He had heard of a Beverly Hills attorney, Murray Chotiner, who was supervising winning campaigns for Earl Warren and William Knowland.

In a recent interview with an aging Chotiner, held in his law office across the street from the White House, this key figure in Nixon's life reminisced to me that he had not been too interested when the young man from Whittier first came to see him. The smallish, sharp-eyed, soft-spoken Chotiner was busy with Hollywood divorce litigation, and his star, Republican Governor Earl Warren, preferred Voorhis. He agreed to accept a $500 fee as a consultant out of habit more than anything else.

He immediately pointed out that Nixon's campaign had been too traditional for the Herculean task he faced. One simply could not expect to beat a man of Voorhis' substance merely by ringing doorbells and shaking voters' hands.

Nixon would have to deflate his adversary. It was essential always to be on the attack, always to answer charges with generalities, so that your opponent could not focus his counterattack on anything specific. It was W.C. Fields bottle-wisdom taken from the silver screen and peddled in the provinces as profundity—"Never give a sucker an even break."

Chotiner felt Voorhis' vulnerability stemmed from the fact that he was being supported by some left-wing Democrats. Since his record in Congress was excellent, that must be ignored and all attention focused on these few "unsavory" men. Nixon labelled them supporters of "Communist principles" and "Communist sympathizers" and left every listener with the understanding that Voorhis had their endorsement because he sympathized with Communism.

The Cold War was beginning to cool off relations between the former allies. Nixon and Chotiner detected this trend before most. And although Nixon's memory had faded enough by 1958 so that he was willing to say "Communism was not an issue in 1946, despite what people have said later. Few people knew about Communism then and even fewer cared," even a casual review of the events of that blistering campaign affirms the opposite.

Nixon came out swinging wildly at his opening rally in Whittier on August 29:

> I want you to know that I am your candidate primarily because there are no special strings attached to me. I have no support from any special interest or pressure group. I welcome the opposition of the PAC, with its Communist principles and its huge slush fund.

What PAC was he talking about? Although he always spoke as if there were only one, in reality there were many PACs. The initials merely stood for "political action committee." There were three PACs that were significant: the CIO-PAC, the National Citizens PAC, and the California PAC—each different, two of them moderate left, one, the California PAC, Communist controlled. Only one of the three endorsed Voorhis, and that was not the California PAC.

The meat that Nixon dispensed at his opening rally was red enough even for Chotiner, but, as is well known, advice is cheap, even five-hundred-dollar advice, and results are what count. Nixon was making little headway. His crowds were modest, and although they responded to the red flag he constantly waved in their faces, there were not enough faces to predict a reversal of the primary results.

The campaign literature attempted to depict Voorhis as a "pink" and was tailored to Chotiner's specifications. There was none of the Quaker sense of fairness reflected in Nixon's vicious assault. At sparsely attended streetcorner gatherings, while Pat handed out broadsides, he constantly spoke of Voorhis as "the PAC candidate and his Communist friends."

Voorhis was confident. Although this type of smear was being used for the first time since the 1930's, he had every reason to think it would backfire. To begin with, he was a member of the House Un-American Activities Committee and had cooperated in the investigation of Communist front organizations. It was just such activity on his part that had cost him the support of the California PAC, which Nixon persisted in implying had endorsed him.

Furthermore, he had sponsored an effective piece of antisubversive legislation, which made him anathema to the Communist left. The Voorhis Act provided for registration of foreign agents who had formerly, in the guise of patriotic Americans, duped innocent liberals into support of front organizations. For this and other heresies, Voorhis was regularly denounced by *The People's World,* the Communist organ in California. It was logical for him to be confident that an amateur rabble-rouser like Nixon would have no more success than his previous opponents.

All that altered suddenly when Voorhis innocently blundered into Nixon's hands. Voorhis was in the habit of mailing to the parents of newborn babies a government pamphlet called *Infant Care*. He would inscribe a message on the cover of each copy. Shortly after Tricia was born on February 21, the Nixons received their copy inscribed, "Congratulations. I look forward to meeting you soon in public."

Nixon and Chotiner, sensing the campaign was going sour, hit on a scheme to put Voorhis on the defensive. Nixon challenged him to a series of public debates. It was a situation in which he had nothing to lose and Voorhis had nothing to gain. Normally such a transparently disadvantageous confrontation could be sidestepped, but in this case Nixon had his *Infant Care* pamphlet, to which he was planning to write an appendix on how to take care of political rivals.

He stumped his district, waving the pamphlet and sarcastically reading the inscription. Was Voorhis afraid to meet him now?

Voorhis rose to the bait. Confident a record like his could not be besmirched, and underestimating the depths to which a striving Nixon was ready to plunge, he accepted the challenge. A series of five debates was scheduled.

Nixon prepared for the battle with his usual thoroughness, which is not to say that he searched out the truth, but rather that he had his debater's strategems worked out and rehearsed to perfection. Evelyn Dorn, who sat in the audience, took down every word her boss spoke. She noted one of his techniques. "I asked why he always repeated a question that had been asked him before answering it. He said it gave him more time to be thinking of the answer."

There was nothing spontaneous in his answers. They were developed in advance and measured to conform to Chotiner's dictum that a successful politician always attacks, never defends.

His favorite prop was a piece of paper, which he displayed in the first debate. He held it aloft dramatically, silently for a moment, then charged that it contained "evidence" Voorhis had received the endorsement of the National Citizens PAC. Waving the paper under Voorhis' nose, he would charge that "In the last four years, out of forty-six issues sponsored by the CIO and PAC my opponent has voted against the CIO and PAC only three times. Whether he wants it now or not, my opponent has the PAC endorsement and he has certainly earned it. It's not how a man talks, but how he votes that counts."

With five minutes' rebuttal time, exactly how do you explain the complexities underlying your decisions on forty-six separate votes? Voorhis found himself sinking as he made fruitless attempts to answer his opponent's hydra-headed charges. Voorhis was gently ineffective in his answers. On the other hand, the young attorney from Whittier was so vigorous, so condemning and his past was so vacant, so spotlessly blameless.

With each passing debate the audiences grew larger, as word of the donnybrook spread. There was something absolutely hypnotic about the sight of a floundering Voorhis vainly laboring to deny an inference here and an innuendo there. Between debates Nixon fired even heavier guns. He accused Voorhis of being "a lip-service American" who was fronting for "un-American elements, wittingly or otherwise. . . ." Finally, three days before the election, he accused Voorhis of "consistently voting the Moscow-PAC-Henry Wallace line in Congress."

Exhausted and disheartened, Voorhis allowed his campaign to stumble to a halt. Nixon won 65,586 to 49,994. It was a Republican year. They swept every doubtful race in California. Across the country they wrestled fifty-five seats away from the Democrats and took control of the 80th Congress that Truman subsequently labelled, with devastating effect, "the Do-Nothing Republican Congress."

While Nixon basked in the pleasure of victory Voorhis seemed to have a similarly positive reaction to defeat. He told reporters later, "I'm frank to say that I felt a little bit this way: I had been a Congressman for ten years. I'd done the best I could. And I really felt if the voters wanted to throw me out, by golly, okay. I'm afraid this was on my mind the whole time, to some extent. I hated a fight like that."

The public-spirited, generous-minded loser could not change the habits of a lifetime. He wrote a long letter to Nixon marked by a tone of helpful Christianity. He encouraged his successor to make a contribution to the nation in Congress, and offered to be of assistance in any way he could. At the conclusion he made the only allusion to the ordeal he had just been through. "I have refrained, for reasons which you will understand, from making any reference in this letter to the circumstances of the campaign."

Millions of people who watched that campaign were not as generous. What they had seen was a new phenomenon, a type of political campaign not unknown in history but relatively rare in democratic America, marked by vilification, obfuscation, smear and lying. All the techniques for which Joseph McCarthy was to become infamous four years later were sharpened to perfection and used without stint during this lamentable campaign. Even the language was McCarthyesque: "I hold here in my hand. . . ." While McCarthy was simultaneously staging his first campaign for the Senate in Wisconsin with the support of the Minneapolis Communist Party, Nixon was practicing to confuse with the "proof" contained in a document no one in the audience was ever given the opportunity to examine.

Under Chotiner's skillful guidance he had bludgeoned his way into

Congress. Using every oratorical trick in the debater's manual, exploiting every audience-milking artifice he had acquired in amateur theatricals, he had adroitly thrust himself onto the national scene.

Yet, what a wrenching it must have caused in the fiber of the man. Unlike the average run-of-the-mill politician, he knew right from wrong. He had been raised on the concept of right-thinking and right-action. However, he was entering a profession where the thoroughness with which a man shed his morality often determined his success. The training of his Quaker boyhood was an encumbrance, a brake on his ambition.

Had he been willing to settle for small stakes, county district attorney or lower court judge, he would have still been ill-suited by upbringing for his calling. However, he chose to gamble for the big pots and this committed him to the destruction of any pretense of a moral posture. Seldom had an American politician begun his career in such a spectacularly unscrupulous manner.

(Stewart Alsop in the February, 1972 issue of *The Atlantic Monthly*, commented on Nixon's choice of a career, "Nixon went into politics the way other young men home from the war went into construction, or merchandising or whatever—for the lack of anything better to do. . . . The fact is that as a candidate for office, Nixon has consistently been a thoroughly second-rate politician simply because he is not a natural politician, because he was made, not born.")

When someone compared the Voorhis campaign to the Jimmy Stewart movie *Mr. Smith Goes to Washington*, in which idealistic Mr. Smith is destroyed by cynical politicians, Nixon responded impulsively and without guile, "Yes, yes—I remember that movie well. Jerry Voorhis was supposed to be Mr. Smith, you know."

Even Nixon cast himself in the role of heavy in that campaign. The extent to which he was permanently marred by the experience can perhaps be gauged by the fact that he seldom voluntarily referred to it. In *Six Crises*, his highly selective fragmentary "autobiography" written for him largely by ghost writer Al Moscow, Nixon did not include the Voorhis campaign as one of these crises, and underscored his inability to look back without pain by devoting less than one thin paragraph to it. "My success in the '46 campaign was probably the result of three factors: intensive campaigning; doing my homework; and participating in debates with my better-known opponent, the veteran incumbent Congressman, Jerry Voorhis."

He commented with a brevity inspired by shame. But he was only at the beginning of his race and to any alert Quaker, it should have been clear that the track immediately in front of him led downward.

VI.

Dick the Anti-Red, or
The Man Who Taught Joe

The 1947 Congress opened on an antic note. Senator J. W. Fulbright of Arkansas, although as good a Democrat as he was ever to be, urged President Truman to appoint a Republican Secretary of State and resign. He said that this act of British parliamentary courtesy would prove Truman's "patriotism."

Nixon was sworn into Congress January 3, 1947, at a particularly hectic moment. The country was grappling with the worst aspects of reconversion from a wartime economy. There was a sharp rise in unemployment as ordnance industries closed down. Rosie the Riveter and G.I. Joe tried to make up their minds what direction their lives were going to take, plagued by the fear that the prosperity of the wartime years was a temporary phenomenon, soon to be replaced by the more durable uncertainties of a recurring depression.

The poisonous anti-Communist hysteria, that had shown itself in the Nixon campaign, had surfaced in enough successful Republican campaigns across the country so that even if Stalin had proved more tractable, destruction of the Grand Alliance of World War II seemed a certainty. The decades of foreign tranquility, which a few months earlier, on the occasion of V-E and V-J Days, seemed assured, now were replaced by fears of a third world war.

Compounding the anxiety on the domestic level was the demand of Republicans, led by conservative Ohio Senator Robert Taft, son of William Howard Taft, twenty-seventh president of the U.S., that all wartime controls be lifted immediately. He wanted the "normal" processes of an unfettered economy to reassert themselves. To Harry Truman, and most Americans, this appeared to defy reason. Millions of workers were unemployed. There was a tremendous shortage of consumer goods, since few civilian items had been manufactured during the previous six years. At the same time, there was a huge reserve of money squirreled away in the bank accounts of the millions who had not gone off to war, but instead had worked overtime. For years they had anticipated the time when their industry on the assembly line would be rewarded with substantial creature comforts.

Taft was proposing that price controls be scrapped immediately. That meant an automobile manufacturer, who marketed a pre-war car for somewhere in the neighborhood of $1,000, would be free to place any price tag on his first eagerly awaited post-war models. There were enough people with bulging pocketbooks who were ready to pay three or five thousand dollars for the same car.

Truman wanted price controls removed selectively at a more moderate pace. As industries retooled and inventories were built, controls would be dropped. In this way the greed of a small group of men who were in position to take advantage of the "free" marketplace in a "normal" capitalistic economy would be held in check. He had the same plan for other wartime economic regulations, such as the all-important rent controls. No new housing had been built since before Pearl Harbor, and with the number of newly married couples at an all time high because of returning war veterans, demand for accommodations was peaking.

Left to the mercy of unleashed landlords, in a seller's market, these young couples were being forced to bribe rental agents for the privilege of paying exorbitant rents. The new rents were not caused by increased labor or material costs. All the apartments had been built and financed years earlier. The money saved by these youngsters, one dollar at a time, was merely being drained off by rapacious landlords with political clout.

Taft largely had his way. Nixon supported him without reservation. The predictable resulted. Prices skyrocketed as the profiteering instinct was given free rein. Inflation got almost completely out of hand for several years and, when prices finally leveled off, they were at a permanently higher plateau.

Savings melted under these twin pressures, a Taft-induced inflation and a reconversion-caused rise in unemployment. Union workers responded by trying to secure contracts with substantial raises. Failure to accomplish this meant their members' standard of living was being permanently cut. Since wage controls were removed with price controls, they were no longer obliged to tailor their desires to the deflationary dictums of the War Labor Board. Union negotiating teams began to demand settlements which would keep their members abreast of the soaring inflation. Industrial leaders resisted these demands. Many of them were retooling slowly and saw no reason to rush into higher labor costs. Others, observing the large pool of unemployed, felt this was a good time to tame the unions.

The result was something approaching economic warfare over a period of two years. Every giant industry in the country was on strike for prolonged periods of time, as the workers demanded and the owners rejected. There has never been a period of greater labor unrest in America. Estimates are that as much as one third of the labor force was on strike each of those crisis years. In the twenty years prior to 1972, during which time many complained about the profusion of strikes, the annual number of man hours lost due to strikes seldom approached 1 per cent. But in 1946-47 millions of steel, auto, coal mining, and assorted craft union workers were often simultaneously walking picket lines.

The temptation for Taft and his followers was to attribute the disruption caused by their premature lifting of controls to "Communist subversion." They did not resist. Unions were described as being under "Communist control." Union leaders were accused of being card-carrying Communists and hauled before Congressional committees for interrogation.

Nixon began his public life at this flash point in our history. He had just won his greatest debate. But instead of receiving yet another plaque his mother could store in the top drawer of her bureau, he had been made a national leader. In a few months he had metamorphosized from a thirty-three-year-old lawyer concerned with resuming his interrupted practice, to one of the country's youngest Congressmen, who now dreamt of someday becoming Speaker of the House of Representatives.

The seniority system, and the normal timidity of a traveler in a strange land, make most new Congressmen hang back while they steady themselves in their untried environment and learn which button to press to make the lights go on. This was drastically and decisively not the case with Richard Nixon. He came to Washington in January, 1947, as the Nixon he was to be, fully grown as a political personality, all his most distinctive characteristics completely defined. His drive, his public relations sense, his grinding determination to succeed and his lack of public shame were as finely honed then as they were ever to become. A hysterical flow of energy seemed to pour from him. He dashed around the capitol building scarcely pausing, as though he felt that a moment's hesitation would allow some other freshman to get in front of him.

Almost his first act was to seek out a group of other freshmen and organize them into the innocently titled "Chowder and Marching Society." There were fifteen charter members, all of whom voted as a unit and therefore lent their colleagues in this legislative union some strength. Nixon was no longer merely a green congressman who had caused some stir by knocking off Voorhis, he was the leader of a minor power bloc that entitled him to some consideration.

His committee assignments were interesting, and formed a perfect platform from which he could launch his career. He was plucked out of the crowd of fresh faces and given a spot on the Education and Labor Committee, which was then struggling with the most publicized piece of legislation of that generation, the Taft-Hartley Act. With Voorhis' departure from the scene, there was a vacancy on the House Un-American Activities Committee, which Nixon filled. HUAC had for years been the loudest, if not the most productive, committee on Capitol Hill.

Young Nixon had every reason to be happy with his assignments. Other members of the class of 1946 were bound over to the Agricultural or Interior Committees, and disappeared into the bowels of the House Office Building, for which they have not since reappeared.

Nixon made a strenuous effort to cultivate the press corps. Since he came to Washington with substantially more notoriety than the rest of his neophyte colleagues and was always available for comment, he was sought out whenever a reporter wanted to flesh out a story with a comment from at least one of the back-benchers. He had caught their eye immediately when, on arriving in Washington, he told a reporter, "I was elected to smash the labor bosses."

Although he has since denied saying that (he has since denied saying many other things, which a substantial number of people persist in thinking he said), he proceeded to act as if that were precisely his intent.

On February 17, barely a month after he burst upon the scene, Nixon's characteristic mode of operation had already become apparent. The House was in the midst of debate on the Taft-Hartley Act, which was the Ohio Senator's way of quieting the hounds of labor he had set howling with his purist application of pre-McKinley economic theories. Hardworking young advocate that he was, Nixon had already begun to take an active role in shaping the final legislation. Since he never believed in hiding any act of his which might accumulate a gram of credit to him, Nixon performed his service to labor reform in the limelight. Taft commented years later that one of the reasons he did not like Nixon was that he was "too much in a hurry." His behavior in this instance may have contributed to Taft's sour attitude.

The New York *Times* reported that on February 17 Nixon called the news corps together and revealed the results of one of a number of "grass roots" inquiries being conducted "individually" on labor matters. This was his effort to rouse support for Taft-Hartley. He went at it with relish. "Mr. Nixon asserted that *talks* [italics added] with men in the Scranton, Pa. district indicated a 'unanimous' feeling that 'some legislation was necessary to restrict the power of certain union leaders who overreached themselves and were harming the union movement.' "

There was something so obviously flim-flam about this performance that he immediately drew the fire of Taft-Hartley opponents. Who was the individual who conducted the grass roots inquiry? How many men were polled? What were the questions they were asked?

His reaction must have pleased Murray Chotiner. *When you are attacked, counterattack.* He called a press conference and read off "excerpts" from his *mail* from Scranton. His correspondents were alleged to agree with him that union members were looking to Congress to protect them from their leaders. With grim satisfaction he held a piece of paper aloft from which he then proceeded to read. "You know these union gangsters will never go for you unless you let them control your vote."

His implication of the previous day that a full-blown field study had been made of the Scranton area to determine what the rank-and-file really thought had degenerated on closer inspection to some letters which he had purportedly received because of his well known championing of the working man's cause. He was on his way.

In the midst of this imbroglio, which called his honesty into question immediately, he gave his maiden speech. On February 18 he was selected to go before the House as a representative of HUAC, and request a contempt of Congress citation against Gerhart Eisler. Eisler was an agent for Communist Russia who had been scoring headlines for the committee by belligerently refusing to answer its questions. He eventually hid aboard a steamer headed for Europe and ended up in East Germany, one of the Communist gauleiters.

Although Nixon continued to work on language in the Taft-Hartley Act to strengthen its chances of surviving an eventual Supreme Court test, he seemed to have reached a decision that it was safer for an aspiring Speaker of the House to stay with the anti-Communist issue and avoid mixing it up with "labor bosses." Joe Stalin was clearly coming to a bad end.

Besides, there were enough domestic and foreign Communist issues around to fully occupy his energies. Chiang Kai-shek was not managing to keep the Chinese Communists bottled up in the north, and a speech devoted to the "subversives" who were "selling out" China was always good for a strong audience reaction. After all, if the civil war was being lost in China, there must be numerous people responsible for that loss, and many fruitful hours could be spent in their pursuit.

Making the task easier for Nixon was the fact that he *knew* who the villains were all along. They were Harry Truman and all those Democrats who wanted to reach some agreement with the Chinese Communists. At the best such men were expedient politicians who would betray any trust in order to win an election. But the worst was more likely true, that they were traitors who under the leadership of Secretary of State Dean Acheson were handing

China over to the Reds, their first move in a plan to deliver all Asia into slavery.

Nixon pioneered in a particularly virulent type of anti-Communism. He did not merely assert that Truman and Acheson were wrong-headed in their policies, he insisted they were deliberately betraying America. Time and time again, he insisted they were "helping the Communist cause."

What made the charges even more reprehensible was the fact that Truman was vigorously anti-Communist. In March, 1947 he issued an Executive Order calling on the FBI and Civil Service Commission to investigate the loyalty of all federal employees. On March 12 he announced the "Truman Doctrine" which offered to "help free people to maintain their free institutions and their national integrity." He simultaneously asked Congress to appropriate $400 million to strengthen the armed forces of Greece and Turkey and halt the spread of Communism in those countries. While Nixon was attacking his administration for being "weak on Communism," he was in the process of developing Cold War strategy along an uncompromisingly anti-Communist line.

An even easier target was the American Communist Party. Never too potent a force in domestic politics, by 1947 the U.S. Communist Party was largely a discredited remnant of its former self. Although it was hardly likely the few thousand well-identified and closely-surveyed American Communists would start a revolution, Nixon hammered away at them as though they were on the verge of seizing power.

Eugene Dennis, General Secretary of the party, was spending more time before HUAC than he was in his subterranean cell planning the overthrow of the government. On April 9, 1947, Nixon proved his vigilance by proposing before HUAC that Dennis not only be cited for contempt of Congress, which crime was penalized only by a fine of $1,000 and one year in jail, but that he be charged with "conspiracy to commit contempt," for which more heinous crime the penalty was $10,000 fine and two years in jail.

In August he made his first trip abroad as a Congressman. Christian Herter was the head of a committee studying problems of foreign aid. Herter subsequently played an important role in Nixon's life, and here, at the beginning of their relationship, the older congressman from Massachusetts was offering his brash colleague the opportunity to strengthen his credentials in the area of "the Communist threat." On his return Nixon was able to speak as a man who had seen what Communism was doing in Europe.

With the passage of the Taft-Hartley Act in June, 1947, after a tumultuous five-month debate, the men most involved with it were able to turn their attention to other matters. Taft began a concerted attempt to capture the Republican Presidential nomination, since his abiding ambition was to duplicate his father's accomplishment. Fred Hartley immediately retired from Congress and went to work in industry, which he had served so well, at a much increased salary. Nixon devoted his full attention to the Communist menace.

So impressed was J. Parnell Thomas, chairman of HUAC, with Nixon's purity of purpose that he appointed the young congressman to be chairman of a special legislative subcommittee of HUAC. (Within a short while Thomas was to be convicted of criminal misconduct and sent to the penitentiary for several years. But at this moment, only the most perceptive challenged his honesty.)

Nixon set to work with his usual vigor. On January 18, 1948, he announced he was inviting witnesses to appear before his subcommittee so that it could draw up legislation to "check Communism." Nixon felt the charge that the committee was ignoring its legislative function was exposing it to legitimate criticism. For years all the committee's time had been spent listening to alleged Communists, some of whom were cited for contempt of Congress when they refused to answer questions. Few pieces of legislation had, however, resulted from these inquisitorial efforts. He wanted to plug up that hole.

For two months and a day Nixon held a marathon series of hearings. Often he was the only member of the subcommittee in attendance as witness on both sides of the issue tried to shape the direction of his report. Immediately after the last hearing he went before the full committee with legislative recommendations "to put the spotlight on Communist propaganda," and to isolate and "quarantine" underground Communism.

He had a vast file of testimony wheeled into the hearing room, and averred that it confirmed his feeling that stronger measures had to be taken against domestic Communists if the nation was to survive. He offered a number of "stiffening" amendments to existing laws covering immigration, naturalization and the issuance of passports. All his recommendations were aimed exclusively at American Communists. He told the attentive committee that his system would depend on the registration of Communists and Communist "front" organizations.

Representative Karl Mundt, of South Dakota, who was also a champion debater in college, applauded Nixon's presentation. He had introduced a Communist control bill the previous winter, but it lacked the comprehensive dimensions of Nixon's recommendations. He and Nixon combined their efforts and the result was the Mundt-Nixon Bill, the only piece of legislation ever to bear Nixon's name.

On April 9 the committee unanimously approved the bill. It provided for $10,000 fines and ten years in jail for anyone found to be intentionally "in aid

of the immediate or *ultimate* objectives of the world Communist movement."
"Front" organizations would have to register. Nixon was identified as the
bill's principal author. At a press conference shortly after the committee's
approval was won, he stated it would amount to a Congressional finding that
the Communist Party of the United States "as it now exists and under its
present policies was conspiratorial." He said if the law passed, present
leaders of the party would be prosecuted.

On May 14 he became floor manager of the Mundt-Nixon Bill. The debate
was acrimonious. Nixon accused the administration of being "soft" on
Communism. Years later he referred to this time, when he was under attack
from his critics in Congress:

> They raised questions about the Vice President [Agnew] , and about
> other people in the Administration, about the rhetoric. And, I know, of
> course, questions have been raised about my rhetoric. . . . The only
> difference is that of all these people, and I refer particularly to some of
> my lively critics in the House and Senate, they have the luxury of
> criticism. I was once a Senator and a House member, and I thought back
> to this when I called Harry Truman today and wished him well on his
> 86th birthday, some of the rather rugged criticisms that I directed in his
> direction.
> They have the luxury of criticism because they can criticize and if it
> doesn't work out, then they can gloat over it, or if it does work out, the
> criticism will be forgotten.

He was able at this point, over twenty years after the events, to describe the
underpinnings of his own approach to public affairs. He criticized lavishly
whenever the spirit moved him. If his criticisms hit the mark he was ready to
step forward and claim credit. If they misfired, as they often did, he assumed
a low profile and waited until the flak died down. But, whereas he showed no
mercy when he was in Congress, and knew no extreme accusation that he
would not blithely hurl, he now asked his critics to consider that the man at
whose heels they yapped had the destiny of their country in his hands. The
fact that *he* had not kept this in mind when he was in their position should
not discourage their better instincts.

The Mundt-Nixon Bill, which looked as if it would sail through an intimidated Congress, was torpedoed by Thomas E. Dewey, governor of New
York, who was in the process of trying to win his party's nomination for the
presidency for a second time. His chief opponent in 1948 was Harold Stassen,
former governor of Minnesota.

Stassen had met Nixon in the South Pacific during the war when he was
Admiral "Bull" Halsey's deck officer. During the Voorhis campaign,

Stassen, once again pursuing his political destiny, which he perceived to be the White House, posed for a campaign picture with Nixon. It is hard to remember that during the early years of his career Nixon was considered a Stassen man, as was Joe McCarthy. Both of them were working for Stassen's nomination at the 1948 convention.

Stassen made his best run for the nomination in 1948. Dewey had managed to lose to F.D.R. in 1944 and was too liberal for many Taft Republicans. Stassen humiliated Dewey in the Wisconsin and Nebraska primaries and by the time of the Oregon primary it looked as if Stassen was coming up fast and would soon overtake him. The climactic point of the Oregon campaign came in a face-to-face debate between the two leading contenders. The key issue was Richard Nixon's Communist control bill. Stassen supported his friend's attempt to destroy the remnants of American Communism. Dewey took the opposite position. He felt Mundt-Nixon was a potential attack on all our freedoms. He dismissed it as "an attempt to beat down ideas with clubs."

The New York *Times* editorialized that it "could be used to impose restraints on freedom such as the American people have not known for one hundred and fifty years." The *Christian Science Monitor* said it would create "precedents and a machinery for the kind of political proscription which could be turned by any party in power against any minority."

Dewey won the debate. He had been bolder and more forthright than Stassen. Many observers thought Stassen should have adopted the Dewey position, which was more in keeping with his liberal reputation. The fact that he did not made him appear an opportunist.

Nixon was beside himself with anger. He told everyone that if only Stassen had taken the time to read his telegram in which he outlined a fool-proof defense of Mundt-Nixon, the candidate from Minnesota would have won. Stassen's loss was a blow to Nixon. His bill was defeated on the momentum of Dewey's attack.

Although he had lost, there were benefits that accrued to his personal cause, his desire to get ahead. He had become the leading anti-Communist in Congress, and this in little more than a year. At a time when Joe McCarthy was still making unnoticed speeches on farm prices and the need for fiscal responsibility, Nixon's name was known by a substantial number of Americans. Furthermore, he had been defeated on an issue whose day was clearly coming. The basic provisions of his law were in fact enacted in the McCarran Act two years later. Out of such defeats is success fashioned.

To alert the nation to the fact that he was not discouraged in his fight against the Red menace, he introduced a resolution which he pretended not to notice was an echo of the Truman Doctrine. It morally committed

Congress to defensive military alliances, and to military aid, for any non-Communist country threatened by Kremlin-directed infiltration. Little more than a year and a half out of the Navy and he was anxious to mold American foreign policy. It would take more than a Stassen blunder to dishearten him.

Chotiner envisioned a new election strategem that year. With the press Nixon had been getting, it was obvious to Chotiner that the real reelection campaign was being won in Washington. He encouraged Nixon's aggressive behavior and told him not to worry about the primaries.

The sureness of his instincts was demonstrated on June 1, 1948. Nixon cross-filed in the Democratic and Republican primaries in the Twelfth and was paid in the coin which he valued most—he won the nomination of both parties.

VII.

Dick's Friend

Richard Nixon made the Hiss Case possible.
—Whittaker Chambers

An orbiting group had formed around Richard Nixon in Washington. Included in it were newspapermen, congressmen of his vintage year and assorted types who thought he might help them, or who he thought might be of help. However, there was not a single person in that group who could be labelled "a friend."

Ralph de Toledano, who owed much to Nixon, wrote of those days with a touch of candor in *One Man Alone*:

> He was too single-minded to be quite at ease with people. Friends whose homes he had visited and whose wives and children he knew would, on seeing Nixon, find themselves plunged into a political dialogue. After a half-hour of this, Nixon would suddenly remember that it was customary to ask a few questions about a man's family. This embarrassing formality having been overcome, there would be a reversion to political matters. Nixon's fleeting awareness of these amenities betrayed his lack of interest in daily life apart from politics.

Nixon was leading an essentially lonely life, made more so than his life had been with Wingert, Bewley and Knoop by his decision to trust no man. There were dark thoughts this apostate Quaker had that could not be shared. "It is true that I'm fundamentally relatively shy," he told Stewart Alsop. "It doesn't come natural to me to be a buddy-buddy boy. When I meet a lot of people, I tend to seek out the shy ones. . . . You know, I try to be candid with

63

newspapermen, but I can't really let my hair down with anyone. . . . No, not really with anyone, not even with my family."

He was spending less and less time at home. His duties seldom allowed him to leave his office before eight at night. Pat was increasingly occupied with the children; their second child, Julie, was born July 5, 1948. During most of their youth, Nixon had little to do with them. He would arrive home after they were in bed. The clearest memory his daughter Tricia had of those days was of seeing her father off at the airport, often accompanied by her mother for long official absences abroad.

On August 3, 1948, Richard Nixon met his friend, and until the death of Whittaker Chambers thirteen years later, sought solace in his presence during moments of great stress.

Whittaker Chambers was an extraordinary man. He was born in Philadelphia in 1901 and brought up on Long Island. His father was a free-lance artist who deserted the family for a period of years. His mother had been in the theater and never lived as comfortably after she married as she had before. She often slept with an ax under her bed while Whittaker's father was not living with them. She forced her two adolescent boys to move into her bedroom because of her terrible fears. Whittaker slept with a knife under his pillow, whose handle he fondled when he was restless. His insane grand-mother was locked in a room in their house, her screams heard by all. On occasion she attacked family members with knives and scissors.

Chambers' relationship with his younger brother was tortured and ended tragically with his suicide in 1926. The brother had tried to get Whittaker to enter a suicide pact. When he discovered his brother with his head in the gas oven, Chambers' first thought was that he had betrayed him by letting him go on alone.

Tormented by the most morbid hauntings, Chambers became a fanatic, atheistic Communist. He had written a play mocking the Resurrection while at Columbia University, and been expelled. He joined the Communist Party in 1925 and, during the next twelve years, he devoted himself completely to its service. At first he helped distribute Party propaganda, eventually becoming an editor for the *Daily Worker*.

In 1931, according to his testimony, he became involved in underground work for the Soviet Union. By 1934 he headed a group based in Washington which he, for many years, described as a Marxist study group, but which he described in November, 1948, as a group that stole government documents which he retyped and microfilmed. They were then passed on to Soviet agents who smuggled them out of the country.

There is no indication that anything he stole was of substantial value. But that was clearly beside the point. For given the opportunity, Chambers would have rifled the national treasury in an attempt to betray the United States most completely to its enemy.

In 1937 he had a sudden change of heart, which he attributed to a religious conversion (he became an Episcopalian in 1939 and a Quaker two years later) and a revelation about what was really going on in Russia.

For two years, after leaving the Party in 1937, he constantly feared for his life, fleeing from one remote hideout to another. His wife, who had also been a Communist, but according to him not involved directly in the theft of government secrets, followed him around the country. Again he slept with a knife under his pillow, and always had a gun within reach. He carried a butcher knife in his belt whenever he went out.

Chambers earned enough to keep his family alive by occasionally translating books for German for American publishers. His substantial talent led him in 1939 to a job with *Time* magazine.

In August, 1939, horrified at the German-Soviet Non-Aggression Pact, Chambers determined to strike a blow against his former comrades. On September 2, in the company of anti-Communist pamphleteer Isaac Don Levine, he went to Adolf A. Berle, then Assistant Secretary of State, although he first tried to arrange a meeting with F.D.R. because he thought that was the "appropriate level" on which his information should be considered. Berle took notes and subsequently testified Chambers said he left the Party "at the end of 1937." "This was not," as Berle put it, "any question of espionage. There was no espionage involved in it. He stated that their hope merely was to get some people who would be sympathetic to their point of view. With that in mind a study group of some sort had been formed. . . ."

Chambers did not speak of *his* espionage efforts for the Soviets. In the strain of international events of that incredible period Chambers' story was heard and then shoved to one side. In 1943, now safely ensconced at *Time* magazine, he repeated his story of Communists in government during the 1930's to the FBI, who had sought him out on his Westminster, Maryland, farm. They returned to him on March 20, 1945, and August 28, 1946, as the interest in any sort of inside information on Communist underground activity grew.

Through each of these interviews, first with Berle and then three times with the FBI, he maintained that he had left the party *in 1937* and had never been involved in espionage. There was every reason to believe that Chambers' past was in the process of being annihilated by time. He had made an effort to be heard, during a time of great personal turmoil, but even the FBI, which exhaustively checked out his story, was uninterested in seeking Justice Department action.

For one thing, no other witness ever came forward to confirm any part of his story, and, even more important, he seemed to be describing a common phenomenon of the 1930's, Communist sympathies on the part of some lower level government employees. Since the lives of most of these men had taken conventional turns, there seemed no reason to believe that, even granting the unverifiable truth of Chambers' accusations, they had not repented their youthful radicalism for exactly the same reasons Chambers so eloquently expressed.

By 1946 he had become one of Henry Luce's senior editors, winning his way largely on the basis of his vast knowledge of Communism, and his ability to turn out long philosophic articles that reverberated with religiosity. During the mid-1940's he had a nervous breakdown which kept him confined to his shade-drawn bedroom for months. Despite his doctor's reassurance, he was convinced he was dying.

Chambers' drift toward obscurity was arrested by Elizabeth Bentley and Richard Nixon at the end of September, 1948. A middle-aged, bizarre-looking woman, Miss Bentley appeared before the House Un-American Activities Committee and named thirty-two people working for the government who, she claimed, had passed government documents to her for transshipment to the Soviet Union.

Nixon commented in *Six Crises,* "The charges were significant and sensational—but unsubstantiated." Miss Bentley became an overnight sensation. Her picture was on every front page in the country, usually under a headline identifying her as a "Spy Queen." In an endeavor to substantiate her testimony, the committee issued a subpoena for David Whittaker Chambers, whom they had heard from FBI sources was a "Communist functionary" during the 1930's.

Richard and Whittaker met in a small HUAC office just prior to the first public session on August 3. The only purpose of that meeting was to determine whether he was a crackpot who would embarrass the committee in public session.

Nixon was negatively impressed:

Both in appearance and in what he had to say, he made very little impression on me or the other members. He was short and pudgy. His clothes were unpressed. His shirt collar was curled up over his jacket. He spoke in a rather bored monotone.

Chambers named four members of his underground Communist group whom he insisted were not engaged in espionage, but were rather interested in "Communist infiltration of the American government."

His accusations were leveled against Nathan Witt, former Secretary of the

National Labor Relations Board; John Abt, former Labor Department attorney; Lee Pressman, former Assistant General Counsel for the Agricultural Adjustment Administration, and Alger Hiss, former State Department official who had helped in the organizational work for the United Nations and was then president of the prestigious Carnegie Endowment for International Peace. (Years later Lee Pressman appeared before a Congressional committee and admitted such a group had existed. He denied, however, that Hiss was a member, or was, to his knowledge, a Communist. He insisted they had only been interested in discussing Marxist literature.)

In response to committee questions, Chambers also added Donald Hiss, Alger's brother, Priscilla, Alger's wife, and Henry Collins, who had worked in the Labor Department. None of the people he named were on Elizabeth Bentley's list. Miss Bentley had pointed the finger at Harry Dexter White, former Assistant Secretary of the Treasury. Since he was the individual who had risen highest in government, the committee members were straining to get Chambers to confirm her charge. All he would say, after prolonged questioning, was that he believed White had been a "fellow-traveler" during the 1930's.

By this time in its history the reputation of the House Un-American Activities Committee was so rank that the only requirement for surviving its accusations was to ignore them. This seems to have been the strategy followed by all save two. Harry Dexter White insisted on denying Elizabeth Bentley's charges several days later, despite a bad heart condition. He made a stirring defense of his reputation, and responded to Nixon's questions with a fervor that was applauded in the hearing room and in the press. Within a few hours after leaving the hearing he suffered a heart attack and was dead three days later.

The other incautious individual was Alger Hiss. The morning after Chambers testified Chief Investigator Robert Stripling, whom Chambers described as having a "flair for showmanship" without which the committee's work "would have been smothered in silence and reduced to nullity," received a telegram from Hiss requesting the opportunity to appear before a public session. He wanted to deny under oath all Chambers' charges against him. Nixon commented: "Hiss was the only one named by Chambers who volunteered in this way."

His appearance was scheduled for the next day, August 5. By this time Nixon realized he had hold of a situation whose publicity possibilities were immense. He engaged the use of a larger room and watched it fill to overflowing in the morning.

Nixon had quickly developed faith in Whittaker Chambers. He said: "I came more and more to realize that despite his unpretentious appearance,

Chambers was a man of extraordinary intellectual gifts and one who had inner strength and depth. Here was no headline seeker but rather a thoughtful, introspective man, careful with his words, speaking with what sounded like the ring of truth."

He was going ahead on a hunch, but the hunch was supported by his sure knowledge that he was once again the focus of national attention. The flash-bulbs exploding in his face were a reliable index. And he had a vested interest in trusting Chambers. The committee was the leading force in the country touting the "Communists in government" line. It could ill afford to turn its back on any witness who supported HUAC and sounded fairly reasonable. Furthermore, there was little risk. In the anti-Communist climate of the day many of Nixon's supporters took accusations as proof. If the accusations against Hiss eventually proved false, Nixon could look forward to easy forgiveness for having committed his error in a good cause. In the meantime, there would be all that priceless publicity depicting him as the defender of the nation against subversives.

Although Chambers was hesitant and barely audible at first, he quickly developed a witness-stand presence. Despite having been an isolate all his life, he unexpectedly found the center of the stage his natural habitat.

This reaction was altogether natural. Chambers was a brilliant, highly emotional man. He was also consumed with the conceit which, at any given point in his life, allowed him to believe he knew what *the truth* was. So that for the twelve years or so when he was a Communist, every scintilla of his intelligence was concentrated on rationalizing the most irrational Party-line positions handed down from Moscow. During those dark years he stole from his government, he betrayed his friends and he cursed the name of God.

Having reversed himself and become, in his own eyes, a moral man and an anti-Communist, he flew to the opposite extreme. He was now willing to undergo the humiliation of exposure in order to destroy the "Red menace." It was "a small price to pay if my testimony helps to make Americans recognize at last that they are at grips with a secret, sinister and enormously powerful force whose tireless purpose is their enslavement."

Not only were the Communists involved in this conspiracy, but so were liberals, New Dealers and most Democrats. The only difference between the troops in F.D.R.'s phalanx and the Communists was that the Communists knew where they were going, while the Washington bureaucrats were marching blindly toward their common goal.

The committee met on August 5, but it was careful not to bring Hiss and Chambers together. Hiss made a complete denial of the charges and was so convincing that when the committee members assembled privately af-terwards they were completely downcast. "We're ruined!" one of them said.

All of them, except Nixon, who had no opponent in the November election, were going to have to face the voters within three months. Congressman F. Edward Hébert said dejectedly, "Let's turn the record over to the Justice Department and let them decide who's lying."

Toledano commented, "Nixon's public relations sense told him that this was no solution." He argued for a continuation of the hearings. They would play it safe but keep the ball bouncing.

There was something about Chambers that struck a responsive cord in Nixon. Perhaps it was that he was extremely shy. Like Nixon he had no friends. On his farm he was close to being a hermit, watching passing cars through his binoculars to see if Russian agents were about to assassinate him. In addition, he was obsessed by the Communist issue, as was Nixon. Since coming to Congress Nixon had become largely a one-issue man and they shared that issue. Chambers was also an authority on Marxism. For the previous year and a half Nixon had been boning up on the subject in skull sessions with Father John F. Cronin, an ecclesiastic who made a specialty of studying Communist infiltration into labor unions. But here was an opportunity to pick the brains of a front line ex-Communist. Short of sitting in on a seminar with Marx and Lenin, this was the closest he could imagine getting to the truth of the twists and turns in the Communist conspiracy.

Finally, Nixon found Chambers' morbidness attractive. It echoed a strain in his own character. By any objective standard, life had dealt harshly with Chambers. There was ample reason to sympathize with him.

When all the other members of the committee wanted to drop the Hiss hot potato Nixon refused to be swept along by their fears. Instead he argued for more time. It was true that Hiss had only denied knowing a man *named* Whittaker Chambers and if they were brought together immediately, he would probably identify him by some alias Chambers admitted using at the time. The air would probably go right out of the balloon the committee had been trying to blow up. But perhaps there was a way to prevent the case from collapsing. Nixon hit on the strategy of keeping the two apart. Let Hiss demand to see Chambers. They would keep him dangling while Nixon prodded and probed, hoping that some facts would emerge to give substance to Chambers' charges. Meanwhile, tension would build up across the country as people debated the interesting but minor question, did they know each other?

On August 7 Chambers was once again called before the committee in private session. He was questioned for hours. Nixon urged him to recall every personal detail he could dredge up about Hiss. The pressure was increasing, for Harry Truman had brusquely labeled the hearings a Republican "red herring" being staged by Nixon and his fellow conservatives to distract the country from the miserable job the Republicans were doing in the 80th Congress. It was three months before the presidential election and Nixon was cheerleading a Republican smear aimed at defeating him.

Herblock, the *Washington Post* Pulitzer Prize cartoonist, had already developed two stereotypes for Nixon, one more deadly than the other. In one version Dick had a five o'clock shadow and the furtive stoop of an assassin. In the other, he had the sleek body of a well-fed black cat, on his face the expression of wicked satisfaction achieved by felines who have swallowed their victim whole.

It is important to note that Nixon was convinced espionage played no role in Hiss's relationship to Chambers. The no longer reticent witness repeatedly stressed that fact. Nixon did not expect to send Hiss to jail. He had no thought that he was dealing with a complex spy network which was a continuing threat to America's security. The service to country was minimal, as usual, the service to self was paramount.

Hiss made every attempt to pin Nixon down on a date when he could confront Chambers. The story dominated the front pages for days on end. The substance of these stories was provided by leaks Nixon shrewdly placed with favored reporters. Carefully rationed tidbits about this or that detail Chambers had remembered about the Hiss household were presented to the readers in a manner that made it seem Nixon was slowly forcing Hiss into a corner. Eventually Nixon would make him admit he knew Chambers.

Becoming increasingly obscure was the fact that Hiss had not denied knowing the man who had suddenly leveled these accusations at him. He was simply not being given the opportunity to see *whether* he knew him.

On August 16 Hiss was again called before the committee, again in private session, again with Whittaker Chambers carefully kept out of sight. The questioning now concerned details of Hiss's memory of his former Georgetown residences, which Chambers had claimed to have visited. Hiss was assured Chambers would not have access to his answers from which he could obtain items to substantiate his claims of intimacy. The hearing, Nixon pledged, was secret. Not a word of what was said would be made public.

Nixon finally yielded to Hiss's demand that he be allowed to confront Chambers. He was informed the confrontation would take place on August 25. The hearing transcript concluded with this final notation: "THE CHAIRMAN: Thank you for coming and we will see you August 25."

Overnight Nixon felt the ground shifting under him. Harry Dexter White's death soon after the committee's badgering had provoked attacks on HUAC in the press, and Nixon decided he would have to produce a sensation which would result in some favorable publicity for the committee. The confrontation between Hiss and Chambers would have to take place that very day. There was no doubt in his mind that Chambers did indeed know Hiss. If this relatively insignificant matter could be presented in just the right light, it might be made to serve as confirmation of other assertions. Besides, no one was going to jail. It was simply a matter of seeing who would land on his feet after this scrimmage.

For greatest impact Hiss had to be kept in the dark about the committee's plans. Committee member John McDowell had his secretary contact Hiss to ask whether they could get together during the afternoon. Hiss thought McDowell, whom he had known before the accusations were made, was proposing a private chat with him in his New York office. He waited there for the Congressman. At 5:30 McDowell called to say that he would like Hiss to meet him and Nixon at the Commodore Hotel. There was no indication of what he had in mind, and since the committee had interrogated him exhaustively the previous day in Washington, Hiss had no thought that at the end of a workday, without notice, without an invitation to bring along an attorney, he was again being summoned to testify. He specifically did not expect that the confrontation with Chambers, which was scheduled for a week later, was about to take place.

When he entered the room in the Commodore, he was astonished to discover it was quickly being converted into a hearing room. Nixon immediately announced that the purpose of the hastily arranged meeting was to bring the two antagonists together. Hiss protested. "I resented the hypocrisy of the elaborate assurances of secrecy that had been given me the day before," he wrote in his 1957 book *In The Court of Public Opinion*, "only to be cynically violated by immediate leaks slanted to injure me. In addition, the disingenuous manner in which McDowell summoned me was displeasing."

He complained about the sub rosa release of selected items from his testimony. McDowell frowned at Nixon and responded, "Obviously, there was a leak, because the story that appeared in the various papers I read was part of the activities of yesterday afternoon. As a member of Congress, there is nothing I can do about that. It is a regrettable thing, and I join you in feeling rather rotten about the whole thing."

Nixon remained silent. Within moments Hiss and Chambers, friends who had not seen each other in over a decade, were reunited. Nixon had his *big* story and had landed on his feet. The evening papers were dominated by the drama of the confrontation. Ignored rather completely was the fact that Chambers reiterated Hiss had *not* taken part in any espionage activity. His accusation remained that Hiss had been a Communist during the mid-1930's. Hiss challenged him to repeat his statement outside the committee room where he would not have Congressional protection to say anything without fear of prosecution. He asserted he would sue Chambers for libel if he would come out from behind the committee's protection.

The world at large had heard Chambers repeatedly deny that espionage was involved in his "Marxist study group." Everyone took it for granted that he was telling the truth. Why should a man publicly exhibit himself as Chambers had, and then hold back on the most crushing charge. After all, Elizabeth Bentley had already admitted to committing espionage, and nothing had happened to her. Furthermore, the Cold War had taken a nasty turn. The Communists had executed a coup against Czechoslovakian democracy in the late spring, and on June 24 our forces in Berlin were blockaded when the Russians cut all roads, canals and railroads between the city and West Germany. Our air force was mobilized to fly supplies into the beleaguered city. For almost a year this airlift continued, as Stalinist policies led to a further deterioration in relations between the two great world powers. It was almost war. In this siege atmosphere it seemed inconceivable that a self-professed anti-Communist crusader would shield Stalinist spies.

The committee was satisfied with the results of the initial confrontation. In the climate that prevailed it was unimportant that Chambers was unwilling to accuse Hiss of espionage. What he had said was serious enough in the minds of most Americans. Nevertheless, Nixon was not completely satisfied. He wanted to gain as much favorable publicity as possible. Clearly another public session was called for.

When Chambers heard of this from Nixon he rebelled. "Another public hearing, especially another confrontation with Hiss in front of hundreds of strange people, was more than I could endure. In two weeks I had been through three hearings. Another great circus under eager, avid eyes, under batteries of news cameras and the hard stares of a prevailingly hostile press was too much."

Nixon was unrelenting. There would be another public hearing, after which the committee would be through with him and he could seek space outside the spotlight.

I asked Nixon why there had to be a public hearing at all now that Hiss had admitted that he knew me. But if another hearing had to be held, why must it be public, why could it not be held in executive session? Patiently, he put me off with reasons that did not seem to me to make sense. When I became insistent, he said reluctantly, "It is for your own sake that the Committee is holding a public hearing. The Department of Justice is all set to move in on you in order to save Hiss. They are planning to indict you at once. The only way to head them off is to let the public judge for itself which one of you is telling the truth. That is your only chance. That is why the hearing must be public." I liked and trusted

Nixon. Clearly, my choice lay between procuring my own safety and the agony of the others. . . . I left Nixon, feeling, in addition to all else that I felt, like a very small creature, skirting the shadows of encircling powers that would not hesitate to crush me as impersonally as a steam roller crushes a bug.

Clearly Chambers had doubts about his new friend. He had a purpose in testifying, cloudy as the real nature of that purpose was to him, but Nixon also had reasons for wanting him to testify and their reasons, he sensed, did not always coincide.

In an addendum he commented, "Regardless of whether or not Richard Nixon was mistaken—and there are many who would claim that he was—I believed him, and his words weighed heavily upon me." Even his friend Whittaker sensed the trickiness which had by now become so integral a part of Dick's nature.

After the August 25 public hearing, at which time he again denied Hiss was engaged in espionage, Chambers accepted an invitation to appear on "Meet the Press." On the August 27 broadcast he asserted that he had known Hiss to be a Communist. Once again, with compelling sincerity, he denied that Hiss had taken part in espionage activity. In fact, the question was now being asked only by those few meticulous individuals who liked to touch all bases.

Chambers was next called before a Federal Grand Jury in New York. The government was intent on determining whether there were some legal action that should be taken against someone. Since it was not illegal simply to be a Communist, the Grand Jury was determined to explore the possibility that espionage, an indictable act, had been committed. Chambers thought the question over carefully and swore to the jury members that no espionage was involved in his relations with Hiss.

On September 27 Hiss finally struck back, filing a libel suit against Chambers in Baltimore, claiming defamation of character and asking for $75,000 in damage. The fat was in the fire. A pre-trial hearing, held to clear away the underbrush in preparation for the trial, at first produced no revelations. After several days of testimony, when it had become abundantly clear that in the absence of any witness to corroborate what he had been saying he was going to lose his case, Chambers suddenly recalled an envelope he had left with his brother-in-law in Brooklyn ten years earlier. The envelope, he thought vaguely, might have something in it to lend weight to his charges. He did not remember what it was, but he *did* recall it had been meant to act as a "life preserver" if his Communist bosses tried to retaliate against him for deserting the Party.

He did not mention his sudden recollection to his attorneys, but traveled north to Brooklyn by himself. The envelope his brother-in-law extracted from an unused, dust-laden dumbwaiter shaft, gave the case a bizarre turn. In it were sixty-five pages of typewritten documents, apparently partly typed on a machine that had once belonged to Priscilla Hiss. There were also four memos in Hiss's handwriting concerning some matters current in the department during the 1930's. The last was a memo in the hand of Harry Dexter White in which he discussed inter-office machinations at the Treasury Department.

Included in the envelope were five rolls of microfilm, three of which were not developed. Chambers showed only the documents to his attorneys, eventually hiding the film in a hollowed-out pumpkin on his farm.

Nixon was euphoric. It did not seem to matter that his only witness had been lying to him for over three months. It did not make him pause and wonder that Chambers had repeatedly lied to Berle, to the FBI, to the House Un-American Activities Committee, to the Grand Jury and to the American public. Sufficient unto him was it that the Lord had provided *some* sort of evidence to justify the act of prestidigitation he had been staging since August 3. He was so relieved that he went off on a Caribbean cruise with Pat.

In mid-ocean he received a cable telling him to get back to Washington, Chambers had come up with another revelation. He was plucked off the boat by a seaplane and swept dramatically back onto the scene.

What was the new sensation? It was the old one. It was the second installment of the contents of the envelope. Chambers had called HUAC investigator Stripling out to his farm and in the night, with flashlight in hand, led him into the fields, where he had extracted the cans of film from history's most famous pumpkin.

The contents of the documents were hardly as sensational as the Pentagon Papers which Daniel Ellsberg stole from the Defense Department and used against Nixon in June, 1971. But the moment in space determines the reaction. Ellsberg was generally viewed as a hero while the criminal who stole those other documents was known for the villain that he was. Except, who was he?

Chambers, and eventually Henry Julian Wadleigh, were the only individuals ever to admit that they were involved in espionage. No witness ever appeared to confirm Chambers' allegation that Hiss and his wife committed espionage.

The documents themselves cast little light on who stole them. They were apparently in one last batch covering a period in 1938 up to April. This in itself caused Chambers and Nixon consternation. For years Chambers had been maintaining he left the Communist Party in the latter part of 1937. Hiss claimed he had not seen George Crosley (the name by which he knew Chambers), a man he said posed as a free-lance journalist, since 1936. How could Chambers have collected these documents from Hiss in April of 1938 when he had repeatedly sworn that he made his last collection from him, before fleeing into hiding, late in 1937?

To a man like Chambers the answer to his problem was not difficult. He simply had a clearer recollection. Oh, yes, it had *not* been in late 1937 that he left the Party, it had been in mid-1938. This was not the first time he had reversed himself and it was not the first time such a dramatic about-face seemed plausible to Nixon. The moment called for belief, and Nixon arose to its needs.

Nixon was drawn to Chambers not only by a desire for publicity. There was an empathy between them that Nixon had never shared with anyone. Nixon described the meeting on which the enduring foundation of their friendship was laid.

> I decided to see Chambers again, this time alone and informally, not so much to get more information from him as to gain a more intimate impression of what kind of man he really was. I thought that if I could talk to him alone, I would be better able to sense whether or not he was telling the truth.

It is interesting to see that even though he was publicly demonstrating his conviction that Chambers was telling the truth, he was apparently still full of doubts.

> To avoid any publicity I made the two-hour trip from Washington to his farm by car. We sat on some dilapidated rocking chairs on his front porch overlooking the rolling Maryland countryside. It was the first of many long and rewarding conversations I was to have with him during the period of the Hiss case, and through the years until his death in 1961. Like most men of quality, he made a deeper impression personally than he did in public. Within minutes, the caricature drawn by the rumor-mongers . . . faded away. Here was a man of extraordinary intelligence, speaking from great depth of understanding; a sensitive, shy man who had turned from complete dedication to Communism to a new religious faith and a kind of fatalism about the future. One thing that especially impressed me was his almost absolute passion for personal privacy.

When Hiss said, at the next committee meeting, that he had been in-formed Nixon had secretly met with Chambers at his farm, Hannah's son hotly denied it. But, although it was now clear that he was placing himself in a compromising position, Nixon continued his two-hour motor trips to Westminster. The serenity and companionship he found there were worth the risk.

For thirty-five years Nixon had held himself aloof from intimate association with other men. Now, he found a man so compelling that he took time away from his busy schedule and risked the possibility people would accuse him of rehearsing the witness, so that he could share some time with him during these increasingly strained days.

Just how strained they were for Richard Nixon was described by his mother. She and Frank had moved to a farm in York County, Pennsylvania, only two and a half hours from Washington. Richard and Pat would occasionally visit them. But he was so distracted by the events in Washington that, "he would not hear me when I called him to meals. It bothered me a great deal because when he did come to the table he ate very little."

Hannah was worried. Her son's strange behavior was alarming.

During those visits he would go to one part of the room and stop and think. Then he would go to another part of the room and stop and think again. Then he would pace nervously and talk to himself. "I just feel that I should get out of it," he would say at one moment. But the next moment he would be saying, "I can't drop it now."

My husband and I stood by, not knowing what to do. I said, "If Richard doesn't give up the case, he won't be here to carry on." But we were reticent about saying anything. Finally, however, I said very quietly one afternoon, "Richard, why don't you drop the case? No one else thinks Hiss is guilty. You are a young congressman. Older congressmen and senators have warned you to stop. Why don't you?"

Nixon's response was the surface one he had been giving for weeks: he thought Hiss was lying. But was that sufficient reason for him to be pursuing the suspected liar with such vigor that it was exhausting him mentally and physically? Establishing that Hiss had been a Communist during the 1930's had become a crusade. Whatever little taste for food he ever had (his favorite dish was cottage cheese smothered in ketchup), was disappearing. He was nervous and testy and had fallen to talking to himself.

Although his ambition clearly played its usual role in driving him on, there seemed no doubt that Chambers himself was a major part of the reason Nixon continued in his lonely pursuit of Hiss. He was fascinated by Chambers. The hokey image of the city-slicker turned farmer, the intellectual turned rube, which alienated so many of Chambers' former associates in the publishing field, struck the tuning fork of Nixon's memory with an intensity which could not be denied. He went to him with his usual intention of scavenging as much as possible, but came away thinking he had finally found a friend.

What sort of man was Nixon befriending?

Fortunately Chambers has revealed himself so completely in his book *Witness* that it is possible to answer that question with some authority. He spoke of his feeling after the first few sessions with the committee:

> This sense of having become the still live prey of forces that were impersonal to me in every way but that of destruction, began with the beginning of the Hiss Case, and never lifted from me until its end, and perhaps not wholly then. One of the torments of the Case for me would be in the days when I was reprieved to return to my family . . . before I must return to that public dock where I was simply living prey existing to be rent. Like any creature that knows it is meant to die, I simply went inert in an animal sense.

Chambers had a death urge that was so pronounced and overriding it seemed to obliterate all other normal thought patterns. When he spoke about anything there was this "fatalism" that Nixon immediately noticed, but it was a fatalism freighted with a longing for death. Despite the ordeal he described so graphically, Chambers did not shrink from the pain. The meaning of everything he had been through hinged on that exquisite torment.

> I believed that I was not meant to be spared from testifying. I sensed, with a force greater than any fear or revulsion, that it was for this that my whole life had been lived. For this I had been a Communist, for this I had ceased to be a Communist. For this the tranquil strengthening years had been granted to me. This challenge was the terrible meaning of my whole life, of all that I had done that was evil. . . . My failure to do so, any attempt to evade that necessity, would be a betrayal that would measure nothing less than the destruction of my own soul.

In this messianic spirit he persisted throughout in maintaining that he had nothing but the warmest feelings for Hiss, whom he described to the committee as "a man of great simplicity and a great gentleness and sweetness of character. . . ." Although he occasionally spoke of his understanding that he was betraying an old friend and that betrayal of this sort was "unforgivable" he more often spoke as if he was still the loyal friend of the man he was in the process of destroying:

> My feeling for Hiss had remained unchanged through the years. I felt

about Hiss and myself as of people whom chance has led to live in different continents, but who had only to be brought together again for their friendship, like an interrupted conversation, to be taken up where it was dropped.

Chambers persisted in deluding himself into thinking he was being merciful toward his former friends. Incredibly he took the pose that he was actually protecting them. He continued to hope Hiss would admit he had been a Communist "so that I might not be compelled to testify to worse about him and the others."

My intention was clear, too. I did not wish to harm, more than was unavoidable, those whom I must testify against, of whose lives in the years since I had left them I know next to nothing, many of whom might no longer be Communists. I would not, therefore, testify to espionage against them. But I must testify that they had been concealed Communists and that an underground had existed in the Government. That was the one indispensable fact.

He felt that once they had all bared their souls the country would "pass on to more pressing things. . . . Most of the witnesses would lapse back into their routine lives." Everyone, that is, but himself. "I felt, with a certainty that I could neither explain nor shake off, that I *was doomed.*"

The incongruity of his thought patterns is barely concealed by his facility with language. For this doom-yearning individual, who claimed that anti-Communism was now the central issue of his life, the "one indispensable face" about the men he was accusing was that they must admit they had been Communists at one time. Once they had made such an admission, they could return to their normal pursuits, as far as he was concerned. "I had tried to shield those who were most deeply involved from darker charge of espionage."

Chambers apparently felt that some of these men were still Communists. He subsequently alleged they stole government documents. He had every reason to believe some of them were still jamming state secrets into that underground pipeline to Moscow. Yet, it was not "indispensable" for him to expose their purported espionage activity, which might destroy the United States, it was merely "indensable" for them to admit he was correctly identifying them. At the very least this was monumental conceit. But it was probably much more.

Nixon did have an instant of great doubt about Chambers and, in terms of his own personal life, that episode is significant.

On December 6, 1948, the Grand Jury had been reconvened in New York to hear the new evidence produced by Chambers, this time about espionage. In his anxiety to get Chambers before the committee and question him on his new charges Nixon scheduled a committee meeting in New York for 9 P.M., after the Grand Jury had had an opportunity to interrogate him. As he was preparing to leave his Washington office for the train a telephone call came through for Stripling. Nixon described what happened:

It was from Keith Lewis of the Eastman Kodak Company. We had asked Eastman to check the microfilm which Chambers had turned over to us and to determine when it had been manufactured. Rumors had been circulated that Chambers might have put the documents on film not ten years ago but only after the Committee hearings of the past summer in order to manufacture evidence to prove his charges. A look of complete dismay came over Stripling's face as he took the call. I heard him say, "You mean this film couldn't have been manufactured before 1945?" Stripling hung up and turned to me. "Well, we've had it. Eastman did not manufacture the type of film Chambers turned over to us until 1945."

Nixon had been faced with many inconsistencies in Chambers' testimony during the previous four months, but this seemed too substantial. At first glance there did not seem to be any way to slip around this one.

The news jolted us into almost complete shock. We sat looking at each other without saying a word. This meant that Chambers was, after all, a liar. All the work, the long hours we had put into the investigation had been useless. We had been taken in by a diabolically clever maniac who had finally made a fatal mistake.

No doubt Chambers was every bit as clever as Nixon thought; however, this was the first time he expressed the thought that his friend was merely a cleverly disguised madman. What was he to do in this emergency? Characteristically he immediately thought of his own best interests, which no longer seemed to lie on a straight line with Chambers'. But first he must make sure. Perhaps Chambers had some way of explaining it all. In the past he had led them around obstacles that seemed almost as insurmountable.

Chambers was visiting in the office of Judge Harold Medina, Jr., who was soon to preside at the trial of the American Communist leaders. Nixon omitted any reference to Medina.

I buzzed my secretary in the outer office and asked her to get Chambers on the phone in New York. Before he had a chance to say anything, I asked him: "Am I correct in understanding that these papers were put on microfilm in 1938?" He answered, "Yes"—obviously mystified by the question. "We have just had a report from the Eastman Kodak Company that film of the type you turned over to us was not made by the company until after 1945," I retorted. "What is your answer to that?" There was a long silence at the other end of the wire. For a moment, I thought he must have hung up. Finally he answered in a voice full of despair and resignation: "I can't understand it. God must be against me."

Then I took out on him all the fury and frustration that had built up within me. "You'd better have a better answer than that," I said. "The subcommittee's coming to New York tonight and we want to see you at the Commodore Hotel at 9:00 and you'd better be there!" I slammed the receiver down without giving him a chance to reply.

Chambers' account of the incident is substantially different.

One day (Dec. 6) when for some reason I was excused from the Federal Building I went down to Wall Street to ask the advice of Harold Medina, Jr. While we were talking, Medina's telephone rang. "He's here now," I heard him say. Then his voice began to rise in surprise, in an incredulous tone, and he began to make brief answers in a conversation that I could not follow. Then he handed me the telephone.

One glimpses here the elaborate mechanism for shadowing Chambers that Nixon had set up. He wanted to speak to him and within moments he was able to pinpoint his whereabouts. The reasons why Nixon hid the name of Judge Medina and the nature of his conversation with him can only be conjectured.

Chambers took the phone as Medina said, "It's Nixon." Now Chambers' account continues

"The Eastman Kodak experts," said Congressman Nixon, "have just reported that the film in those undeveloped rolls was manufactured in 1945. If you got them in 1938, how do you explain that?" "It cannot be true," I said, "but I cannot explain it." "The subcommittee's going to New York tonight," said Nixon, "and we want to see you at the Commodore Hotel at nine o'clock. We're going to get to the bottom of this." "I will be there," I said. "You'd better be there," said Nixon. His voice was harsh with the just anger of a man who has placed his confidence in another man who turns out to be an imposter.

Omitted from Chambers' account is any reference to his lame explanation for the glaring discrepancy, which, according to Nixon, was, "God must be against me." Likewise missing is Nixon's furious and frustrated response.

Instead Chambers moved that quote around a little, as is the habit of editors seeking a somewhat more effective way of presenting their story.

> I had felt that Richard Nixon was one of the few friends who really understood what was going on. I put up the receiver slowly. As I did so, I saw Medina's eyes rest on me with a scrutinizing glance. He had learned from Nixon about the film. I knew what unpleasant thoughts must be hovering behind his eyes. I walked out of the broadloom and heavy oak hush of his office into the teeming Wall Street crowds. "God is against me," I thought.

His "friend" had other thoughts on his mind. As he slammed down the receiver, Nixon turned to Stripling, who asked, "What'll we do now?"

> "There's only one thing we can do," I answered. "I want you to have the staff call the reporters who cover the Committee and ask them to come to my office in thirty minutes for a statement I will make at that time." I have made some decisions in my life more difficult than this one, but none could approach it in terms of personal embarrassment and chagrin. But there was no other choice.

Nixon's commitment to himself was never clearer than at this moment. He had made a mistake. He had, for almost the first time in his life, extended his hand in friendship—what a colossal error. But, perhaps it was not too late. If he could get out *his* version of the story first, then perhaps some profit could still be gained from his display of weakness.

> I tried to collect my thoughts and put down some notes for the statement I had to make. . . . Five minutes before the time scheduled for the press conference, after some of the reporters had already arrived in the reception room of my office, the buzzer sounded on the intercom. I answered and my secretary said, "The man from Eastman Kodak is on the phone and wants to talk to Stripling again." He picked up the phone and I saw the expression on his face change to one of sheer joy. He shouted into the receiver, "You mean you were wrong? You did manufacture that film through 1938 but then discontinued it during the war?"
> I had no need to hear the answer. Stripling put the receiver down, let out a Texas rebel yell, grabbed me by the arms, and danced me around the room.

Disaster had been averted. It was unnecessary to seek an explanation of why the error had been made. The mouths of gift horses should never be explored too thoroughly. Still, one without Nixon's overwhelming commitment could not help but wonder at the blinding speed with which this reversal came. Surely Eastman Kodak had checked out every possibility for error before phoning Nixon to explain that what Chambers was saying could not possibly be true. In the face of the exhaustive checking process they must have gone through, to have come up with conclusive evidence of the reverse within the few minutes that it took to summon the reporters from the press room must have convinced Nixon that the gods were smiling on him.

However, Chambers did not know that his salvation had followed so closely on the heels of his disgrace. Nixon tried to reach him, but was unsuccessful this time. Where was the former Communist courier?

> I toted my frozen core about the streets of the financial district. I was not going anywhere. . . . By informing against the conspirators, I had misunderstood God's purpose, and God was making that clear to me. . . . I knew absolute defeat.

Chambers had previously contemplated suicide during the earlier stages of the hearings, as his sense of shame over what he perceived to be the unforgivable sin of betraying his old friends became too much for him to bear. The feeling now returned with a vengeance. He walked "in the Wall Street maze, a man who had nowhere to go in heaven or on earth, sometimes stepping off the narrow sidewalks, more by instinct than by sight, to avoid colliding with the busy people."

Before leaving Medina he had promised to phone later in the afternoon, for a reason that was no longer clear to him. He stumbled into a phone booth and dialed. "Say," Medina said, "Nixon called again and wanted me to tell you that that was all a mistake. The expert was mistaken. They manufactured that kind of film in the 1930s and then discontinued it. In 1945, they began to make it again."

Chambers heard the news, "but my mood did not change." Nixon had plunged him into a depth of despondency few men experience. Although the technical error had been corrected, the experience "continued to shake the soul. All of the suffering of which I had been the cause and witness . . . all that pointless pain continued to roll me under in a drowning wave."

Deserted by his God, vilified by his friend, Chambers had reached a dead end. He went to a seed store in lower Manhattan.

> I strolled among the sprays and insecticides. . . . I was looking for that poison one of whose ingredients is a cyanide compound. At last I asked a clerk if they stocked it. From some hiding place, he brought me the big

round, tan-colored tin. I paid for it and went out. I went to another seed house. Again the poison was not displayed. I had to ask for it. "Is there any danger in using it?" I asked. "Be very careful," said the clerk, "if you breathe enough of it, it will kill you." I thanked him.

He stored the can away in his bedroom in his mother's house on Long Island. Time passed and still his sense of dejection did not lift. "When I sought prayerful guidance, there was none." His Communist faith had failed him, now his Quaker faith was failing him. "I could not free my mind from an organic revulsion that I should have had to denounce those men and women, none of whom, as human beings, I would ever have raised a hand to injure."

In his strained condition, his logic matched the sham nobility of his language. "I could spare the others," he reasoned, "by removing myself as the only living witness against them. As men and women, they would then be free of my charges. But my witness against the conspiracy [he should have said, *against them*] would remain. It would remain in the form of the documents and microfilm."

Chambers was refusing to face his own morbid motivation. He was describing a diseased mental disposition as humanitarianism. In reality what he proposed, at this stage of the game, was not to dispense humanity to those he had accused, but rather to give himself the relief of oblivion. He had always had an inclination toward self-destruction. And as his younger brother, who had marked the way twenty-two years before, he would wipe out his pain with gas.

I wrote a letter addressed simply: To All. In it I said that, of course, my testimony against Alger Hiss was the truth (time would certainly bear me out) , but that the world was not ready for my testimony. I wrote that, in testifying, my purpose had always been to disclose the conspiracy, never to injure any individual man or woman. . . . My act was not suicide in the usual sense, for I had no desire to stop living. It was self-execution.

The self-deception apparent in this note *To All* was not apparent to Chambers years after the event when he made it public. The eminent British jurist Earl Jowitt remarked in his book, *The Strange Case of Alger Hiss,* when considering the difference between suicide and self-execution, he found that Chambers had made "a subtle distinction which I fail to appreciate."

Chambers wrote a letter to his wife in which he poignantly remarked (and duly recorded for *All* to note in *Witness*) , "I could not get back to you. . . ." However, he had managed to get back to his mother's house. This was the place for dark acts to be committed, where the walls still resounded to the screams of an insane old woman and he still might find an ax under a bed or a knife under a pillow.

> I poured some of the chemical in the cover of each tin. But I was afraid that the fumes might be diffused in the air of the room. I thought to concentrate them by rigging a receptacle for my head. I moistened the chemical. The fumes began to rise. I prayed for my mother, my wife and my children. I felt that I had no right to pray for myself and did not do so. On my bureau, there was a small picture of each of my children. I took one picture in each hand to have them with me through the night. Then I lay down with my head inside the receptacle, which I closed with another damp towel draped across the front.
>
> The fumes were somewhat sickening, but, perhaps because of them, and because I was very tired, I fell asleep almost at once. Some time during the night, I half-awoke, as if I had been stabbed in the chest and my body had jack-knifed against the pain. I suspect that at that moment the fumes had begun to take effect, that my body had bucked against them, and that when it did so, the towel fell from the front of the receptacle; the fumes poured out and air moved in.

And so the night passed. When he awoke in the morning, he began vomiting. His mother heard the sound of his retching and entered his room when he did not respond to her frantic knocking. "Perhaps," Chambers added, "with the memory of her other son in mind, this possibility had tormented her since the Hiss Case began."

But her advice was harsh and practical. "Oh, how could you, how could you? The world hates a quitter. They would never forgive you." With this motherly nudge Chambers was able to face the future, never brightly, but rather with a grim determination which was always threatening to disappear. Nixon claimed to understand what had motivated his friend:

> Looking back, I think I can understand how he must have felt. His career was gone. His reputation was ruined. His wife and children had been humiliated. But all this would not have mattered to him if the cause for which he had taken these calculated risks had some chance to prevail. And now it did seem that "God was against him." From the time he testified on August 3, through the months of summer and fall, I had been the one public official who had stood by him and on whom he thought he could count. And now I was deserting him. Chambers was to go through many crises during Hiss's two trials, but this proved to be his most difficult moment. It seemed the height of irony that I was the one who found it necessary to put him through this ordeal. . . .

Nixon apparently felt he was responsible for Chambers' attempted suicide.

In this he was undoubtedly mistaken. Had it not been Nixon who pushed him over the edge, someone else would have performed that service. In fact, Dr. Meyer Zeligs, in his book *Friendship and Fratricide,* strongly suggests that Chambers did finally commit suicide in 1961.

Hiss's defense counsel produced psychiatric testimony at the first trial, which resulted in a stalemated jury, and at the second, which resulted in his conviction of perjury. The testimony tried to establish that Chambers was a psychotic. There seems little doubt that if the psychiatrists had had Chambers' autobiography, which did not appear until after Hiss's conviction, their task would have been much easier.

The book is peppered with references to the fact that Chambers felt he had "ceased to be a person," that "a dead man could scarcely have been more divided from the living world than I felt." Faced with what he was going through, he said, "most men will retreat, make peace at any price, or kill themselves." He spoke of "an air of death" that clung to his thoughts during those days.

Even after the inconclusive first trial, when it was apparent the government was no longer seriously thinking of indicting him for the crimes he so readily confessed (or for the crimes which he had been observed committing, such as his perjury before the New York Grand Jury), he was still ready to answer a newsman's question with the dark narcissism of a martyr. "I am a man who, reluctantly, grudgingly, step by step, is destroying himself that this country and the faith by which it lives may continue to exist."

His acute sense of public display allowed him, even at this low point, to pose repeatedly for movie camera crews who came to his farm, and morbidly rehearse his theme: "I am a man who . . . is destroying himself. . . ."

But Chambers' tormented soul had moved the soul of Richard Nixon. Toledano described the phenomenon:

> The relationship between Nixon and Whittaker Chambers that began then was a poignant one. At times of stress, even when he was Vice President, Nixon would drive to Westminster for a visit, informing only friends such as myself and the most reliable members of his staff. It was not only counsel that he sought from the older man, but a kind of intellectual replenishment and emotional stability. . . . Chambers was also a man of great insight, and he quickly assessed Nixon's abilities and limitations. Nixon, never one to open his heart or his mind unstintingly, came as close to this with Chambers as he has with any man. . . . To Nixon's credit, he never allowed his rapid rise in the world of affairs to interfere with his friendship and loyalty to Chambers. . . .

What Chambers finally said about Hiss may be true. Liars sometimes tell the truth. Truthful men occasionally lie. However, barring the testimony of some other witness to lend weight to Chambers rainbow-hued charges against Hiss, the historical jury, which sits now, remains out, still deadlocked, examining a voluminous record, which, despite Richard Nixon's faith, does not often make his friend seem credible. One thing that makes one hang back from reversing the verdict of January 21, 1950 is the enormous hideousness of the fact that Hiss served several years in Lewisberg jail and that his life was ruined. Surely it is easier to think that he deserved this fate than to accept the horror that such an injustice was allowed to take place.

Nixon has had few public displays of uneasy conscience. Usually he has handled the occasional sticky hangover from the case with the arrogant assurance of a lawyer whose faith in his client was confirmed by the prompt payment of his fee. A case in point was the sensation created by the publication of Nixon's autobiography.

The single item that had seemed to weigh most heavily in the jury's deliberations and tipped the balance in favor of conviction was the Woodstock typewriter that belonged to Priscilla Hiss. In the absence of any witness to corroborate Chambers' charges, the typewriter seemed to lend support. *Some* of the documents appeared to have been typed on it. Others were not. Chambers claimed that all the typed documents were copied by Priscilla on her Woodstock. Expert testimony by the FBI contradicted this.

The typewriter was missing and presumed by all to have gone into some recycling pot years ealier. It was the persistent detective work of Hiss's investigators that finally uncovered the Woodstock in April, 1949, six weeks before the first trial. Determined not to suppress anything that had a bearing on the case, Hiss instructed his lawyers to turn the machine over to the FBI.

Subsequently the Woodstock took its place next to Chambers as a silent, often contradictory, always suspect, but nevertheless potent accuser.

Imagine the shock of Hiss, *et al*, when in 1962 *Six Crises* was published with the following statement on page 60. "On December 13 [1948] , FBI agents found the typewriter."

That was six months before Hiss's attorneys thought *they* had found it on a junk pile, where it had supposedly lain for years. It was, according to Nixon, really found by the FBI during the most crucial moment in the New York Grand Jury's attempt to make up its mind whether to indict Hiss or Chambers.

In an endeavor to tell the whole story, Nixon elaborated on his statement:

It was still touch and go. Hiss and his lawyers fought down to the last hour of the life of the Grand Jury. On December 15, the critical last day, an expert from the FBI typed exact copies of the incriminating documents on the old Woodstock machine and had them flown up to New York as exhibits for the members of the Grand Jury to see. A typewriter has one characteristic in common with a fingerprint: every one is different, and it is impossible to make an exact duplicate unless the same machine is used. The evidence was unanswerable.

Hiss subsequently claimed the typewriter had been forged, and had an expert go to the trouble of doing what Nixon claimed was impossible, reproduce an exact duplicate of the old Hiss Woodstock. But whether an expert could forge a typewriter is a matter for scholarly debate. What was suddenly beyond debate was Nixon's 1962 assertion that the FBI had the typewriter secretly in its possession and had, in fact, "typed exact copies of the incriminating documents on the old Woodstock machine and had them flown up to New York as exhibits for the members of the Grand Jury. . . ." No wonder Hiss detected that the Grand Jury's attitude suddenly altered on that last day. He was still confused by this change in 1957, when he wrote his own book claiming forgery by typewriter. In *Six Crises* Nixon cleared up the confusion.

Beleaguered by newsmen who had immediately detected that this was new evidence, Nixon smiled broadly and made a flat denial that what he had written was true. It had all been a "researcher's error" he claimed smoothly and then refused ever to discuss the matter again. In subsequent editions of his book, the incriminating passages were deleted and we were given another example of how history can be rewritten with an eraser.

Nixon has erected an immense wall of silence surrounding any doubts he may have entertained about the Hiss case. It is as if he were determined to insist that there can be no questions about this most questionable affair. Almost as if he were afraid to contemplate the idea that perhaps the last word was *not* yet in. With the leisure of hindsight an observer might conclude that the strident, uncompromising stance he took in 1948 was part of what a young man regrettably had to do to get ahead in politics, and that like most Americans in 1949 and 1950, as Hiss moved toward the jailhouse door,* he had his nagging doubts.

While the battle was going on and since its end, however, there has been no slightest public suggestion of self-doubt. He had found a dramatic cause that propelled him onto the front pages of America's newspapers almost every day for a period of two years. And even more important, he had found a friend.

Newsweek reported, April 24, 1972, that Alger Hiss, now a stationery salesman, had received a letter from Nixon's finance committee which began, "Dear Fellow American," and asked for any small contribution that might help the man who had profited so much already from their relationship. Describing the reaction Nixon always caused in him, Hiss commented, "It gave me a bit of a jolt."

VIII.

The Pink Lady Campaign

A reporter came up to Nixon after the announcement of Hiss's conviction and said admiringly, "Dick, if you play your cards right, you can be President of the United States."

Although he recorded that Nixon reacted by laughing, it was very likely the laugh of the Green Island hustler who knew he had a winning hand. Nixon began the Hiss trial as one among many Congressmen. When it was over he was the best known member of the Lower House.

He set up his lightning rod immediately and started sending up incantations in the hope that a bolt of luck might strike. On June 20, 1949 he issued a statement calling for an "exhaustive inquiry" into school textbooks to detect instances where the "Communist conspiracy" had infected them. He drew up a list of citizens he considered reliable censors. Lo, General Dwight David Eisenhower's name led all the rest. Ike was then briefly head of Columbia University, and the most astigmatic Congressman could see that he was being groomed for the Presidency. There was nothing wrong with Nixon's eyes.

And they quickly focused on a new and more immediate objective, a seat in the Senate. Senator Sheridan Downey, a veteran of many California slugfests, was up for reelection at the end of 1950. Since Downey was elderly and in poor health, it seemed likely he would retire gracefully. It was not difficult to foresee the bitter Democratic primary that would take place in the spring of 1950, as the party's left and right wings sought to determine who would be the nominee. No matter who survived, the Democrats were bound to be splintered and working at cross-purposes as the November election approached. This made the Republican nomination even more attractive to Nixon, since it was clear that if he wanted it he could probably have it without significant opposition. Furthermore, the most attractive California

Republican of them all, Earl Warren, was running for a third term as governor. He was bound to strengthen the entire ticket.

Nixon began to assemble his campaign team in mid-1949. At its head was Murray Chotiner. Since 1946 he had often consulted him on political matters. The advice Chotiner portioned out was directly to Nixon's taste. It was extremely practical and preoccupied with only one possibility, victory. There was never a moment in a conversation with Chotiner when Nixon would be jarred by a cautionary note that a certain action should not be taken because it was unfair or immoral. His official title was to be *campaign coordinator and manager*, in charge of the whole shooting match. His first maneuver was to contact all papers in the state and ask for their advertising rates. He claimed this would make them treat stories about Nixon favorably in anticipation of lucrative ads.

On October 17, 1949, one month before the second Hiss trial was scheduled to begin, Nixon went back to Whittier for what was officially described as a "homecoming" celebration. In reality, this was Nixon's attempt to round up support for the candidacy which he expected to announce momentarily. Chotiner relayed the information to him that the field was open. Only two minor league Republicans had indicated they might be interested in opposing him. Even more joyous news was the fact that Sheridan Downey had withdrawn from the race.

On November 3 Nixon announced his candidacy in Pomona, California. The clear outline of Chotiner's campaign strategy was already apparent. "The issue," Nixon said bluntly, "is simply the choice between freedom and state socialism." Keeping his elbows close to his sides, as his high school debating coach had always advised, he chopped the message out at his audience of committed Republicans. "They can call it planned economy, the Fair Deal, or social welfare—but it is still the same old Socialist baloney, any way you slice it." Always ready with innuendo of treason, he finished his message to the faithful by accusing the Democrats of "selling the American birthright for a mess of political pottage."

For the next few months Nixon coasted, as Republican leaders from all over the state contacted Chotiner to record their presence on board the bandwagon. Hiss's conviction in January, 1950, gave Nixon's stock a boost. The Communists-in-government issue was clearly a winning one.

The spring primaries in Florida clinched it. Claude Pepper had been the Senator from that state for years. He had been one of Franklin Roosevelt's lieutenants in the Senate. Pepper was on the left wing of the party. However, he had always been a tremendous vote gatherer. He was a phenomenal stump speaker and popular in every section of the state, except in the offices of Ed Ball, squire of the billion-dollar Florida Du Pont interests.

Ball secured the services of Congressman George Armistead "Smooch" Smathers to run in the all-important Democratic primary against Pepper. Smathers had previously been an ardent Pepper supporter.

Smathers' campaign was pitched at the crudest anti-Communist level he could reach. It was watched most carefully and received the widest publicity all over the country. Smathers accused Pepper of being "the leader of the radicals and the extremists" in Florida. That was a relatively mild opening and had he remained in the vicinity of that allegation, the Committee on Campaign Decency might have looked the other way. Pepper, he said, "is now on trial in Florida. Arrayed against him will be loyal Americans. . . . Standing against us will be certain Northern labor bosses, all the socialists, all the radicals and all the fellow travelers. . . . Florida will not allow herself to become entangled in the spiraling spider web of the Red network. The people of our state will no longer tolerate advocates of treason."

Like Nixon, he had been a college debater of renown. And like him, Smathers had a tendency toward exaggeration. "The outcome," he continued, "can truly determine whether our homes will be destroyed, whether our children will be torn from their mothers, trained as conspirators and turned against their parents, their home and their church. I stand for election on the principle of the free state against the jail state."

Smathers was taking the popular anti-Communist theme of the day and carrying it to its extreme. Short of calling for a firing squad for Pepper, he knew no limits to what he would say about the Florida Senator. The deliberately fraudulent nature of Smathers' campaign can be seen in the speech he made in Northern Florida in the early spring.

"Are you aware," he asked his back-country audience, "that Claude Pepper is known all over Washington as a shameless extrovert? Not only that, but this man is reliably reported to practice nepotism with his sister-in-law, and he has a sister who was once a thespian in wicked New York. Worst of all, it is an established fact that Mr. Pepper, before his marriage, practiced celibacy."

A man who could read off lines like that probably deserved to sit in the Senate. William Buckley characterized Smathers' technique in this speech as "making Claude Pepper a pervert by assonance." Smathers nicknamed his opponent the "Red Pepper" and doffed his hat to Nixon by accusing Pepper of being a "graduate of Felix Frankfurter's Harvard Law School and classmate of Alger Hiss."

Bebe Rebozo, still a long way from the respectability of the Key Biscayne Bank presidency and not yet even introduced to Nixon, acted as Smathers' errand boy during this campaign. Preparing for his future role in life, he trailed after Smathers, assuring him of his infallibility.

Smathers won the Democratic nomination, which in this Southern state was then tantamount to election, by more than 67,000 votes. This was a lesson in success that was bound to be noticed by aspiring politicians. *Time* magazine, then super-conservative under the able leadership of Henry Luce, commented: "Republicans joyfully saw the result as a harbinger of a national conservative trend . . . a blow to the Fair Deal nationally and a warning of the Communist issue which Republicans are sure to raise this fall."

Richard Nixon did not wait that long. He admired Smathers' campaign so much that the Florida Senator became one of his closest friends. In later years their business deals threatened to compromise Nixon. Along with Bebe Rebozo, Smathers became Nixon's chief Florida playmate.

Nixon was nothing if not a quick study. The Democratic primary in California laid the foundation for his exploitation of the Red menace issue. Helen Gahagan Douglas, the forty-eight-year-old mother of two, and a six-year member of Congress, announced for the Democratic nomination. She was a former movie star, the first of that Hollywood line which eventually produced tap-dancing Senator George Murphy and second-lead-lover Governor Ronald Reagan. In the House she had fought hard for the Marshall Plan, for reciprocal trade treaties, for the mutual aid program and for measures to aid Korea. They were all substantial anti-Communist positions of some importance. In 1949 she voted for a 70 group Air Force and for expansion of Army and Air Force manpower. Furthermore, during the 1948 Presidential campaign, when Henry Wallace had marshalled the support of all of the left-wing Hollywood Democrats, she remained staunchly behind Harry Truman. (And this despite Truman's loyalty-security program instituted in 1947 which alienated the Democratic left.)

Mrs. Douglas's opponent in the Democratic primary was Manchester Brody, ultra-conservative California newspaper publisher. Brody pulled out the stops against his attractive opponent, and in so doing wrote the scenario for the upcoming Nixon campaign.

Nixon's electioneering was moving along briskly while the two Democrats battered each other. He sent a handbill to all registered Democrats headlined, "As one Democrat to Another." This was a minor lie compared to what was to come.

The rush to exploit the Communist issue took on a full head of steam after Hiss's sentencing at the end of January, 1950. Within two weeks Joe McCarthy made his first venture into this verdant field. He delivered his sensational speech in Wheeling, West Virginia, in which he claimed "I have in my hand" the names of (each tax-paying American is allowed to fill in his own number here, since McCarthy never used the same number twice) card-carrying members of the Communist Party who were, McCarthy claimed, on the State Department payroll. He demanded the firing of Secretary of State Dean Acheson and suggested that impeachment for Harry Truman was the only reasonable course of action for a patriotic Congress to pursue.

Overnight McCarthy replaced Nixon as Congress' chief anti-Communist. Although the Wheeling speech had been made with a casualness that suggested McCarthy did not sense the tenderness of the nerve he was jabbing, he quickly came to see its nature and began exploiting it with a shameless recklessness.

Nixon had been introduced to McCarthy at a Harold Stassen party. They were both protégés of the Minnesota "golden boy." With the rise of McCarthy's star, their relationship grew closer. It was based on mutual admiration. It would be difficult to overestimate Richard Nixon's responsibility for McCarthy's success in intimidating the nation during the next four years. He laid the groundwork for the excesses of McCarthyism and when its most successful exploiter finally arrived on the scene, he did everything in his power to advance and protect him.

The announcement of Nixon's candidacy brought out the card-carrying members of the lunatic fringe who might be expected to be attracted to an anti-Communist symbol of such potency. Gerald L.K. Smith, notorious anti-Semite, started delivering speeches for Nixon early in the year. He was apparently excited by the fact that Irish-born Helen Gahagan Douglas was married to Melvyn Douglas, movie idol of the 1930's and 1940's. Douglas's father had been Jewish and guilt by association, for Smith, also took in the religious question.

On February 27, 1950, he told a meeting that the man who uncovered Alger Hiss "is in California to do the same housecleaning here. Help Richard Nixon get rid of the Jew-Communists." Nixon did not seek such support. It came to him without effort.

Meanwhile Manchester Brody was going after Helen Douglas with hammer and tong. In his signed Los Angeles *Daily News* column at the end of May he attacked a "small minority of red hots" who, he claimed, were using the election to help "establish a beachhead on which to launch a Communist attack on the United States."

It would be a mistake to say, as some of his biographers have, that Nixon merely used the line Brody had laid down during the primary campaign. Nixon's November 3, 1949 speech, in Pomona, announcing his candidacy may have well been the deciding influence that convinced Brody to try to smear his way to victory.

Even before the results of the June 6 primary were in, Nixon was campaigning on "the Americanism theme with sharp attacks on Communism," according to Toledano, who worked actively for Nixon that year in California.

Helen Gahagan Douglas won the primary, but the personal cost had been high. There is a strong probability that Richard Nixon could have won the election against her if he had conducted a straightforward honorable campaign based on a discussion of issues. However, this was not the Nixon-Chotiner style. Such an approach would be founded on the assumption that the average voter was intelligent, an assumption that they never made.

Earl Warren seemed to become increasingly disenchanted with Nixon as time passed. Undoubtedly the Voorhis campaign had left a bad taste in his mouth, and the intervening years had done nothing to change his opinion.

On June 18, less than two weeks after the primary, Warren held a press conference. He attacked McCarthy and McCarthyism. Noting that the Wisconsin Senator's figures on Communists in the State Department kept changing, he said he was not aware of any evidence produced against anyone. He was the first major Republican to attack the Wisconsin witchhunter. When Senator Margaret Chase Smith tried to get her fellow Republicans to sign a "declaration of conscience" condemning McCarthy in 1950, only six of her Senatorial colleagues could summon up the courage to join her. McCarthy, uninterested in party labels, immediately began to smear them with the Communist brush.

In response to reporters' probing Warren said that he was not endorsing Nixon, even though he had won his party's nomination in the recent primary. Such an endorsement was almost automatic, and in withholding it Warren was underscoring his displeasure with the campaign he had seen Nixon run during the previous eight months. He said they would mount their separate drives. Clearly Nixon was not going to be given a free ride on Warren's broad coattails. "Well, we'll just run independently," he said in answer to continued questioning.

Then as if to indicate why he was not offering Nixon aid, he said he hoped no California Republican would adopt McCarthy's tactics or inject the State Department issue into their race. This was exactly what Nixon had already done.

He officially began his campaign on September 18 with a well-rehearsed speech he delivered with minor variations until election day. He spoke in San Diego, Los Angeles, Fresno, and San Francisco, all within the space of a few hours. The speech hit rock bottom immediately and did not rise much above that level. He described Mrs. Douglas as "a member of a small clique which joins the notorious Communist Party-liner Vito Marcantonio of New York in voting time after time against measures that are for the security of this country."

His campaign workers joined in the hue and cry. One sheet issued by them and addressed to Mrs. Douglas charged, "You, and you can't deny it, have earned the praise of Communist and pro-Communist newspapers for opposing the very things Nixon has stood for."

There were many who took part in the security madness, the political immorality and the know-nothingism of the Nixon campaign that year. A demagogue is not an isolated phenomenon. He flourishes in an atmosphere conducive to his brand of lying. Just as the McCarthy weed grew in the ground fertilized by Nixon, he now found his assault on Helen Gahagan Douglas buttressed by men and women of hysterical temperament, easy conscience, or simple minds who mistook his witchhunting for a crusade.

The story Ralph de Toledano tells about the time Murray Chotiner and he drew up a particularly inflammatory piece of campaign material is typical:

> I was present at a discussion between Chotiner and novelist Adela Rogers St. John, active in Democrats for Nixon, over a leaflet that stressed the "soft on Communism" theme and emphasized Mrs. Douglas' record. Mrs. St. John fought hard to tone down the leaflet and to delete much of its tougher material. Chotiner mollified her and got her out of the room. Then he took off his jacket, rolled up his sleeves, and said, "Let's get to work." The leaflet appeared as originally planned.

One can assume Chotiner did not require any special fuel to stoke his partisan fervor. But the final product must have been several degrees more savage than it would have been because of the frenzied atmosphere of the moment, which allowed excess after excess to be viewed merely as means to an end.

And the means were never straightforward where they could be devious, never illuminating where they could be confusing. Chotiner got together a manual for Nixon workers which illustrates his goal—death to the opposition by innuendo: "We must appeal to Democrats to help win the election. Therefore, do not make a blanket attack on Democrats. Refer to the opposition as a supporter of the socialistic program running on the Democratic ticket."

Helen Gahagan Douglas was not going to have an easy time with men like this. Politicians of almost every hue were running scared in the face of the Nixon-McCarthy stampede tactics. Truman's Attorney General, J. Howard McGrath, caught the spirit of the times when he said in April, 1950, "There are today many Communists in America. They are everywhere—in factories, offices, butcher shops, on street corners, in private business—and each carries in himself the germs of death for society."

Chotiner analyzed Nixon's skill in exploiting the mood of 1950 in his assault on Mrs. Douglas:

> Practically everybody in the organization told Dick, "You must not talk about Communism. It has been overworked." And I remember in case after case, Dick Nixon told audiences, "I have been advised not to talk about Communism; but I am going to tell the people of California the truth and this is one thing we cannot stop talking about as long as the menace of international Communism faces us here in the United States."

Nixon constantly tried to sell the idea that the Russians were about to launch an attack on the continental United States, the groundwork for which was being laid by domestic Communists who would rise up in revolt when Stalin gave the signal. If that was an honestly held opinion, it was surely a variety of paranoid delusion. The United States was in sole possession of the hydrogen bomb, and we had the capability of delivering it to any part of the world. Governor Edison of New Jersey had been demanding for years that we drop it on Moscow, and there were people who thought this a sensible suggestion. Our armed forces were poised on the Russian border, but Russian armies were separated from us by thousands of miles of water and ice. The Russian economy and countryside had been blighted by a war which also resulted in the death of millions of their young men. The United States had come out of the war untouched by shot or shell, with a fraction of the Russian casualties and with an invigorated economy which had permanently shaken off the effects of a devastating depression.

It took myopic men, most often led by dishonest men, to think that either we were going to attack the Soviet Union, or the Soviet Union was going to attack us. Still, men who were guillible enough to allow McCarthy to convince them that the dentist, Major Peress, was successfully drilling away at the foundations of our society were capable of believing many of the things Nixon said about his opponent.

And these were the usual mixture of facts and omitted facts, all calculated to sell the product, the most glaring example the infamous "pink sheet." This scurrilous piece of political poison was concocted by Chotiner and staff writers and immediately delighted Nixon, who saw in it the perfection of his techniques.

Five hundred thousand copies of the pink sheet were printed and distributed over the entire state. Nixon quoted from it constantly, as though it were a footnote to the Ten Commandments. It made an attempt to link Congresswoman Douglas with Congressman Vito Marcantonio. Such a connection was bound to be damaging to Mrs. Douglas. Marcantonio was an apologist for every act committed by the Soviet Union. He represented an area of Manhattan that took in a corner of Spanish Harlem, black Harlem and a poverty-stricken Sicilian community near the Harlem River. There was probably no poorer constituency in the North than Marcantonio's. Bowing to the requirements of his electors, he tended to see the brighter side of Soviet life, and to be a ready critic of bankers and industrialists, none of whom had the pleasure of punishing him at the ballot box.

Marcantonio was the protégé of Mayor LaGuardia, who, although a Republican, had an eclectic attitude toward politicians. During World War II, while we were allied to Russia, Marcantonio had sat in Congress side by side with other patriots and not seemed out of place. However, the Cold War created a new orthodoxy and Marcantonio became everybody's pincushion.

The headline on the pink sheet read: *Douglas-Marcantonio Voting Record.* Although the pink sheet never lived up to the headline, it did get its distorted message across. "Mrs. Douglas and Marcantonio have been members of Congress together since January 1, 1945," it began. "During that period, Mrs. Douglas voted the same as Marcantonio 354 times." It went on to falsely maintain that Nixon had voted "exactly opposite to the Douglas-Marcantonio Axis!"

Actually Nixon had voted the same way as Marcantonio 112 times since he had entered Congress in January, 1947. Since he had served less time than Mrs. Douglas, a pro-rated calculation indicated that he voted with Marcantonio over 50 per cent of the time.

No wonder that as he increasingly resorted to the pink sheet the campaign took an uglier turn. On September 29, 1950, in a small Southern California paper, the *Independent Review,* the label "Tricky Dick" was first placed above the candidate's picture—and it stuck. It was too appropriate to be ignored. Although the Institute for Journalistic Studies at Stanford University reported that Nixon had the overwhelming endorsement of California papers—the circulation advantage was six to one—it wasn't long before references to Tricky Dick appeared widely.

He had earlier found what he considered an appropriate label for Mrs. Douglas. He referred to her as "The Pink Lady," a variety of "Smooch" Smathers' "Red Pepper." He added weight to this stigma when in speech after speech he accused Mrs. Douglas of voting "against citing recalcitrant Communists for contempt of Congress." This was an outright misstatement of fact. She had voted for some contempt citations and against others.

Determined to leave no stone unturned, Nixon welcomed McCarthy into the state on his behalf on October 10. The Wisconsin Senator was in rare form. Riding the crest of his popularity, which meant he had finally intimidated most of the *respectable* men of the day, McCarthy pulled out all the stops for his friend Dick. Speaking over a Los Angeles network, he agreed with his Congressional colleague, whom he expected soon to welcome into the Senate chamber, that Secretary of State Dean Acheson must be forced to resign if the nation were to survive.

"He must go," McCarthy growled. "We cannot fight international atheistic Communism with men who are either traitors or who are hip-deep in their own failures. . . ."

He gave the Democratic Administration its Hobson's choice. Acheson could either admit he was a traitor or, if he preferred, McCarthy would allow him to merely concede he was a failure.

"Ask the basket-cases if they agree that Acheson is an 'outstanding American,' " he continued shamelessly. "I am sure the mothers of America will notify the Administration this fall that there is nothing 'outstanding' about washing away with blood the blunders and traitorous acts of the crowd whom the Democrat candidates have pledged to protect if they are elected."

McCarthy's inherent callousness is apparent in that passage. However, he had learned a central truth about people: They will not often come to the aid of people under attack. The more ferocious the attack, the more likely the noncombatants are to hide under the bed, praying the assailant will not discover them. It is the Kitty Genovese syndrome.

Hitting full stride, he finished his effort for Nixon. "The chips are down between the American people and the Administration Commicrat [sic] Party of Betrayal."

There were few men in the country who could mouth hogwash like that and be listened to respectfully. Nixon had the leader of those men in his corner.

As was true of every campaign in which the poor boy from Whittier was ever involved, he was never short of money. Even a casual perusal of his voting record offers a rather complete understanding of why millionaires have always found him attractive.

As the campaign drew to a close, it became obvious that there was still some loose change clanging around in the treasury. Chotiner suggested a huckster's touch that appealed to the perennial pitchman in Nixon. He proposed that in the last few days of the campaign California voters be told that if they answered their phone with the greeting "Vote for Nixon," and the person phoning them was a Nixon staff worker, they would win a prize. Newspaper ads appeared. *"Prizes Galore!!!* Electric Clocks, Silex coffeemakers with heating units—General Electric automatic toasters— silver salt and pepper shakers, sugar and creamer sets, candy and butter dishes, etc., etc. *Win With Nixon!"*

One would have to be a fanatical Acheson-lover to refrain from answering his phone "Vote for Nixon." If it was your mother calling you could always quickly add, ". . . for worst dressed man of the year."

As Election Day approached the New York *Times* commented, "Nowhere in the country will the outcome of the Nov. 7 election show more conclusively than in California the effectiveness, or lack of it, of the constant hammering on Communism as a campaign issue."

When push came to shove, it was these tactics that won for Nixon. He beat his liberal opponent by 680,000 votes, and, although Warren beat James Roosevelt for the governorship by a substantially wider margin, the Whittier Kid had every reason to be proud of his showing.

In 1957 British publisher David Astor interviewed him and asked him to explain his campaign against Helen Gahagan Douglas. Astor later wrote, "Nixon looked up from his desk with dignified sadness and said, "I'm sorry about that episode. I was a very young man.' "

There is every reason to believe that Nixon was merely supplying the answer and the tone called for by the occasion. For Nixon, it was the result that counted. The means he used were unimportant. During the four years he had been in public life he had risen to the heights by selectively using facts, by creating *facts* that he needed when they did not exist, by exaggeration, by a willingness to smear the reputation of patriotic, well-meaning men that was clearly beyond the limits of the conventional standards of decency he had been brought up to accept. He cannot be excused on the basis of ignorance. Richard Nixon knew what he was doing. He constantly practiced and refined his sleazy techniques so that they would be more effective. Nixon was rapidly ridding himself of all restraints. In an endeavor to reach higher, perhaps even someday to the Presidency, he was destroying the most valuable quality a President needs, the ability to exercise a judgment that would leave behind self-interest and consider only the interests of the larger community. By 1950 it had become obvious Nixon could see no interest beyond his own.

IX.

Reaching for the Brass Ring

When Richard Nixon was sworn in at the beginning of January, 1951, he was the youngest Senator sitting in that body. But although the man with the least seniority, he was somehow the one with the brightest prospects.

He had the electrifying quality of a young fast-ball pitcher or a novice opera singer with a giant voice. There is an intensity about such people that rivets the attention. The arm may wear out quickly from overuse, and the voice may sputter and crack from too great a strain, but while they last they are spectacular.

Although Dick had no curve or change-of-pace, he threw hard and the fans screamed their delight each time he hurled the blazer past some befuddled Democrat. He might not last, there was something too flashy about him to convince the real pros he had the necessary staying power, but if he faded, there was always some bush leaguer warmed up and ready to take his place. Right now he was a phenomenon.

Joe McCarthy, looking for someone he could depend on, maneuvered to get Nixon on the Government Operations Committee, whose Permanent Investigations Subcommittee was his power base. In order to do that he had to create a vacancy on the committee. Since Margaret Chase Smith was in his doghouse for issuing her "Declaration of Conscience," he drove her into the wilderness and filled her seat with a willing Nixon. McCarthy's committee had been established to look into the operation of the executive branch. He was supposed to keep Truman and Acheson, and all the rest of those bungling bureaucrats, honest. What a wonderful spot for a man who liked the limelight.

McCarthy viewed Nixon as an established lawyer views a law clerk. He was going to do the spade work on new cases and see that the allegations were lined up neatly, so that they would not get in the way of each other. He would plod along meticulously cross-examining witnesses, attending all of those boring committee sessions, and when the television cameras were turned on, McCarthy would step forward.

In most respects the two men were complete contrasts. Although Nixon was down sloshing around in the political mud of Washington, he was still essentially the neat young man who had stood in front of Hannah for that crucial daily inspection. He was still the social isolate he had always been. McCarthy was a different, more gregarious type of Irishman. He loved to drink and to socialize. Personally he was a charming casual companion. We met once at a cocktail party given on the occasion of the publication of a new William Buckley pro-McCarthy book. He made pleasant small talk, listened attentively, was completely disarming and then autographed the book in a wild sprawling handwriting—"Good Luck and Best Wishes to you. . . . ," then signed "Joe McCarthy" with only half as many flourishes as John Hancock had used to sign the Declaration of Independence.

For all he knew he might have been expressing those warm sentiments to the cleverly disguised head of the Soviet secret police. One sensed that it would not have mattered. He was a man completely devoid of scruples. He was also capricious, which made Nixon cautious in his presence. They were both essentially lone wolves, which had a further tempering effect on their passion for each other. But within these narrow constraints they worked together as two tense and highly trained tandem horses might, going step by step in the same direction but exhibiting enough nervous tension so that an observer might conclude they were on the verge of snapping their harnesses and dashing off in opposite directions.

Chotiner, who was in charge of Nixon's California operations, and visited with Nixon in the national capital at least once a month, approved of the partnership. He viewed them as essentially the beneficiaries of the same phenomenon, frenetic anti-Communism. Their destinies were linked.

By the time he entered the Senate, Nixon had become obsessed with our foreign policy toward China. When Chiang Kai-shek was defeated in 1949 and the Chinese Communists took control of the mainland, Nixon decided that he had a weapon of enormous potency to use against the Democrats. While the Democrats have been in power since World War II, he would say morosely, 700,000,000 Chinese have fallen captive behind the Iron Curtain. He would ignore the $3 billion Truman had given Chiang in an endeavor to help him defeat Mao Tse-tung, and suggest that the defeat had been the result of secret Democratic sympathy for Mao. Such a disaster must have been the result of treason.

Truman had made every reasonable effort, short of sending American troops into China, to bolster up the Nationalist government. When Chiang retreated with the remnants of his armies to Formosa, Truman stationed the American fleet in the Formosan Straits to keep Mao from overrunning the island.

Although our subsequent experience in the much smaller area of South Vietnam suggested that there was very little we could have done to change the course of events in China before 1949, Nixon persisted in vociferously maintaining that a Republican President, supported by a patriotic Republican Congress, would have moved history in a different direction.

This urge toward military vigor, which characterized the Republican Party since World War II, ran counter to its more ingrained desire to hold down government expenses. So that in early 1950 when Truman requested millions of dollars to bolster the defense of Korea, then divided between the Communists in the North, supported by the Russians, and the non-Communists in the South, supported by the United States, Richard Nixon and the preponderance of his Republican colleagues, voted against the measure. He later explained that he wanted money for the defense of Formosa included in the bill, and had voted against it only for that reason.

When the Communist North Korean army, encouraged by the Russians, crossed the 38th parallel and invaded the South on June 25, 1950, Nixon must have had a twinge of personal regret that he had compromised his hawkish posture by his earlier vote. However, he made up ground fast. Although Harry Truman did not ask for a declaration of war from Congress, as is mandated by the Constitution, Nixon fell in behind Taft and other Republican leaders in full support of the "police action."

However, never one to praise the opposition for long, he began his carping criticism as soon as the going got rough. Why was General Douglas MacArthur, an open candidate for the Republican Presidential nomination in 1948, being shoved back into a narrow defense perimeter at Pusan? There could be only one answer. Clearly he was not getting enough supplies and his brilliant advice was not being followed.

When MacArthur's troops made their successful amphibian landing at Inchon and American troops advanced north over the 38th parallel, Nixon praised his Republican general for his wisdom and courage. MacArthur's efforts to mold American foreign policy from the battlefield were applauded by Nixon. Why shouldn't a successful Republican general tell a ward-heeling President what to do?

When Truman found it necessary to travel halfway around the world to meet MacArthur on Wake Island, on October 15, 1950, in order to curb his propensity to make policy statements, Nixon maintained that this was a reasonable compromise for the President to make. And MacArthur's news for the President seemed to support Nixon's appraisal. The war was going so well that it would be over by Thanksgiving, he told a skeptical Truman. What about the intelligence reports that the Chinese Communists were about to intervene, Truman asked? Nothing to it. The boys would be home by Christmas. Truman finished by ordering MacArthur to make no further statements on foreign policy. With that message from his Commander-in-Chief, MacArthur flew back to Korea.

Had Nixon been informed of Truman's order, cries of "muzzling the military" would probably have followed. However, MacArthur was supremely confident that the flow of events was in his direction and as soon as his victory was recorded in Korea, it would just be a matter of time until he was nominated by a grateful Republican Party. Ike might be confused about whether he was a Republican or a Democrat, but Herbert Hoover's Chief-of-Staff had known his party affiliation for decades.*

The Chinese Communist intervention in the Korean War, within two weeks of the Wake Island confrontation, left MacArthur high and dry. Our soldiers had almost reached the Yalu River, the border between North Korea and Manchuria, when their overextended supply lines were cut by Chinese Reds dressed in quilted uniforms. The subsequent retreat, which did not end until the Communists had re-invaded the South, left MacArthur with a badly damaged reputation as a soothsayer.

MacArthur's desperation was clearly visible. That representative of the Pendergast politicos was gloating over his disgrace and just waiting for the moment to finish him off. He needed time to turn things around. Nixon and the China Lobby sought to provide him with that time by lifting the burden of blame from his shoulders. The defeat in North Korea was not MacArthur's fault, it was the responsibility of those soft-on-Communism toadies who refused to give MacArthur what he needed to win.

MacArthur wanted to bomb Red Chinese supply bases inside China. Some of these depots were just over the border, but others were thousands of miles inside China. Truman felt that such a move would escalate the war, turning it from an essentially local war involving limited losses, into World War III, involving the possible destruction of mankind.

Nixon came down hard on MacArthur's side. The Democrats clearly did not want victory. And their half-hearted attempt to gain a stand-off was bound to result in another debacle such as the loss of China.

Nixon's stand in favor of MacArthur was his coded signal that he wanted China bombed. Chiang and the entire right wing of the Republican Party, which is to say the more influential section of the party, had been calling for such action for months.

*See *The King Makers* (New York, Coward, McCann & Geoghegan, Inc., 1971), pp. 99-115.

At the beginning of April, 1951, little more than four months after Nixon entered the Senate chamber for the first time, MacArthur was relieved of his command in Korea, ending his forty-year up-and-down career in the army in disgrace. However, the bellow of support from the minority on the right who saw perfection in his every move obscured that fact for many months.

Upon returning to the country for the first time since before the Japanese attack on Pearl Harbor, MacArthur received a hero's welcome wherever he went, and for a while he kept moving rapidly. On April 21, in an attempt to damp down some of the enthusiasm for the general whom he had stripped of his gold braid, Truman had some of the secret documents covering the talks on Wake Island leaked to the *Times*.

Nixon hit the roof. He immediately demanded all the records of that meeting be released. "The new test for classifying secret documents now seems to be not whether the publication of a document would affect the security of the nation," Nixon said in a manner that would have made Daniel Ellsberg proud, "but whether it would affect the political security of the Administration."

Nixon demanded the complete report be made public. Let the people judge whether the *Times* was right in concluding that General MacArthur had miscalculated in Korea. This was a common pattern in Nixon's dealings with the White House. During the four years he had served in Congress he had repeatedly gotten into arguments with the executive branch over his desire to get information and the President's refusal to supply it on the grounds of "executive privilege." Truman had always refused to knuckle under to Nixon's demands. What reason did Dick have to imagine he would agree in this case? His request had been what it always was, an attempt to create a diversion, a smoke screen behind which the real, embarrassing issue could be hidden. The *Times* story had hurt MacArthur. If only the public could be distracted by the thought that the remaining documents contained items which would show the general in a good light, then a service would have been performed for the potential 1952 Republican Presidential nominee by his humble servant, Richard Nixon. Such a service surely would not be forgotten.

On May 3, Truman, as he took pleasure in doing, gave Nixon an unpleasant surprise. He turned over the collected documents, entitled "Substance of Statements Made at Wake Island," to the Senate Armed Services and Foreign Affairs Committees. More horrifying to Nixon, the committees promptly made most of the records public.

The general was quoted as telling Truman there was "very little" chance the Chinese would intervene. Of course, if they did, he boasted, they would be "slaughtered."

The Joint Chiefs of Staff, who had sat in on the Wake Island talks, reported

MacArthur's assurance that, "We are no longer fearful of their intervention." He was absolutely confident. "I believe that formal resistance will end throughout North and South Korea by Thanksgiving." That meant in approximately one month. Instead, by Christmas we were desperately evacuating 105,000 United Nations troops from Hungnam on the North Korean coast.

Nixon had responded to the original *Times* story by saying that "one of the most vicious smear campaigns in history" was being mounted against five-star General MacArthur. One would think, with the experience he had had in smear campaigns, he would have been able to distinguish between the bogus and the genuine. However, it was important to keep your hand in. Criticizing Harry Truman was clearly one of the greater responsibilities he had at that time. Calculated only on the basis of the time devoted to it, one had to conclude it was surely one of the more important reasons he was collecting a government salary. The Tammany dogma, that it doesn't matter what they say about you as long as they spell your name right, seemed to be Nixon's guide in matters of this sort.

Years later, at a March 4, 1971 press conference in the East Room of the White House, President Nixon commented on executive privilege, and issued another installment in what had become an endless apology to Harry Truman for the way he had behaved to him. The reporter asked, "Do you see any limit on the exercise of executive privilege?" (Henry Kissinger had been repeatedly refusing to accept Senator Fulbright's invitation to appear before the Foreign Relations Committee to discuss the invasions of Laos and Cambodia.)

Nixon responded philosophically. The words came tumbling out in a rush, and, as on such occasions, he was not entirely coherent: "The matter of executive privilege is one that it always depends on which side you're on. I well recall—and, Mr. Teiss, you were covering me at the time when I was a member of the House—that I raised serious questions as a member of an investigating committee about the executive privilege that was at that time, looking back in retrospect, properly insisted upon by President Truman, and, as President, I believe that executive privilege is essential for the orderly processes of government."

No doubt the view determines the perspective. Later in the same month he was asked again about the "age-old conflict between the Executive and Congress." Again his tender conscience had been touched. "When I was a Senator and a Congressman, particularly when I saw a Senator and a Congressman with a President in the other party in the White House, I played all of those games, too, with very little success."

He was underestimating his success, partly because he had forgotten the purpose of his "games." He had never been interested in securing information or in fulfilling any Constitutional responsibility. He had, from the moment he entered Congress in January, 1947, been playing only one "game," and that was a variety of Monopoly, in which the boxes around the board were labelled with the names of state delegations, instead of Park Place and Marvin Gardens, and the prize was not possession of money and hotels, but nomination to higher office. In his quest for that prize, Nixon was always successful.

X.

Lucky Dick

Shortly after his disconcerting duel with Truman over MacArthur's ability as a seer, Nixon turned his attention to another general. On May 14, less than two weeks after the Wake Island documents were released, Nixon attached himself to a Congressional delegation programmed to attend the World Health Organization conference in Geneva. Not too surprisingly, in view of his apathy toward world health and his interest in politics, Nixon ended up in Paris for a covert visit with the then commander of NATO, Dwight Eisenhower.

It would be a mistake to conclude that Nixon was making a direct appeal to Ike for second place on the Republican ticket in 1952. To begin with, the general had by no means finally concluded that he was going to run for the Presidency,* and although he was a Republican by temperament (he voted for Dewey in 1948, the only time he had ever voted for President), he had not publicly revealed his party preference. More important, the men who were going to select the Republican nominee were not in Paris. Tom Dewey, the governor of New York, was the man to see if you were interested in a place on the ticket, and Murray Chotiner was already plotting the best approach to the head of the Eastern Establishment. (Nixon had addressed the prestigious Women's National Republican Club in New York on February 27, 1951, less than two months after taking his Senate seat, in an endeavor to put flame to fuel for his nomination drive.)

Nixon was simply introducing himself to the general. There was only so much mileage a stranger could make by proposing long distance honorariums. A personal contact had to be made.

When he answered the Senate roll call on May 21, Nixon unexpectedly

---

*See *The King Makers* (New York, Coward, McCann & Geoghegan, Inc., 1971), pp. 7-12.

revealed that he had dropped in on Eisenhower in Paris. The general, he confided, felt his hardest job was to convince our allies to put "first things first." Since this was Nixon's supreme talent—he had never been known to put second things first—it is easy to understand why the general found him pleasing.

There is something fundamental that a candidate for the Presidency or Vice Presidency must understand before he has much of a chance to win. The people have little to do with selecting the men who will fill those positions.

Although each citizen is a potential voter, a scandalously high percentage of those eligible never bother to exercise their franchise. But more important, those who do vote have as little to say about the man who will be President as those cynical, bored, uninvolved citizens who use election day to catch up on their sleep. And it is not simply a matter of the impotence of the individual voter. Our Presidents are chosen by a handful of people across the country, who resemble no one more closely than the aristocrats of the *ancien régime.* They are never kings themselves, but they are the king makers, and it is they who benefit most from the power exercised in their behalf by the man they place in the White House. In return for their support, the President provides them with favors that are often monetary, but in whatever form, are always serviceable.

The selection of the President usually takes place more than a year before the voters walk into the polling booths and it is made by not more than three hundred people in each political party. They are the men and women who control the delegations that go to the quadrennial national party conventions. This group usually includes the two national committee members from the more important states, the single most influential political leader in the more populous states, and the moneyed aristocracy which will be called on to supply the millions of dollars needed to finance the frolic that passes for the democratic process.

These three hundred political patricians in each party have usually surveyed the field, and been prospected by embryonic candidates, up to two years before the convention. This leads to a winnowing out of the potential candidates as they wet their finger and hold it aloft only to discover the wind is not blowing in their direction.

This explains the seemingly inexplicable fact that men like Senators Harold Hughes, Fred Harris, and Birch Bayh toured the country for months in 1971, a year and a half before the Democratic convention, and then dropped out of the race before a single voter pulled down a lever in the polling booth. They seemed attractive, vigorous fellows with many remarkable strengths. Perhaps the voters might have preferred them, if they were given the chance to express their true preference. But that is exactly the point. The nominating nabobs seldom present the electors with the man for whom they would most like to vote. Instead, they have bestowed on them every four years the candidates of the party oligarchies. The real choice has been made by that time. They are given the largely ritualistic opportunity to choose between two men, one of whom is usually so repellent to them, because of abstract philosophical differences summed up in the wrong party label, that they must vote for the other. Their driving force is a fear that if they do not vote for anyone they will be committing a mortal civic sin.

But long before that simple act of self-deception has taken place, the American aristocracy has made up its mind that the President will either be this Democrat or that Republican. They use the party system and the quadrennial conventions to achieve their purpose. It is amazing that this should be so, since the Constitution never mentioned political parties or national conventions, and our founding fathers had an active hostility toward such shenanigans.

So disinclined are our actual rulers to formalize the codes that govern our Presidential selection procedure, that they have never even bothered to amend the Constitution to legitimize their power. There has been time to amend it for every other reason except this. More disquieting, there is no hint that any disaffected bloc, dissatisfied isolated militant, or institutional watchdog of the commonweal has devoted much time to considering the need for the reform of our Presidential selection process.

The average citizen is happy to have the opportunity to watch the festivities in convention city and to feel somehow superior to the clowns romping in front of the cameras for their summertime diversion. But before the convention cameras were ever turned on the serious work of choosing a President has been done, and the citizen's right to choose has been undone.

Richard Nixon always understood this fundamental truth about the Presidential selection system. He therefore seldom wooed anyone *except* the king makers, and seldom, as a result, ended up far from the mark.

By November, 1951, he had returned to Paris, joining a flood of industrious politicians who were trying to get the general to throw his hat in the ring. They have both reported that the substance of that meeting was concerned with the general's enthusiasm for the Senator's role in the Hiss affair.

Nixon's pursuit of the Vice Presidential nomination is a classic in opportunistic politics. Philosophically he should have been tied to the right wing of the Republican Party. His issue, Communism in government, was their issue. In terms of domestic policy, he was as right wing as the most troglodyte of Robert Taft's supporters. His role in fashioning Taft-Hartley and Mundt-Nixon made him an obvious partisan of the Ohio Senator. Although in foreign affairs he took an internationalist position in support of the Marshall Plan and the United Nations, his pro-Chiang speeches occupied the largest part of the time he devoted to that subject. His position on China was completely in keeping with the stance taken by the Party's extreme conservatives.

Little wonder, then, that when Taft decided to make his last run for the Republican nomination, he expected to have Nixon behind him. It is easy to imagine the distress Taft experienced when he first discovered, in early 1951, that Nixon was reaching out to the Eastern Establishment.

Nixon was an important delegate from Taft's point of view. For one thing, he was so clearly identified as a conservative who should have been supporting Taft that his absence would be noted. In addition, he had become an important national figure and was bound to be influential at the 1952 Chicago convention.

After several informal probes by his friends in Congress and by Tory members of the press who acted as liaison between the two, Taft felt he must speak to the young Senator himself. He went to see Nixon in his Senate office and was bluntly told that Nixon's personal feelings were not going to sway him. Ike was going to be the next President. Taft went away annoyed with this freshman Senator who was "too much in a hurry."

The one factor that led Nixon to this break with his spiritual leader in Congress, besides his shrewd, but not too startling, conclusion that Ike was likely to be the next occupant of the White House, was the byplay that was taking place between him and Dewey. The governor of New York, having decided that he was finished with Presidential daydreams, was spear-heading the drive for Eisenhower. Recognizing Nixon's devotion to himself above all else, he decided to concentrate on this weak link in the conservative chain. Men like Senators Everett Dirksen and John Bricker were too personally and ideologically bound to Taft to expend energy in a fruitless effort to win them over. How much more rewarding to look in Nixon's direction. He was already signalling not reluctance but anticipation at the prospect of lining up behind Eisenhower.

In order to clear the air between them, Dewey sent Herbert Brownell, a reliable retainer who had done his bidding for many years in New York, to deliver a message. Barring Eisenhower's active opposition, which was not expected to develop, Dewey was committed to placing Nixon on the ticket as Vice Presidential nominee. Implicit in this offer was the understanding that Nixon would lend his good offices to securing the nomination for the general.

This was not a gratuitous offer made by a quixotic Dewey in some moment of weakness. It was doubtful Eisenhower would be able to win the nomination without Nixon's support. Despite the fact that a substantial majority of the voters preferred Eisenhower for President, there was every reason to believe they were never going to get the opportunity to vote for him. The men who were in absolute control of the convention were determined to nominate Taft. He had been thwarted twice by Dewey and the liberal wing of the party, and twice his conquerors had gone on to defeat. It was Taft's turn.

Had the selection process been democratic, there is no doubt Ike would have been nominated almost unanimously. In 1948 he had been offered the nomination of both parties. He was clearly the most popular man in the country. But so little are the opinions of the people considered in these matters that Eisenhower had to race Taft down to the wire, and then barely nose him out. The 1952 Republican convention provides the most searing indictment of our Presidential nominating process. The ruling oligarchy in the Republican Party almost brought it off. They almost stole the nomination. It took the overwhelming popularity of America's greatest military hero to prevent that injustice.

Nixon also played an important role in winning the nomination. Wherever he went he spoke with sorrow about his "good friend Bob Taft," who would make a fine President if he could get elected, but unfortunately, "He can't win." It was this nagging suspicion, which Nixon did everything to encourage, that cut most deeply into Taft's strength. In short, it was not simply that he was withholding his support from Taft, who had every right to expect it, he was betraying the Ohio Senator at every turn.

In order to prove to him that he was not committing a *faux pas* in getting aboard the Ike bandwagon, Dewey invited Nixon to address the May 8, 1952 annual meeting of the New York State Republicans at the Waldorf-Astoria. Nixon always had a fond place in his heart for the Waldorf after addressing the main force of the party's liberal wing there. He was a hit. He delivered his well-rehearsed Communists-and-corruption speech and found himself applauded by the 2,500 New York Republicans. Many agreed with his sentiments but those Republicans who had doubts about the content extolled the vigor and competence of the delivery.

Immediately after the speech, Dewey summoned Nixon to his suite and informed him personally that Brownell had represented his true sentiments. Nixon was to be the Vice Presidential nominee. Since the March New Hampshire primary Eisenhower had been a candidate for the Republican nomination and, although still in Europe, he had registered no demur to Dewey's decision in favor of Nixon.

Nixon now redoubled his efforts for the absentee general, concentrating on the California delegation. As a result of the June primary it was committed to Earl Warren as a favorite son. Warren had every reason to think he might win the nomination. It had become clear Eisenhower and Taft were headed for a probable deadlock. In view of the fact that Warren had been the 1948 Vice Presidential nominee on the Dewey ticket, and was looked on with favor by liberals in both parties, his strategy of working toward such a deadlock seemed promising.

However, at this point in their relationship, Nixon and Warren clearly owed each other no favors. Although formerly committed to Warren, as was the rest of the seventy-man delegation, Nixon now did everything in his power to undermine him. Shortly before heading for Chicago Nixon mailed out 23,000 queries to California Republicans asking them to name "the strongest candidate the Republicans could nominate for President." The results of this slyly worded poll were predictable. Eisenhower was selected as the "strongest" candidate, Warren's drive was weakened, and Nixon lost forever something he never had, Warren's friendship.

Nixon worked hard at the convention to make sure nothing weakened Dewey's determination to fulfill his privately proffered pledge. As the train-load of California delegates approached convention city on the *Sacramento Special,* Nixon joined them at Denver. He immediately tried to stampede them on the basis of information he claimed to have acquired during the previous few days in Chicago. Warren did not have a chance was his theme. Better to jump on board the Eisenhower bandwagon while there was still room left.

By the time he and Chotiner had settled down at the Stockyard Inn adjacent to the Amphitheater, Nixon was completely alienated from the Warren forces and close to Dewey's heart, or at least as close to it as any politician was likely to get.

Even as he was trying to torpedo Warren, he was publicly professing to be his supporter. During the Warren demonstration on the convention floor, sparked by Senator William Knowland's nomination speech, Nixon was wild with feigned ecstasy. He was the first man up when the signal went out from grim-faced Knowland and the last man down after the music and the hoopla ended.

But all the time he was following Chotiner's plan to destroy Warren and nominate the general. Crucial to his strategy were his efforts in the California caucus when the pivotal Langlie Amendment was being discussed. Dewey had maneuvered Taft into a corner on the basis of allegations he had been immoral in rounding up delegate votes, especially in the Texas and Georgia primaries. The Langlie or "Fair Play" Amendment, as Ike's supporters liked to call it, seemed to concern itself only with a narrow moral question about the destiny of less than a hundred delegates. In reality, since the contest between Eisenhower and Taft was so close, *these* were the very delegates who would decide the issue.

Warren's best hope was to employ this amendment squabble to bring about his sought-after stalemate: In an endeavor to achieve that, and not show preference for either of the two leaders, Warren had determined to split the seventy California votes down the middle, half for Eisenhower, half for Taft. Nixon struggled to prevent this. At a pivotal point in the caucus he got up and emotionally pleaded for "fair play." Since the delegation was made up of men who believed in that principle, and, incidentally, had Eisenhower as their second preference all along, Nixon's plea won the day. The California delegates decided to cast a unit vote for fair play and Ike.

With the narrow success of the Langlie Amendment and the subsequent seating of the contested Eisenhower delegates, the fight was just about over. But for Nixon, the tension had become acute. He had known for months that he was being seriously considered for the nomination, yet he had been forced to act as if he knew nothing about such a development. Though assured by Brownell and Dewey that the prize was his, he could neither publicly allow himself the luxury of revealing it, nor privately allow himself to accept the inevitability of such good fortune. To every inquiry he responded, with his usual frankness, that he knew nothing about "the talk" that he was to be nominated.

Immediately after the general's convention victory Brownell sought Chotiner out on the floor. Chotiner knew both Knowland and Nixon, Brownell began. He worked for both of them. Brownell asked for a candid opinion. Which would be the better campaigner? It is hard to imagine what sort of answer Brownell expected from one of Nixon's paid employees. In any case, Chotiner was happy to endorse Nixon. With the quest for a Vice President of the United States narrowed down to these two, Chotiner could answer in good conscience. Nixon was more effective on the campaign trail.

Chotiner immediately left the floor and informed Nixon of Brownell's question and his reply. However, Nixon continued to inform reporters that "such things don't happen."

The night of July 10 Nixon presented himself with a bogus moral question. Pat was not enthusiastic about the nomination. She had always preferred the peaceful period of her husband's private law practice, and now, to make the prospect more attractive, the New York firms he had once sought out so fruitlessly were anxiously wooing him.

But Nixon was never as interested in money as power. The former high school debater wanted to persuade people, to bend them to his will. The former Quaker respected money but knew that someday he was going to make a lot more of it because of his political career than he would have made had he remained behind a law office desk.

Years later when asked if he planned to voluntarily become a one-term President, much in the fashion of Lyndon Johnson, he responded with a grin.

"The idea of what you call voluntary retirement, I would suggest, is quite premature where I am concerned, and I would say that anybody who reads my life would perhaps take that kind of story with a grain of salt."

Anyone who read his life would understand that Richard Nixon never faltered in his relentless run for power.

However, all night on July 10, 1952, he engaged in a sham debate with Pat and Chotiner as to whether he should accept the nomination if it were offered him. Chotiner remarked that there had been "constraint between Dick and Pat" when he entered their room. However, he was not as anxious to bring about a peaceful reconciliation as he was to convince Nixon to run, if, indeed, the slightest doubt remained. He pointed out, in effect, Nixon had nothing to lose.

If he won he would become Vice President and the prospect of his someday becoming President would increase enormously. He was not one to downgrade the office of Vice President. On the other hand, if Eisenhower lost the election to the Democratic nominee, an unlikely eventuality, Nixon would have improved his image in the losing campaign. He would still be a Senator with more than four years to serve in his present term. When he left the Nixons at 5 A.M., July 11, Chotiner had not been told by Nixon that he would accept the nomination. However, he was not concerned that the wrong decision would be made.

When Brownell called Nixon later the same afternoon to inform him that Dewey and a few of the boys had picked his name out of the hat, he no longer displayed any coyness. Brownell did not even bother to ask him if he would accept, the thought never having occurred to him that he might not. And so anxious was Nixon to nail down the offer that he neglected to shave in his determination not to waste a minute getting to Ike's side.

He was so eager to please, so eager to adore the man who had made his future look so bright, that he overplayed his hand from the beginning. The general recognized that quality of self-abasement that inferior ranks so often display toward commanding officers. He had taken advantage of it throughout his military career, but he had never learned to respect it. He preferred men like Lucius Clay and Bedell Smith, men who had convictions and expressed their opinions forcefully.

Eisenhower was irritated immediately. He had been told that Nixon was forty-two, which was extremely young for such responsibilities, but he had subsequently discovered that he was actually thirty-nine. More serious disappointments with his political partner were to follow. I sensed, as I stood a few feet from the two candidates and their wives as they appeared on the podium in the Amphitheater to accept the nomination, that Ike was not completely comfortable sharing the moment with this young stranger. As Nixon grabbed the general's wrist and pulled his arm above his head displaying him to the multitude as the victor, a touch of annoyance flickered across Ike's face and it was obvious that Richard Nixon's humiliation was about to begin. He had become an aide to a commander who knew how to teach ambitious subordinates to know their place.

XI.

Tell Us a Dog Story, Dick

Nixon had been placed on the ticket, if the practical purpose of buying his California support for Eisenhower can be ignored, because of the balance he seemed to add to the team. The general was from the East, he was from the West. The general was old, he was young. The general was an eminent statesman who could make convincing speeches on moral themes, he could be counted on for low-note speeches laced with innuendo and buttoned up with implications of treason.

There was a place for each of them and each of them was to be in his place. Nixon stated what he thought that place was when on September 2, shortly before the campaign was officially opened, he made a four-day trial run through Maine. He warned he would make "Communist subversion and corruption the theme of every speech from now until the election."

Since the Democratic candidate was Adlai Stevenson, a man of unimpeachable integrity who could be expected to run a campaign based on reason, Nixon's decision to run against Stalin and the Mafia seemed somehow inappropriate. But the last thing Nixon intended to do with Stevenson was carry on a reasoned dialogue. Besides, Stevenson had given a character deposition for Hiss after he was indicted, which for Nixon, labelled him a personal enemy. "If the record itself smears, let it smear," Nixon called out to his audiences. "If the dry rot of corruption and Communism, which has eaten deep into our body politic during the past seven years, can only be chopped out with a hatchet—then let's call for a hatchet."

He had laid the foundation for a moral posture the previous year when between September 31 and October 5 he held hearings on influence peddling in government and pointed the finger at the private legal activities of the Republican National Chairman Guy Gabrielson. Gabrielson had responded that what he did was not of "personal" benefit to him. And Nixon had countered that in Gabrielson's exalted position he must be, like Caesar's wife, above suspicion.

Of course, the fact that Gabrielson was a Taft partisan may have had something to do with his judgment that Gabrielson should be read out of the party. This close to the Chicago convention, Nixon considered such men little better than Democrats. However, he repeatedly used this episode to prove his political neutrality when it came to corruption. Democrat or Republican, public officials should be unimpeachable. If the Democrats would not adopt a similar high-minded approach and cooperate with him, then he would chop them out, if necessary with a hatchet.

In a series of speeches delivered in New England, while he slowly made what he described as his "shakedown cruise" back to Washington, Nixon rejected the idea of a "nicey-nice little powder-puff duel." He had his hatchet and he intended to use it.

In mid-September he flew out to Denver to put the finishing touches to the mechanics and strategy of the campaign. Before leaving Washington he had rented office space and set Murray Chotiner up as his campaign manager. His greeting by the general at the Brown Palace Hotel left him feeling uneasy, with the beginning of an understanding that Eisenhower was not taking to him. He remarked that Ike "had a quality of reserve which, at least subconsciously, tended to make a visitor feel like a junior officer coming in to see the commanding general."

The campaign strategy was outlined. Ike would take the high road, and Dick was to pick up whatever votes there were along the low. "The plan was," he said candidly, "for General Eisenhower to stress the positive aspects of his 'Crusade to Clean Up the Mess in Washington.' I was to hammer away at our opponents on the record of the Truman Administration, with particular emphasis on Communist subversion because of my work in the Hiss case."

Nixon was by no means only interested in "Communism, corruption and Korea." He was strangely concerned with the question of giving the federal off-shore oil lands to the states. The Supreme Court had ruled that all underwater land beyond the three-mile limit off the coast belonged to the federal government. Since most of the oil rich coastal fields were adjacent to the states of Texas, Louisiana and California, those states had been attempting to get the federal government to transfer ownership to them.

Why should states which were notoriously negligent of dry land within their boundaries be so concerned about underwater acreage usually not visible from any point on their shoreline? The answer lay in the area of political payoff, patronage and graft. These priceless underwater oil reserves were to be turned over to the petroleum barons of Texas and California at a fraction of their true value for their private exploitation. There was enough natural wealth in the continental shelf, had it been retained in the hands of the federal government, to pay off the national debt. And it was clear beyond question that once the states got control of these national treasures they would immediately sell the mineral rights to men like H.L. Hunt, and his friends, who were generous with Republican and Democratic politicians alike, as long as they protected their interests. Once the states wrenched control of those oil pockets away from the federal government, the big giveaway was on. Governors and state legislators in both parties were ready to accept the oil magnates' first offers for the state franchises. For private oil drillers this potentially meant billions. For the people of Texas, Louisiana and California, it meant polluted beaches, and the dubious honor of underwriting the success of drillers with tax write-offs under the unequitable provisions of the oil depletion allowance. The oilmen of Texas, Louisiana and California could not lose, and the American people could not win.

Stevenson had taken a strong position in support of the Supreme Court decision that the federal government had "a paramount interest" in the oil rich offshore lands. This seemed to infuriate Nixon. "A vote for Stevenson," he warned on August 26, "will be a vote for the hungry and insatiable Truman program of building up federal power by tearing down states' rights. But a vote for Eisenhower will be a vote to safeguard the rights and responsibilities of the states as set forth in the Constitution."

He was pleading for the safeguarding of the *rights* of states, but ignoring the more central rights of the people, which were going to be despoiled by his proposed giveaway. He was, in reality, proposing the biggest single payoff in American history.

There was no suggestion that Nixon was profiting "personally" from this foray. It seemed merely an example of how a poor boy from Whittier found it easy to sympathize with the problems of millionaires and work for their commercial interests without any apparent monetary benefit to himself.

It is against the background of these Nixon statements and positions that the events of September, 1952 take on a new dimension.

On Thursday, September 18, the city room of the New York *Post* was humming with activity. The galleys of a sensational story had just been delivered from the composing room and knots of reporters, copyreaders and rewrite men clustered around Editor Jimmy Wechsler as he pored over them. "This should blow that moralizing, unscrupulous, double-dealing son-of-a-bitch out of the water," he said with some satisfaction. "I'd love to see Ike's face when he finds out that Tricky Dick, his partner in the fight against Democratic corruption, has been on the take for the last two years."

Wechsler was referring to a story wired to the *Post* from Los Angeles the previous day by Leo Katcher. Katcher has been described by Nixon as a "Hollywood movie writer" and by Nixon's friends as a Hollywood gossip columnist. In reality, he was a top-notch newspaper man. He had been a New York political reporter for years and had been an assistant city editor at the *Post* before heading West.

Katcher had been tipped off by Dan Green, pro-Democratic publisher of the *Independent Review,* that Nixon had been soliciting money from rich California Republicans to make possible the grandiose political expenditures which would help him advance his political fortunes. Green told Katcher he received his information from a disgruntled Warren supporter who had been unhappy with the way Nixon had undercut the California governor at the convention.

Katcher, and two other Los Angeles newsmen who had also been contacted by Green, now set out to carefully document the charge. On Monday, September 15, they went to see Dana Smith, in whose name the Nixon bank account was registered.

Smith was Nixon's finance manager during the Helen Gahagan Douglas campaign. He had been alerted to the fact that the story was breaking by a long distance call from columnist Peter Edson that morning. Edson had heard rumors about the fund, and had asked Nixon the previous day, after interviewing him on "Meet the Press," to explain "the fund we hear about." He said that he had refrained from asking him about it on the television program because he had not yet checked it out. Nixon smoothly referred him to Smith. So that by the time Katcher got to Smith, Smith was well aware of the fact that there was no way to suppress the story.

However, the frankness with which he discussed the fund was unexpected, and was subsequently described by Nixon partisans as an example of his political naivete. "Our thinking," he said about the men who helped him organize the collection, "was that we had to fight selling with selling, and for that job Dick Nixon seemed to be the best salesman against socialization available. That's his gift. Frankly, Warren has too much of the other point of view, and he never has gone out selling the free-enterprise system. But Dick did just what we wanted him to do."

It was heartening, at least, to see that Nixon was rendering satisfactory service. Too often men who pay with honest metal are rewarded with a false measure.

"He told us," Smith continued, "he needed money. . . ." And then Smith went on to describe how Nixon had persuaded the organizers of the fund to support him. The sales pitch was centered around the idea that he had to make long-distance calls, use airmail stamps, make recordings for use on radio, and make trips from Washington to California several times a year.

"Here we had a fine salesman," Smith said in describing this United States Senator, "who didn't have enough money to do the kind of selling job we wanted, so we got together and took care of some of those things. Between fifty and a hundred people put up the money [actually seventy-six] , and we put a limit of five hundred dollars per person on the amount anyone could give in a single year . . . just so no one could say that we were buying a senator."

Apparently that possibility seemed likely enough that even this group of promoters thought hard on how to avoid the stigma. Although the contributions were limited to $500 a year for each person, the violators of the Hatch Act had already worked out a strategem for bypassing such an apparently restricting provision. The way to make $500 per individual add up to much more than that was to have Poppa and Momma, plus Aunt Mary and Uncle Andy, each kick in what was in effect a family contribution. Furthermore, this was not envisioned as a one-shot arrangment. Had Nixon not won the Vice Presidential nomination and the impropriety of the arrangement then seemed too blatant, the contributions to the Senator would have gone on as long as he continued to satisfy the wildest hopes of his benefactors.

After four days of meticulous checking, Katcher's story appeared in the *Post* under the headline *Secret Nixon Fund*. The sub-headline read "Secret Rich Men's Trust Fund Keeps Nixon in Style Far Beyond His Salary."

An amazing aspect of this story, which colored the rest of Nixon's career, was that despite the millions of words that have been written about it, no one, least of all Richard Nixon, has ever denied the facts originally revealed by Katcher. Nixon had a secret fund, registered in a Pasadena bank under someone else's name. Furthermore the $18,235 had been collected from, among other rich men, oil entrepreneurs Earl Gilmore, R.R. Bush, Thomas Pike, Leland K. Whittier, Donald Whittier, Paul W. Whittier and Tyler Woodward. How many of the remaining sixty-nine were relatives or business associates of these seven petroleum plungers has not yet been determined. However, there was probably not another politician outside of Texas who had such a high concentration of oil men contributing to his campaign kitty. His mighty efforts to get the tidelands oil turned over to them made this statistic seem utterly reasonable.

Wednesday morning, September 17, Nixon started on his first campaign trip from Pomona, northward in California by train. The trip was scheduled to end in Portland, Oregon, five days later. He was somewhat out of touch with the rest of the world, as there were no direct telephone connections with the mainland past which this grimy vessel cruised. When stops were made for speeches, the schedule was so tight that occasionally the train would start while Nixon was still speaking.

The trip had begun on a euphoric note. Nixon had developed his speech on the shakedown cruise through Maine and he was delivering it with precision. For the first time as a campaigner he felt no pressure. As Vice Presidential nominee he felt he had no responsibility for winning the election. "The head of the ticket wins or loses," he said.

He had felt so relaxed that he invited along William P. Rogers, eventually to be his Secretary of State, but at this point a counsel to a Senate investigating committee. He thought this would be a fine opportunity for the shy, lisping Rogers to find out what a campaign train was like. Jim Bassett, press secretary on the train, told Nixon before they left Pomona that a reporter had tipped him off "that his paper had a story scheduled for Thursday about a Nixon fund." Nixon brushed aside the hint of trouble.

Herb Klein was so completely satisfied with the way things were going that he dropped off the train and headed back to California headquarters, the Ambassador Hotel in Los Angeles. Murray Chotiner was similarly bored and was talking about following Klein back to the Ambassador.

In August, 1971, he told me in a long pleasant interview, "I felt there wasn't anything for me to do. I would be more useful back in Los Angeles. Rogers talked me into staying. He said that he thought the story might mushroom into something."

However, on the Eisenhower train rolling through the Middle West the full impact of the story hit at once and with devastating force. Emmet John Hughes, Eisenhower's speechwriter and philosopher-in-residence from the center of the political spectrum, described the general as being "staggered and shaken" by the event.

Eisenhower had convinced himself there was an unusual "mess in Washington." He had allowed himself to be persuaded that he was seeking the Presidency in order to purge the government of corruption. Suddenly the fantasy of Democratic depravity and Republican chastity exploded. His own running mate was being accused of accepting money, for his own personal benefit, from men who had an interest in the way he voted. Furthermore, there was no explanation forthcoming from Nixon.

Nixon accounted for his decision to remain silent in the face of this massive assault on his integrity with cold political logic. "The consensus that night among our little strategy group was to ignore the attacks, on the theory that answering them would simply give them more publicity and play into the hands of those making the attacks. This, I knew, was generally sound political strategy. 'Let's wait and see what they do,' I said."

Nixon's honor had been attacked, but he thought the best political strategy was not to defend himself. Thursday afternoon, as the ruinous effect of the story became more apparent to those on the Nixon train, Chotiner and Rogers sat down and composed a two-hundred-word statement which Nixon approved for distribution. It was merely descriptive of the general purposes of the fund, asserting that the Senator had done nothing illegal.

The independent *Sacramento Bee* rejected all rationalizations. "The man who the people of California believed was actually representing them is the pet and protégé of a special interest group of rich Southern Californians. To put it more bluntly, Nixon is their subsidized front man, if not, indeed, their lobbyist."

Nixon and his cabal decided he would continue to refrain from any comment. "I was still convinced that because the attack was entirely partisan, it would not stand on its merits. I thought it would eventually run its course and be forgotten, provided I continued to play it down."

However, Nixon was misstating the nature of the adverse comments. They were not "entirely partisan." A survey of the nation's press, which was overwhelmingly Republican, showed a two-to-one reaction against Nixon. Cries were heard on all sides for Nixon to step down from the ticket. Emmet Hughes described emotions in National Republican headquarters in New York as "ranging from a cool and somber concern to an instant and heated exasperation with the man causing all the trouble."

Herbert Brownell, who had played such a crucial role in placing Nixon on the ticket, began a poll of headquarters people to determine what their answer would be to his blunt question, should Nixon be dropped from the ticket? In the context of the campaign being waged, the question seemed insane. In the long history of political electioneering no candidate had ever dropped off a national ticket. Yet, here were the members of his own party urging that course of action.

It reflected the ambivalent attitude, especially of the party's Eastern wing, toward the youthful Vice Presidential candidate. The reasons they had supported him for a spot on the ticket had all been political. There was not an ounce of affection or commitment toward him on the part of the king makers. His connections with McCarthy made them suspicious. His campaigning techniques made them uneasy, as if they were turning loose a Frankenstein monster of their own making, whom they were not sure they could control.

General Lucius D. Clay, one of Ike's oldest friends and closest advisors, was, according to Hughes, particularly "angry and vehement, for he felt particular responsibility—and disenchantment—as one who had urged upon Eisenhower, at the Republican Convention, the choice of Nixon as his running mate."

Brownell collected all these "largely hostile opinions" and reported them in person to Ike. On the Eisenhower train the members of the press, who were the most prestigious journalists in the country, some with influence in the Republican Party, were letting Ike's press secretary, Jim Hagerty, know that they thought Nixon should be dropped from the ticket. Hagerty concurred with them. At one point Ike called the press into his compartment and listened to the mini-speeches that preceded their rhetorical questions. He wanted them to know he would not take any hasty action. That was the closest he came to defending Nixon. On the other hand, he said with some heat, Nixon would have to prove himself innocent of all guilt before he would be allowed to continue on the ticket. He would have to be "clean as a hound's tooth."

Friday morning, September 19, Nixon woke up after a terrible night's sleep. Eisenhower's failure to contact him and the reports of anti-Nixon sentiment on the general's train were beginning to take their toll. It had become clear that sitting back and waiting for the dust to settle was not going to work. Chotiner, always the activist in political campaigning, was now urging that an offensive be mounted. Nixon listened and agreed. "Instinctively I knew I had to counterattack. You cannot win a battle in any arena of life merely by defending yourself."

The first speech Friday morning was in Marysville, a tiny mining and lumbering town in Northern California. As he concluded his speech a heckler called out, "Tell us about the $16,000." The train had already started. Nixon called out, "Hold the train!" Chotiner signalled desperately and the locomotive screeched to a stop one hundred yards down the track.

Nixon prepared to give his first explanation of the fund as the crowd moved down the track to where the train had stopped. He began by calling attention to the heckler, chewing him out while pointing his finger at him. Then, excited and relieved at last to be fighting back, he said:

> You folks know the work that I did investigating Communists in the United States. Ever since I have done that work the Communists and the left-wingers have been fighting me with every smear that they have been able to.

His defense had been outlined by Chotiner. "An attack is always a smear when it is directed against you." It was immaterial that the story had been broken by anti-Communist sources and was being commented on unfavorably by many Republicans, it was all a Communist smear.

> Even when I received the nomination for the Vice Presidency I was warned that if I continued to attack the Communists and the crooks in

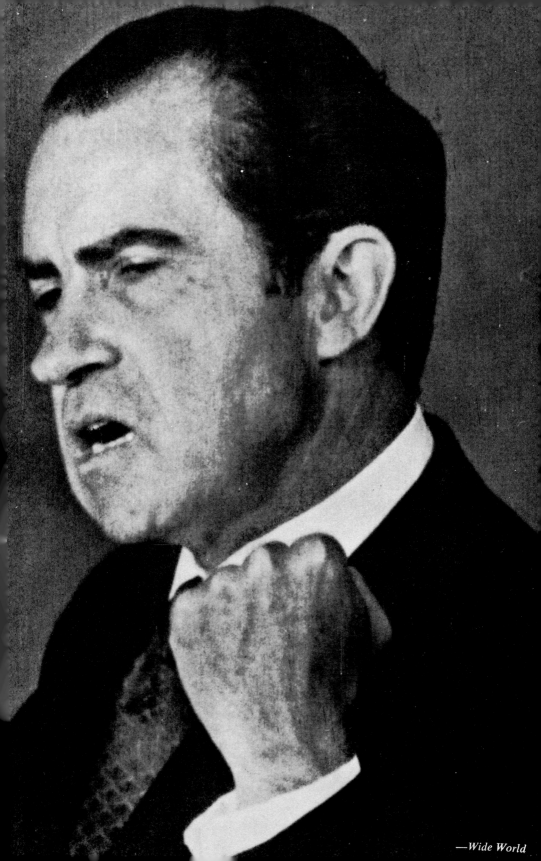

—*UPI*

The Whittier College second team picture, 1933

On his first day as a Congressman, January 3, 1947, Nixon poses for
a publicity picture in the empty House Chamber

—*UPI*

Wide World

THE NIXONS (left to right): Harold, Frank, Donald, Hannah, and Richard, at four, in 1917

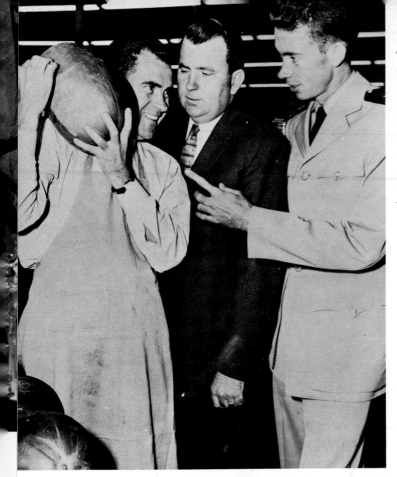

Temporarily on leave from the Republican convention in 1956 to visit his dying father, Dick took time out to pose for a picture in brother Donald's supermarket. Brother Edward, in ensign's uniform, watches approvingly —*UPI*

Nixon at bay, in his Chicago hotel room, October 13, 1958, preparing to flee rather than be photographed in front of such an obvious advertisement of his ambitions —*UPI*

"I have in my hand a document..." Joe McCarthy defending his —*UPI*
chums (left) Private G. David Shine, (right) Roy Cohn, June 7, 1954,
before the Senate's Army-McCarthy hearings

Two years after he had been
censured by the Senate, October 1, 1956, and long after most,
Nixon was still smiling at
McCarthy, who wears a Nixon
campaign ribbon in his button-
hole

—*UPI*

The Army's attorney, Joseph
Welch, in tears after climax of
McCarthy's hearing, June,
1954, when he accused the Wisconsin Senator of "cruelty" and
called down the wrath of God
on him

—*Wide World*

Nixon trying to sell a point to Khrushchev in the famous Moscow "Kitchen Debate" during the summer of 1959, as Leonid Brezhnev sneers his opinion in the background
—*Wide World*

A woebegone Vice President announces the official results of the 1960 election to a joint session of Congress   —*Wide World*

this government they would continue to smear me. They started it yesterday—you saw it in the morning papers.

Groups were being mixed and matched. Who was it who had warned him? Was it the Communists through some intermediary? Was it Chotiner in his wise old political way? And who was it who was continuing the smear? That, at least, the audience completely understood. It was the *Communists*. But the Washington *Post* was calling for his resignation and the conservative *World-Telegram* said he had done wrong.

They have tried to say that I had taken $16,000 for my personal use [he continued boldly]. What they didn't point out is what I was doing was saving you money, rather than charging the expenses of my office, which were in excess of the amounts which were allowed by the taxpayers and allowed under the law, rather than taking that money, what did I do? What I did was have those expenses paid by the people back home who were interested in seeing that the information concerning what was going on in Washington was spread among the people of their state.

His explanation in Marysville had all the conviction of a confessed felon trying to make his crime seem plausible. Nixon, in effect, admitted everything. Yes, such a fund had been collected. Furthermore, it would have been illegal for him to charge the expenses, paid for out of the fund, to the government. Although he seemed to deny that the fund had been collected for his "personal" use, his description of what the money had been used for made it abundantly clear that the fund had been employed exclusively for that purpose.

An audit of the fund disclosed that every cent of it had been spent on him: $6,166 for stationery, $3,430 for traveling expenses, $2,107 for radio and TV broadcasts, $1,281 for mailing list address plates, $1,188 for telephone, telegraph and messenger service, $1,109 for postage above senatorial allowance, $920 for "extra office help" (he received $70,000 a year from Congress for office expenses), $764 for advertising and publicity, $605 for meals for Washington visitors, $387 for costs of meetings, $294 miscellaneous.

It is true he did not use any of the $18,235 on booze or girls, neither of which appear to be important to him. But he was using it to advance his political career, which was *personally* important to him.

Years later Chotiner spoke freely to me about the fund. It had been his idea, along with Dana Smith. He saw it as a necessary source of the money Nixon needed to advance his political career. If he was going to have a chance for the Vice Presidential nomination in 1952 he would have to keep his name in the news. He would have to travel widely and keep in touch with people all over the country. When the fund was set up Chotiner traveled around the state talking to potential contributors. In an effort to prove how much of a tempest in a tea pot the whole affair had been he said, "Besides, there was very little money collected. No one could contribute more than $500."

It was pointed out to him that the limit was $500 *per year* and that the fund had been set up as a permanent addition to Nixon's salary. It stopped only when he received the Vice Presidential nomination. However, had he remained a Senator, the donations to the fund would have mounted. In addition, Chotiner had spoken to large numbers of persons. True, only seventy-six had responded. However, if three or four times that number had succumbed to his appeal, the fund might have easily been over one hundred thousand dollars. "That would have made you perfectly happy?" he was asked. "That's right," he admitted.

But Chotiner's admission was superfluous. Obviously there was no limit on the fund and only the hearts and pocketbooks of the generous contributors determined the amount that went into the pot.

The pressure to force him off the ticket was mounting. Harold Stassen sent a three-hundred-word telegram, in which he insisted Dick must relieve the general of the unpleasant duty of kicking him off the ticket by submitting his resignation. He even included proposed language he thought would be appropriate.

Reports from the Eisenhower train were now filtering through at a more rapid pace. They were unrelievedly dismal. Everyone except Arthur Summerfield, the National Committee chairman, was calling for his head. (Karl Mundt, holding the fort in Washington at National Committee headquarters, issued a statement of support, but on the train Summerfield stood alone.)

The major blow came when the New York *Herald Tribune* called for his resignation. "This one really hit me," he said. A reporter mentioned it to him in the train corridor, Friday night around ten o'clock, just as he was about to try to get some sleep. He called for Chotiner and Rogers to join him in his compartment. "I knew that if the reports with regard to the *Herald Tribune* were accurate, I had been hit by a real blockbuster . . . when Republicans as well as Democrats began to demand my scalp, the roof caved in."

He described the *Herald Tribune* as "the most influential Republican newspaper in the East." But that in itself would not have driven him to such a depth of despair. Other important Republican papers were attacking him.

I also knew that the publishers and other top officials of the *Tribune* had very close relations with Eisenhower and with some of his influential supporters. I assumed that the *Tribune* would not have taken this position editorially unless it also represented the thinking of the people around Eisenhower. And, as I thought more about it, it occurred to me that this might well be the view of Eisenhower himself, for I had not heard from him since the trouble began, two days before.

When Chotiner and Rogers arrived they were confronted by a shaken Nixon. They admitted they knew about the editorial and had been withholding the news from him because they wanted him to get a decent night's sleep. He was reaching the end of his rope and they were worried.

Chotiner showed him a copy of the editorial. Nixon read and reread the section devoted to his future. "The proper course for Senator Nixon in the circumstances is to make a formal offer of withdrawal from the ticket. How this offer is acted on will be determined by an appraisal of all the facts in the light of General Eisenhower's unsurpassed fairness of mind."

Nixon was being invited to put his head on the block. Eisenhower would judge him and execute his own decision. "I knew now that the fat was in the fire," Nixon said. "That sounded like the official word from Eisenhower himself."

Chotiner, protective of Nixon's interests as usual, and deeply implicated in the creation of the fund, was furious. "Why do the Republicans have to play right into the hands of the enemy? How stupid can they be? If those damned amateurs around Eisenhower. . . ." and on and on. He was the professional and professionals admit nothing, deny all, and hope that the newspapers spell their name right.

Nixon's chief concern now was how best to handle Eisenhower. The General was not cooperating with him, but somehow he must be brought around. Even at this point, when he was completely overcome by the depressing news, he only posed the question of resigning to Pat in the role of devil's advocate. This was his favorite technique of sounding out all sides of a question. To Pat's vigorous "You can't think of resigning," he responded, "I was never to receive any better advice, and at a time when I needed it most."

But the heat increased. His determination not to quit was reflected in the business-as-usual face he showed to the public. The whistle-stop tour continued into Oregon as if nothing had happened. The signs held up in the crowds inflicted their wounds but he smiled and waved. "Will the Veep's salary be enough, Dick?" "No Mink Coats for Nixon—Just Cold Cash," and "Sh-h-h, anyone who mentions $16,000 is a Communist."

Chotiner was informed that Knowland was ordered to fly back from Hawaii immediately and join the general's train. It was apparent he was being warmed up as a potential replacement. Warren was also being held in reserve.

When Nixon arrived in Portland, Sunday night, September 21, he made his way to the Benson Hotel through a hail of pennies pitched into his car. It had been four days since the story broke and still Eisenhower had not been willing to talk to him. Sherman Adams had left word at the switchboard that Nixon was to call as soon as he arrived, but Dick, apparently feeling he had nothing to lose, told Chotiner to let Adams know that he would only talk to the general.

There was also a message from his mother. There is something to learn about Nixon from this episode. In *Six Crises* he says of it: "There was a message from my mother, who was staying with the children in Washington. It was a simple one: 'I will be thinking of you.' This had been her Quaker way through the years of saying that she would be praying for me."

Straight, simple and to the point, or was it? Here is his mother's version of the same episode.

> I was at Richard's home in Washington, baby-sitting with Tricia and Julie. Richard and Pat were in Portland, Oregon, campaigning. I knew he was going to make a speech at the Temple Beth Israel's men's club in Portland. I decided to send him a message. A lot of words would make it even harder for him, I thought. So all I said was: "Have faith. Mother."

Hannah Nixon was telling her son to rely on God. She then went on to describe how Richard reacted to her injunction, something which has been described by other people, but which he was never able to speak of.

> When Richard read my message, I was told, he rushed into an empty room and wept. This surprised me, for as I have said, Richard is not demonstrative and does not weep easily. But I suppose it was the combined effects of tension and sentiment that made him break down.

Contrary to Hannah's analysis, the emotions visible here in such a raw state seem to be guilt and regret. The one person he was closest to, at this crucial moment in his life, was recommending, with the pure innocence of her soul radiating from those two words, a course of action no longer open to him. She was pointing up an even greater guilt than the one for which he was being accused by the public. His fall from grace, something of no great moment to most imperfect men, was being called to his attention by the one person whose words could not be ignored. In complete innocence, the purity of which he had no way to challenge, she urged to *have faith,* the one thing he could not have.

Like the Faustian figure he was, Richard Nixon, conscious of the bargain he had made, faced his real doom—the private one of which none but he was aware—with a sense of finality. Having made up his mind years earlier that the God of the silent void does not vote and must therefore be discounted, he had no recourse to the remedy offered by his mother. Her advice to have faith rang out as a final denunciation, and all he could do was weep.

Pat Hillings, who had been picked by Nixon to take his seat in Congress in 1950, said he was so affected by the sight of his benefactor in tears that he had to avert his eyes. Nixon was so shaken by his mother's telegram that he still cannot speak of it without completely misquoting it.

After he delivered the speech, he returned to his hotel room and tried to relax. Chotiner and Hillings were among a handful of people in the room. In the previous four days he had rehearsed with them what he would say to the general when they finally confronted each other. Chotiner stiffened his resolve with advice from what Nixon called "his keen political mind." His final statement, "This is politics. The prize is the White House." Chotiner wanted Nixon to make an appeal directly to a nationwide television audience. He was convinced this was the only way Nixon could make his way back. "What we have to do," he insisted, "is to get you before the biggest possible audience so that you can talk over the heads of the press to the people. . . . The press is killing you." Most of the rest of Nixon's advisors were skeptical about consigning his fate to the outcome of a single telecast. Chotiner advised against accepting an offer from "Meet the Press." He felt the format was bad. It would not give Nixon an opportunity to state his case "alone, without interruption by possibly unfriendly press questioners."

Nixon constantly maintained the chief reason he was not willing to remove himself from the ticket was that if he did Eisenhower would lose. This was a form of supreme self-deception. In fact, there was little doubt from the beginning that Nixon lost more votes for the ticket than he won.

By this time Chotiner was the advisor getting through to Nixon most consistently. He had learned to respect Chotiner's practical counsel through the years. However, in this case their destinies were intertwined. The one man in Portland with him who was most involved in setting up the fund and collecting the money was Chotiner. If he was destroyed, Chotiner would be dragged down with him. Chotiner knew the nature of all the arrangements, was privy to most of the Nixon state secrets. The advice of such a man could not be ignored.

Suddenly red-headed Rose Mary Woods, Nixon's private secretary for the previous two years, who was to become the most durable member of his office staff, entered the room. "General Eisenhower is on the phone," she said crisply.

Nixon was slumped on the couch, his legs propped up on a coffee table. He tried to compose himself and then picked up the phone.

At first their conversation was casual. The call could not have been easy for the general. As he indicated to Nixon, much of the advice he had been getting was to dump him. Nixon quotes him as saying, "You know, this is an awfully hard thing for me to decide." The one clear thing was that it was the general who was going to have to decide. However, over a period of four days he had been unable to make up his mind.

Nixon then quotes him as saying, "I have come to the conclusion that you are the one who has to decide what to do." He was throwing the ball back to Nixon. And Nixon has the general explain why he was placing the decision in Nixon's hands. "After all, you've got a big following in this country and if the impression got around that you got off the ticket because I forced you to get off, it is going to be very bad. On the other hand, if I issue a statement now backing you up, in effect people will accuse me of condoning wrongdoing."

If the accuracy of the statement is accepted, then it is easy to understand why Nixon was infuriated with Ike and why his opinion of him was lowered after this conversation. This was hardly the stance of the giant who had conquered Fortress Europa, who had compelled Hitler to put a gun in his mouth and pull the trigger. This was a wheeling-dealing politician who was concerned only with appearances.

He had been having dinner with some friends, the general said. There had been a good deal of disagreement. However, they all agreed he should have an opportunity to tell his story to the country. "I think you ought to go on a nationwide television program and tell them everything there is to tell."

Nixon was prepared for that. It fit into the Chotiner strategem. However, the important thing was to get a commitment from the general. Dewey had called and suggested he make such a speech, but if the response was not 90 per cent in his favor after four days, he resign. This sounded like the same suggestion. He finally had Eisenhower on the phone and this was the time to pin him down. "General," he pitched it in hard, "do you think after the television program that an announcement could then be made one way or the other?"

The general had already indicated he did not want to make a decision. He squirmed. "I am hoping that no announcement would be necessary at all, but maybe after the program we could tell what ought to be done."

Nixon was infuriated. Barely under control, he reverted to his Green Island days. "General . . . there comes a time when you have to piss or get off the pot!"

In *Six Crises* that uncivil sentence came out of the cleaners as, ". . . you've either got to fish or cut bait." However, everyone in the room, including Nixon, has subsequently confirmed the authenticity of the first version.

What an incredible way to speak to the commander of all Allied troops in Europe. Was it really possible to address the friend of Winston Churchill in this manner? It seemed to have been a desperation move. Nixon had not really slept for three nights. He had been eating little and he had been maintaining a rugged speaking schedule. Backed into a corner, there was nothing much for him to lose by being direct.

However, as Nixon pointed out, "One of Eisenhower's most notable characteristics is that he is not a man to be rushed on important decisions." Which was another way of saying that if Franklin Roosevelt was not able to rush him, he was not going to be rushed by this California politician.

"We will have to wait three or four days after the television show to see what the effect of the program is," Ike insisted logically. Certainly there would be no way to accurately measure reaction immediately after the speech. By this time Nixon's temper was completely out of hand. He brusquely warned Ike against taking the advice of "some of those people around you who don't know a damn thing about it."

The conversation ended on this arrogant note. Two things had come through. Nixon was to have his chance to state his case, and the general was not going to be rushed into a decision. He would make the decision himself but it would be about four days before he made up his mind. However, at least some of the suspense was over for Nixon. They had finally talked and there was a course of action for him to follow over the period of the next few days. Amazingly, he had made no effort to explain the fund to Ike. One would have expected most men to describe its innocence, how very little was collected and contributions strictly limited. But it apparently did not occur to Nixon to waste his precious moments with the general in such a defensive posture. Even more amazingly, during their fifteen minutes of rambling conversation Eisenhower did not think of asking him for an explanation.

Chotiner got in touch with Arthur Summerfield, Nixon's most stalwart ally. During the next few hours the details of the broadcast were ironed out with Summerfield and Sherman Adams. The National Committee finally agreed to underwrite the $75,000 needed for a half hour of prime evening time, two days hence, on Tuesday, September 23. The telecast was to originate from the stage of the El Capitan Theater in Los Angeles.

From this point on Nixon's every move was calculated to heighten interest in what he was going to say. Although he never seriously considered voluntarily removing himself from the ticket, and was now utterly committed to waging an all-out battle to retain his nomination, he gave no hint of this in public. "I made up my mind," he confided later, "that until after the broadcast, my only releases to the press would be for the purpose of building up the audience which would be tuning in. Under no circumstances, therefore, could I tell the press in advance what I was going to say or what my decision would be."

The speech itself was carefully prepared. He began to work on it in the plane as he flew from Portland to Los Angeles. "I took some of the picture postcards from the pocket of the seat in front of me and began to jot down my first notes for the speech."

Each and every item in the telecast that scandalized, or moved his listeners to tears, although appearing to have come from some instant, unrehearsed, gut reaction, was carefully selected, weighed for its appropriateness and considered for its effect. Cats and dogs and Pat's Irish ancestry were all fitted in and orchestrated to an exact pitch.

"For most of Monday afternoon and all day Tuesday, I outlined the speech and gathered facts for it," Nixon recalled.

On Monday afternoon the Chicago *Tribune,* his staunchest supporter in the Midwest, tried to make things easier for him. It front-paged the story that Adlai Stevenson also had a fund. As Nixon put it, "The money in his fund had gone for the personal use of members of his Administration in Illinois, while the money in my fund had been used solely for mailing, printing, travel, and other political expenses and not for my personal use."

Stevenson had organized a fund out of which money was paid to supplement the salaries of state employees. These were experts whose services were in such high demand that they could command salaries two and three times as much as the state of Illinois was willing to pay. In order to attract them to state service, and not to penalize them excessively for their civic responsiveness, Stevenson had devised this technique of softening the financial impact. It had brought able men into state government.

Stevenson had obviously acted out of his usual concern for the people he represented as governor. He had not supplemented his own income from the fund. The reason this story did little to affect Stevenson's standing with the voters, aside from his obvious purity of motivation, was the high opinion everyone, friend and foe alike, had of Stevenson's honesty. His opponents may have thought he was too eloquent, perhaps too indecisive, but his probity was never challenged.

On the other hand, despite Nixon's attempt to make black appear to be white, it was clear his fund was gathered with only one purpose in mind, and that was for his "personal use." Furthermore, there were few people in the country on Monday night, September 22, who would trust Nixon with the church collection box.

He slept only four hours that night, getting up while it was still dark to work at his speech. He was "edgy and short-tempered." He could not eat. He was badly in need of sleep. As the day wore on the tension increased. The broadcast was scheduled for 6:30 Pacific time, 9:30 on the Atlantic coast.

An hour before Nixon was to leave for the studio, Rose Mary Woods received a call from "Mr. Chapman" in New York. That was the code name for Tom Dewey. He wanted to speak to Nixon. Knowing her boss's condition, she attempted to put him off. "Don't give me that," Dewey growled, "it is essential that I talk to him." He was still *unavailable*. Mr. Chapman said, "I'm not going to get off this phone until I speak to him. It's essential."

At this point Chotiner was summoned. "He's out someplace and I can't reach him," Chotiner said with great sincerity, having just come from his room. "Well," Dewey responded patiently, "I'll hold the phone."

The idea that Mr. Chapman would stoically wait on the long distance phone for Nixon's return was too much even for Chotiner to contemplate. He returned to Nixon with a report of his failure to put Dewey off.

Nixon described the moment in *Six Crises*. "I knew that Dewey would not have called at this hour unless a matter of the highest urgency was involved. I left Rogers and Chotiner to continue their discussion and went into the next room and picked up the telephone."

Dewey was blunt, perhaps a bit more so than he might have been if Nixon had come to the phone immediately. He told him that he had polled the party leaders and the overwhelming majority felt he should resign. "There has just been a meeting of all of Eisenhower's top advisers. They have asked me to tell you that it is their opinion that at the conclusion of the broadcast tonight you should submit your resignation to Eisenhower."

Nixon recalled, "I was so shocked by what he said that I could not say a word for several seconds."

Dewey tapped the receiver: "Hello, can you hear me?"

Finally Nixon collected his thoughts. He asked what the general wanted him to do. Mr. Chapman did not want to give the impression that he had spoken to Eisenhower directly, but, according to Nixon, "he went on to say he was sure that, in view of the close relationship between those with whom he had talked and Eisenhower, they would not have asked him to call unless this represented Eisenhower's view as well as their own."

Nixon was completely flustered. "It's kind of late for them to pass on this kind of recommendation to me now," he said.

Dewey suggested he go on and deliver the prepared speech but at the end he should add, despite feeling he had done no wrong he was submitting his resignation. He would explain it was being done out of a desire not to be a liability to the Republican ticket, and he would insist that the general accept it.

"What shall I tell them you are going to do?" Dewey asked inquisitorially.

Nixon remembered, "My nerves were frayed to a fine edge by this time and I exploded, 'Just tell them that I haven't the slightest idea as to what I am going to do and if they want to find out you will have to watch the show to see. And tell them I know something about politics too!" Whereupon he slammed down the receiver.

When he told Chotiner what Dewey had said, *the keen political brain* was "shocked." "You certainly aren't going to do what he suggests, are you?" he asked the numbed Nixon.

He chased Chotiner and Rogers out of the room, telling them to "give me a chance to think." It was now less than a half hour before he was to leave for the studio. "I moved around in a daze," Nixon said. He shaved and showered, then put on the suit he planned to wear and began reviewing his notes again. "Dewey's telephone call had only shaken my equilibrium but had robbed me of time enough to get the whole outline in my head. I decided to speak from notes rather than from memory." There was never a moment in which he thought of following Dewey's advice and altering his carefully prepared explanation.

Chotiner suddenly stuck his head in from the other room. Nixon commented, "I looked up, irritated that *even* he would interrupt me at such a time."

But Chotiner had decided that something had to be done to break the tension. "Dick," he said with some bravado, "a good campaign manager must never be seen or heard. But if you're kicked off this ticket. I'm going to break that rule. I'm going to call the biggest damn press conference that's ever been held. I'm going to have television present. And I'm going to tell everybody who called who, what was said—names and everything."

"Would you really do that?" Nixon asked guilelessly.

"Sure I'd do it," Chotiner retorted, like a Samson ready to pull the world down about his head. "Hell, we'd be through with politics anyway. It wouldn't make any difference then."

Nixon appreciated the visit. He stuffed five pages of notes into his pocket and went across the hall to pick up Pat. The two of them walked through the hotel lobby and rode down in the elevator in perfect silence. "No one bothered us or spoke to us. It seemed like the last mile."

The twenty-minute drive to the El Capitan Theater was made in a similar icy silence. Nixon rode alone in the front seat so that he could study his notes. The 750-seat theater was empty, as he had instructed. The cameramen and technicians were the only persons allowed on stage with him and Pat. He specifically asked Chotiner, Hillings and Rogers to leave so that they would not become a possible distraction as he spoke. His only instructions to the director were ". . . just keep the camera on me."

In the last few minutes before the telecast, "I tried to read my notes again but by now the tension was too great. Three minutes before the red light blinked on he turned to Pat and said, "I just don't think I can go through with this one."

She reassured him with "firmness and confidence."

Nixon was seated behind a desk, his notes in front of him. Pat was placed in an armchair approximately seven feet to one side of the desk on his left. She did not vary the position of her body once during the half hour of her agony, nor did she alter the fixed semi-smile on her face.

He watched the big clock next to the camera during the last two minutes before air time. Suddenly the director pointed to him and he began to speak. "My fellow Americans, I come before you tonight as a candidate for the Vice Presidency and as a man whose honesty and integrity has been questioned."

He stumbled when he reached the word "integrity," as if embarrassed by it. Back in Washington Hannah "shuddered" as she heard those words and "was grateful that Tricia and Julie were asleep." Richard on the other hand claimed to feel that "all the tension suddenly went out of me. I felt in complete control of myself and of my material."

Watching from Cleveland's Public Auditorium was General Eisenhower and approximately thirty members of his staff, all of whom had been increasingly insistent that he demand Nixon's resignation. Ike was scheduled to address the crowd after Nixon's speech was flashed on a large screen in the auditorium. He waited in the manager's office, a pad in front of him, intent on taking notes as Nixon spoke.

Stewart Alsop interviewed one of the staff members who spent his time watching the general's reactions while everyone else was watching the television set. The view was equally dramatic in both directions.

The speech was unbelievable. It was a melange of lies, half-truths, distortions, clever sallies, maudlin sentimentality and evasions, delivered out of the depths of hurt sensibilities, which occasionally looked as if they would produce actual tears. The speech was not aimed at the logical man. It made no attempt to reason and explain. Such explanation was impossible. Nixon was aiming at the one corner of the target it was possible for him to hit. Dewey and Eisenhower knew the nature of this self-serving fund. Its purpose was so clear in their minds that they did not even bother to discuss it with him. They had both indicated that the only matter of consequence to them was the public reaction. Therefore, his speech was aimed most directly at arousing to fiery action that segment of the public which was susceptible to a direct appeal. He must stir them so that they would fill the air with shouts of "Save Dick!" And in a country of a hundred and seventy-five million people, it shouldn't be too difficult, if the pitch was right, to shake loose a sizable reaction.

Sixty million people watched Nixon that night, the largest television audience to that point and a record which stood for eight years. They turned off their wrestling matches, and the movies, to catch this more absorbing spectacle. Nixon did not disappoint them. He pointed out that they had all "I am sure" read charges that he had taken $18,000 from a group of his supporters. The pitchman in him took over immediately.

> The question is was it morally wrong? I say that it was morally wrong if any of that $18,000 went to Senator Nixon for my personal use. I say that it was morally wrong if it was secretly given and secretly handled. And I say that it was morally wrong if any of the contributors got special favors for the contributions that they made.

That is called taking the bull by the horns. But the question then becomes, how do you handle the bull now that you have him. Some experts feel that the best way to handle this situation is to throw the bull.

> And now to answer those questions let me say this. Not one cent of that $18,000 or any other money of that type ever went to me for my personal use. Every penny of it was used to pay for political expenses that I did not think should be charged to the taxpayers of the United States.

Whose political expenses were being paid by Dana Smith if not his *personal* political expenses? He was the only man in the country who could draw on the account in Smith's name.

In Marysville he had pointed out that he could not "legally" charge these expenses to the United States taxpayers. But in this moment of desperation that legal prohibition was not even mentioned. Instead it became a matter of personal choice—"I did not think . . ." it should be charged to the taxpayers. He went on to repeat this distortion of his actual position a few moments later when he said, ". . . the purpose of the fund simply was to defray political expenses that I did not *feel* should be charged to the government." Repetition fastens an idea in the mind of the listener and it was important to drill home the thought that he refrained from charging his personal political expenses to the government because he was fair-minded, rather than because it was illegal, and if he tried it he might end up in jail.

So intent was he on making an asset out of a damning liability that he returned to it again.

> Do you think that when I or any other senator makes a political speech, has it printed, should charge the printing of that speech and the mailing of that speech to the taxpayers? [sic]

> Do you think, for example, when I or any other senator makes a trip to his home state to make a purely political speech that the cost of that trip should be charged to the taxpayers?

Do you think when a senator makes political broadcasts or political television broadcasts, radio or television, that the expenses of those broadcasts should be charged to the taxpayers?

The answer was clear. Well, then, if you could not charge such expenses to the taxpayer, what was the alternative? He could do what Senator Sparkman, the Democratic Vice Presidential nominee, was doing. He could put his wife on his office payroll as a secretary, and supplement the family income in this manner.

At that period in his life it was impossible for Dick to make a speech without smearing someone. It was Sparkman's turn. "Now just let me say this. That's his business and I'm not critical of him for doing that. You will have to pass judgment on that particular point." But he had never done such a thing with Pat, although "My wife's sitting over here. She's a wonderful stenographer. She used to teach stenography and she used to teach shorthand in high school. That was when I met her." Then why not use her sterling talents? The answer came from his generous and selfless nature. "But I have never done that for this reason. I have found that there are so many deserving stenographers and secretaries in Washington that needed the work that I just didn't feel it was right to put my wife on the payroll."

But, at least it would not have been illegal.

There were other ways to pay for purely personal political speeches aimed at advancing your own career. He pointed out that it would not have been illegal to practice law, taking only those cases not touching on his responsibilities as a member of Congress. He apparently would have been willing to consider supplementing his income that way but for two reasons. "I'm so far away from California that [sic] I've been so busy with my Senatorial work that I have not engaged in any legal practice." [sic]

Since he was not independently wealthy, and his personal political activity drained all his time and energy, the alternatives were, to his mind, limited. "And so I felt that the best way to handle these necessary political expenses of getting my message to the American people . . . this one message of exposing this Administration, the Communism in it, the corruption in it, the only way that I could do that was to accept the aid which people in my home state . . . were glad to make."

Omitted from Nixon's list of possible methods of getting his message across were all the conventional ones his colleagues employed. As a well-known public figure in 1950 and 1951, he was often asked to appear on national television interview shows. In addition, he had complete access to the press and was masterful in using that publicity resource. Individual groups of local Republicans around the country were anxious to have him speak to them, and they traditionally paid the expenses for such speakers, including transportation, lodgings, and distribution of the speaker's remarks by radio and television.

This apparently was not enough for Nixon. His ambitions were making him overreach the bounds of propriety.

Having admitted, in effect, all the charges made against him during the previous six days, although hoping they would be viewed in a new light now that he had explained how they *should* be viewed, he devoted the middle part of the speech to describing his assets. Since he was never a hoarder of money, preferring rather to hoard fame and power, he was on strong ground here and dawdled leisurely over a detailed listing of his small capital accumulations. "I have no life insurance for Pat," he said sadly, as he turned and nodded in her direction.

Of course, to the average man the list of Nixon's assets did not appear so meager. He had two houses, a car, money in the bank, but clearly, had he been interested in money, he could have done better.

Always keeping in mind that he was trying to win over the man sitting in his modest, mortgaged living room, Nixon reached for homey little items that would appeal to his humanity. "I should say this—that Pat doesn't have a mink coat. But she does have a respectable Republican cloth coat. And I always tell her that she'd look good in anything." As he finished, he smiled weakly, as if to clinch what he had imagined would be a winning point. But the smile quickly faded, and he clutched at the bridge of his nose, hiding his eyes behind the palm of his hand and looking downward for a moment, as though this was too much even for him.

The quality of this famous Nixon remark is distinctively his. There is the partisan political note. The cloth coat was Republican, although it seemed likely that more Democrats than Republicans wore coats made of cloth. Furthermore his willingness to exploit anything to advance himself is clear.

The tasteless reference to his wife's coat was followed immediately by the most famous part of the speech.

> One other thing I probably should tell you, because if I don't they'll probably be saying this about me too, we did get something, a gift, after the election [sic]. A man down in Texas heard Pat on the radio mention the fact that our two youngsters would like to have a dog. And, believe it or not, the day before we left on this campaign trip we got a message from Union Station in Baltimore saying they had a package for us. We went down to get it. You know what it was? It was a little cocker spaniel dog in a crate that he sent all the way from Texas. Black and white spotted. And our little girl Tricia, the six-year-old, named it Checkers. And you know the kids love the dog and I just want to say this right now, that regardless of what they say about it, we're gonna keep it.

To this point the speech, henceforth "The Checkers Speech," was merely remarkable. He had been called on to give an explanation which would clear up accusations about a "secret fund" and had turned it into a soap opera. The moment had called for honest simplicity. He had served up a salad of evasive, complicated rationalizations.

Even as he did it, he could not avoid commenting, "It isn't easy to come before a nationwide audience and air your life as I've done." Even this look into his tormented soul had its elements of self-exploitation. Although it was understood by all that he was undergoing an unpleasant experience, he could not resist bringing it to the viewer's attention and asking for his pity.

From this point on the speech was a series of attacks, fulfilling Chotiner's fondest wish. It began pompously: "And now I'm going to suggest some courses of conduct." Having come to explain his conduct, he was now prepared to advise others:

> First of all, you have read in the papers about other funds now. Mr. Stevenson, apparently, had a couple. One of them in which a group of business people paid and helped to supplement the salaries of state employees. Here is where the money went directly into their pockets.

He wanted Stevenson to come forward and explain his fund. "I don't condemn Mr. Stevenson for what he did. But until the facts are in there is doubt that will be raised." As in the case of Guy Gabrielson, everyone in politics, seeking public trust, must be above suspicion—everyone, that is, except himself.

> And as far as Mr. Sparkman is concerned. I would suggest the same thing. He's had his wife on the payroll. I don't condemn him for that. But I think that he should come before the American people and indicate what outside sources of income he has had. I would suggest that under the circumstances both Mr. Sparkman and Mr. Stevenson should come before the American people as I have and make a complete financial statement.

At this point Alsop's informant said the general stabbed his pencil point into his pad. Nixon had not mentioned it but there were four candidates on the national tickets. One of the poorly kept secrets in the narrow world of the well-informed was that Ike had asked for a special tax write-off on his best-selling book, *Crusade in Europe*, during the Truman Administration. In receiving permission for his profits to be considered capital gains, instead of ordinary income, he had taken advantage of a tax loophole made available to no one else. This canny business arrangement saved him hundreds of thousands of dollars and made him a millionaire by the stroke of a pen. This was not something Ike wanted to explain to a nationwide television audience. And, although he had watched two-thirds of the speech in skeptical, immobile silence, in contrast to the growing enthusiasm of his staff, his first mark on the pad was a black puncture.

Nixon moved on quickly. Alger Hiss was never far from his mind and now found his place in this speech.

> I'm going to tell you this. I remember in the dark days of the Hiss case some of the same columnists, some of the same radio commentators who are attacking me now and misrepresenting my position were violently opposing me at the time I was after Alger Hiss.

His detractors were Hiss-lovers. Since he had explained how innocent his fund was, it must be obvious to all that the men who raised the charges, and those who saw merit in them, must be acting out of a desire to punish him for his pursuit of Hiss. And then, as if to make an aside of interest to the millions who had been watching him since 1948, he added: "I can say to this great television and radio audience that I have no apologies [to make] to the American people for my part in putting Alger Hiss where he is today." It sounded a little like whistling in the dark. But whatever it was, at this terrible moment in his life it was clear that the things closest to the surface of his mind were emerging into view.

Back to the attack—slash right, slash left. No one within reaching distance was safe, and Ike leaned forward, unsmiling. It was time for Nixon to belt the Democrats. "I say look at the record. Seven years of the Truman-Acheson Administration and what's happened? Six hundred million people [in China] lost to the Communists, and a war in Korea in which we have lost 117,000 American casualties. . . . And I say that those in the State Department that made the mistakes which caused that war and which resulted in those losses should be kicked out of the State Department just as fast as we can get 'em out of there."

Men who commit mistakes must go, that is, as long as they are not Richard Nixon.

Again he returned to praising Ike. "And so I say, Eisenhower, who owes nothing to Truman, nothing to the big city bosses, he is the man that can clean up the mess in Washington." The usual exaggeration, the always present, ever so slightly distorted viewpoint, was there. Truman had offered Ike the Democratic nomination in 1948. He had placed him in command of NATO. He had honored him on every occasion. Surely the general's gratitude was of a finer quality than his running mate's.

"And I say that any man who called the Alger Hiss case a 'red herring' isn't fit to be President of the United States." A gratuitous remark in view of the fact that Truman was not running for reelection. On the other hand, he pointed out, there was an alternative to Truman, and it was not Nixon, although his enemies had tried to make him the central issue in the campaign. "And I say that the only man who can lead us in the fight to rid the government of both those who are Communists and those who have corrupted this government is Eisenhower."

He had buttered him up, but not won him over. The grim older man watched the web being spun, and realized he was the intended victim. He might be caught, but he was not going to act as if he liked it.

The masterstroke came at the end. Eisenhower had told him directly and repeatedly that he was going to make up his mind whether Nixon should remain on the ticket. Dewey had instructed him to place his destiny in the general's hands, and Nixon said he felt this represented the general's viewpoint. The *Herald Tribune* had urged him to present himself for the judgment of "General Eisenhower's unsurpassed fairness of mind." And to Nixon "that sounded like the official word from Eisenhower himself."

Despite the fact that he clearly understood his fate was in the general's hands, Nixon decided to take one last monumental gamble. He would wrench that decision away. The general was too unconcerned about his fate, too concerned with his own image. He had to find a more sympathetic judge. Obviously the professionals in the party would be most sympathetic. Unlike the general, they had been forced to compromise all their lives. They had dirtied their hands in the everyday activities of the political marketplace. They understood the reasons for the fund that Nixon had not even voiced, and they were the minority of Nixon's defenders who had been declaring their support in isolation during the last five days.

"And now, finally," he began with determination, "I know that you wonder whether or not I am going to stay on the Republican ticket or resign. Let me say this. I don't believe that I ought to quit because I'm not a quitter."

In Washington, Hannah shouted back at the set, "No, and you never have been!" Along with Mother Chambers she abhorred quitters.

"And incidentally," Nixon continued, "Pat's not a quitter. After all, her name was Patricia Ryan and she was born on St. Patrick's Day and you know the Irish never quit."

It was a minor lie. Pat was not born on St. Patrick's Day, but a day earlier. However, if it would help to mention St. Patrick, why hold back because it was not true? There was something more important at stake.

Now looking directly into the camera lens, attempting to appear most direct when he was being most devious, he said:

But the decision, my friends, is not mine. I would do nothing that would harm the possibilities of Dwight Eisenhower to become President of the United States. And for that reason I am submitting to the Republican National Committee tonight through this television broadcast the decision which is theirs to make.

At this point, in the last thirty seconds of the telecast, after hearing Nixon through, Eisenhower made a second angry notation on his pad. He jabbed the pencil violently against the paper, this time so forcefully that the point was crushed. Alsop's observer commented about his feelings as he watched the irritated general try to find an outlet for his frustration: "Before that, I'd always liked and admired Ike, of course, but I'd often wondered how smart he really was. After that, I knew—Ike got what Dick was getting at right away, while the others were weeping and carrying on."

Nixon was telling the general that he was not leaving the decision up to him. He was turning it over to the Republican National Committee. Even before the speech a majority of the National Committee favored keeping Nixon on the ticket. He was submitting the decision to a packed jury, and contemptuously shoving Ike aside with the statement that it was a decision "which is theirs to make."

"Let them decide," he continued boldly, "whether my position on the ticket will help or hurt." This was rank insubordination. But Nixon would not stop. "And I am going to ask you to help them decide. Wire and write the Republican National Committee whether you think I should stay on or whether I should get off. And whatever their decision is, I will abide by it."

Again he was playing with a stacked deck. Who would be most likely to wire the Republican National Committee? Certainly not the thirty or forty million Democrats in the audience. Democrats did not expect to have their views receive an impartial hearing before such a tribunal. So that the people who had listened to him most impassively and with the greatest doubt, those who were least likely to extend their forgiveness, were also those most likely to refrain from following his advice.

The people who immediately rushed to their phones, those who knew where to find the National Committee, even though Nixon had not had enough time to give them the address, were just those party regulars, those soldiers in the field who could be depended on to rally to such a call.

His last word was reserved for Ike. "And remember, folks, Eisenhower is a great man. Believe me. He's a great man. And a vote for Eisenhower is a vote for what's good for America."

The red light blinked off. He had been cut off, he claimed, just as he intended to give the address of the National Committee. The upward curve of his tension was broken. Five days of maneuvering and preparing for this moment were over. All the bravado of the previous thirty minutes drained out of him in an instant. He threw his notes on the floor and told Pat, "I loused it up and I'm sorry. I couldn't do it. I wasn't any good." When Chotiner came rushing in to tell him how successfully he thought he had presented his case, Nixon waved him off—"I was an utter flop." He went swiftly back to his dressing room and burst into tears.

Hannah testified to the persistence of his feeling that somehow the speech represented a failure for him. "Richard, who never thinks he has done anything quite as well as it should have been done, later told me he thought his television talk had been a failure."

What he was ignoring in this period of slackening tension, when the sharp edge of his determination no longer cleared a path for him through his normal pessimism, was that the judgment mechanism he and Chotiner had constructed was fail-proof. As the one-out-of-thirty, or sixty, who had watched him rushed out to record their vote, and as the grinning tally masters at Republican headquarters all over the country prepared to give their version of the count, Chotiner was able to reassure Nixon that he had won. Professional pollsters maintain that the most inaccurate form of polling is the voluntary type conducted by phone or through the mail. This was precisely the poll Chotiner and Nixon decided to employ.

Within a few hours the National Committee announced that over two million people had voted 350-1 in favor of Nixon. How it was possible to count, much less read two million communications in such a short period of time has never been satisfactorily explained. The National Committee voted that same night 107-0 that Nixon should continue on the ticket. There were 138 members on the committee, so 31 of them quite possibly still had doubts.

The *Times* reported its switchboard lit up "like a Christmas tree" as soon as the broadcast was over. However, the *Times* also indicated that the switchboard lit up "like a Christmas tree" an hour later at the conclusion of the Rocky Marciano-Jersey Joe Wolcott fight.

On his way back to the hotel Nixon was morose. He described Pat as being "particularly pleased that I had not stayed on the defensive but had needled Stevenson. . . ." Once back at the hotel, he was surrounded by people who assured him they had just heard a speech more powerful than any ever made, with the possible exception of the Gettysburg Address.

Eisenhower, ever the realist, sensed the tide had turned. Nixon's detractors of a half hour earlier in the manager's office were now singing his praises. He could tell from the cheering of the party stalwarts in the auditorium that they had been convinced. Hagerty came in to tell him he would have to throw away his speech on inflation and tell the crowd how he had reacted to Nixon's presentation. Ike immediately got a new pencil and composed a few lines. A few minutes later he was telling a cheering crowd what they wanted to hear. "I am probably reverting a little bit. I have been a warrior and I like courage. . . ." there was a roar. "Tonight I saw an example of courage. . . . I have never seen anyone come through in such a fashion as Senator Nixon did tonight." Then he quickly added, "I do not mean to say that there will not be some who will find new items on which they will want further explanation, possibly."

At the very least his pride had been hurt and he had to reassert his paramount position in their relationship. "It is obvious that I have to have something more than one single presentation, necessarily limited to thirty minutes, the time allowed Senator Nixon." The folks back home might like what they had seen, but clearly it was not enough for the President of Columbia University.

"I am not going to be swayed by my idea of what will get most votes," he said righteously. He was trying to make up his mind. Everyone must know, therefore, despite Nixon's brazen remarks, that he had not passed his decision-making power over to those politicians on the National Committee. "I am going to say: Do I myself believe this man is the kind of man America would like to have for its Vice President?" He was not going to decide on the basis of what kind of man would be best for America, merely on the basis of whether the man had proved his popularity.

Then he said he was wiring Nixon to come the next morning to Wheeling, West Virginia, so that he would have an opportunity to speak to him and render his judgment.

When Nixon got the news of Ike's first reaction from a wire service bulletin, "I really blew my stack." His conclusion was that "he was being completely unreasonable. I had been prepared for a verdict. I was expecting a decisive answer."

He might have *hoped* for a decisive answer, but certainly he had no right to expect it. Ike had made it unmistakably clear he would want to wait for at least four days before reaching any decision. Furthermore, Dick had just finished telling the nation he did not expect the general to make any decision. He looked to the National Committee to perform his absolution. He had been hurt by the fragmentary press reports which indicated the general was allowing his unresolved doubts to be publicly aired. When the full text arrived, he did not feel any better.

"I announced to everyone in the room that if the broadcast had not satisfied the general, there was nothing more I could or would do. I would simply resign, rather than go through the stress of explaining the whole thing again."

He called in Rose Mary Woods and dictated his resignation from the ticket, then ordered her to send it to the Eisenhower train. This was the closest Nixon came, since the story of the fund had surfaced, to resigning. But it was not really that close. He did not, for example, instruct that the message be released to the press.

He said that he was motivated "to demonstrate that I meant exactly what I said. . . ." And that was precisely what he was doing, demonstrating, like a petulant child who had been thwarted at the last minute. Chotiner, who prided himself on knowing Nixon better than he knew himself, followed Miss Woods out of the room and took the copy from her. With complete self-assurance, he tore it up. Had he not, and had the telegram gotten through to Eisenhower, the general would have been forced to tear it up. The verdict was really out of his hands. What Nixon failed to realize was that the general understood he had been outflanked and had adjusted to it. He was merely trying to arrange his surrender gracefully, so that at least the appearance that he had not lost control of the decision could be sustained.

Chotiner returned to the room and began nursing Nixon back to stability. Dick was quite right. He was not going to have to humble himself. Nixon conceded that perhaps he had gone "off half-cocked." Well, Chotiner assured him, nothing had been lost. The speech was a smashing success. Eisenhower was the one who was going to have to come to him, not the other way around. The next morning when the general wanted him in Wheeling, he was going to be in Missoula, Montana, campaigning as though nothing had happened. Nixon called the reporters in, and, now confident of the accuracy of Chotiner's analysis, blurted out, "If he thinks I'm going to get down on my knees and crawl to him, he's got another thought coming."

The first call that came through from Cleveland was from Arthur Summerfield. He was elated over the way things had gone, and was calling at Ike's instructions to make arrangements for the meeting the next morning. He had left the general's train, which was now making its way over the mountains to Wheeling. For the first time in days he no longer felt isolated on the train among a group of hostile Nixon scalp hunters. His suspicions were scarcely aroused when Rose Mary Woods would not put him through to Nixon, and finally told him to speak to Chotiner.

"Well, Murray, how are things out there?" he asked tentatively.

"Not so good," Chotiner responded coolly.

"What in hell do you mean, not so good?" Summerfield shot back.

Playing from strength, Chotiner unhesitatingly broke the news to the general's emissary. "Dick just wrote out a telegram of resignation to the general."

"What!" Summerfield exclaimed in disbelief. "My God, Murray, you tore it up, didn't you?"

"Yes, I tore it up," Chotiner continued calmly. "But I'm not so sure how long it's going to stay torn."

There was a pause as Summerfield tried to pull himself together. Finally he managed to ask, "Well, Dick is flying to Wheeling to see the general, isn't he?"

"No." Chotiner passed on the rest of the message to the general. "We're flying tonight to Missoula."

"What? My God, Murray, you've got to persuade him to come to Wheeling."

Sensing that the surrender was near Chotiner dictated his last condition. "Arthur, we trust you. If you can give us your personal assurance direct from the general that Dick will stay on the ticket with the general's blessing, I think I can persuade him. I know I can't otherwise."

Summerfield was in a frenzy. There was no way to get through to the train except for the brief periods when it stopped at some station. After hours of exhaustive effort he managed to reach Sherman Adams at 9 A.M. in a trackside telephone booth in Portsmouth, Ohio. Summerfield gave Adams the bad news. Nixon had the whip hand. The general would have to capitulate, and then find some way to make his surrender look like a victory. Adams climbed back on the train with the humiliating news. After a moment of sour reflection the general gave his assent. Adams then led him off the train to the telephone booth where Ike assured Summerfield that as far as he was concerned Nixon could remain on the ticket.

Summerfield managed to reach Chotiner in Missoula, where Nixon had gone to make his bluff seem more believable. Summerfield told Chotiner the good news and insisted that the trip to Wheeling would be viewed by everyone as a triumph. Dick was on the ticket with no ifs, ands or buts. Under those circumstances, Murray responded, he thought he could guarantee Nixon would be there.

Chotiner then got in touch with Fred Seaton, Ike's aide, and wondered aloud where Nixon would meet Ike. Would the airport do? That sounded fine to Murray. "We arranged," Chotiner said, "that he [Seaton] would signal me from the bottom of the staircase, after the plane landed, as to where Ike and Dick would meet. If they were to meet at a certain place, he would raise one hand. If it was in another place, he would raise two hands. If in yet another place he would raise two hands and one foot."

The flight to Wheeling was a celebration. The reporters who had been following the action from Pomona on, and Nixon's staff members, were, according to Nixon, "singing songs with familiar tunes but with improvised and somewhat pungent words." Nixon was literally on top of the world. The victory was his, but now what was he to do? How was he to handle a brooding Eisenhower now that he had rubbed his face in the mud?

When the plane touched the ground at Wheeling, Chotiner stationed himself at the door. As the plane rolled to a stop and the door opened, he glanced down the staircase which had been hastily pushed into place. "Fred Seaton," Chotiner recalled to me, "was standing at the bottom of the staircase. I stood looking down at Seaton when suddenly the general stormed up the staircase."

He called out to Nixon in the back of the plane to warn him, "The general is coming up the steps."

Eisenhower brushed past Chotiner saying brusquely, "Where is he?"

The general caught sight of Nixon. He walked up the aisle toward him and Pat with his hand extended and the infectious public smile on his face.

And suddenly Nixon recognized the disparity in their ranks and began the genuflection that was to be never-ending. "General, you didn't need to come out to the airport."

And the conqueror of Hitler heard the note that had been struck. "Why not?" he grinned broadly. "You're my boy."

XII.

The General's Doghouse

Ike escorted Dick into his limousine, which was the vestibule of the doghouse he was to occupy for the better part of the next eight years. Dick was so tense he was jumping out of his skin. He found himself sitting to the right of the general. "I apologized for what I, with my Navy training, knew was an inexcusable breach of political as well as military protocol, and tried to change places with him," Nixon recalled, still shell-shocked. "He put his hand on my shoulder and said, 'Forget it. No one will know the difference with all the excitement out there.' "

The ride from Wheeling Airport to City Island Stadium, where 6,000 Republicans awaited them, lasted twenty minutes. They made the trip in near silence. Sherman Adams, another passenger in the car, reported that Ike did not take this opportunity to ask Nixon anything more about the fund. "Eisenhower never said a word in his conversation with Nixon about the strain that had been put on their relationship by the Nixon fund controversy or about the pressure that had been exerted on him to drop Nixon from the ticket. Nor did he mention Nixon's refusal the night before of the request for a meeting in Wheeling."

It was almost as if he knew that the slightest probe extended in Nixon's direction would collapse the flimsy structure of his explanation. Besides, no one seemed to notice the difference in all the excitement. Why ask questions no one appeared to want answered.

At the stadium Ike made the first speech. Determined to surpass Nixon's demonstration of irrelevance he quoted from an Arthur Summerfield telegram indicating that the National Committee thought Nixon was an honest man. Then, reaching for another witness of the same neutral quality, he read from a telegram Hannah had sent him. She wanted him to know she had faith in Richard. Any man who could get two such testimonials, the

151

general seemed to be saying, had obviously vindicated himself. Ike was publicly proud to have such a man on his ticket.

With his part of the program concluded he sat down and Nixon rose to praise him. "This is probably the greatest moment in my life," he began with just a touch too much enthusiasm to sound completely sincere. He went on to anoint Eisenhower with the oil of greatness. He was not like Truman. When the charges were made against him, Eisenhower had not rushed to his defense as was characteristic of Truman when his "cronies" were accused of wrongdoing. No, Ike had wanted to know the facts. Vindication from a man like this was far more valuable than the instant defense of a Truman.

Ike slipped away as the crowd pushed onto the stage. Pat and Dick shook hands with his well-wishers. "I spoke to each of them almost mechanically. . . ." Then Bill Knowland came up to him and grasped his hand. Had Nixon played his cards less aggressively, Knowland would have been the man standing in his place. "That was a great speech, Dick," Knowland said with the strength of earnestness that he brought to everything he said.

Nixon burst into tears. Knowland put his arm around him and Dick hid his head on the Senator's shoulder. And there he stood, sobbing, as hundreds of Republicans gaped in bewilderment, wondering how this could be their hero who had appeared so invincible, so challenging on television.

He had managed to survive politically, but only by severely scarring his private personality. The fund crisis was behind him, he remarked, "But Pat and I were to live with its consequences for the rest of our lives."

"I feel Dick was badly affected by that story," Chotiner told me years later. "I don't think he ever got over it. I remember that after he was elected he was invited to be the honorary head of the Pasadena parade. He felt that people were going to hoot and jeer at him and he did not want to do it. Later in 1953 he was invited to attend the Boy Scouts' jamboree. But he thought the Scouts would remember the speech and treat him badly."

His defense had been specious and unconvincing to all but the most committed. Some true believers might accept his word that none of the money had been spent for his personal use, but he knew better. He had told Peter Edson after the September 14 "Meet the Press" program, before such admissions were no longer advisable, that had it not been for the fund he could not have made the down payment on his Washington house. The burden of paying for his political ambitions had been partly lifted from his shoulders, and his standard of living was improved by exactly that much. Other ambitious congressmen put aside part of their salaries for the purpose of paying political expenses. He avoided that obligation and paid the price of that avoidance from that day forward.

(On March 11, 1971, as a result of a completely unrelated question from

Barbara Walters during a television interview for the "Today" show, Nixon began to talk about the fund. Explaining why Pat never enjoyed politics again after that, he said, "The criticisms at that time and the problems that we went through, of course, had somewhat of a marring effect on anyone who was deeply involved." No one was involved more deeply than Nixon.)

After drying his eyes, Nixon made his way to the general's campaign train, where, in the privacy of the general's quarters, he began to understand that henceforth he was a man always to be suspect. Ike wanted to know whether the rumors his staff had relayed to him about his spending $10,000 to decorate his Washington home were true. Nixon did everything, short of handing him the key to his front door, to prove that Pat had made the curtains herself.

Nixon and Eisenhower went their separate ways along the campaign trail. Nixon's crowds were substantially larger than they had been, but the experience was no longer pleasant. He felt on display, an object of curiosity. His red-baiting speeches became more intense. "We can assume because of the cover-up of this Administration in the Hiss case that the Communists, the fellow-travelers, have not been cleaned out of the executive branch of the government," he told audience after audience.

He referred to Stevenson as "a weakling, a waster and a small-caliber Truman." Echoing McCarthy, he called him "Adlai the appeaser . . . who got a Ph.D. from Dean Acheson's College of Cowardly Communist Containment." Tactics of this sort led historian Arthur Schlesinger, Jr., to describe "Nixonism" as "a kind of kid-gloves McCarthyism. . . ."

Nixon's notoriety resulted in numerous crank calls and repeated personal humiliation. At his hotel in Seattle the Secret Service received a report his tomato soup, sandwich and tea had been poisoned. Even at such ostensible moments of rest, his life was thrown into turmoil. If he switched on the radio, he was bound to hear popular comedians using Checkers for a laugh. *Variety* reviewed the Checkers Speech as if it were any other entertainment. The critic described it as a combination of "Just Plain Bill and Our Gal Sunday."

As the month of October wore on, his attacks on Stevenson became sharper. Stevenson had described Eisenhower as being "a khaki-colored package being sold by the political hucksters." Nixon responded, "If we're going to have color in this campaign, I'd rather have good old U.S. Army khaki than State Department pink."

In mid-October in a nationwide television speech he claimed to have grave doubts about Stevenson. "The question is one as to his judgment, and it is a very grave question. He has failed to recognize the threat of Communism as many have failed to recognize it around him."

Eisenhower made no such charges. He spoke instead about the need to clean out corruption, which sounded like a particularly loathsome disease when he warned of it. Emmet John Hughes, Harold Stassen, Herbert Brownell and C.D. Jackson were pounding out his speeches in a ninth floor suite of New York's Commodore Hotel, which they referred to as "The Cliché Factory." One has to search these speeches for any but the most oblique reference to his opponent, and one searches without success for the names of Truman and Acheson.

Not so in Nixon's case. "The word of Truman and Acheson, as well as that of Acheson's former assistant, Adlai Stevenson, gives the American people no hope for safety at home from the sinister threat of Communism."

There was always the hint in what he said that Truman and Acheson were traitors. "I charge that the buried record will show that Mr. Truman and his associates, either through stupidity or political expedience, were primarily responsible for the unimpeded growth of the Communist conspiracy within the United States. I further charge that Mr. Truman, Dean Acheson and other Administration officials for political reasons covered up this Communist conspiracy and attempted to halt its exposure."

The tone of his charges became shriller as Election Day neared. It was almost as if he were trying to drown out the sound of a barking dog and the rustle of a cloth coat. In Texarkana, Texas, on October 27, he left all restraint behind. He told a crowd that "President Truman and Adlai Stevenson are traitors to the high principles of the Democratic Party." He asserted that they "tolerated and defended Communists in the government."

Truman was in a rage. He was never to forgive this remark. He felt that Nixon was implying he was a traitor. He did not quite say it, but the implication of treason was clear.

Chotiner, who watched Nixon deliver that speech with approval, commented later, "Sure, he said Truman was a traitor to the high principles of the Democratic Party, but that did not mean he was a traitor. . . . He was always hard-hitting. I admit that."

Hard hits of that sort were Nixon's specialty.

Two days later, Friday, October 29, his thin skin was punctured by James Heavey, one of the sixty million who could not forget Checkers. He called out from the audience in San Mateo, California, "Tell us a dog story, Dick." Nixon froze for a moment, but then managed to struggle through to the conclusion of his speech. As his audience rose to leave he told them to sit down and ordered the Secret Service men at the door to restrain Heavey. As Heavey tried to pull away, Nixon tongue-lashed him.

"I would be ashamed if any member of my party wouldn't allow a speaker to address his audience," he said, although that was not what Heavey had done. He said he had toured twenty-two states and made two hundred speeches "and this is the first time I've been heckled."

Surely the pressure of the moment had made him depict his audiences as more polite than they had been. The hoots and heckling that had followed that first outburst in Marysville had never really ceased. "When we're elected," he shouted at Heavey, "we'll take care of people like you." Finally grabbing hold of the edge of his anger, Nixon concluded by ordering Heavey's custodians: "OK, boys. Throw him out!"

Heavey, then a twenty-nine-year-old San Francisco draftsman, filed a $150,000 damage suit against Nixon, charging that he had been seized by twelve men under Nixon's supervision and they had "assaulted him, battered and falsely detained him." Nixon had reacted to the matter with such deadly seriousness that the slender control he had over himself was suddenly evident. He was a man stretched too far, ready to snap at the first sharp sound, the first threatening gesture.

As the campaign entered its last phase it became apparent that Stevenson was coming on. He was a strangely compelling man, who spoke direct to the voter's mind, in a way few politicians ever dared try. His brilliance, often cloaked in laughter, put few people off. He was an intellectual without a touch of snobbishness. There was about him a feeling that he could lead the country.

Ike felt him breathing on his neck. There was in Stevenson's campaign the makings of a miracle. For Eisenhower should have won the Presidency without a struggle. He was America's darling. In that generation, only F.D.R. challenged his popularity. His smile was loved in every corner of the land. At one time or another, every public figure, including Truman, Acheson and Stevenson, had said pleasant things about him. And there seemed to be such a durable body of accomplishment behind him. It was not just the smile—*he had won the war.*

Then why were the polls revealing Stevenson closing fast? Part of the reason was that Ike's glamor had been rubbing off during the campaign. His tentative handling of the Nixon affair had been noticed by some men who had previously failed to detect a chink in his armor. McCarthy had also managed to tarnish his reputation; perhaps it would be more accurate to say that McCarthy gave Ike the opportunity to tarnish his own reputation.

In preparation for a campaign trip into Wisconsin in early October Eisenhower had decided to deliver a speech in which he would praise his old friend and comrade General George C. Marshall. Dewey had objected to the idea. He felt Ike's appearance there might be misconstrued as an endorsement of McCarthy, who was running for reelection. Conservative National Chairman Summerfield was pivotal in convincing Ike to go to Wisconsin.

George Marshall had been Ike's overall commander during the war, but he had also been Secretary of State during the early years of the Truman Administration. It was in this capacity that he had become an inevitable target for McCarthy, who had referred to Marshall as being among a group of government leaders who were "half loyal" or "disloyal." No great damage was done because Marshall rode too high above the battle. Nevertheless, Ike, who had already developed a strong distaste for the Wisconsin senator, decided he wanted to speak up for his friend.

Emmet Hughes wrote the speech in late September and its text was delivered to the campaign train in early October as it made its way toward Wisconsin. The following paragraph, much to Eisenhower's liking, was to be delivered on the night of October 3, in Milwaukee.

I know that charges of disloyalty have, in the past, been leveled against General George C. Marshall. I have been privileged for thirty-five years to know General Marshall personally. I know him, as a man and as a soldier, to be dedicated with singular selflessness and the profoundest patriotism to the service of America. And this episode is a sobering lesson in the way freedom must not defend itself.

As Dewey feared, when the Wisconsin-bound train reached Peoria, Illinois, Governor Walter Kohler of Wisconsin and McCarthy stepped smilingly aboard. They were allowed to remain and traveled into the state with Ike as honored guests.

The text of the Marshall speech was released to the press even as Governor Kohler was trying to convince the general's advisors that he should not make such a dramatic denunciation of the Milwaukee mauler in his own backyard.

At first Ike snarled with irritation over their timidity. However, after Sherman Adams and Jerry Persons returned to the subject tentatively Ike snapped, "Take it out!" The capitulation had been too public this time. Furthermore, his reason for retreating, the desire to maintain the good will of the local politicos of Wisconsin, seemed insufficient justification for abandoning his friend of thirty-five years.

In short, Nixon and McCarthy had provided the first opportunity for the public to see another facet of the general's character.

Emmet John Hughes sensed something dramatic would have to be said to halt the slide toward Stevenson. Without consulting Eisenhower, who was too busy acting out the scripts written for him, Hughes decided the general must make a speech, approximately ten days before the election, committing himself to go to Korea if elected. Ike was merely to pledge "himself to look at the arena personally," Hughes explained. "The statement, it seemed to me, was, for him, natural and appropriate, almost to the point of being banal."

When he finished writing the speech, he showed it to Brownell, who was enthusiastic. Stassen was dispatched to the campaign train personally to act as an advocate should opposition arise; none did. As a result, two days later, on October 24, Ike delivered Hughes' speech in Detroit.

The response was overwhelmingly affirmative, even though Eisenhower had done nothing more than promise to take a trip. To the voters it implied Ike would do something to end the festering Korean War. Peace talks had been going on between United Nations representatives and Chinese and Korean Communists for almost two years. Facing each other across a plywood table in a shack in Panmunjom, they had not even neared agreement. Truman, under the constant fire of Nixon and his supporters on the right, was unable to make any gesture toward the Communists that might be misconstrued as appeasement. They forced him into this untenable negotiating position. And as Truman tried to find some way out of his dilemma, American boys continued to die, in a war no one wanted to continue, but no one seemed able to end.

The next day Nixon found himself in Wisconsin. The final devastating effect of Ike's pledge, "I shall go to Korea," was not understood. Nixon, preoccupied with his own struggle to round up every last vote, was tightening himself down for one last push. Hugging McCarthy to him in a fashion that must have made Eisenhower more dubious than ever about him, Nixon called out a ringing endorsement of "my good friend McCarthy."

On such things do elections turn. Candidates in the numbing pursuit of votes, extended beyond human capacity, are reduced to puppets mouthing other men's words, thinking other men's thoughts, often no longer in contact with what is best in themselves. For Nixon this had become a way of life, but for Eisenhower, conditioned by wartime mind-fixes to think his every act was motivated only by patriotism, there was something new and degrading about the process.

On Election Day, November 4, Ike received 33,936,234 votes to Stevenson's 27,314,992. Despite his overwhelming pre-campaign popularity, despite the fact that he ran against a man who was largely unknown to the American public before his nomination, Ike received only 55.1 per cent of the vote.

Nevertheless, he had won the prize, and with it the dubious satisfaction of knowing he had made Richard M. Nixon Vice President of the United States. There was in this victory a trace of the bitterness of defeat. The cause of that bitterness was Nixon, and the general was not the man to forget it.

XIII.

Apprentice to the President, or *Why Pat Wanted Dick to Chuck It All*

The inauguration took place on January 20, 1953. At 12:23 P.M. Nixon took the oath of office, which was given by Senator Knowland. He had several decisions to make about the ceremony. He had chosen Knowland to administer the oath, indicating that he was the senior Senator from his home state and therefore deserved the honor. And he had borrowed the Milhous family Bible, brought to America in 1729, for the occasion.

He had been also given his choice as to the oath's wording. As a Quaker he was entitled by tradition to substitute the word "affirm" for the word "swear." Quakers have a religious objection to swearing any oaths, and Herbert Hoover had affirmed his oath in 1929. Nixon recited, "I Richard Nixon do solemnly swear that I will support and defend the Constitution. . . ."

Harry Truman looked on stonefaced as Nixon rested his hand on the passage from the Sermon on the Mount, "Blessed are the peacemakers: for they shall be called the children of God."

The Eisenhower trip to Korea had taken place the previous month and the President-elect had returned aboard the cruiser *Helena* in late December with no sign of any concrete accomplishment. However, peace as an election issue had demonstrated its effectiveness to Nixon, and his choice of the Biblical quotation suggested the lesson had not been lost on him. Murray Chotiner sat nearby, tears of pride welling in his eyes.

Richard Nixon had become the second youngest Vice President of the United States. His fortieth birthday had taken place the previous week. Only James Buchanan's vice president, John Breckenridge, at thirty-five had been younger on inauguration day.

Once in office, however, Nixon found himself isolated completely from General Eisenhower. The men of the White House inner circle, Assistant to

159

the President Sherman Adams, Press Secretary James C. Hagerty, Special Assistant Major General Wilson ("Jerry") Persons, did not know him personally and disliked what they knew of him. The President apparently felt Dick would be out of place at these affairs which were a combination of barracks' parties and men's club gatherings, where Robert Frost might read his poetry, or leaders from the business community might share food, drink and conversation. Their interests, their tastes, their personalities moved them in opposite directions.

Ike loved golf, even going so far as to have a section of the White House lawn ripped up so he could have a putting green built for the frequent occasions when he would dash away from his desk and practice. Nixon loved to watch sports on television, his major form of relaxation. His coordination had not improved with age.

Ike enjoyed a good joke, pleasant companionship and was most at ease with a large crowd of amiable extroverts. Nixon felt uncomfortable in the presence of people, and he was constantly concerned with how people were reacting to him. He was a self-confessed introvert (shades of Smooch Smathers) , forcing himself to smile when he preferred to frown, to speak when he would have preferred to remain silent.

His name almost never appeared on the daily appointments calendar. His meetings with Ike were formal and stiff. He took up golf, hoping against hope that this was the way to the general's heart. He brought the same furious dedication to golf that characterized his political activity. There was no grace in his stroke, no skill or finesse. However, as he efficiently absorbed the professional instruction he received, his score showed a steady improvement. But as in politics, there seemed to be no fun in doing it well. Golfing companions, among whom he rarely numbered Eisenhower (who was willing to play with almost *anyone* else)' , describe the fury with which he struck out at the ball; the frowns, the grimaces and the fierce determination to do better at the next hole.

As Ike's coolness was revealed in numerous ways, Nixon studied how to melt his commander's reserve. He seemed determined to convince Eisenhower that he would do anything to win his friendship. There were many ceremonial things about being President that Ike found unpleasant. Dick was ever-ready to step forward. For example, Ike made it a rule not to accept any dinner invitations. However, there were occasions when the pressure for his presence was intense. At times like that Adams discovered the heat could be turned down by offering the Vice President and Pat as substitutes.

Similarly, on September 29, 1953, when Senator McCarthy finally at age forty-three decided to end his bachelorhood, and take his secretary, Jean

Kerr, as his bride, Mr. and Mrs. Nixon were the top representatives of official Washington at St. Matthew's Cathedral. Ike and Mamie had declined an invitation with regrets. He was in Washington but too busy entertaining the President of Panama.

However, in terms of legislative responsibility, Nixon was almost never consulted. He did not have the confidence of key legislators that would have made him as valuable on Capitol Hill, as John Nance Garner had been to F.D.R., or Alben W. Barkley to Truman.

In terms of foreign affairs, which Eisenhower viewed as the area of his greatest responsibility and competence, Nixon was excluded with something approaching contempt. Ike needed no advice here from his callow subordinate. He was likely at any moment casually, and without any suggestion of concern about its impact on the listener, to refer to some personal characteristic of Churchill or Adenauer. What could such a man learn from Richard Nixon? In addition, he had John Foster Dulles as Secretary of State. As the years wore on, Dulles came to be the jealous custodian of American diplomacy, expending as much time in protecting his power as he did in executing foreign policy decisions. As a result, Nixon's only attitude on foreign affairs had to be one of attentive self-effacement.

In such a situation, the normal impotence of the Vice President was exaggerated dramatically. In those first years as Vice President, Nixon had fewer responsibilities, and was offered a less respectful hearing than most men who had held that office. He was so inconspicuous that he almost disappeared from view.

Ralph de Toledano and I appeared together on Public Broadcast television in Baltimore on October 14, 1971. We discussed the factors which molded Nixon's personality. Toledano felt that aside from his youth in Whittier, "the second controlling factor was the Eisenhower years where he worked for a man, and I know you shouldn't say this kind of thing—but he worked for a man who in my book was just a complete sadist, and who really cut Nixon to pieces."

Toledano shook his head and continued:

> He would cut him up almost just for the fun of it and I don't think Nixon ever really survived that. I don't think I am talking out of school and I say that when he was Vice President and I saw him quite frequently, he would come back from the White House and as much as he ever showed emotion you'd think he was on the verge of tears.

Left largely to his own devices, and being a man of exceptional nervous energy, Nixon began to cultivate the new Republican members of Congress.

They were birds of a feather. The floor leaders did not have time to spend with the fledgling congressmen, just as Ike did not seem to have time to squeeze Dick in between practice tees.

The Vice President began to hold seminars for them where he would pontificate on Administration policies. As in the case of the Chowder and Marching Society of 1947, he was cultivating friendships which would be of incalculable value in the years to come.

With the passage of time, Nixon grew increasingly restless. The cruelty of the situation was that no matter how he might wish relations between him and the President to mend, there was nothing he could do to improve them. He must be patient, Chotiner advised. All he could do was faithfully act out his role and hope Ike would relent.

It was a part of his nature to make things seem better than they were, and he could not abide the estimate of the well-informed that he was a fifth wheel on the vehicle of government. On July 26, Arthur Krock, conservative *Times* columnist and Nixon partisan, wrote an essay obviously inspired by the Vice President, or his friends. He pointed out the source of his information at the beginning by writing, ". . . persons familiar with the Vice President's helpful activities have told this correspondent that they consider them unique in the records of his high office." He then went on to build up Nixon's purported role in Eisenhower's inner councils. After describing how busy Nixon was, he mentioned, "The leaders of the House and Senate are too deeply engrossed in their heavy duties on the floor to give the time he can to trouble-shooting and to keeping the back-benchers posted on the reasons for decisions of the leaders."

In short, he was incredibly busy, but not too busy to do errand work for Congressional leaders who were truly busy.

His trouble-shooting activities, referred to so positively by Krock, consisted of doing anything that other more finicky members of Ike's staff abjured. Chief among these was the necessity to deal with the increasingly disruptive and disreputable McCarthy.

Nixon quickly discovered that in being willing to associate with McCarthy, he was filling a vacuum; no one was willing to snatch that particular glory away from him. Like any scavenging animal who finds healthy sources of nourishment denied him, Nixon turned to the carrion of the irresponsible right.

Ostensibly he was the bridge between the two camps. He performed the function that the Swiss government performs for the United States in Havana. Bereft of any diplomatic ties, but occasionally forced by circumstances to communicate, the neutrality of a party friendly to both sides was required.

There was, for example, the occasion on which McCarthy, in a burst of constructive energy, decided he was going to take a hand in shaping American foreign policy. Greek shipowners had concluded there was money to be made by trading with Communist China. McCarthy refused to consider this merely as an example of the free enterpriser discovering a new way to make a buck. Instead, he viewed it as a form of betrayal by citizens of a country the United States had befriended when they were under assault from Communist guerrillas.

He had by this time come to believe he was close to being a sovereign power himself, so it seemed natural to him that he should begin negotiating with the Greeks to end their unprincipled trade. Eisenhower and Dulles were furious. If there was to be any negotiating they wanted to do it. Stassen, now a White House Assistant on Disarmament, issued a blast against McCarthy's interference, one of the few Administration acknowledgments that someone named McCarthy existed.

While Ike clenched his teeth resolutely in the background, Stassen claimed that McCarthy was infringing on executive function. McCarthy bellowed that he was just doing what any patriotic American would do in his place. Nixon willingly intervened to break up this impending jurisdictional dispute.

He brought together F. D. Flanagan and Herman Phleger, respectively counsels to McCarthy and Dulles and had them negotiate a peace agreement which was formalized in a communiqué. Then Nixon invited Dulles and McCarthy to a luncheon, after which the communiqué was released. In it Dulles stated that McCarthy's activities were in the "national interest." The net effect was that Stassen had been undercut and the possibility of mobilizing a fight against the Wisconsin witchhunter was aborted.

To some this seemed constructive work for the Vice President. Dulles, for one, was happy with his role. The Secretary of State was perfectly willing for McCarthy to continue as a force in the country. He just wanted him to understand the ground rules. He was to aim his blunderbuss only at Democrats, and preferably Democrats of the previous Administration who were no longer in any position to retaliate. He could harp endlessly on Yalta, Potsdam and Tehran. Those were Dulles' favorite subjects, too. And if he wanted to call for the "unleashing" of Chiang Kai-shek so that he could reconquer mainland China, that fit in well with Dulles' priorities. Blessed are the peacemakers, as Nixon knew. And the best kind of peace was that existing between fellow Republicans, so that they could more effectively wage war against the Democrats.

It seems incongruous that any effort had to be made to get Republicans to pull together. However, for the new Eisenhower Administration this was a number one objective, and, to Ike's never-ending horror, it was seldom achieved. The Republicans had been out of power for twenty years. During that time they had developed a *modus operandi* that consisted almost exclusively of criticizing the Democratic President. Their criticisms seldom contained a hint of alternative constructive policy.

In foreign affairs Republican Congressional leaders always suggested that Roosevelt and Truman were in the process of giving away America's wealth, motivated almost exclusively by a desire to betray the country they led. In domestic affairs they accused the Democrats of being spendthrifts who were determined to run the economy into the ground, something for which the Republicans under Hoover had displayed far greater talent.

Having perfected the skill of carping criticism, the Republicans seemed reluctant to abandon it after they took over the White House. No longer having a Democratic target, some of them hesitated about altering the direction of their criticisms. It was almost as if they were victims of a habit which had them inescapably in its grip.

Consider the manner in which Ohio Senator John Bricker tried to amend the Constitution. Bricker, along with Taft, Knowland, Bridges, and the top Republican leadership in the Senate, felt some restrictions had to be put on the treaty-making powers of the President. Years of know-nothing criticisms of the Yalta Pact and endless denunciations of "sellouts" led Bricker to compose an amendment that would strengthen the hand of Congress in foreign affairs, at the President's expense. Bricker formally proposed his amendment on January 7, 1953, before Eisenhower was sworn in.

The threat to the new President's ability to function in the one area of government in which he was most competent was clear. Dulles cautioned that the amendment "might seriously impair the treaty-making power and the ability of the President to deal with current matters, notably U.S. troops abroad, etc., through administrative agreements."

Once again Nixon intervened. He pointed out that a man with his talents could move Bricker toward a more reasonable version of his amendment, his implication being that old John probably just wanted an amendment passed with his name on it so that he would be better remembered in the history books. Nixon marshaled all his selling ability to convince Eisenhower to temporize with Bricker. He was convinced a compromise could be worked out that would be satisfactory to both sides.

A series of delaying tactics was adopted by Eisenhower and Dulles in an attempt to give Nixon the opportunity to effect such a compromise. The effort went on for over a year, until it became clear that Bricker and his supporters were not interested in compromise. At that time a full-scale attack was made on the amendment and it was subsequently defeated.

However, the consequences of Nixon's meddling were not lost on the White

House. He had postponed action against a proposition that was aimed at destroying Eisenhower's effectiveness. He had prolonged the fight and caused tremendous energy to be expended over a long period of time that could have been used constructively on other projects. At the same time, he had made Ike look bad, as if he were weak and vacillating. The Bricker Amendment was so obviously against Ike's best interests that it was hard for observers to understand how he could refrain from waging an immediate, all-out fight against it. Nixon's advice had led to months of fruitless negotiating and had resulted in failure. Eisenhower made it a point never again even to seem curious about Nixon's opinion on foreign affairs.

Nixon was at his wits' end to know how to occupy his time. On August 31, 1953, in an attempt at constructive activity, he addressed the American Legion Convention in St. Louis. He had his white Legionnaire cap set firmly on his head and rendered the first of a long series of apologies to Harry Truman. "Regardless of the argument over the conduct of the war . . . let's recognize right now that the decision to go into Korea was right . . . . And let me say that in the past I had occasion to disagress with the former President of the United States, Mr. Truman, on some issues, but on this issue President Truman was right, and he deserves credit for making that decision, and I'm glad to say it in his home state."

Back in Washington Nixon was frequently visited by Chotiner. The Beverly Hill lawyer found Nixon chafing under the bonds of his ceremonial office and the obvious White House disinterest in his opinions. He tried his best to keep up his friend's morale, but the odds were against him.

Besides, Chotiner was a busy man in Washington. Unlike Nixon, whose future depended completely on the whim of another man, Chotiner was busy fashioning his own destiny. He was not on any government payroll and had no such ambitions for the future. Nixon might be interested in fame and power, but Murray was concerned with money. While Nixon was frozen into an attitude of attentive impotence for at least four and, if his fondest wishes were realized, eight years, Chotiner was free to make his way in the world. Everywhere he looked his prospects seemed promising.

He set himself up as an "influence peddler." The term is indelicate, but accurate. Most lawyers are in the business of peddling influence and knowledge. However, influence peddling in Washington, a business engaged in by only the most important lawyers in the Capitol district, had a par-ticularly unsavory connotation.

In effect, the clients who made their way to the door of Chotiner's law office were not in search of a skillful advocate who understood the intricacies of Blackstone. They were interested in paying him retainer fees because he knew Richard Nixon, and claimed to have influence in the White House, which he was willing to exercise in the interests of his paid-up clientele.

Sherman Adams wrote of one instance in which trying to help Chotiner resulted in personal embarrassment. Chotiner had contacted him in early 1953, claiming that his client, North American Airlines, was being discriminated against by a ruling made by the Civil Aeronautics Board. He asked Adams to "inquire into the situation."

Adams said, "I did not hesitate to ask the Board about its policy and for a statement in the case that I might use in replying to Chotiner. I had known him as Nixon's campaign manager in the 1952 campaign, and felt that his request was a reasonable one and deserved a courteous reply."

Adams expressed "surprise" when, years later, a House Committee discovered an exchange of letters between him and Chotiner on this subject and felt he acted improperly. He instantly pointed out that the CAB's decision had not changed and claimed that "Chotiner's client did not benefit from my inquiry."

What he overlooked was the fact that Chotiner benefited substantially. He was able to demonstrate to his client, who no doubt paid a handsome fee for the demonstration, that he could bring the White House into the case on his side. A normal client could be expected to be dazzled beyond recovery from such an exchange of messages, apparently on his behalf, on White House stationery.

During the next few years, Chotiner built up a substantial practice based on exactly this mixture of White House and Department of Justice letterheads and suggestive spiels to gullible, often desperate, clients. Nixon understood what was happening, since Chotiner at this time was his closest confidant. However, he did nothing to restrain Chotiner, who apparently felt that he had access to a cookie jar which was out of reach of his protégé.

This first year of the Eisenhower Administration was a rugged one for Richard Nixon. He seemed to come down on the wrong of side of every issue. He was extravagantly wrong in the advice he gave on the economy. When Ike took over, the economy was going strong. Truman's Fair Deal fiscal policies and the stimulation of the wartime economy brought about by our involvement in Korea produced close to full employment. Price stability had not been achieved until wage and price controls had been instituted. Between the outbreak of the war in June, 1950 and February, 1951, when controls were enacted, prices rose by a staggering 8 per cent. During the first year controls were in effect, the price index rose only 4 per cent. By 1952, Truman's last year in office, the rate of inflation had been reduced to 1 per cent per annum. In effect, inflation was nonexistent. Truman had introduced an element of fairness when he slapped on these controls by simultaneously introducing a tax on excess profits and levying a temporary increase in upper-bracket personal income taxes.

To Republican politicos these measures, to make the economy act rationally under the extreme pressure of a war they supported, were insufferable. Nixon joined his conservative colleagues in Congress to urge the elimination of all these Democratic devices to destroy the free enterprise system. At a Cabinet meeting, on February 6, Ike went along with this advice and abolished all wartime controls over wages and prices. A bill abolishing rent control was passed on July 31.

The results were predictable by a high school economics student. The Korean War was still on. It was soaking up two-thirds of the budget. The same pressures that had existed in the economy after World War II were current in the country as controls were lifted in early 1953. The results were the same. Prices rose dramatically, before the ink on the President's order had dried. Within a month of assuming office, Ike was confronted by an inflationary spiral of his own making which threatened to do the United States in much more effectively than the "Communist sympathizers" Nixon claimed had been left in key government positions by Truman-Acheson.

In an endeavor to correct a situation he had created, Eisenhower approved a recommendation of Secretary of the Treasury George Humphrey to tighten credit. Humphrey was the Cabinet's arch-conservative and could be expected to resolve questions about the economy in favor of high interest rates for his banking friends.

By mid-summer the recession of 1953-54 began. It was a direct result of the inept economic manipulation of hard line, pre-Keynesian Republicans. The incredible thing is that this normal activity of Republican Presidents who want to control inflation, and reject other fiscal tools made popular during the New Deal era, always causes recessions and always seems to surprise them when it does.

By the end of the year Humphrey was ready to admit he had tightened credit a little too severely. As Adams put it, "Instead of fighting inflation he found himself with deflation on his hands." A lot of people, as a result, found themselves with unemployment on theirs.

In a panic by the end of 1953 over what he had done to the economy, Ike accepted the advice of traditional economist Arthur Burns and applied the Keynesian solution for a sluggish economy. He primed the pump by allowing the excess profits tax and the emergency increase in personal income tax to expire. As usual with Republican Presidents, relief came first for the rich. Ike had fought vigorously against the Democratic idea to stimulate the economy by giving a $25 across the board tax cut which would have been appreciated most by the poor.

Strange as it may seem, the group of men Eisenhower brought with him to Washington were largely ignorant of how the government operated. They were mostly from the business world and had a simplistic faith that techniques used in pushing automobiles could be used to make government function more efficiently.

Charles Wilson, Secretary of Defense, was the chief propagandist for this viewpoint. At the height of the recession, trying to explain that unemployed workers should leave their homes and travel to other areas of the country where the possibility of getting a job was greater, he observed, "I've always liked bird dogs better than kennel dogs myself. You know, one who will get out and hunt for food rather than sit on his fanny and yell."

Wilson had probably said that a hundred times when he was encouraging some General Motors' executive to view as a priceless opportunity his transfer from the Detroit main office to the Zilch Gulch hubcap supply depot. Since none of his executives had probably ever had the nerve to speak of their agony over leaving their relatives and friends, Wilson thought his reasoning was flawless.

The Eisenhower cabal was immature in the ways of Washington and ill-equipped to run the largest government in the world. It is indeed remarkable that the ship of state stayed afloat long enough to survive their panicky efforts to learn where all the buttons were and what happened when you pressed them. Ike had been so angry with Truman that he spent scarcely twenty strained minutes with him in bleak silence before taking office. And Dulles was so intent on not being trapped by "secret" agreements which all good Republicans knew F.D.R. and Truman had made with the enemy, that he spent a large part of his first months in office vainly searching for them in the sub-basement of the State Department building.

Emmet Hughes commented on the level of Republican inefficiency in those days and the inability of most informed observers to see it for what it was.

> Thus, at the end of a day of administrative disorder in White House or State Department, there was an almost tonic effect in reading, in the evening's news columns, a most tidily organized account of all that had happened. And it was a particularly reassuring experience, for example, to scan a thoughtful commentator's analysis of the subtle reasons why the Administration shrewdly avoided or deferred certain action—when anyone within the government might have been naive enough to have thought it a simple case of someone failing to finish his work.

Among this dazzling array of incompetents, Nixon suffered no invidious comparisons. It was not lack of competence that made Eisenhower avoid him. It was personal distaste. Men like Humphrey bumbled along for years, never losing a whit of Ike's trust. They managed this miracle by charm alone. Ike liked them—that was enough. And it was enough that Ike did not like Dick to guarantee Nixon's side-lining.

It was only in the field of domestic politics that his advice was sought and occasionally heeded. He was, in fact, thought of as the expert in campaigning. His methods were not admired, and he won no personal respect for them. However, they were considered successful, and it was in his role as hatchet man that Dick got his toe in the door.

On April 17, 1953 he presided at a Cabinet session. The previous day Eisenhower had delivered his memorable "The Chance for Peace" speech before the American Society of Newspaper Editors in Washington. It was being cheered world-wide. Favorable editorial response was flooding in, but queries were also being made as to what concrete steps were going to be taken to lend substance to the President's lofty generalizations. Ike and Sherman Adams had gone off to Atlanta, Georgia, to relax on the golf course after the exertion of delivering his major policy statement. It had been announced that the meeting of the Cabinet was "special" and the world waited for some momentous announcement.

Emmet Hughes, in whose debt historians will always be for allowing them to capture some of the flavor of these sacrosanct Cabinet meetings, described Nixon in the chair. "The main order of business for this Cabinet meeting was stated and discussed at length by Vice President Nixon. 'The time, the right time,' he declared with sincere urgency, 'to start winning the 1954 elections is right *now*.' "

He warned against any of those present allowing themselves to be quoted as acknowledging the fact that the Democrats in Congress were giving Eisenhower more help than the Republicans. He did not deny that it was true; he merely wanted them to avoid the truth. And he ended by urging them not to get "your public-speaking schedules all crowded with engagements in Congressional areas where there will be no contest next year." Hughes closed his diary entry for that day with the comment, "I suppose a lot of people thought we spent this day in the White House talking about the peace of the world."

The nightmarish quality of Nixon's existence came from the fact that the harder he tried to please, the more he displeased. There was no task he was unwilling to undertake if it would earn him a few brownie points with Ike. Although Ike was willing to use him in this manner, it further lowered his opinion of him. The consequent strain in their relations caused Nixon to tighten up as he pasted his jolliest smile on his face in preparation for stepping through the doorway into the Oval Room. And Nixon's obvious inability to relax in his presence made the general view his infrequent visits with increasing reluctance. It was a deadly circle.

One would have imagined that a young man, scarcely forty years old, who had been in politics for only seven years and had achieved the lofty status of

Vice President of the United States, would be supremely happy. This was not the case with Richard Nixon. He looked forward to an uncertain future, and lived each moment in the grip of an anxiety which had been with him from childhood, but with which he dealt less adequately from day to tormenting day.

XIV.

My Good Friend McCarthy

At his October 18, 1953 press conference, Ike obliquely told Dick how little use he hoped to have for him in the future. Fed up to his twinkling blue eyes with McCarthy, and apparently beginning to sense that the charge of Communists controlling the government was good for an opposition party, but no way to run 1600 Pennsylvania Avenue, he told a somewhat skeptical press corps that he hoped the Communists-in-government issue would be "a matter of history and memory by the time the next election comes around."

At this point in his development it was like telling Nixon that he was soon expected to be obsolete. He concluded by saying he was "unhappy" about the allegations that Communists were in key positions and about "the suspicion on the part of the American people that their government services are weak in this regard."

That Nixon was going to have difficulty adjusting to this viewpoint was apparent when he invited McCarthy to visit with him in Smathers-Rebozo Land at Christmas time. This confirmed his role as McCarthy's friend in the Eisenhower councils, but it suggested he was being a bit slower than usual in noticing that the wind had changed.

He was mesmerized by the fact that he had influence with McCarthy—the man no one seemed able to influence. After all, hadn't Jerry Persons, the White House staff's chief defender of the theory of conciliation with McCarthy, come forward earlier in the year with praise of Nixon. His fine work in attempting to get Charles E. Bohlen's nomination as Ambassador to the U.S.S.R. past an aroused McCarthy, who knew when he met a disguised Communist, had led Persons to cite Nixon as proof of the possibility of working with McCarthy. Persons had moved around the White House seeking converts and saying, "On the Bohlen case, for instance, McCarthy had two speeches ready to use in fighting us. Both were pretty rough, but one

171

was *real* dirty. So he went to Dick Nixon to ask which he ought to give. So Dick told him—and he didn't use the real *dirty* one."

Victories such as that gave Dick his major sense of usefulness on the Eisenhower team. He was not likely to easily relinquish such a pleasure.

Balancing off McCarthy's friends in high places was one indefatigable enemy, himself. In the absence of this one powerful opponent it is unlikely that his influence would have ever waned. At that time brave men were remarkably scarce in a country where everyone could trace their lineage back to courageous ancestors. By 1953 McCarthy had succeeded in intimidating almost all men of influence. The fingers on one hand were not fully employed in counting the senators who had risen to mildly criticize their out-of-control colleague. Eisenhower's treatment of McCarthy encouraged the most abysmal displays of cowardice. He hated McCarthy with a passion, which he often privately displayed. He was, however, too timid to fight it out with him. Instead he invented a number of rationalizations for avoiding an open confrontation perhaps best expressed by his famous remark, "I will not get into the gutter with that guy."

It had a high-minded ring to it, but the practical result was catastrophe. McCarthy roved at will along the gutters, following their paths into government agencies, private industry, the State Department and finally the Army, destroying morale wherever he went. In three short years he had become the most powerful single individual in the country, with the possible exception of the President. If anyone were to stop him, it was going to have to be the general. As Truman said looking up from his desk when a hard decision had to be made, "The buck [passing] stops here."

Sherman Adams described how Ike handled this monumental example of buck passing. "If Eisenhower could have had his own way in dealing with Joseph R. McCarthy, he would have ignored the Senator completely. . . . Eisenhower would have preferred to look steadily at a point at least two feet over McCarthy's head." The problem was that the danger lay two feet below Joseph R. McCarthy's head, to be exact, in the hand that held the dagger.

Nixon, conversely, saw too much of himself in McCarthy to place him beyond the pale. They were really practitioners of the same black art, character assassination. McCarthy was catching everyone's eye at the moment, and his charges were stated ever more flamboyantly, more recklessly. But this seemed a matter of chance, character and training. Nixon was inherently cautious, always projecting the image of a man who hoped to get out of town before the target of his invective could rally a necktie party. And somehow his legal training had taken better than McCarthy's. He was always shading his remarks so that libel would be hard to prove. Tom Dewey characterized him as "a respectable McCarthy." The nature of those times can perhaps be measured by the fact that Dewey, weighed down with what was for him an unforgiveably negative opinion, was the most influential individual responsible for procuring the Vice Presidential nomination for his "respectable McCarthy."

There were brave men who spoke out. Chief among them was radio commentator and journalist Elmer Davis, at whose grave Democrats should give grateful thanks. His lonely voice, heard for fifteen minutes each weekday night, gently, firmly, often with scathing humor, spoke out for sanity. He was eventually joined by Edward R. Morrow and others.

The lack of organized opposition caused McCarthy to lose control. Freed of all restraints, there seemed little he was not capable of saying or doing. Occasionally he was challenged because of the activity of his underlings. He had hired J.B. Matthews, formerly with Nixon's House Un-American Activities Committee, as the director of his committee's investigations. Matthews, in his tireless pursuit of "Commonists" [sic], had written an article for *The American Mercury,* July, 1953, which began McCarthy-style, "The largest single group supporting the Communist apparatus in the United States today is composed of Protestant clergymen."

This might be a sentiment to cheer the hearts and tighten up the muscles of men in Southern Ireland, but WASPish America recognized a Papist threat when they heard it. There was an instant outcry against Matthews, which eventually led to his firing by McCarthy. However, so confident was McCarthy of his invincibility that for several days he stood by his renegade investigator, and, as a result, suffered self-inflicted wounds other men would never have thought of causing him.

McCarthy's downfall began that very July, but from a cause completely unrelated to Matthews. Another of McCarthy's sidekicks, a young man named David Schine, was called by his draft board to serve his country. Such is the democratic nature of the draft that although Schine was the scion of the hotel Schines and the close friend of the most powerful United States senator, when his turn came, he was bound to go. McCarthy, and his indefatigable committee counsel Roy Cohn, Schine's bosom buddy, tried everything they could to save David from the horrors of egalitarian sacrifice.

McCarthy tried to soften the blow by getting Schine, otherwise an investigator for the committee, a commission in the Army, the Navy or the Air Force. None would have him. Black mutterings from McCarthy about what would happen if Schine was forced to don the uniform of his country as might any yeoman's son, left his draft board unmoved. On November 3 Private Schine took his place in the ranks.

In early December, shortly after making a speech against *that man in the White House,* except this time it was not F.D.R., McCarthy informed the

Secretary of the Army, Robert T. Stevens, that the day of retribution was imminent. He had divined that there were Communist employees working at Fort Monmouth, New Jersey. McCarthy intended to subpoena several members of the Army's loyalty-security board the next morning, at which time he was going to force them to reveal what their secret files contained about the men he suspected.

Nixon and William Rogers, now Assistant Attorney General under Brownell, but already the Vice President's closest ally in his dealings with McCarthy, were enlisted in an attempt to turn McCarthy aside. It was during this period that McCarthy made his Christmas visit to Nixon in Miami.

If McCarthy had a master plan to take over the government, Nixon's counsel at this point might have been more closely heeded. Nixon surely pointed out to him that he was attacking the wrong group. His chief supporters were to be found strolling the halls of the Pentagon. However, McCarthy was never a revolutionary, intent on organizing a coup d'etat. He loved and hated intensely. One of his favorites had been dealt with cavalierly. General Bedell Smith had even refused to find Schine a place in the Central Intelligence Agency, among all those secrets. Executive orders protecting the security of the loyalty board files would have to be scrapped in the face of his enraged demand to know all.

Henry Cabot Lodge told Eisenhower he felt it was time for the Administration to take "a more thoughtful look" at its conciliatory attitude toward McCarthy. A meeting was scheduled for January 21, 1954, in the Attorney General's office, and Nixon, Rogers and Persons, McCarthy's friends in the White House, were excluded. Lodge, Sherman Adams, by now Eisenhower's surrogate in all matters of importance, Brownell and John Adams, the Army's chief counsel, were in attendance.

That the issue had been settled, and an open break with McCarthy finally decided on, was clear. There was no talk of how McCarthy might be convinced to back off, no suggestion that Nixon's conciliatory service might be required. Instead, the Schine file was reviewed and Sherman Adams ordered that the Army was to put every request for preferential treatment from McCarthy and Cohn into chronological order and see that a copy was placed in the hands of each member of McCarthy's investigating committee. "Not entirely by accident," Adams commented with gleeful self-satisfaction, "the Army's report on its troubles with Schine fell into the hands of a few newspaper correspondents before it was seen by the subcommittee, and their stories built up a backfire against McCarthy, as intended."

McCarthy fought back with his characteristic diversionary tactics. A dentist, Irving Peress, previously noted only for his ability to fill cavities, became McCarthy's instrument. Peress had been inducted into the Army the previous year under the provisions of the Doctors' Draft Law. He had been commissioned Captain and promoted to the rank of Major according to standard procedure aimed at correlating civilian earnings with military pay. During this period when Peress was reluctantly making his way up the career ladder, the Army's loyalty-security board had been unable to get him to answer questions about his alleged Communist associations. He had subsequently been labeled a "security risk," which apparently meant he could drill teeth on no one above the rank of sergeant. Sensing that this strictly limited the quality of service Peress was able to render his country, the Army had determined to discharge him. At this point someone connected with the loyal-security board tipped off McCarthy that a threat to our national security was being harbored in the Camp Kilmer, New Jersey, dental office. On January 30, Major Peress was summoned before the Grand Inquisitor. He immediately pleaded the Fifth Amendment, which was enough to confirm the worst that McCarthy feared about his lethal potential for Cold War damage. McCarthy demanded Peress be court-martialed. Instead, three days later, in an energetic display of sweeping the dirt under the carpet, he received an honorable discharge.

On February 18 McCarthy summoned General Ralph Zwicker, Camp Kilmer's commander, and possessor of a splendid military record, to discover why Major Peress was allowed to escape the firing squad. Finding his answers unsatisfactory, McCarthy proceeded to call him "ignorant" and growl that he was "not fit to wear that uniform." He told him he should "be removed from any command" and that he was forced to question "either your honesty or your intelligence." He informed him that he had "the brains of a five-year-old child."

When John Adams tried to end the general's mortification, McCarthy evicted him from the hearing room. After the hearing, Stevens announced no Army officers would be allowed to appear before McCarthy's Permanent Investigating Subcommittee.

In the meanwhile Roy Cohn, still primarily concerned with his friend Schine's comfort, was continuing his attempt to pull strings. He told Stevens that if Schine did not start receiving elitist treatment, McCarthy's investigation into the Army would get tougher. He suggested the Secretary would be performing a national service if he appointed Schine his special assistant in charge of uncovering subversives in the Army. Stevens' refusal then led to a Cohn suggestion that Schine be transferred to West Point, where he could make a study of Army textbooks to ferret out Communist propaganda.

There was here such a tender concern for a friend that Cohn's and McCarthy's efforts are almost appealing. In a fit of Byronic fervor they were willing to rip down the pillars of the world in order to provide him with a moment's pleasure. Cohn went so far as to phone Army counsel John Adams one night in Massachusetts to demand that Schine be excused from KP the next day.

At this point Nixon stepped forward. He arranged the famous "fried chicken luncheon" on February 24 in Senator Dirksen's office. Being feted were Stevens, McCarthy, and McCarthy's close Senatorial friends, Dirksen, Mundt and Potter. Ike was out of town, playing golf at Palm Springs.

Nixon was convinced some sort of accommodation could still be reached. C.D. Jackson, McCarthy's chief opponent in the White House, described him as still believing that "the Senator is really a good fellow at heart." However, Nixon's sense of caution, which was never to relax after the fund fiasco, led him to make a point of absenting himself from the slaughter of the innocent. Stevens had to go into that den of wolves alone, although Nixon was next door in his office, perhaps with his eye pressed to the keyhole.

Stevens had gone to the luncheon only after Nixon pledged it would be kept secret, and instead found over a hundred reporters milling around in front of Dirksen and Nixon's offices. After this surprise he never regained his footing.

Stevens nevertheless went back to the Pentagon convinced he had arrived at an honorable agreement with McCarthy. Henceforth the Senator would not bully Army officers before his committee. The ability of men to deceive themselves was never more clearly illustrated than in this instance where Stevens found it possible to accept McCarthy's word that he would be capable of acting with such uncharacteristic restraint.

Mundt, deputy for the residue of conferees, immediately called a press conference in which he announced the *capitulation* of the Army, in what he referred to as a "memorandum of understanding." The Secretary, he announced, would make available to Senator McCarthy the names of those who had made possible the promotion and honorable discharge of the dentist major. Furthermore, Stevens's prohibition against Army officers testifying before his committee, specifically General Zwicker, was rescinded. Mundt made no references to the assurances he had given Stevens.

Mundt's announcement made Nixon realize how far out on the limb he really was. He had been assuring Eisenhower that a coexistence pact could be worked out with McCarthy. However, Mundt's betrayal made such a supposition insupportable. Stevens was roasted in the press for showing "the white feather." He was pictured as a weakling who had been lured into a trap by McCarthy's friends. Stevens allowed himself the comfort of publicly complaining about the "timid souls" in the White House, a direct reference to Nixon and Persons, who had pressured him into attempting to reach an agreement with McCarthy and his friends.

Adlai Stevenson contributed a cutting blast against the Administration's handling of McCarthy. At the same time, President Eisenhower fulminated in private that McCarthy's headline-hunting was actually impeding the search for subversives in government agencies, an unintentional confession that despite the most strenuous efforts of every new Republican department head to discover hidden Communists on their payroll, they had been unsuccessful. He added that McCarthy was doing such a job of disorganizing and demoralizing the federal government that "the Kremlin ought to put McCarthy on its payroll."

Nixon finally understood that he had gone as far down the road with McCarthy as he could. On March 13 he announced his formal break with his "good friend McCarthy." In a speech answering Stevenson and, in effect, announcing a new Administration position, he said, "Men who have in the past done effective work exposing Communists in this country have, by reckless talk and questionable methods, made themselves the issue rather than the cause they believe in so deeply."

The break was obviously being made in sorrow and with reluctance. Even in parting Nixon could not resist paying his friend, and inferentially himself, a compliment. McCarthy, he said, had "in the past done effective work in exposing Communists." Nothing on the record supported that contention. Ike's older brother, Arthur B., executive vice president of the Commerce Trust Company of Kansas City, had hoisted a signal that Nixon should have seen when he labeled McCarthy "the most dangerous menace to America" and said he "has never been responsible for the conviction of one . . . Communist."

The Army formally filed its chronological report on the McCarthy-Cohn attempt to gain preferential treatment for Schine on March 11, two days before Nixon's speech. It formed the basis for the most sensational Congressional hearings of the twentieth century, which began April 22 and lasted through thirty-six days of actual testimony. Every minute of that hearing was telecast live to every corner of the country. The American people sat as members of the jury that judged McCarthy.

McCarthy's own Permanent Investigating Subcommittee held the hearings. Senator Karl Mundt, Nixon's co-worker from HUAC, temporarily replaced McCarthy, who stepped down to alternately take the witness stand with Roy Cohn and David Schine and act as defense attorney. Stevens presented the Army's case. However, his most successful tactic was to hire Joseph N. Welch to bolster his legal staff.

Welch was an elderly Boston lawyer, a wise, patient, friendly man. When he spoke the listener knew he was bound to hear some witty remark. The contrast with cold, sarcastic McCarthy was complete.

From the beginning it was clear McCarthy was vulnerable. In an attempt to change the focus of the hearings he broadcast an appeal to federal employees to disregard Eisenhower's orders and give him security information from confidential files. Even Knowland broke with him on this point. On May 29 he warned that McCarthy was on "dangerous and doubtful ground." Nixon did not rise to the defense of his chief.

The turning point in the hearings came on June 9. Roy Cohn was on the stand and Welch had been closely questioning him. As usual, the hearing room was jammed. The television cameras captured the anxiety on Cohn's face as Welch patiently probed. Irritated by the questioning which had exposed the frivolous nature of Cohn's and Schine's behavior as committee employees, McCarthy suddenly injected a charge.

He mentioned the name of Frederick G. Fisher, Jr., a young lawyer working for Welch's law firm. He stated that Fisher had been a member of the National Lawyers Guild "long after it had been exposed as the legal arm of the Communist Party." He accused Welch of recommending Fisher as counsel to the committee for this investigation.

Mundt, worn down, as was everyone else, by McCarthy's obvious duplicity, chose this moment to make an isolated anti-McCarthy gesture. He interrupted to volunteer that he "had no recognition or no memory of Mr. Welch recommending either Mr. Fisher or anybody else as counsel for this committee."

Mundt's remark made McCarthy look like a liar who had attempted to relieve the pressure on his partner by dragging the name of an innocent young man through the mud. It was a rampant demonstration of McCarthyism before the eyes of millions. McCarthy leaned forward over the large committee table, suddenly at bay. Welch, stunned by McCarthy's unexpected accusation, reacted instantaneously. Almost in tears, bent in McCarthy's direction as if so severe a blow had struck he could not remain erect, he told McCarthy that "until this moment, Senator, I think I never really gauged your cruelty or your recklessness." He asked him if any "sense of decency" remained in him.

The room was utterly silent. Welch gasped almost convulsively. "If there is a God in heaven," he said, his voice gentle, pained, sincerely angered and, yet, somehow full of compassion even for McCarthy, "it [the attack on Fisher] will do neither you nor your cause any good."

The spectators burst into applause, the sound echoed in millions of homes across America.

The hearings were soon over. The true meaning of McCarthyism had been exposed and the exposure had destroyed him. His credibility had been demolished and the atmosphere of invincibility that had developed around him during the years when powerful men had allowed him to go unchallenged was exploded.

The truth of the matter was that there had been a failure of nerve on the part of most Democrats during the last two years of the Truman Administration, as they saw Nixon and his Republican allies making increasingly more effective use of Communist-smear tactics. On the other hand, the Republican leadership was closely allied to McCarthy. They had used him to win elections and when Eisenhower went into Wisconsin in 1952 and endorsed McCarthy, despite his personal antagonism toward him, all alert Republicans knew the pact was sealed. Had McCarthy been able to recognize his friends and work with them, the pit he fell into could easily have been avoided. As Sherman Adams pointed out, "Eisenhower and Dulles were ready to go along with this attempt at coexistence [by Richard Nixon] , provided that McCarthy would keep his investigations and his accusations within reasonable bounds."

It was an incredible admission, but a true measure of the attitude of the Republican leadership. When Senator Ralph E. Flanders, Republican of Vermont, introduced his motion to censure McCarthy in July, 1954, as a direct result of the Army-McCarthy hearings, it was still not certain the Republican leadership could be convinced to abandon McCarthy. In fact, when the special Senate committee headed by Republican Arthur V. Watkins of Utah recommended in December that McCarthy be censured "for conduct unbecoming a Senator," Knowland, the GOP majority leader, Dirksen, Bridges and Millikin voted for McCarthy. Senator Leverett Saltonstall was the only top Republican to vote against him. This was despite an overwhelming Senate condemnation of McCarthy, sixty-seven to twenty-two.

McCarthy rapidly disappeared from the scene after the censure motion had been adopted. His old friends fell away, and on the rare occasions when he took part in Senate activity before his death in 1957, he was morose and frequently incoherent. Six months after he was censured McCarthy's influence had dwindled so completely that the introduction of a resolution by the Wisconsin Senator led Nixon to remark, according to Adams, that "it was a matter that the President did not need to take very seriously." And, although there is no witness who has testified on this matter, he undoubtedly joined the assembled Republican leaders in laughing when Ike asked if everyone heard the one going around Washington about McCarthyism now becoming McCarthywasm.

All these men who had been so instrumental in advancing McCarthy, in using his magic when it had potency, were now eager to wash their hands of him. And as the years passed they did everything they could to change the perspective on their roles in this sad period in American history. Their close alliance with McCarthy became something they never spoke of voluntarily. When their supporters brought it up, it was with guile, to differentiate between McCarthy and the men he had always considered his friends.

Years later Chotiner explained Nixon's attitude toward his former comrade: "He thought that McCarthy painted with too broad a brush. He liked McCarthy. But it finally got to a point where McCarthy would not listen to anyone. Not even to Dick. And when even Dick could not get through to him, everyone knew that there wasn't any use in trying any more."

In his office next to the White House, Herb Klein told me on August 5, 1971 of Nixon's attitude toward McCarthy in remarkably similar words. "Well, his reaction to McCarthy was that he was too broadbrush. . . . He thought McCarthy was not specific but too general."

If only McCarthy had been a little more careful, they seemed to say, then, like Nixon, he might have gone on to a brighter destiny. After all, in their heyday they were the Pollux and Castor of the anti-Communist smear. They made their way not on legislative contributions or bold plans for the nation's economic or social improvement. They made their reputations by destroying those of other, mostly decent men, and when Nixon looked back in 1954 and saw that his friend McCarthy had fallen among the victims, he must have been pleased at having avoided the trap himself, and eager for a great new day to come.

XV.

Soldier Dick, or *How Dick Heated Up the War*

The history of the Vietnam war has been obscured by its length and the desire of politicians to avoid accepting responsibility for their follies. No one has been more intimately involved in the decisions surrounding that war than Richard Nixon. It is hard to find a single important Vietnam option he did not help initiate, either by direct participation or the weight of his forcefully expressed opinion.

The French had been holding Indo-China as a colony since the reign of Louis Napoleon in the mid-nineteenth century. They had ruled it in the tradition of rapacious imperialists of all languages and color throughout history, showing their final contempt for their subjects by maintaining their emperor on his throne as a puppet. At the beginning of World War II, while France was being defeated by Hitler in Europe, and temporarily becoming his imperialist victim, the Japanese occupied the defenseless French colony. As the war's end approached it became apparent to the victorious allies that some provision had to be made for all of reconquered Southeast Asia.

Franklin Roosevelt's strongest impulse was to grant independence to the area. He did not approve of French colonialism. We were in the process of liquidating our forty-five-year-old imperialist venture in the Philippines. Roosevelt saw no reason why we should support a reimposition of French rule, which had never been as enlightened as our own, on a people whose nationalism had been reawakened by Japanese propaganda during the previous decade.

At Yalta in 1944, he proposed that Indo-China be granted to France as a trusteeship. Similar arrangements were being made with other former League of Nations mandated territories. He envisioned a short period during which the French would help prepare the Vietnamese for self-government, then they would supervise free United Nations elections and withdraw. He urged DeGaulle to accept this proposal, arguing that it would allow the French to strengthen their commercial ties with Indo-China while avoiding the expense of large armies of occupation and the possibility of insurrection. This prospect never appealed to the Elysée potentates who thought rather in terms of the glory inherent in imperial domain.

With the advent of the Cold War, plans which had seemed to hold out the prospect of reducing tensions became the first casualties. The prime U.S. objective under Truman's leadership was to assume a condition of alertness against Communist aggression anywhere in the world. Despite Nixon's constant clamor that the Democrats were being soft on Communism, each foreign affairs decision was measured to conform to that requirement. Unfortunately, this put us in step with French militarists, who had never agreed to Roosevelt's dream of an independent Indo-China.

They had been fighting against Communist leader Ho Chi Minh and his nationalistically inspired native guerrillas since the end of World War II, determined to reimpose pre-war French rule. At first our role was one of passive support as the French appeared capable of handling their own problem. However, as the years went by, Truman began to take on part of the financial burden incurred by the French army. The fall of China to the Communists in 1949, and the Republican outcry that it was solely his fault, hardened Truman's determination to avoid Communist conquest of Southeast Asia. The Korean War, which dominated the last two years of his Administration, further reinforced his resolution to "contain" Communist aggression.

By the time Eisenhower took over, we were paying the French $400 million a year, which represented about half their budget for fighting the increasingly violent war. During all this time, Nixon supported every measure to heat up the war, although he couched his support of help to the French in a way that would not give the impression he approved of anything Harry Truman did.

After Eisenhower and Nixon took office, the situation in Indo-China went from bad to worse. Communist supplies which had gone to help the North Koreans fight American troops were diverted to the southern battlefields. Although Ike managed finally to wring an armistice out of the North Koreans and Chinese Communists on July 27, 1953, by implying he was ready to use the atomic bomb to achieve peace if they refused, he was dismayed to see that the position of his French ally in Southeast Asia was deteriorating.

On August 4, 1953 he explained his reasoning to the Governors' Conference: "If Indo-China goes, several things happen right away. . . . The tin and tungsten that we so greatly value from that area would cease coming, and all India would be outflanked. Burma would be in no position for defense."

It was a frankly imperialistic statement, revealing businessman's and soldier's logic. Nowhere was the element of practical idealism that had motivated Roosevelt, nor Truman's anger at Communist duplicity.

One month later, on September 2, Dulles told the American Legion Convention, "Communist China has been and now is training, equipping and supplying the Communist forces in Indo-China." Then he expressed a veiled warning to the Communists. Further aggression in the area "could not occur without grave consequences which might not be confined to Indo-China." Bomb-rattling, which had produced some results in Korea, was being tried again. Private sources were allowed to convey to Communist China the American government's clear intent not to let Indo-China fall behind the Bamboo Curtain.

On February 6, 1954 Eisenhower, with Nixon's enthusiastic support, took the decisive step that was eventually to involve American soldiers in direct combat. Acting as Commander-in-Chief of the Armed Forces, he sent two hundred "technicians" to Indo-China. They were the first uniformed Americans to set foot in Southeast Asia. Ostensibly they were there to service the planes we had been sending to the French. From this moment on, an American military presence was always felt in the area.

At the same time, with the approval of the National Security Council, of which Nixon was the only other prominent elected official, Ike upped our contribution to the French. Henceforth we were to annually pay them $785 million, which completely relieved them of any financial responsibility for the war.

Three days later Defense Secretary Charles Wilson was asked at a press conference, "Do you think a military victory can be won in Indo-China or that peace will have to be negotiated there?" His answer, characteristically blunt, was, "I would think that a military victory would be perhaps both possible and probable."

It was an amazing statement for two reasons. It implied an American participation in achieving a military victory. This remark came only six months after we had concluded a bloody war in Korea, when citizens of every persuasion were determined to put on the garments of pacifism. In addition, the course of events to date would force most men to admit that the Indo-China war was going badly indeed and a military victory was improbable.

Consequently the President's press conference the next day was awaited with tremendous anticipation. He was immediately asked, "There seems to be some uneasiness in Congress that sending these technicians to Indo-China will lead eventually to our involvement in a hot war there. Would you comment on that?"

Ike, speaking with that intense sincerity which marked even his simplest statements, said, "Well, I would just say this: No one could be more bitterly opposed to *ever* getting the United States involved in a hot war in that region than I am. Consequently, that [sic] every move that I authorize is calculated, so far as human can do it, [sic] to make certain that does not happen."

He was not being entirely candid. For months Eisenhower had been trying to organize some form of "united action" in Indo-China with France and Great Britain. The French resolve to fight was weakening and he felt if a stand were to be made against Communism in Southeast Asia, it would require some form of American intervention to bolster the French. However, recognizing the difficulty of convincing the American people to support another military venture so soon after Korea, Ike felt intervention would require, at a minimum, the support of our two anti-Communist World War II allies. Such a move would symbolize common and equal sacrifice for a cause all supported. By early March, the final form of the French defeat was beginning to take shape and Dulles was desperately trying to convince the French and English governments to endorse Ike's plan. However, the American public was not being apprised of these efforts, partly because they never looked very promising.

On March 10 another question on the growing American involvement in Indo-China was asked at Ike's weekly press conference. "Mr. President, Senator Stennis said yesterday that we were in danger of becoming involved in World War III in Indo-China because of the Air Force technicians there. What will we do if one of these men is captured or killed?"

This question reflected popular anxiety over Eisenhower's decision to send American soldiers to Saigon. The President answered: "I will say this: There is going to be no involvement of America in war unless it is a result of the Constitutional process that is placed upon Congress to declare it. Now let us have that clear. And that is the answer."

With the firmness of a commanding officer he refused to countenance further discussion. In view of the fact that he had already taken the first long step into a war which inevitably flowed from his action, his answer was evasive, and of a kind with many such answers given by future Presidents.

The French had now committed themselves to the final battle of the war at Dienbienphu. Ike told his press conference on March 25 that the defense of Indo-China was "of transcendent importance." He watched the battle reports apprehensively. The French had, in effect, staked all on one last cast of the dice. They had lost the war of hit-and-run jungle tactics. They now determined to offer Ho Chi Minh such an inviting target in the recesses of the north that he would be tempted to fight a conventional battle of fixed positions against them, which they hoped their superior fire power would enable them to win. As their miscalculation became apparent, Ike and Dulles, with cheerleader support from Nixon, determined to increase American aid.

Speaking before the Overseas Press Club in New York City on March 29, 1954, Dulles said, "The imposition on Southeast Asia of the political system of Communist Russia and its Chinese Communist ally, by whatever means [apparently free elections were already out] would be a grave threat to the whole free community. The United States feels that that possibility should not be passively accepted, but should be met by united action." He was preparing to fly to England and France in one last-ditch effort to gain support for his grand design.

Finishing ominously, he said, "This might have serious risks, but these risks are far less than would face us in a few years from now if we dare not to be resolute today."

It was clear that the Republican leadership had resolved on a military solution in Southeast Asia if such a course of action could be made palatable to our allies. At a meeting in his upstairs study in the White House at the beginning of April, according to Sherman Adams, Ike agreed with Dulles and Admiral Radford that American troops should be sent to Indo-China, "under certain strict conditions."

However, the enigma remained. Having made the decision, how was that fact to be conveyed to the American public? At his April 7 press conference Ike tried to simplify the problem. He used an imaginary row of dominoes to illustrate his point. Indo-China was the first in the row, which once having tipped would foreshadow the fall of the last. Now that the explanation had been given it was necessary to find out if anyone was convinced.

What Nixon said to the American Society of Newspaper Editors on April 18 can be viewed in two ways. It was either a carefully thought out Administration trial balloon which was merely floated aloft by the exhaust from the Vice President's conveniently timed statement, or it was an example of Nixon once again extemporizing himself into trouble.

After delivering his prepared address, he agreed to answer questions if the answers were considered off-the-record. He stipulated that he could be quoted only as "a high administrative official." In short, he was not foreclosing—indeed, seemed to encourage—the publication of his remarks. It was just that he did not want his name associated with his opinions.

Assured of anonymity, he launched into a long answer about the probable course of American action in Indo-China.

The United States as a leader of the free world cannot afford further retreat in Asia. . . . If France stops fighting in Indo-China and the situation demands it, the United States will have to send troops to prevent the Communists from taking over this gateway to Southeast Asia.

He was calling for a major escalation of the war. In fact, it was the first open declaration that Americans should start fighting in Southeast Asia. From this moment forward Richard Nixon was the spokesman for that hawkish point of view.

American newspapers honored their commitment to erase Nixon's name from the record. However, the London *Times* made clear in its story who had been responsible for these sensational remarks. *France-Soir* was less delicate. It identified him by name. Within two days American newspapers were openly connecting him with his opinions, often a disservice to politicians.

And so it proved on this occasion. Democrats, preparing for the upcoming Congressional campaign, denounced him for "whooping it up for war." Although his hawkish California rival, Bill Knowland, came to his support, most Republicans discreetly kept their silence. Senator Hubert Humphrey expressed immediate and complete opposition, but even such leading Republican Senators as Saltonstall and Hickenlooper opposed Nixon. Saltonstall said: "From the information that has been given me thus far, my opinion is that we should not send men into Indo-China."

The trial balloon, if it had been one, had been shot down. Dulles, the chief architect of intervention, quickly issued a statement that the use of American troops in Southeast Asia was "unlikely." Ike, playing golf at his favorite course in Augusta, said nothing.

Nixon seemed strangely undisturbed by the clamor. The reason was simple. Ike approved of what he had said. Sherman Adams is the source for the intelligence that Ike called Nixon after the public uproar informing him of his positive reaction to his statement. This communication was doubly important to Nixon since it was known Ike disliked using the phone and avoided it whenever possible. Showing his preoccupation with the Indo-China War, the President tried to reassure Nixon, telling him the outcry over his comment had been "all to the good because it awakened the country to the seriousness of the situation in Indo-China."

Ike had actually called him to murmur soothing words into his ear. The battle at Dienbienphu might be going poorly but progress was being made in Dick's battle for Ike's approval.

Emboldened by this first affirmative sign, and hoping for better things to come, he refused to retreat four days later when he spoke at a University of Cincinnati dinner. "The aim of the United States is to hold Indo-China without war involving the United States, *if we can*," he said boldly.

There was no indication this time that he wanted the alumni to withhold the identity of the *high administrative official* from whom they had received this information. "We have learned that if you are weak and indecisive, you invite war. You don't keep Communists out of an area by telling them you won't do anything to save it."

He was not standing by himself. At about the same time Senator John Kennedy stated that "Indo-China independence must be guaranteed." Although it was not voiced in the same belligerent tone, the similarity of the position of the two future Presidents on escalating the war was unmistakable. However, at this time Nixon was in a better position to affect events.

Support for this stand also came from mercurial Cambodian King Norodom Sihanouk. He branded the Communists in Cambodia as "invaders" and led the international press through a lecture on how he was going to eliminate them. Years later, after his overthrow by a military junta, Sihanouk fled to Peking, where his legitimate title and the Communists' indisputable power made them willing to endure each other's political idiosyncrasies.

The whole matter was being settled at Dienbienphu. As April dragged on it became apparent the Vietminh troops clustered in the hills around the French bunkers were in possession of enough heavy artillery to pick the French to pieces. Confronted with this sad intelligence, and the Allies' unwillingness to join in "united action," and the failure of Nixon's proposal to win any but Knowland to its support, the Administration was faced with the distasteful job of negotiating with the Communists.

On April 25 the Big Four foreign ministers agreed to hold a peace conference at Geneva. The original conferees were France, the U.S.S.R., Great Britain, the United States, and Communist China. On April 27, in an advance concession of defeat, the French signed an agreement with Bao Dai's puppet government granting "total independence" to Vietnam. Within a week the big powers at Geneva sent invitations to the Vietnam and the Vietminh to join the talks.

It was not difficult to get the Vietminh to come to Geneva. They were in the process of defeating the French at Dienbienphu, but one battle does not make a war. The French seemed discouraged after nine years of fighting, but Eisenhower, Dulles and Nixon were making ominous sounds about picking up the slack. There was no telling what those crazy Americans were capable of doing. Besides, the French still occupied most of North and South Vietnam. They held all the important cities. Even a year later, long after the

French had agreed they had been defeated, the job of evacuating their forces from the North was so great that they still had possession of Haiphong harbor, the chief port of Ho Chi Minh's new government. A bird in Ho's hand was still worth more than a bird in the Vietnam bush. If he did not like what came out of Geneva, he was always free to resume fighting. Besides, there was something appealing about forcing the French to negotiate with the "natives" they had previously treated with such disdain.

From the beginning, the conference was a disaster for the United States hardliners. Knowland said he would lead a fight to send U.S. troops to Indo-China if Ike said it was necessary. He warned of a "Munich" sell-out at Geneva. But since Nixon's avowal of that position before the editors, the Administration had disavowed the possibility of such action. The best Ike could convince himself to say publicly was that he ruled out a Geneva settlement based on partition of Indo-China.

By May 4 Dulles returned to Washington and rumors began circulating that he had left Geneva so as not to dirty his fingers with compromise proposals. Republican hawks were attacking him for "abject surrender," and Senator Lyndon Johnson, proving once again that he who lives by the sword will die by the sword, charged American foreign policy was suffering a "stunning reversal" in Vietnam.

Making the situation infinitely harder for Ike was the fact that the Army-McCarthy hearings were in full swing. While the French legionnaires were being slaughtered at Dienbienphu and we were being pressed at Geneva, he was being tormented by the vision of the American Army besieged by a Wisconsin Senator.

The conference dragged along indecisively during May as the Communists allowed the full impact of the French May 7 defeat at Dienbienphu to be felt along the side streets of Paris and Marseilles. On June 12 the Laniel government fell. Mendes-France became the new Premier and pledged to end the war, regardless of terms, within thirty days. Knowland, seeing the handwriting on the wall, demanded an end to the conference, but he was too late, and too unrepresentative of the American consensus that any price the French had to pay for peace was not too high.

As France's role in Indo-China was about to end, Bao Dai announced the appointment of Ngo Dinh Diem, one of his chief opponents, as premier. Diem's advocacy of Vietnam nationalism had made it inadvisable for him to remain in Indo-China while the French were ruling. Since he was a Roman Catholic, and anti-Communist, there was likewise no place for him in Ho's camp. Diem had to return from a Belgian monastery to take charge of the tottering Bao Dai government. The emperor then took off for the Riviera, announcing no plans to return.

Within the week an agreement was reached at Geneva. The country was going to be split into four separate governments, with North and South Vietnam divided, despite Ike's wishes, at the 17th parallel. Dulles' chief victory was that he was not forced to sign the agreement. Despite China's demand that the U.S. join in guaranteeing the settlement, the ceremonies on July 21 were not graced by his presence. He did, however, announce that although we were not becoming one of the signatory powers, we would not do anything to upset a reasonable settlement.

By this time Nixon had taken the lowest possible profile on the whole question. The closest he could come to commenting on the Indo-China war, on the day the Geneva accord was being inked, was to urge public support for the CARE package drive to aid war refugees.

It was a degrading day for Republicans. They were being pinned with the donkey's tail. Republicans were suddenly the men who lost territory to the Communists. It was during their Administration that an additional twelve million people had fallen behind the Iron Curtain. The reliable campaign issue of China falling to the Communists was about to lose its potency.

From Nixon's point of view, it was happening at the worst possible time. The 1954 Congressional campaign was about to get under way, and he had finally been given a major role to play in Ike's Administration. He was going to spearhead the Republican drive to hold on to control of Congress. The signals going up over the Geneva peace conference indicated that his job had been made harder. The question was, how was he going to handle himself?

XVI.

To the Well Once Too Often

Despite Eisenhower's clearly stated declaration in October, 1953, that he was hopeful the Communists-in-government issue would have no place in the 1954 campaign, it was by no means certain he would have his way.

An issue that had been so helpful in electing Republicans in the past seven years could not lightly be cast aside, especially since the new Republican rulers of America had not done an especially effective job in running the country. How could the Democrats be routed when they campaigned on the issues of a Republican recession, and foreign policy defeats, except by pointing out that they liked to "coddle Communists" in the Army.

Leonard Hall, the Republican National Chairman, tried to get Ike to understand this simple political fact of life. McCarthy, on November 24, 1953, in a nationwide radio and television broadcast, still six months short of his public humiliation by Welch, gruffly disagreed with the President. The "raw, harsh, unpleasant fact," he told his audience, was that "Communism is an issue and will be an issue in 1954."

However, the 1954 off-year Congressional campaign did not get under way until after McCarthy's disgrace, when Eisenhower was once again completely in control of the party's political apparatus. One would have imagined that his known reluctance to use the Communists-in-government issue would have been enough to keep it from being exploited by aspiring Republicans. However, this was not the case. The reason was simply that Richard Nixon had been given the responsibility of heading up the campaign in 1954 and he had concluded the soft-on-Communism issue was still the strongest, if not the only issue the Republicans had going for them. In this conclusion he was undoubtedly wrong. However, he based his actions on that assumption. At the June 4, 1954 Cabinet meeting, while the Geneva conference was winding toward its gloomy conclusion, he urged all department heads to stress the Administration's handling of subversion in speeches and press releases.

Two events in Nixon's life in early 1954 indicated there were rewards as well as penalties for being so prominent. On January 10 Checkers gave birth to five pups, three days before Nixon's forty-first birthday. Then on January 23 he was designated "Salesman of the Year" by the Los Angeles Sales Executives Club.

However, there were also reversals. On April 5 the Duke University faculty by a vote of 61-42 turned down a recommendation of a secret committee that the Vice President, their most conspicuous alumnus, be awarded an honorary Doctor of Laws degree. The secret committee had apparently informed Nixon this honor was coming his way in advance of the faculty vote, and, in an attempt to reciprocate, he had agreed to deliver the commencement address. With the announcement of the faculty vote, his secretary revealed that the press of business was suddenly too great; he would be unable to deliver his planned speech. However, on June 13 he found time to travel to Whittier College and deliver a commencement address, after being awarded an honorary degree there. Feelings were so divided on Nixon, Earl Mazo reported, that two reception lines had to be set up by the college administration. Those who wanted to greet the Vice President stood on one, while those who desired to avoid that honor stood on the other.

His presence in California drew attention to the upcoming campaign. He had earlier chosen Murray Chotiner to represent him in all his political dealings in California. By mid-summer it became apparent Nixon was planning even beyond the 1954 election, all the way to the Presidential campaign in 1956.

Nixon wanted to control the California delegation. Opposing him was a group led by Knowland, Governor Goodwin J. Knight and Senator Thomas H. Kuchel. Knowland was beginning to imagine himself as a good stand-in should Ike decide not to run for reelection. The confrontation between the two camps came over the selection of a relatively minor functionary, the vice chairman of the Republican State Central Committee. The position was anointed with importance for only one reason. During the 1956 Presidential campaign, the vice chairman would automatically become the chairman who controlled the California party apparatus.

Murray Chotiner was in charge of the Nixon forces. For Chotineresque openers, he charged "brute force" was being used against his candidate, Ray Arbuthnot, a Los Angeles fruit grower, who had been Nixon's advance man in 1952.

Governor Knight, a free-swinging original, counter-attacked by accusing Chotiner and "the Nixon crowd" of breaking an agreement. He called

Chotiner a "liar." Chotiner suddenly found himself on the defense, which must have whispered to him that he was going to lose. He decided to cut Dick's losses. He denied he had discussed the matter with the Vice President, or that Nixon was even interested in the contest. When Arbuthnot lost, after Knowland took a personal hand in the fight, Chotiner had a statement released saying that Nixon had been "a little too busy being the greatest Vice President in the history of the United States to take any part in this controversy." A modest enough claim.

These incidents underscored the fact that Nixon was not achieving the status and power he might have hoped for as Vice President. Instead he had become a lightning rod attracting hostile behavior, contemptuous comment and suspicion concerning his motives.

By mid-summer of 1954 Eisenhower had managed to disguise his lack of affection for Nixon. The young man was so anxious to please that it did not make much sense for Ike, who was content to compromise with intransigents like McCarthy, to openly bicker with such a willing servant.

At his June 30 press conference Edward T. Folliard, of the *Washington Post,* asked Ike the following question: "Vice President Nixon made a speech the other day. His thesis was that the Acheson foreign policy was to blame for the loss of China, and from that flowed the war in Korea and the difficulties in Indo-China. The Democrats didn't like it very much. [He had also violently attacked Truman.] I wonder if you had any observations to make about it?"

Ike scarcely paused for breath. "Well, now, first of all, let's recognize this: Each individual in this country is entitled to his own opinions and convictions."

Nixon must have found a moment of consolation when he read the transcript of the press conference and discovered that Ike had referred to him as a "splendid American." However, the joy was fleeting, for Eisenhower went on to say: "I think my own job is to look at America today and to look ahead. I carry administrative and executive responsibilities and planning responsibilities that don't fall on some other individuals; so that I just simply haven't the time to go back."

There was here a subtle downgrading of Nixon that typified Ike's way of referring to him. He concluded by reiterating, "My belief is this: We must seek agreements among ourselves with respect to foreign policy that are not confined to any party." He also wanted it known that "I have never seen his [Nixon's] speech, but, as I said, everybody is entitled, I think, to his own opinion."

It was on such meager gruel that Nixon had to nourish himself. Seeking satisfaction in other directions, he crammed for the Naval Reserve test to qualify for the rank of Commander. It might seem incongruous for the man who was one heartbeat away from being Commander-in-Chief to strive so stubbornly to become a Commander in the Naval Reserve. Each man has his own style. The disappointment must have been considerable when on July 14, while the bad news was coming in from Geneva, he was informed he had not earned sufficient points for promotion.

Fortunately the time for the 1954 campaign was at hand and nothing distracted him from his troubles so much as hitting out at the opposition. Besides, this election gave him a rare opportunity to dominate the center of the stage. Ike had turned the campaign over to him in a way that suggested only part of his distaste for the whole process. He had often felt "dirtied" by having to associate with politicians seeking public office. How nice to have this eager young man, who had at least achieved a reputation for success in this field, willing to take on the burden of getting all those Republicans elected.

During the last weeks of the campaign, as a Democratic victory was being forecast by the pollsters, Ike allowed National Chairman Leonard Hall to convince him to make some speeches. The high road strategy of 1952 prevailed. While Nixon explored the switchbacks of subversion, Ike devoted himself to the farm problem and the dangers of a government split between a Republican executive branch and a Democratic Congress. He stressed his Administration's accomplishments abroad and spoke of far-off places called Iran and Guatemala.

Sherman Adams remarked that Ike "told Nixon and others, including myself, that he was well aware that somebody had to do the hard-hitting infighting, and he had no objections to it as long as no one expected him to do it."

Apparently the absence of McCarthy as a hair shirt constantly reminding him of the unfairness of unsubstantiated charges, and the willingness of Nixon to do "the hard-hitting," made Eisenhower less concerned about barring the Communists-in-government issue from the campaign. In any case, Nixon concluded he was free to put on his brass knuckles and swing out without seriously risking Eisenhower's displeasure.

In mid-September he hit the campaign trail. During the next forty-eight days he traveled 28,072 miles to ninety-five cities in thirty-one states. He made two hundred and four speeches and held over one hundred formal news conferences. In each and every one his central theme was that the Democrats loved Communists, or, alternatively, did not know how dangerous they were.

In St. Louis, on September 17, he said the Democrats "either did not understand the magnitude of the [Communist] threat, or ignored it." Three days later in Omaha he contrasted this sorry record of Democratic malfeasance in the area of subversion control with the splendid record of the Eisenhower Administration. The Eisenhower Administration was, he claimed, "kicking Communists, fellow-travelers, and bad security risks out of the federal government by the thousands. The Communist conspiracy is being smashed to bits by this Administration. . . . Previous Democratic administrations underestimated the Communist danger at home and ignored it. They covered up rather than cleaned up."

This issue heated up the campaign. Lyndon Johnson, then leader of the Senate's Democrats, and by far more loyal to Eisenhower than most of the members of Ike's own party, answered Nixon's charges. He said the Republicans were using Nixon to lead "a fascist-type" attack on Democrats. He singled out for categorical denial Nixon's repeated assertions that "thousands of Communists, fellow-travelers and security risks" had been kicked out of government since the Republicans had taken over.

The issue was crucial for Nixon. It was *his* issue, and it went beyond winning the campaign. In New Bedford, on September 27, he boasted: "We have driven the Communists, the fellow-travelers, and the security risks out of the government by the thousands. I stand by the statement."

Then, in response to charges that he was smearing the Democrats with loose, unsubstantiated, generalized charges à la McCarthy, he decided to become specific. At Rock Island, Illinois, on October 21, he told a cheering Republican rally, "The President's security risk program resulted in 6,926 individuals removed from the federal service. . . . The great majority of these individuals were inherited largely from the Truman regime. . . . Included in this number were individuals who were members of the Communist Party and Communist-controlled organizations."

If charges could be made to appear more substantial by including figures, then he would provide them. And just to show how much more careful he was than McCarthy, he would use the same figure consistently, rather than alter it with each new speech. On November 1, he told a Denver audience, "96 percent of the 6,926 Communists, fellow-travelers, sex perverts, people with criminal records, dope addicts, drunks, and other security risks removed under the Eisenhower security program were hired by the Truman Administration."

One of the things that made this campaign a low point in Nixon's career was the fact that he was lying. The figures were impressive, but they were bogus. Philip Young, Eisenhower's personal selection for Chairman of the Civil Service Commission, revealed, but only after the election, that he knew of no single government employee who had been fired by the Eisenhower

Administration for being a Communist or a fellow-traveler. What a contradiction between the statement of an honest Republican and what Richard Milhous Nixon had been telling the electorate for over two months.

Even later Young published a more devastating analysis of 3,746 government workers who were dismissed, or handed in their resignations after being accused of being possible security risks (almost all alleged homosexuals or alcoholics), from May, 1953 until mid-1955. It showed that 41.2 percent had been put on the payroll by the new Republican Administration.

Manipulation of the truth in this case was not being done by a callow Navy veteran anxious to take fullest advantage of an opportunity unexpectedly handed him. The lying was being done by the Vice President of the United States. No doubt the pressure was great. He had an enormous responsibility—to preside over the election of a Republican Congress. Failure at that would be inexcusable; everything else could be explained if he succeeded. In fact, he knew by now that success made explanations unnecessary.

On October 13 Nixon made his way to Van Nuys, California, where he had determined to try out a new theme. The polls had indicated his pitch was not working too well. Looking confidingly at his audience, he said, "When the Eisenhower Administration came to Washington in January 20, 1953, we found in the files a blueprint for socializing America."

People in the audience gasped, as did most Americans when his charges appeared in the newspapers. He went on in his best accusatorial tone. "This dangerous, well-oiled scheme contained plans for adding $40 billion to the national debt by 1956. It called for socialized medicine, socialized housing, socialized agriculture, socialized water and power, and perhaps most disturbing of all, socialization of America's greatest source of power, atomic energy."

It seems hard to understand why he was so solicitous of the private atomic energy developers, since almost a generation later there were still few enterprisers who seem interested in turning away from conventional polluting power plants to "America's greatest source of power."

However, the heart of his message was that Truman and his subversive cronies had been busy in some subterranean hideaway, plotting the socialization (a Nixon code word synonymous with communization) of vital areas of the economy: medicine, housing, agriculture and power.

The Republican press was aghast and created the usual illusion that most of the people in the country were too. Reporters were sent to Nixon headquarters to get copies of the "blueprint." The Vice President was suddenly unavailable. He was "resting." However, a discreet inquiry by his press secretary delivered the intelligence that the Vice President was not speaking about a specific document when he used the term "blueprint." He had been using figurative language to describe the true meaning of Truman's proposals. Did Mr. Nixon still want to use the term "blueprint" in view of this newest information, the reporters wanted to know. Yes, certainly, Murray Chotiner's spokesman stated. The Vice President would continue to use the word "blueprint" in future speeches.

Van Nuys proved a bad stop for Nixon. Having put his foot in his mouth, he was placed in the position of having to raise the ante on his charges in order to conform to Chotiner's dictim that he should never allow himself to be forced onto the defensive. But the tension was clearly mounting. It revealed itself when he made a speech before an audience at the Valley Junior College that day. In an attempt to pace his delivery, one of the members of his party was signaling to him as the television time lapsed. He made an error and Nixon completed his prepared text one minute before the end of the telecast. At a loss to know exactly how much time he had left, he was forced to extemporize.

When the picture on the monitor finally went off, so did he. "Who the hell did that?" he demanded. Although the picture was off, the sound was on, and within seconds the switchboards at the station and the local newspaper were overloaded with protest calls. Running a gauntlet of reporters, Nixon demurred, "It wasn't me. I used no such language."

In one day he had managed to malign the former President of the United States and blaspheme the Lord. Such a man was bound to repel the conventional. It was at this time that tongue-in-cheek pictures appeared showing Nixon standing in front of a lot filled with old cars, a toothy smile on his face. The caption read: "Would you buy a used car from this man?"

In Los Angeles, the Vice President quoted Adlai Stevenson as saying that "while the American economy has been shrinking, the Soviet economy has been growing fast." He went on to accuse Stevenson, in best McCarthy manner, of being "guilty without being aware that he was doing so of spreading pro-Communist propaganda."

Stevenson had merely stated a self-evident truth. Since the Republicans had taken over, the Soviet economy had expanded in relationship to ours. In addition, our budget was farther away from being balanced than it had been during Truman's six years of direct responsibility for it. Truman had managed to reduce the national debt by $3,733,000,000. In the first full year of Eisenhower's responsibility he had run up a deficit of $3,117,000,000. Stevenson had not suggested that he was pleased with the news of Soviet industrial progress. In fact, it was clear he was pointing to this situation with alarm and calling for the election of Democrats so that a brighter day for the American economy might dawn.

It was distortions of this sort that led Walter Lippmann to describe Nixon as a "ruthless partisan . . . [who] does not have within his conscience those scruples which the country has the right to expect in the President of the United States."

Driven on as if by a demon that stung him from one excess into another, he made his most memorable slander in 1954 in a telecast in which he was defending the Eisenhower-Dulles foreign policy. For several minutes he read from his script, laboring only to communicate his sincerity. Suddenly he looked up from the text, a technique he used to convince his audience that what he was saying really came from his own mind and heart. Ad libbing with gusto, he blinked and said, "And incidentally, in mentioning Secretary Dulles, isn't it wonderful finally to have a Secretary of State who isn't taken in by the Communists?" Stewart Alsop referred bitingly to this slur. "It had all the earmarks of the classic Nixon low blow—a rhetorical question delivered with carefully calculated spontaneity, suggesting a falsehood without actually stating it."

The remark not only attempted to begrime Dean Acheson, who had been made immune to slights of this sort by repetition, but George C. Marshall, Ike's old friend of thirty-five years. Had these men really been "taken in" by the Communists? Had they devoted their careers to advancing Soviet ambitions? The implications were damning, not of Acheson and Marshall, but of the man who had made them. Far more unsettling for the future of the country was the possibility that he sincerely believed what he was saying. A liar was bad enough, but a liar and a fool, that was a combination of calamities that seemed to threaten the very safety of the Republic.

On Election Day it became apparent the Chotiner-Nixon strategy had not worked out the way it had been plotted on the drawing board. After controlling Congress for only two years, the Republicans were displaced, losing eighteen seats in the House, making the count 232-203 in favor of the Democrats. In the Senate the Democrats led 49-47. A Democratic newcomer named Edmund Muskie had so thrived on running against Nixon that he had won the governorship in rock-ribbed Republican Maine.

Nixon quickly characterized the results "a dead heat." Had he not made such a herculean effort, and stooped so low for such scant results, his appraisal might have been more valid. More important, had the loss of a few seats not meant the complete shift of Congressional control from his party, his casual tone might have been more convincing. However, he had gone all out, employing every technique in Chotiner's manual for winning—and he had lost. The only thing left to do was to act as if he had won. In this farce Eisenhower was willing to play his role. He wrote Nixon a warm letter of praise for his efforts, throwing in a kind word for Pat's help as well (the note was delivered several days before the election) .

At a Cabinet meeting afterwards on November 4, Nixon was given the floor to provide the official version of what had happened. "There were too many turkeys running on the Republican ticket." Telling half the story, as usual, he failed to point out that the quality of the Democratic candidates had not been any higher. Then, as if he had to provide a graphic illustration of his point, he pulled out of his pocket a toy drummer. Setting it carefully on the table, as the leaders of the American government watched in wonder, he released the toy's mechanism and the uniformed figure went marching stiffly across the large oval table, banging on its drum.

Summing up inanely, Nixon said, "We've got to keep beating the drum about our achievements."

Nixon had been speaking before a friendly audience and although some of them could not repress a smile of startled amusement at his curious display, it was nothing like the roar of disapproval that greeted him from Democratic ranks. When the 84th Congress reconvened on January 5, 1955, Nixon was not left in the dark about their reaction to his "hard-hitting" campaign.

Sam Rayburn, the venerable Texan who was Speaker of the House of Representatives for longer than any other man in American history, made the keynote speech of the new session. His fury toward Nixon boiled over. As a stunned House listened, he said, "We Democrats do not indulge in personalities. We are not the accusing kind of people. We do not have to be that way. . . . It matters not what the heat may be. . . . We are not going to indict people en masse. We are not going to say that just because we do not like somebody politically he is soft on Communism or that he believes in subversion."

Nixon had gone to the well once too often. He had ridden the anti-Communist tidal wave after World War II, but had failed to detect that, with the excesses of McCarthyism fresh in the voters' minds, and with the failure of the Eisenhower Administration to prove any of the charges the Republicans had been making for years, that wave had crested. He had extended himself all the way, testing the power of his one issue, and he had failed. He had no victories to offer his party and had accumulated enough hatred and distrust to bury the ambitions of more talented men. With a morbidness which for once seemed justified, he told Murray Chotiner that he was not going to run again in 1956. Pat breathed a sigh of relief and looked forward to happier days.

XVII.

The New Nixon

"Mrs. Nixon realizes there is always an enormous conflict between the public side of a family where the man is in public life and the private side, and it is necessary to choose," Nixon said in 1971, "and I think she felt at times that it would have been best if we were to leave public life."

One of those times was in the first half of 1955. It was a dreary period for Nixon. Being Vice President had solved few of his personal problems. Ike was distinctly uninterested in closing the gap between them. Except for an occasional pat on the head, usually evoked after Nixon had made some faux pas by the need for public display of the President's non-existent trust in him, the older man did nothing to comfort his associate. In the third year of their relationship, gregarious Ike, whose Gettysburg door stood open to any head of America's top two hundred corporations, had not found time to spend a single social evening with Nixon.

The Vice President had established no close ties with anyone in an exceptionally harmonious and socially active Cabinet, a slight for which he was able to avenge himself when choosing his *own* Cabinet. If only the contrast between the two were not so complete. Everyone liked Ike, but one could search for days before filling a jury box with people who would admit to a similar passion for Dick. If he had only been Lyndon Johnson's Vice President, life would have been much happier for him. But there was always the feeling when Ike and Dick were in the same room that someone had made a mistake and routed these uncongenial strangers into an embarrassing confrontation.

It was during this period that Nixon visited Dr. Arnold A. Hutschnecker for the first time. Dr. Hutschnecker had written a book on psychosomatic medicine in 1951. Although he was practicing "internal medicine" in 1955, he was in the process of becoming a psychoanalyst. In an article for *Look* magazine, printed July 15, 1969, he remarked that, "By 1960, I had largely changed my medical practice to psychotherapy."

Hutschnecker's article is fascinating for what it says about Nixon's mental health, and for what it implies. The article is entitled, *"President Nixon's Former Doctor Writes About the Mental Health of Our Leaders."* Dr. Hutschnecker explained his decision to speak publicly about this most famous patient. "In this live-or-die situation, we want to know what kind of a human being the man is who had set his goal as high as that of the Presidency." He felt that men "who are driven by hostile-aggressive impulses make up the majority of leaders in all areas of life." They "are the ones most likely to break down under stress. Therefore, they become a risk in social and certainly in political positions of responsibility."

Although he was generalizing at this point, his generalizations are disturbing because of the fact that for several years during the mid-1950's he was regularly visited by the Vice President.

Hutschnecker felt that, "the hostile-aggressive type is, however, often strongly passive-dependent on deeper emotional levels." Nixon would drive up to his Manhattan office escorted, on occasion, by Secret Servicemen, who would stand about conspicuously waiting for their charge to return.

"When a man seeks excessive power, what moves him is an urge to fulfill neurotic needs," Dr. Hutschnecker wrote. "Most of these needs go back to the child's feelings of smallness and a compulsion to compensate for his helplessness by attaining omnipotence. Napoleon went from conquest to conquest motivated by a desire to win approval from a mother who never fulfilled his needs."

Dr. Hutschnecker said Nixon came to him "for physical checkups, none of which showed evidence of any illness." Nixon often boasted during the 1950's that he never missed an engagement because of sickness. He was proud of his physical health. However, he has been equally frank in describing how depressed he was during this period.

Hutschnecker wrote of Nixon's mental health directly. "During the entire period that I treated Mr. Nixon, I detected no sign of mental illness in him." He had a good deal of opportunity to reach this diagnosis. "As I came to know him over the years, we developed a trusting professional as well as amicable personal relationship. . . . We became friends and, as such, we discussed many subjects in an open and relaxed manner."

Although he felt that his friend showed no signs of "mental illness" he did not choose to openly discuss his neurotic patterns. Instead he tried to reveal as little as possible. In fact, he became aroused when dealing with the accusations that news about Nixon's mental health had come from his office. ". . . the assumption had been made that there had been a leak from my office. This challenge, and I must state this categorically, is without founda-tion. There was no leak, and there was no violation of the sacred obligation a doctor has to safeguard the privacy of all of his patients."

Why all the secrecy? If all Nixon had was a little high blood pressure or allergies, surely the matter could have been discussed more openly.

In any case, Pat was worried. She took every occasion to insist he give up politics. As his morale sank to a low point she had reason to think she was making headway. She had a strong talking point when she urged him not to run for reelection. He had a hard offer from a New York law firm, which guaranteed him in excess of $100,000 a year. Even before he wanted to be President, he wanted to be a senior partner in a Wall Street firm. And Pat loved New York, where she had spent some happy days as an X-ray technician before meeting Dick.

Why should they remain in Washington, the scene of so many bad memories. Their personal life was solitary, the moments together broken only by the sound of the television set and visits from Murray Chotiner. And Murray was not always available for solace. The National Committee prevailed on him to tour the country addressing gatherings of local ward heelers, and dispensing his brand of wisdom. He prepared a 14,000-word speech which he usually delivered in the back room of some Republican clubhouse.

There was about his standard spiel a flavor of larceny that made it a dish for a strictly limited audience. One of Chotiner's beguiling qualities was his willingness to openly express a preference for sewer politics. He did this with a smile on his face and a suggestion of sharing some valuable understanding. He always pointed the way for other men, in a gesture that implied generosity. But the finger with which he pointed was so crooked that one trembled at the thought it was showing the way to future leaders of the United States.

He urged the junior league Chotiners across the country in 1955 to have their candidates ignore attacks. After a while, no matter what the nature of the charge, the opposition would run out of steam. "But if you find the attack has reached such proportion that it can no longer be avoided in any way, when you answer it, do so with an attack of your own against the opposition for having launched it in the first place."

The candidate was under no circumstances to answer the charges directly. Chotiner was actually dealing with situations in which the candidate was clearly in the wrong and could not possibly answer. His advice was not to resign, admit all, plead repentance, beg forgiveness and offer restitution. His advice focused on beating the rap.

"May I suggest to you," he offered, "that I think the classic that will live in all political history came on September 23, 1952, from Los Angeles, California, when the candidate for the Vice Presidency answered, if you please, with an attack against those who made one on him!"

By this time Nixon had become so imbued with Chotiner's techniques that when he spoke about tactics he even *sounded* like his mentor. Addressing the Radio and Television Executives Society in 1955, he offered some free advice on how to be effective on television. This was the pre-Marshall McLuhan era and these apostles were in search of a prophet. He stressed the importance of projecting sincerity, advising, "Use your fireside chat, a straight-forward, sincere type of presentation." The impression conveyed to the viewer must be of informality. But this was not easy to achieve. "A good off-the-cuff informal speech takes more preparation than a speech you read, and the candidate must realize that he can't just get up there and talk off-the-cuff without having spent hours in preparation." It was vintage Chotiner.

By the middle of the year Pat had every reason to believe she had made progress in her campaign to get Dick out of politics. She had even forced him to sit down and commit his resolve to paper, something she was to do again after the disappointments of the early 1960s.

The tedium of rank without power, of title without honor, seemed to be grinding him down. Ike was making life even more uncertain by acting coy about seeking renomination. On August 6 he told Arthur Krock he had some reluctance about the idea of running again. He spoke of the "erosion" of his mental and physical health and said he would make up his mind on the basis of whether he felt he could adequately perform his duties. Krock commented that Ike was giving Republican politicians "an emotional Turkish bath."

The low point for Nixon was, perhaps, reached on September 17, when a dispute, magnified out of all proportion because of the doubts people had about him, broke into the open at the San Francisco Art Festival. Artist Victor Arnautoff had created a cartoon entitled "Dick McSmear," which had been accepted for exhibition. It showed a figure, unmistakably Nixon, wearing a black mask, and holding a red-daubed paintbrush and pail in one hand. The pail was, in the not-too-subtle manner of the cartoonist, labelled "smear." In Dick's other hand was a pumpkin. Arnautoff called his work "A Political Comment on McCarthyism," and thought twenty-five dollars was all it was worth.

Had the Festival's director consulted Chotiner, he would undoubtedly have been told to ignore the lampoon and have his publicity releases stress the Jackson Pollack imitations. However, his decision was to remove it from the exhibit wall. It was at this point that the matter came to national attention. Once again Dick was made to understand his function in our society.

However, within a week any thoughts of apartment hunting in New York were thrust aside. Dwight Eisenhower, at the age of sixty-five, suffered a major heart attack. He had been vacationing in Denver when stricken on September 24. For a while his life hung in the balance.

Overnight Nixon found his status had dramatically changed. All those people who had been giving him the cold shoulder were suddenly attentive. This was the real magic of the office of Vice President. At one moment you are a supernumerary at cocktail parties, with time hanging heavy on your hands. Then by an act of God you are President, or likely to be so elevated by the next ring of the hot line.

It was necessary for him to hide his understandable pleasure. Undue eagerness to take over the functions of his fallen chief might alienate Ike's coterie, and should the chief recover, their enmity could be mortal. Patience was the ploy. If he were to be President, a show of humility would serve him well.

For the next two months Eisenhower remained in near isolation. The actual operation of the government was exercised by a council consisting of Nixon, Dulles, Brownell, Humphrey, Persons and Sherman Adams. Adams, the only official given access to the convalescent's room, assumed the most important role, a role whose duties (as Mrs. Woodrow Wilson discovered) were nowhere defined in the Constitution.

He commented, "As I expected, Nixon, in particular, leaned over backward to avoid any appearance of assuming Presidential authority." The Vice President made a point of sitting in his own place at Cabinet meetings, directly across from the invitingly vacant Presidential seat.

Although his role, in the eyes of the men charged with the responsibility of keeping the sinking ship afloat, had increased, Nixon's status with Eisenhower and Adams had altered very little. It was some time after Ike began to accept visitors, and resume a light work load in the Denver hospital, before Nixon was invited to fly out from Washington to spend a few moments with his chief. By this time, Ike's heart specialist, septuagenarian Paul Dudley White, was predicting full recovery, and Nixon sensed a cooling in the ardor of the Washington cognoscenti.

It was during this interregnum that "the New Nixon" emerged. The style suitable for a hatchet man was highly improper for a probable President.

James Reston called attention to this deliberate metamorphosis. "Vice President Richard Milhous Nixon is now making a conscious effort to modify his reputation as a fiercely partisan and highly controversial figure in American politics. Ever since the illness of President Eisenhower a month ago, Mr. Nixon's friends have been urging him to couch his public speeches in less extreme terms, and to concentrate on themes that will unify rather than divide the country."

When he now spoke he used prepared texts which had an optimistic tone.

His approach seemed balanced and thoughtful. He avoided partisan attacks and, in fact, went out of his way to praise Lyndon Johnson for his "magnificent" support of Eisenhower's foreign policy program in the previous Congress. On October 17 he delivered a speech before the *Herald Tribune* Forum in which he said, "We must at all costs avoid the bluster which might blunder us into war." This from the man who had a year earlier called for American intervention in Indo-China.

This speech was also marked by a complete switch in his feeling about the possibility of compromising with Communists. "We can be thankful that on October 27 the foreign ministers will meet in Geneva [a second summit] in an atmosphere which at the outset, at least, will be more cordial and therefore will hold more promise for resolving differences than any similar conferences between East and West in the past ten years."

He was displaying here an ability to do an about-face on a fundamental issue—an ability which showed itself dramatically during his Presidency. As in 1971, his partisans claimed he was merely displaying flexibility. Times change, and so does Richard Nixon. However, as Ike lay in bed struggling for life, the thought suggested itself that Nixon was perhaps less scrupulous than some people had previously believed. Surely anti-Communism—*his* issue— was a point of principle on which it could be expected he would never compromise. How could it be that one day Nixon was shouting to the nation that Communists were inplacable enemies plotting our destruction, whose subject people we were duty-bound to "liberate," and the next he was thankfully looking forward to "resolving differences" between these two incompatible philosophies.

Harry Truman did not find the New Nixon any more appealing than the old. He told a Seattle audience on November 26 that the Geneva conferences did not "amount to a damn" and went on vigorously to attack Nixon. "I don't like him. He called me a traitor and if I was a traitor, then the country is in a hell of a fix."

Ike's slow recovery brought about another change in Nixon's fortunes. It forced the President to seriously contemplate the possibility that the man he had allowed to be placed on the ticket with him in 1952, with a casualness that approached irresponsibility, was likely to be his successor. The prospect did not please him.

He left the Denver hospital in November and spent the next few weeks at Gettysburg, with plenty of time to contemplate the bleak winter landscape and torment himself about the decision that soon had to be made as to whether he would seek reelection. If he had doubts about his health allowing him to carry on when speaking to Krock one month before his heart attack, surely his physical breakdown had ended them. A vacation in Key West, according to Sherman Adams, lightened his depression. On January 13, 1956 he was back in the White House.

That evening he called together a group of his closest advisors for a frank discussion of the problem. In attendance were Dulles, Lodge, Brownell, Hall, Persons, Humphrey, Summerfield, Hagerty, Tom Stephens, Howard Pyle, Milton Eisenhower and Sherman Adams. Nixon was deliberately excluded. There were too many questions in Ike's mind about Dick's future to allow him to play any role in determining what the President's plans should be.

An informal dinner was held and then they retreated to the upstairs study, where Ike invited each of them to express his opinion. In a sense Ike had programmed the advice he was to receive. With the possible exception of his younger brother, each of the men in the study had already expressed the opinion that Ike should run. The consensus seemed to be that retirement would be bad for Ike; he would get bored hanging around. It was as though they visualized the Presidency as a method of diverting an ailing man, of keeping him active in his declining years.

It is likely, especially after the Congressional election fiasco of 1954, that men such as Leonard Hall, Herbert Brownell and Arthur Summerfield felt the Republicans were dead without Ike. It was fairly obvious Stevenson was going to be a repeat candidate for the Democrats. With a man of his caliber leading the opposition, the main chance for victory lay in utilizing Ike's potent magic.

Strange as it may seem, the only real alternative was Nixon. The young man was the darling of the conservative National Committee and local potentates across the country who would select the nominee, should Ike decline the honor. Because of Ike's resplendent reputation, no other Republican had developed in the previous three years as a possible stand-in. Dulles, the man with the most power in the Cabinet, had never cultivated the political cabbage patches. In addition, his dour style had kept popular enthusiasm for him to a minimum. Sherman Adams, who was in reality running the country during this period, was too genuinely modest and too satisfied with his role as major domo to entertain any thought of giving free rein to his ambition.

Incredibly, it was going to be either Ike leading the Republicans to victory, or Dick leading them to defeat. And that was not what Ike had in mind. In fact, his thoughts about the Vice President had taken a dark turn.

He called Nixon to the White House almost immediately after the January 13th meeting. Having made up his mind about his own plans, although he was not yet making that decision public, he now turned his attention to the second spot on the ticket. During his conversation with Nixon he spoke almost paternally. He wanted to discuss Dick's future with him. He knew he had Presidential ambitions. Fine, Ike said, but he thought his career would be strengthened if Dick decided not to run for Vice President again.

He had apparently done some serious thinking, perhaps even research before their tête-à-tête, and did Dick know that the Vice Presidency was considered by some as a political dead end? Not one Vice President in this century had gone on to the Presidency except on the death of the President. Furthermore, all Dick's public service had been in the field of politics. Think how he could advance himself in the esteem of his countrymen if he took a Cabinet post and got all that difficult, exacting and valuable executive experience. He bolstered his argument by pointing out that Herbert Hoover had been nominated after he had served with distinction as Coolidge's Secretary of Commerce. In order to make his proposition more attractive, Ike offered Nixon any job in the Cabinet except Secretary of State. So well thought out was his presentation that he specifically mentioned the Defense Department. Dulles was indispensable, but Charlie Wilson could easily be replaced by a rejected Vice President. (Did he have any idea how many Secretaries of Defense in the twentieth century had gone on to become President?)

This had been a difficult personal task for Eisenhower. He had performed extraordinary mental gymnastics to demonstrate the undemonstrable—that being Vice President of the United States was not a good job for a man who wanted to become President. Edited out of his thinking was the fact that if he were to die during this conversation, *President* Nixon would be the first witness to the catastrophe. The possibility that Nixon would ever convince a majority of voters in this country to make him President at the ballot box was remote. He would be running as an unpopular candidate of the minority party. However, since September 24, 1955, it had become tantalizingly clear that he might reasonably expect at any moment to be President.

Ike's proposition destroyed the momentary serenity of the "New" Nixon. Ike was trying to break the news gently, but the message was clear. He wanted him off the ticket.

Dick listened quietly. Ike told him to take his time and think over what he was proposing. Dick got up and politely assured the President that he would give his remarks careful consideration. But when he walked out of the President's office he knew he had been tactfully shown the door.

Within a week the primary season began. Ike was forced to tell the New Hampshire Secretary of State that he was willing to allow his name, which had been submitted by overeager partisans, to remain on the primary ballot. This was not a public announcement that he would seek reelection, but it was enough presumptive evidence for some cynics. They were now ready to turn their attention to the question of who would be his running mate.

At the end of January Ike resumed his weekly press conferences, the last of which had been held in August, just before his heart attack. His reelection plans preoccupied the reporters. For weeks he put them off with one answer or another. Finally at his February 29 conference he ended his coyness. He would be a candidate and he was going on television that night to explain to the American people how he had reached that decision.

The very first question asked after this announcement was, "Would you again want Vice President Nixon as your running mate?" This question had been asked at each press conference since the end of January, and he had started the rumors flying by avoiding the answer. No longer able to duck the issue, he declared that Nixon himself was undecided. It was not quite a lie, but then again, it was not quite the truth. Ike was avoiding any sort of admission that it was his suggestion that Dick depart which had caused the Vice President's indecisiveness. Then to compound this masterpiece of evasion, Ike told the astounded newsmen that he had advised the Vice President "to chart his own course."

Clearly, it was not Nixon who was undecided, but Eisenhower. It was preposterous to think hard-driving Dick would voluntarily step out of the line of succession. It was even more ludicrous to suppose that if Ike wanted him on the ticket he would have advised him "to chart his own course." No, Dick was being dumped, and that was the next day's story in every paper in the country.

There is built into Nixon an automatic response mechanism triggered by opposition. Offer him the element of competition, tempt him with a fight, hint that someone might want to deprive him of some prize and a tiger emerges from the camouflage he normally shows the world. If Ike wanted to give his shot at the Presidency to someone else, he was going to have to wrestle him for it.

As the weeks passed Nixon's depression deepened. Ike made no attempt to see him again, apparently reasoning that he had said enough. But every hint coming from the President's direction confirmed he had not changed his mind.

Once Ike had indicated his intention to run for reelection, the pressure on Nixon increased tremendously. He could not show himself in public without prompting questions about his future. He told his associates that unless Ike changed his mind, he would retire from politics and accept an offer to practice law. Under no circumstances would he accept a demotion.

Years later Chotiner recalled those difficult days. Dick had been "very hurt." He paused and grimaced. "How would you feel if you were asked to step off the ticket?"

Nixon received an unexpected boost in the March New Hampshire primary. There was, what the newspapers called, a large write-in vote for him. The word "large" must be used advisedly since only a fraction of the state's voters even bothered to go to the polls (22,202 party faithfuls wrote in his name). However, Nixon suddenly had an affirmative sign, and he was never one to let the slightest advantage slip by. He began organizing his supporters on the National Committee. Leonard Hall, National Chairman, had been working actively for him in New Hampshire. Word got to Ike that Nixon partisans wanted him to name the Vice President for renomination immediately. The President sent back word he would prefer to let the matter ride until the national convention met in San Francisco in August. The general knew how to fight a war of attrition. F.D.R. had shown him the way in the 1944 Democratic convention when he took no position on the redesignation of Henry Wallace for a second term until the convention was in session, and then just sat back and watched Wallace's enemies do the job of dispatching him.

The pressure on Ike mounted. The predictable questions at the weekly press conferences intensified his discomfort. Each time he hesitated, each time he gave an evasive answer, his embarrassment became more apparent. He was finally tripped up at the April 27 morning session. Once again he was questioned about Nixon's plans. He responded, almost plaintively, "Well, he hasn't reported back in the terms in which I used the expression that morning, no. He hasn't given me any authority to quote him, any answer that I would consider final and definite."

Nixon saw his opening. Within minutes he was on the phone with Adams arranging an early afternoon appointment with Ike. Once again Nixon was forcing Eisenhower into a corner. He was putting pressure on a man most people treated with nothing but respectful admiration and obedience. But experience had afforded him a special insight. Ike showed him in the Checkers episode that he would yield to a man who acted firmly when not to yield might cause him some public embarrassment.

He entered the President's office aggressively, like a well-prepared advocate. Since Ike had indicated he did not know whether Dick wanted to continue as Vice President, he would clear that matter up. He would be honored to remain in that taxing office. The only reason, he assured Ike, that he had withheld his answer since their January heart-to-heart was that he wanted to make sure Ike really *wanted* him on the ticket. Now that his misunderstanding about Ike's attitude was cleared up, he was happy to remove any doubts about his availability. He was pleased to report, he said confidently, showing Ike the tip of his blackjack, that he had the near unanimous support of the National Committee in his quest for renomination.

Ike was suddenly all business. It was time to clear up any doubts that had arisen over his ambivalence toward Nixon as his running mate. He called Jim Hagerty into his office and told him Nixon had a statement to make to the press. Hagerty was to get the press together in the White House and Nixon's statement would clear up for once and all the fact that he was willing to run with Nixon again, *should the convention nominate him*. It was not an endorsement, but the circumstances surrounding it, and its presentation, made it appear to be one.

Nixon soberly told the agitated newmen, who had been given thirty seconds' notice, "I informed the President that in the event the President and the delegates to the convention reach the decision that it is in the best interests of the Republican Party and his Administration for me to continue in my present office that I would be honored to accept that nomination again as I was and as I did in 1952."

He spoke with such a lack of enthusiasm that it almost sounded like a concession of defeat. Hagerty, trying to elevate the tone of the moment, broke in, "The President has asked me to tell you gentlemen that he was delighted to hear of the Vice President's decision."

The pact was sealed. Once again, at a crucial moment, Dick had his way. Adams commented: "It was one of those times when the President was pressured out of a previously prepared position by political clamor and harassment."

Nixon had forced Eisenhower to yield, and as in previous similar incidents, had undoubtedly declined even further in the older man's affections. However, he had once again proved that an ambitious politician who was not part of the inner circle could still survive if he followed his predatory instincts remorselessly. The new Nixon, when not on public display, seemed much like the old, and at forty-two the prospect for him successfully changing his spots seemed remote.

XVIII.

How Chotiner, Stassen and Truman Tried to Do Dick In

The year 1956 began on a disturbing note. Chotiner was forced to file a libel suit on January 11 against *Behind the Scene* magazine for calling him "Nixon's secret link to the underworld."

Why was it that Chotiner drew that sort of lightning? He considered himself "colorless." His style was self-effacing and shy to the point of obsequiousness. He was 5'7", chunky and, although he liked expensive suits, they somehow looked rumpled and off-a-bargain-basement-rack when he wore them. He had been divorced the previous year after twenty-three years of marriage, and belonged to no social organizations. But why connect him with the underworld? That was a serious charge even for a scandal magazine.

Perhaps it was the type of law practice Chotiner had put together. Until 1952 he had been associated with his brother Jack in a general practice which included a number of bookmaking cases. Murray had gone off on his own after Nixon was elected Vice President; however, the nature of his clientele had not improved.

Chotiner hired Jerry Giesler, the flamboyant Hollywood divorce lawyer, to handle his libel suit. He told reporters he had spoken to Nixon about it. Dick had read the article and told him "if it contained libel I should go ahead and sue those responsible for it." Having turned the matter over to his attorney, Chotiner tried to avoid any further comment.

The matter seemed to be slipping into the background, lending credence to his oft-stated advice that attacks were to be ignored. Nixon's name had been associated with the underworld, but no one seemed to give too much weight to the charges. Dick had not yet developed a taste for the things money could buy. His outwardly austere mode of living, by Washington standards, belied any such speculations.

When Harry Truman attacked Nixon on February 3 he made no allusion to *Behind the Scenes*'s charge. He just wanted everyone to now that Nixon had, in effect called him a traitor during the 1954 campaign and he was not likely to forget such a libel. Stevenson, intensifying his drive for the Democratic nomination, followed Truman's lead on February 13, in Salt Lake City, by scoring Nixon's campaign tactics and calling him a man of "very easy verbal virtue."

That same night Nixon fumbled the ball again. Speaking about the Supreme Court, he said, "a great *Republican* Chief Justice, Earl Warren, has ordered the end to segregation in schools." This focused attention on his propensity to view every act in terms of partisan advantage. Warren had been a notoriously indifferent Republican before Eisenhower placed him on the court; however, from that day forward he never considered himself a Republican and was not thought of in that respect by anyone, with the apparent exception of Richard Nixon. It was possible that this lapse of taste was occasioned by Ike's invitation to Dick to retire from the Vice Presidency three weeks earlier. Such a blow might unsettle anyone.

Ike's half-hearted endorsement of Nixon on April 29 came just in time. Luck plays a decisive role in the careers of successful men and there is every indication that if Ike had managed to hold his ground for another week or two, his desire to be rid of Nixon would have been fulfilled.

On May 3 Murray Chotiner was summoned before the Senate Permanent Subcommittee on Investigations. McCarthy, though still a member of the committee, had been forced to relinquish the chairmanship when the Democrats took control of the Senate after the 1954 elections. The committee's young counsel, Robert F. Kennedy, half-apologetically, according to Chotiner, told him, "We were not investigating you. It's just that we came across your name and thought we would look into it."

Kennedy had been investigating alleged pay-offs to armed forces purchasing agents by Herman and Samuel Kravitz, Atlantic City garment makers. The Kravitzes had refused to tell the committee whether, in order to secure contracts, they had bribed government officials. Chotiner's name had come to Kennedy's attention when Herman Kravitz had testified he retained Chotiner in the belief the California-based attorney had political influence. Kravitz revealed he had paid Chotiner $5,000 and that he retained him although he was being represented by other lawyers.

Under Kennedy's relentless questioning, Chotiner confirmed that he had gone to the Department of Justice on his clients' behalf to confer on legal questions raised in the fraud and bribery investigations. Several people in the department had been helpful.

As Kennedy probed, the dimensions of Chotiner's law practice became clearer. He admitted seeking aid from the White House for two airline clients who had lost appeals before the Civil Aeronautics Board. Under questioning he revealed he was the lawyer for Marco Reginelli, a former uniform contractor whom Kennedy described as "the top hoodlum in the Philadelphia and New Jersey area." Chotiner told the committee he had accepted many cases since 1952 from clients with whom he had no desire to associate personally.

At this point an echo from the past was heard. Joe McCarthy roused himself to speak. He defended Chotiner, an old ally, and told the committee chairman, Democrat John L. McClellan, he was "wasting time" and had produced no hint of misconduct against Chotiner.

McCarthy had lost so much of his clout that McClellan scarcely bothered to notice he had spoken before turning back to Chotiner. "Do you have any information," he asked in the best manner of investigating members of that committee, "that the Attorney General or his deputy issued an order or memorandum to attorneys in the Justice Department that they deal with you cautiously when you had business in the Justice Department?" Chotiner answered with a simple denial, to which McClellan responded grimly that he knew such orders had been issued.

Chotiner admitted he went to the White House in 1954 to service the accounts of two of his clients, North American Airlines and California Central Airlines. He had seen aide Charles F. Willis, Jr., who had been cooperative. Later he had spoken to Maxwell M. Rabb, also high up in White House councils, about the California cases.

Chotiner was excused from the stand, to be replaced by William A. Parzow, of Miami Beach, who had been convicted of jury tampering in 1941. Parzow described himself as a "non-worker" who lived on "borrowed money." There were $74,000 in canceled checks in the possession of the committee which passed through Parzow's hands on their way from uniform contractors to government workers. McClellan sternly asked, "Were you a pay-off man in bribery looking to contract-getting?"

Parzow, apparently more concerned with his freedom than his reputation, refused to answer on the grounds that it might incriminate him. He admitted knowing Chotiner, but refused to discuss their relationship.

The story created an immediate sensation. The next morning at Eisenhower's press conference Edward P. Morgan, a respected radio commentator, pointed out that Chotiner had admitted two White House aides had "given him some assistance in some business he had with the government." Would the President care to comment?
the government." Would the President care to comment?

Ike was clearly flustered. He answered angrily that he had instructed his aides if anyone tried to use influence, even members of his own family, "he is to be thrown out instantly." Having expressed himself forcefully on this academic aspect of the subject, he went on to discuss the not so academic Murray Chotiner. "In no case did any connection he had with the White House benefit him one bit, and if it ever does, if ever I—I can't believe that anybody on my staff would ever be guilty of an indiscretion." He was choked up with emotion. "But if ever anything came to my attention of that kind, any part of this government, that individual would be gone." Poor bosom buddy Sherman Adams was not listening closely enough.

Ike did not say Chotiner had not tried to profit from his connections in the White House, just that he had not succeeded. Once again, as in the case of other influence-peddling cases, Chotiner had benefitted from his White House intimacy, although his client benefitted not a whit. Chotiner was in the business of collecting legal fees, and so, as he deposited his retainer in his bank account, he must have concluded, despite Ike's apparent inability to understand this point, that his trip to the White House had been eminently successful.

Later that day the affair began exuding an even riper aroma. The chief of the Secret Service, U.E. Baughman, revealed he had asked the FBI in 1954 to investigate a company Chotiner administered, the National Research Company of Los Angeles and Washington. Baughman wanted NRC prosecuted because it was using forms styled to give the impression it was a government agency. Although Chotiner had managed, at that time, to soothe the Secret Service, the nature of his efforts was now becoming public knowledge.

At this point in their friendship, when Chotiner shook Nixon trembled. The Vice President suddenly became unavailable for comment. There were rumblings from the countryside. Jacob Javits said he had "reservations" about Nixon for Vice President, observing, "He has been bitterly partisan in some areas which I think are subject to criticism."

Stevenson, speaking the day after Eisenhower's bout of apoplexy over corruption in high places, hit out at Nixon. He said Nixon, with intemperate talk, had "poisoned four successive election campaigns," had confused United States foreign policy before the world causing "incalculable harm," and had affronted the nation, the Supreme Court and its Chief Justice by imputing partisanship to the court's desegregation decision. He concluded, "That distasteful technique has worked three times. It did not work in 1954 and it will not work in 1956." Nixon, he said, was disqualified by his "irresponsibility" to be "America's number two spokesman."

It seemed likely Ike was kicking himself around his office because he had prematurely endorsed the one man in his Administration who had, from practically the first day he had known him, proven a political embarrassment. On May 13 the embarrassment became acute. Bobby Kennedy informed Chotiner the committee would like to restudy his relations with William Parzow.

His name had been in the papers for ten days and Murray was clearly sweating it out. Chotiner revealed to the committee that Parzow had referred four clients to him, all of whose firms were involved in government cases. An accountant in the employ of one of these firms testified Chotiner had been hired only because of his "influence." McClellan indicated he was convinced these four clients had sought Chotiner out only because of his supposed ability to pull strings. Each of the four clients had other attorneys handling their affairs when they reached out for Chotiner. Nixon's friend had visited people in the Department of Justice on behalf of these clients.

The crunch came. Chotiner was told Parzow had refused to say why he recommended the four clients to him. Would Chotiner, the Senators wanted to know, explain why Parzow had come to him?

Chotiner decided to take the lawyers' Fifth Amendment. He claimed Parzow was his client and he was compelled to silence by the lawyer-client relationship, unless released from that sacred vow by Parzow.

Well, the committee wanted to know, what fees had he collected from Mr. Parzow? Chotiner had previously listed fees paid by his other clients, so that to claim privilege in this case would have done him no good. He responded that Parzow had never paid him. In fact, he had never required his services.

The committee members were astonished. In view of the fact that he had never collected a fee or performed a service, why did he assume Parzow was his client? Chotiner conceded Parzow never asked "in so many words" to be added to his not-so-exclusive list of patrons. However, he came "to the very definite conclusion that he was confiding in me." Apparently the shocking nature of what Parzow had told him convinced Chotiner no sane man would say such things to another person unless he was talking to his lawyer, or asking the forgiveness of his priest.

The affair Chotiner dragged on into the next year. The committee seemed only vaguely interested in finding out why Parzow recommended clients to Chotiner and why Chotiner considered him a client, and finally decided to adjourn its meetings on the subject until after the 1956 elections, since the hearings' political overtones were inescapable and McClellan proclaimed he did not want to be accused of taking partisan advantage. It was, perhaps, the first time in the history of that notorious committee that such fine sensibilities had surfaced.

Dick's conduct toward Chotiner can only be explained by reference to their previous intimacy. Although Chotiner described his relationship with Nixon as that of "a friend," his monthly trips to the nation's capital abruptly ceased and Nixon's discrete silence on Chotiner's troubles gave the impression they had parted company, an impression he tried to strengthen. There were, however, too many secrets shared through the years to allow this Svengali and his Trilby to go their separate ways. In 1958 Nixon allowed an edge of his feeling about Chotiner to show when he told Stewart Alsop, "It was a tragedy that he had to get involved in the kind of law business that does not mix with politics." That was the closest he came to criticizing his associate and it indicated his flawed sense of morality.

Chotiner's law practice was unusual. Many of his clients had not hired him because of his legal talents. There is no evidence he ever drew up a contract for them or pleaded a single one of their cases in court. The kind of non-law business he got involved in was influence peddling.

Nixon busied himself with affairs of state. Ngo Dinh Diem arrived in Washington on May 8 at Ike's invitation. They both announced that they saw a "large build-up" of North Vietnam military forces. Nixon did his share to entertain the South Vietnamese dictator, who was announcing he had no intention of taking part in the July 20 elections called for by the Geneva accord. He was no party to that agreement, Diem pointed out, and besides, there was no way to guarantee a democratic election in the part of Vietnam controlled by Ho Chi Minh.

By this time we had completely replaced the French in Indo-China. Hanoi radio claimed we had 2,000 troops in the South, but our General Williams put the actual figure at 342. Whatever the figure, it was clear we were building our troop strength. We were also training and supplying the South Vietnamese army. Thailand, under contract to our government, was training whole units of the Diem army. Ike had pledged in February and March of 1955 to defend Laos and Cambodia against Communist aggression.

In short, the whole outline of our future role in that beleagured country was clearly established. We had already suffered a fatality the previous May when an American soldier, Everett (Dixie) Reese, 31, had been shot down while photographing the fighting in and around Saigon. Rebel fire brought down his light plane in flames. He was head of the U.S. Photo Section. About that time Ike had described the situation in Vietnam as being "strange and inexplicable." In short, he was confused.

Nixon did his best to clear up the President's confusion. On July 6 he visited Saigon to help celebrate the second anniversary of Diem's rule. Always a poser of simple solutions, he addressed the Saigon Assembly and hailed Diem's successful resistance to Communism. He did this as turmoil continued: assassinations took place regularly, the Diem guillotine was in constant operation, there were clashes with Cambodian troops, internecine warfare with Buddhists, and unceasing charges of corruption. The deadline for the Geneva-sponsored elections occurred two weeks after Nixon's visit. It passed without the elections taking place.

Diem defined the nationalist nature of his regime on August 31 when he ordered all South Vietnamese with French first names to change them.

When Nixon made his way back to Washington he could only privately report on the American disaster in Southeast Asia. In essence, Ike, Dulles and Dick had presided over the dissolution of Indo-China as an anti-Communist bulwark. Half of it fell under Communist control while they were in a position to do something about it. From this point on they twisted and turned desperately to avoid being credited for that failure. Nixon applied a new coat of paint by referring to the remnant of the country still under American sway as "the free nation of Vietnam."

Judgment of this sort became more ominous on the night of June 8, 1956, when it was suddenly announced by the White House that the President was being operated on for ileitis at Walter Reed Hospital. This was major surgery and for a short while it was uncertain he would survive. For the second time in less than a year Ike had suffered a major medical breakdown.

Ike was probably incapable of serving as President after his heart attack. Yet he allowed himself to be sweet-talked into running for reelection. He soothed his conscience by frankly telling Americans he would always be a bad insurance risk, and that he could only work part of the day, with frequent rests and prolonged vacations. If they wanted him for President, he wanted them to know, this was the only way they could have him.

Years later the former British Prime Minister, Harold MacMillan, caustically remarked that Ike had been pushed into running again in 1956 when he was clearly incapable of serving in that office for the last five years of his Administration. He claimed Dulles was the real power in foreign policy, making it without consulting Ike.

The ileitis attack, which necessitated the removal of a large section of his intestine, took place almost two months before the San Francisco convention. Ike was in a position to give a second sober look at his decision to run for reelection. Instead, like a punch-drunk fighter who could not stay out of the ring, he told Sherman Adams, while he was still at Walter Reed, that "this was the last time he would go through such a period of uncertainty and crisis; the next time, he warned, if he had any doubt about his physical ability to do the job as President, he was through."

There were other men who were not as sanguine at the prospect that Richard Nixon would some cold night inherit an office the majority of his countrymen would never think of giving him. Harold Stassen became their spokesman.

On July 21 he entered the White House, determination reflected on his pasty white face. He went directly to Adams' office and informed him he was planning to start a move to win the Vice Presidential nomination for Christian Herter, governor of Massachusetts. Ex-Congressman Herter was a well-respected figure in the Republican Party, white-haired and tall, soft-spoken, the image of what a Vice President should be.

After informing Adams of his intentions, and being warned he should in no way involve the President, he was ushered into Ike's presence to perform the ceremonial courtesy of revealing his plans to the chief. He was apparently listened to impatiently. He was, after all, touching a sore nerve. Ike did not want Nixon on the ticket any more than Stassen; however, he had made his attempt to bump him, and was not about to be lured into another scrape with tenacious Dick. It was ridiculous to think that if *he* had not succeeded, with all the prestige and power at his command, the largely discounted Stassen would do better. There were too many other things for a sick President to do to allow him any pleasure at the thought of wasting his energy in this patently foolish endeavor.

Stassen then went to visit Dick to try to talk him out of seeking the nomination. This was, perhaps, the most fruitless conversation to take place between two adult men in the United States that year.

From this bitter little conference, Stassen went before the press and once again the country was told there were Republicans who thought the White House would be a better place without Nixon.

Ike held his peace, refusing to express publicly who he thought the nominee should be. It was all up to the convention. This lent support to those who dreamt of dumping Dick. Faced with this minor crisis, Nixon's conservative supporters on the National Committee, led by Leonard Hall, moved to squelch the rebellion.

Hall proposed that Herter be pressured into nominating Nixon. That would put an end to Stassen's mischief. Herter, overjoyed at the prospect of being suddenly in the middle of a situation which might make him Vice President, went to the White House to find out Ike's pleasure. Adams, operating with a sureness that stemmed from the possession of real power, and convinced of the silliness of trying to bring any plan of Stassen's to life, offered Herter a glimpse of rosy prospects. He told him "in making his future plans, he could take into account the fact that he could be given favorable consideration for a position of responsibility in the State Department." Since Herter's lifelong preoccupation had been foreign policy, Adams' offer was calculated to achieve results.

Herter went home and considered Adams' proposition. He placed the two offers on the scale, a promise from Adams on one side, and on the other, a serving of Stassen optimism. Being a practical man, he called Adams to say he would make the nominating speech for Nixon.

Stassen continued the Herter campaign even without Herter. But it was an aimless journey, of the sort in which he had come to specialize. After the convention opened, however, he saw the light and prepared a statement "cheerfully and wholeheartedly" supporting Nixon, and the Vice President had the final pleasure of witnessing Stassen reduced to seconding his nomination. Chotiner remembers watching Stassen scrambling to snatch the microphone so that he could publicly complete his humiliation. Not until John V. Lindsay was to second the nomination of Spiro Agnew in 1968 was the nation to witness such an abject surrender of principle to expediency.

Nixon frequently used his father in a manner which did not please the old man. He often referred to Frank's having been a menial worker during much of his life. He would always bring the matter up when speaking of the need for laborers to work hard and appreciate the mystical qualities of sweat. He would quickly list some of the simple jobs his father had held at one time or another. Frank preferred, as most men do, to remind people of his more elevated endeavors. But Dick always made his points where he could, and Frank's willingness to dig ditches and pump gas went over big in Labor Day addresses and before gatherings sponsored by the National Association of Manufacturers.

During the convention Frank made his last major contribution to Dick's career. He had been ill for some time. In a move that was unprecedented, and roused great sympathy, Dick left the convention on August 22 soon after it started, to fly to his father's bedside. He said he would not return unless his father's condition warranted it.

During the same press conference in which he announced Stassen's capitulation, Ike expressed hope for the rapid recovery of Dick's father. Stassen, eager to discover a way to please, held a news conference a few minutes later and expressed his sympathy for Dick because of his father's illness. Immediately after Nixon was nominated unanimously, Joe Martin was directed by the convention to voice its regrets about Frank's illness. The major topic of conversation at this colorless convention, with its foreordained results, was the health of a seventy-seven-year-old man few of the delegates had ever met.

Hannah described Richard's return to Whittier. "As soon as he entered . . . he sank into his characteristically deep silence. For he realized that his father, who had been ill with a kidney ailment and with the arthritis that had plagued him all his life, was very much worse than he had known."

But the rest of the country had been led to believe Richard had known how seriously ill his father was before he left the convention. What other possible reason could there have been for all the attention and sympathy everyone was being asked to direct toward Nixon's father?

The day after his nomination a story was released from California saying that Frank was improving and wanted Dick to return to the convention to make his acceptance speech. Never one to disobey his father, Dick boarded a plane immediately and flew back to San Francisco, working on his notes all the way.

Immediately after the speech it was announced Frank had suffered a setback and Dick was returning to his bedside. On August 25 he stopped in to see his father, then held a news conference in which he commented on Frank's condition. Having finished with the medical aspect of his visit, he went to his brother Donald's supermarket and donned a grocer's apron for a few minutes. While the photographers recorded the moment, he regaled them with stories of working in the store as a boy.

The next day he left to go on about his business. It was announced that Frank's condition was worsening and on August 29 he was put on the critical list. Dick spent that day on the golf links with Billy Graham, no doubt seeking some spiritual assistance for his father. On August 31 he flew back to California. Frank Nixon died on September 4, having been the involuntary vehicle for advancing his son's fortunes to the last minute of his life. Ike sent condolences, as did the American Legion, whom Dick made a point of singling out for thanks.

Harry Truman, direct as ever, did not wait until after Frank's funeral to blast Nixon. On a television panel show in Milwaukee he cited "evidence" that Nixon had accused him of "treason." Leonard Hall had offered to contribute a thousand dollars to any charity named by Truman if he could produce such evidence. Gleefully Truman referred to an Associated Press story from Texarkana on October 2, 1952 in which Nixon was quoted as telling a cheering crowd that Truman, Acheson and Stevenson were "traitors to the high principles in which many of the nation's Democrats believe." He went on grimly to quote Nixon as saying, "real Democrats" were "outraged by the Truman-Acheson-Stevenson's gang's toleration and defense of Communism in high places."

The questioning took another turn, since certain aspects of Nixon's career were being explored. Truman told the panel he did not believe Alger Hiss had been a Communist spy. Hiss, he pointed out, "was never convicted of being disloyal to the Government of the United States." A Professor Anthony T. Bouscaren, of Marquette University, interrupted to inject the orthodox opinion that Hiss had not been indicted on espionage charges because of the time lag between the time his alleged acts had been committed and Chambers' charges against him.

Truman shook his head. "It wasn't that the statute of limitations ran out," he replied. "It was that they could not prove anything."

Apparently not one to give up easily, Professor Bouscaren shot back, "Do you think he was a Communist?" Without a moment's hesitation the man who had complete access to the FBI's most secret files said, "No, I do not."

On September 12 Nixon made his first semi-social call at Gettysburg. The occasion was a huge gathering of the Republican faithful from the forty-eight states, plus all Cabinet members, to open the election campaign. Ike made his usual high-minded speech, ignoring the Democrats completely and devoting himself mostly to a call for a large citizen turn-out on Election Day. Dick, on the other hand, lashed out at Truman. He challenged Stevenson, once again the Democrat's nominee, to "repudiate" Truman's defense of Hiss. In keeping with his image as the new Nixon, he said Communism "should not be an issue in this campaign," but he intended to use it if Stevenson did not hasten to repudiate Truman's remarks. He told the nation's Republican leaders he would not make "personal attacks on the integrity of our opponents," but added something for the admirers of the old Nixon when he said, "you don't win campaigns with a diet of dishwater and milk toast."

Ike journeyed out to Washington National Airport on September 18 to see Dick off on a thirty-three-state tour. Dick was going to have to do the bulk of the campaigning for the sick President. Ike made a little speech, in the manner of a football coach sending the team out on the field. He told Dick to "stick to the truth," and to "avoid exaggeration." In delivering this message to Nixon he was merely reflecting the nation's uneasiness. Dick responded that Republicans would take Ike's advice, although he insisted it was more difficult to stir people to enthusiasm for a positive cause than it was to arouse them to "be against something."

A sign in the crowd had more meaning to Dick than Ike's paternal advice. It read, "Bring Home Votes." As a morose Tricia tried to hold back the tears she shed when seeing her father off on his frequent long trips away from home, Dick smiled at the assembled faithful. He was eager to get on about the business of trying out his new campaign style.

On his way out of the airport Ike read signs held by Democrats, which he was to see constantly during the campaign, "You Can Still Dump Nixon."

In a Presidential race it is impossible to expect the Vice Presidential nominee to carry the campaign's full burden. In fact, most people vote for the top man on the ticket despite the man party moguls have determined to jam into the second spot. It was no different in 1956. Ike had accepted the nomination after two major illnesses only under the condition that he would not have to engage in a barnstorming, whistle-stopping campaign. The slack was to be taken up with a massive advertising campaign. Batton, Barton, Durstine and Osborn had handled the 1952 campaign and had been on retainer during the years since. Now they were engaged full time and turned loose. Leonard Hall indicated what he had in mind when he said, "You sell your candidates and your programs the way a business sells its products."

Dick was trying to sell his candidate in a new way. He stressed uncontroversial themes, emphasizing praise for Ike. He called him the leader who "got us out of one war and kept us out of others without loss of principle or territory." The exaggeration and distortion were still there but in a muted form. Ike, he enthused, had done so much for the economy that American workers could look forward to a four-day work week in the "not distant future."

Stevenson claimed not to be taken in by the new Nixon. In accepting the Liberal Party nomination in New York in mid-September he said,

> I know of no instance in which a man has so energetically tried to convince the electorate that everything that he has said and done in past years bears no relation to himself and that, until further notice, he is to be considered a new man.
> Now you may not agree with him, but you have to be awed by the lack of conviction which makes so swift a transformation possible.
>
> I don't wish for a moment to deprecate the Vice President's new personality. But I do wish that we might hear some word from him repudiating the irresponsible, the vindictive and the malicious words so often spoken by the imposter who has been using his name all these years.

Pat Nixon also had doubts about the new Nixon. Questioned by reporters during the campaign as to whether she had observed this new Nixon, she replied, "Not at any time. He's the same. He'd never change." Although she had wanted him to get out of politics a year earlier, once the decision had been made to seek renomination, she pitched in with alacrity. Father John Cronin, his advisor on Communism, doubling as a speechwriter during this period, described her dedication to the cause.

"I don't think Pat helps him," he said with what may be no more than a cleric's occupational suspicion of women. ". . . in the 1956 campaign, Dick prepared the last draft of a speech on a tape recorder; but some aide had not fixed the recorder properly, so nothing was on the tape. After all that work, he had to deliver an earlier draft—mine. His heart was not in it, so he gave it a poor delivery. And Pat chewed the hell out of him in front of the staff."

As the campaign proceeded, Nixon's friends called attention to his transformation. They were so enthusiastic about the new layers of reasonableness which had been exposed to the public that they knew no limits to the praise they heaped on him. They began to claim he was the greatest Vice President in American history and better qualified for the office than his predecessor. On October 8, in Pittsburg, Truman took note of this latest slander. He said that when he heard reports that Nixon was better qualified for the office of Vice President than Alben Barkley, who had entered "the house of the Lord" the previous May, he experienced a feeling of "personal disgust."

For a while in September and early October it looked as if Stevenson was closing the gap. However, the outbreak of the Suez War ended whatever hope he had for victory. Ike, proving once again that in a democracy, decisive action, even if it is wrong, often wins votes, told the British and the French he would not countenance their use of force in trying to retake the Suez Canal from Nasser. His actions further weakened the trust our two major European allies had in us and increased the possibility of future Middle East wars, but it put the election out of reach for the Democrats. Ike defeated Stevenson by an even more decisive margin than in 1952.

Interestingly, although he carried 329 Congressional Districts across the country, the Republicans were only able to win 201 seats in the House of Representatives. Once again the Democrats were to control Congress. Stassen, feeling entitled to say I-told-you-so as he was being retired from active national Republican politics, told a television audience the Republicans would not have lost Congress had they nominated Christian Herter for Vice President.

Dick was too elated by his personal victory to be seriously concerned by the party's disaster. On November 13 he arrived at Rebozo's residence in Key Biscayne for two weeks of "just plain relaxing." Pat and the children were to join the two men in a few days. The losers had to spend time thinking of some new way to make an assault on success. The winners could afford to spend that time basking in Miami's strong mid-winter sun. For Nixon the dream of becoming President had moved a giant step closer to reality.

XIX.

Changing Dick into
a Butterfly

"There's something special about standing up there before a lot of people and taking the oath," Nixon confided to a New York *Times* interviewer shortly before the January 21, 1957 inauguration. "You want to get this through and do it without any boo-boos in the process."

He was feeling mellow, and more mature than he had been in 1953. "Four years ago I was really as green as I could be regarding the responsibilities of the Vice Presidency."

One listened to Richard Nixon at such times with a sense of disbelief. Here was a man who confessed he had not been in any way prepared for the country's second most important job, yet such knowledge had not kept him from pursuing it relentlessly. He might have become President at any time during those four years, confident in his own heart that he could not handle the job.

On the eve of being sworn in for a second term he was highlighting one of the most enduring weaknesses in our democratic form of government. A man with no other talent but the ability to prevail was capable, if the cards fell his way, of assuming national leadership. And, dishearteningly, Richard Nixon was not the first man to be put in that position.

Nixon guilelessly continued, "Looking back, my knowledge of world problems four years ago was pretty much limited. . . ."

He seemed to be suggesting that he had now mastered their intricacies. The world with its problems was his oyster. Yet, the troublesome question remained: How capable was he of conducting American foreign affairs should that awesome burden fall on his shoulders. Could a man of his proven expediency conduct a consistent foreign policy that was not molded by the exigencies of his personal politics?

He summed up the changes over the previous four years by saying with a grin, "And, of course, Checkers is four years old, too."

On Inauguration Day Nixon once again swore rather than affirmed his oath. Again Knowland was chosen by Nixon to administer it. Again the family Bible was open, but this time Dick's hand rested on the fourth verse, second chapter of Isaiah: "And he shall judge among the nations and shall rebuke many people . . . and they shall beat their swords into plowshares and their spears into pruning hooks . . . nation shall not lift up sword against nation, neither shall they learn war any more."

The selection of this portion of the Bible suggested either that Nixon was insensitive or insincere. For at this moment in his odyssey, Nixon was a relentless hawk, coming down aggressively on the militarist side of any international conflict. Although Ike was suspicious of what he labelled "the military-industrial complex," Nixon constantly supported every proposal for beefed-up military expenditures. Had he been true to himself, the passage selected might have begun, ". . . an eye for an eye and a tooth for a tooth," for Hammurabi, more than Isaiah, accurately represented his gut reaction to any conflict situation.

Intent on showing his second term was going to be different from the first, Nixon bought a $75,000 home in Washington on January 26. He was now sure of one thing: he would never again have to scramble for the Vice Presidential nomination. Ike was not eligible for renomination, being the first victim of Taft's amendment limiting Presidents to two terms in office. Nixon's goal was now the Presidency, there was no intermediate step. Whereas his first term in office had, of necessity, required him to bow and scrape, he now attempted to display the bearing of a crown prince. He set out to learn how to act as Presidential nominee pretender. In March he went on a two-week tour of Africa, during which he jumped out of his car repeatedly to shake hands with startled natives. Clearly he had not yet mastered the regal manner.

Back home he began privately to express "disenchantment" with Ike. Dick's close associates reported to friendly newspapermen that the Vice President felt the President was playing too much golf, seeing too many rich businessmen, while ignoring Republican politicians. They also revealed, in the strictest confidence, that Dick felt Ike was letting himself be outmaneuvered by those Texas sharpies, Sam Rayburn and Lyndon Johnson, majority leaders of the House and Senate.

Causing Nixon some discontent was the economic recession the country was experiencing for a second time in less than five years of Republican rule. The indexes started their downward slide in late 1956. Fear of "inflation" had led Treasury Secretary Humphrey to institute tight money policies earlier in the year and, predictably, his simple nostrums had ended the short period of Republican prosperity. Nixon began to let light show between him and the party's conservative wing.

It was obvious that the building-up-Ike era had passed, to be replaced by the era of the distinguished "progressive conservative," Richard Milhous Nixon. When Bebe Rebozo now entertained him at Key Biscayne, which he did again in April, he saw a man no longer exhausted by the tension caused by constantly having to stare down the incredulous. Instead he saw a man made tired by the need to resist the advances of men intent on seducing the next President of the United States.

Once again, though, McCarthy threatened the smooth realization of his plan to become respectable. During the early part of the year the decline in McCarthy's health became apparent to all of his colleagues. He often did not show up in the Senate for days on end and when he did, his appearance caused a stir. His face had a ghastly pallor and he tended to stagger slightly. He would sit for a while, gazing vacantly into the distance, and suddenly rouse himself by breaking into a series of disjointed questions. Finally, in the face of his colleagues' obvious annoyance, he would break off, struggle to his feet and leave the hearing room.

When he was finally admitted to the Naval Hospital in Bethesda, Maryland, his wife said it was for treatment of an old knee injury. However, he was housed in the neurological ward. When his death was announced, the official cause was listed as "hepatitis," which the authorities pointed out was "a liver ailment." The *Times* described the cause of his death as "mysterious." Drew Pearson was not so cautious. He said Joe had died of the effects of acute alcoholism.

Dick was suddenly faced with a painful choice. How was he to react to his old friend's death? Dean Acheson, experienced diplomat that he was, instructed him on the proper etiquette. When asked how he felt now that his enemy was dead, Acheson said, "No comment at all. *De mortuis nil nisi bonum.*"

Dick now issued a carefully worded tribute in which Acheson's guidelines were assiduously observed. "Years will pass before the results of his work can be objectively evaluated, but his friends and many of his critics will not question his devotion to what he considered to be the best interests of his country."

Nixon was certainly speaking for McCarthy's friends, but it seems doubtful that the Wisconsin witchhunter's enemies would be as generous. Rounding off his tribute handsomely, the Vice President became one of McCarthy's honorary pall bearers.

Most of the rest of the year was spent in happier pursuits. He appeared at dozens of banquets, attended baseball and football games, and tinkered with politics as best he could without Chotiner. In 1971 Murray reminisced that "After 1956 we just drifted apart. We spoke to each other every once in a while, but I was back in California and he was in Washington. There wasn't much chance to see each other. We still remained on good terms."

It continued to be a bad year for Chotiner. After the prolonged indecisive tussles of 1956, the Senate Permanent Subcommittee on Investigations subpoenaed his law practice records. However, when they arrived at the Capitol they were delivered to the House Government Operations Sub-committee, a group estimated to be more friendly to errant Republicans. By September 5, 1957 the House committee had not yet decided what to do with them, and the Senate committee concluded it might just as well issue its report.

It was fifty-eight pages long and reviewed two years of hearings. It blasted "a nefarious group of contractors" who used bribery, delivered substandard goods and collected "unconscionable" profits on military uniform contracts. Chotiner had appeared as counsel for Samuel Kravitz and Joseph Abrams, mentioned in the report as major culprits. Nine contractors had been fined or imprisoned, a hitherto unheard of consequence of the committee's efforts.

Politicians are by nature restless. By the autumn of 1957 Bill Knowland was ready to move on to bigger and better things. After the death of Robert Taft from leukemia in mid-1953, Knowland became Republican Senate leader. In that capacity he had been at constant loggerheads with Eisenhower. The Republican President, conditioned by a lifetime of association with obedient subordinates to having his orders carried out promptly, discovered in Knowland a man of a different stripe—of independent wealth and point of view. Knowland took every opportunity to thwart any move Ike made in the direction of "modern Republicanism." It had gotten to the point whers Ike was absolutely pained to be in Knowland's presence. Particularly galling was the fact that while the Senate leader of his own party was causing him endless aggravation, the leader of the Senate Democrats, Lyndon Johnson, was becoming a close confederate, even a friend.

The truth was that Ike had chosen the wrong party. He should have opted in 1952 to become a Democrat. Personal antagonism toward Truman and a sentimental loyalty to the symbols of the Kansas Republicanism of his youth had conspired to mislead him. He would have been a splendid example of a moderate Democrat, in a party where that breed was common. Instead he became a progressive Republican in a party which did not easily tolerate such heresy.

Knowland saw no reason why the former junior Senator from California should become the Republican Presidential nominee in 1960 when the senior Senator was perfectly amenable to shouldering that responsibility himself. In an attempt to strengthen his claim Knowland declared on October 3 he would give up his Senate seat and, instead, seek the governorship of California. He reasoned that as governor he would be in a position to control the California delegation to the national convention. Although we were on the threshold of an era in which the U.S. Senate was to become the most frequent source of Presidential candidates, in 1957 fashion dictated that state governors were more persistently sought out for that honor.

Goodwin Knight, the incumbent Republican governor, did not much like Knowland's cavalier attitude. When he looked in the mirror in the morning he saw a fine prospect for the nation's most important office. In this struggle of wills Nixon came out on the side of Knowland. He owed big Bill a favor. In the spring of 1956, Knight, Knowland and Nixon had each controlled one third of the state delegation to the San Francisco convention. Knight had wanted to deprive Nixon of the state's support for his bid to be renominated. He was the only prominent Republican to support Stassen's dump-Nixon drive. Had Knowland thrown in with Knight, the Vice President would have faced the peril of attending the convention without the support of his home state. There were too many assassins waiting in the bushes for Nixon to enjoy that prospect.

As the dispute between Knowland and Knight made bigger and bigger headlines, Nixon made a move, aimed apparently at helping Knowland, which was much more likely to help himself. Sherman Adams was sent to California to urge Knight to withdraw from the primary race in order to avoid a major split in the party. Not lost from sight was the fact that, win or lose, Knowland would be out of the Senate. After arguing the logic of his position, Adams wheeled his big weapon into position. He invited Knight to Washington to discuss the matter with Ike. A cardinal of the Church was as unlikely to turn down an invitation to visit the Pope as a Republican politician was likely to reject such a call.

On November 5, 1957 Knight entered the White House a candidate for governor of California. He emerged a candidate for the Senate. Nixon immediately told a press conference, "I shall give my full support to the nomination and election of Bill Knowland as governor and Goodwin Knight as United States Senator."

Paul M. Butler, Democratic National Chairman, said the whole thing seemed to be a "Nixon-engineered deal." He seemed quite happy about the way feuding California Republicans had settled matters. He predicted that Nixon's "scheme" would make a Democratic victory in both races "more certain than ever." In an endeavor to explain Nixon's reasons for arranging the Knowland-Knight switch he said their defeat would "leave only one big frog in the California pond in 1960—the sly Mr. Nixon who engineered today's deal."

Presidents are made by such deals. They are also made by accident, and on November 25, 1957 it looked as if Nixon was about to be the beneficiary of such an accident. It was announced that Eisenhower had suffered a stroke, or, as the medical bulletin put it, "a small blood clot or blood vessel spasm of the brain."

His secretary had seen its first sign. "He tried to tell me something," Ann Whitman explained on the verge of tears, "but he couldn't express himself. Something seemed to have happened to him all of a sudden." When she called the President's doctor Ike refused to leave his desk. He kept trying to say, "Go away from me."

Finally persuaded to go upstairs to his living quarters, Ike slept for a while but when he awoke he was still unable to speak without stammering. His voice would falter in mid-sentence. Clearly upset by this latest sign of deteriorating health, he still rejected the idea that Nixon host the dinner he was scheduled to give that evening for the King of Morocco. After a frustrated few moments he blurted out to his staff, "If I cannot attend to my duties, I am simply going to give up this job. Now that is all there is to it."

Nixon was that close to becoming President on the evening of November 25, 1957. The Vice President, once again playing a cool hand, announced that the President was "fully capable" of making necessary decisions. That was a long way from affirming that Ike was capable of fully handling the multitudinous responsibilities of his office. However, Nixon's statement was not aimed as much at reassuring the nation that Ike would be President the next day, as it was to disarm his many critics.

That some doubts still remained may be sensed from what *Times* reporter Russell Baker had to say about Nixon's behavior the next day: "The consensus is that he has seen his goal—the White House. . . . The question most frequently asked by those with reservations is whether there is any genuine conviction behind the series of stands he has taken or whether these have simply been dictated by political expediency and may be changed, like suits, to serve the shifts in the climate."

Few men in America believed that Dick Nixon had undergone any sort of genuine metamorphosis. He had been a caterpillar crawling along the underside of the decayed vegetation in the political jungle, and it was going to take more than a public relations cocoon woven by Madison Avenue to change him into a butterfly.

XX.

The Old Nixon

Nixon realized he had achieved a new status on January 4, 1957, when it was announced that a secret helicopter landing site had been built near his home so that he could be evacuated rapidly in case of a missile attack. Some cynics felt the money might better have been spent on relieving the economic distress caused by the Republican Administration. Sharp tax cuts in 1954 for corporations and millionaires had limited the effectiveness of our progressive tax laws. The needed sources of revenue to run the government had been reduced. At the same time, the conservatives in charge of the Federal Reserve Board and the Treasury Department had opted in 1956 for fiscal decisions which slowed down the economy in order to prevent any possible threat to the "soundness" of the dollar.

The only people the Republican planners could conceive of paying for that desirable aim were the American workers. During 1957 and the first half of 1958 unemployment was up sharply and Arthur Burns, the President's chief economic advisor, was telling Ike the anti-inflationary restraints placed on credit had to be eased. Secretary of the Treasury Humphrey, proving once again that Bourbons of his stripe learned nothing from experience, tried to oppose Burns' unorthodox advice by assuring Ike the recommended remedies would not have much effect on the situation.

Humphrey's unfortunate advice in 1953 and 1956 caused Ike to view his guaranteed cure for the nation's economic ills with considerable skepticism. He came down on Burns' side, and toward the middle of 1958 economic activity began to pick up. However, the President's affection for Humphrey never diminished and the Southern conservative continued to set economic policy for the government until the day Ike stepped out of office. His final advice to Ike on the 1957-1958 recession was that he should refer to it, when forced to comment publicly, not as a recession but as "the side-slip in the economy."

It was not only the economy that was causing the President restless nights. His Administration had been subjected to charges of corruption which exceeded those made against the Truman Administration; the Ike of the 1952 *Crusade Against Corruption* was particularly embarrassed by such allegations. The 1955 Dixon-Yates power scandal had rocked his government for months. There were constant charges of bribery and corruption in the letting of garment contracts, the procurement of airline routes and the issuance of licenses for radio and television stations. But more vexing than any of these was the charge of influence peddling. Ike had, after all, pledged in 1952 that if elected, he would ruthlessly purge the government of that corrupt breed.

In early February of 1958 rumors began to spread that influence peddlers were operating on the highest level of his government, in fact, inside the White House itself. And, incredible as it may seem, the name mentioned was Sherman Adams. Hearings before a Congressional committee explored letters Adams had written on White House stationery in 1953 urging the Civil Aeronautics Board to postpone a decision its members had made which would have had an adverse effect on one of Murray Chotiner's airline clients.

Adams appeared before the committee and "explained" why what he had done was not improper, although similar activity by Truman aides had, at an earlier time, caused him to spill over with righteous anger. Ike indicated his complete trust in the man the newspapers referred to as "The Assistant President." However, the investigating committee concluded his activity in Chotiner's behalf had been "grossly improper." They were at a loss to suggest an appropriate punishment.

When Dick left Washington with Pat at the beginning of May for an eight-nation tour of South America, black thoughts about Adams were churning in his head. He had to stand by his friend Murray, but he owed nothing to Adams. Eisenhower's friends should not be allowed to jeopardize Richard Nixon's future.

South America proved a fortunate disaster, one any politician worth his salt would give up an uncontested primary to experience. When Nixon landed in Lima, he was confronted by enormous hostility. Impoverished Latin Americans had never worshipped at Washington's shrine. Elements of jealousy, mixed with conflicting attitudes about religion, and U.S. economic imperialism had conspired to keep relations cool.

The bad judgment that sent Richard Nixon to South America to remedy this situation is hard to imagine. The students, in particular, were well aware of his domestic reputation as a political assassin. To them, his arrival seemed a further insult from, at best, a paternalistic Washington that had no understanding of their aspirations or sensibilities.

When Nixon attempted to visit San Marcos University his car was stoned; he was shoved, booed, and spat on by throngs of milling demonstrators. The same scene was reenacted in front of his hotel in Lima. The Nixons' treatment was potentially dangerous and utterly distasteful. Cloistered in his suite, Nixon issued a statement calling the mob action an affront, not to him (perish the thought) but to Peru. A career of practicing distortion had allowed Nixon to conclude this was the right way to look at it.

The next day he visited Quito, Ecuador, where the same thing happened. Prudence would have dictated the trip had gone sour and should be terminated. Episodes of this sort tend to feed on each other, and it seemed doubtful that things were going to improve in the countries still remaining on his agenda. Instead Dick decided to put a brave face on. There was always the possibility that there were points to be made in these distant climes. He issued a statement after the Quito debacle saying he had been cool, unafraid and was, now that combat had been broken off, without anger. To prove how normal things were, on May 10 he made a call to Hannah in Whittier during the flight from Quito to Bogotá. The occasion was Mother's Day.

In Bogotá he was warned an assassination attempt was going to be made when he reached Caracas, Venezuela. He was advised by the Secret Service, and the South American governments involved, that it would be dangerous to continue the trip. In terms of benefit to the United States, there was absolutely nothing to be gained from its continuation. It was problematical from the beginning what gains a Nixon visit to these countries would bring. Clearly at this point the visit had become counterproductive to American interests and should be terminated.

Nixon demurred. He was not going to be run out of town. There was some discomfort, a lot of heckling, but think of all those U.S. voters who for the first time in his career were identifying with him. At this moment, he represented the flag and the flag was under siege. The feedback from Washington was that the press was unanimously sympathetic. That had *never* happened before. Certainly there was risk in going on, but it was worth the gamble. Now that everyone was alerted, the precautions would be greater and the chances were excellent things would not get out of hand. There might be a little more spitting and stone throwing, but hopefully just enough to make a few good pictures.

There was a lot more than spitting and stone throwing in Caracas on May 14. Howling mobs surrounded his car and the following car in which Pat sat in terror. They rained stones on it, beat the roof with sticks, smashed the windows and rocked the car back and forth for minutes in an attempt to overturn it. The Venezuelan police were helpless. Secret Servicemen placed their bodies between the mob and Nixon. Beyond a doubt, if the demonstrators had been able to get their hands on Nixon, they would have torn him to pieces.

At this point Nixon made what he described as "a command decision." He ordered the driver to give up attempting to get to the location of his next speech and turn tail for the United States embassy. Once inside the embassy, which was soon surrounded by a huge crowd of demonstrators, he issued a statement saying the Communists were to blame for everything. He canceled his remaining appearances and holed up.

Back in Washington Ike was preparing to send the Marines to Caracas to rescue the Vice President. He was saved from that when Nixon was swiftly smuggled out of the country and flown back home. On May 15 he was greeted at Washington airport by an estimated 100,000 people led by Ike, the Cabinet, a Congressional delegation and representatives of most Latin American nations. It was a disaster for United States relations with the people of Latin America, but a publicity triumph for Richard Nixon. He was now a worldwide symbol of conflict, a status he had long since achieved in the United States.

Envoys of twenty Latin American republics announced they were going to hold a banquet for the Vice President, and Ecuador declared its intention to issue a stamp commemorating his visit. A neighboring republic had previously issued a stamp commemorating the eruption of a volcano which had killed thousands.

His South American tour was scarcely allowed to drift off the front pages when Sherman Adams once again occupied his thoughts. In mid-June Adams' name was suddenly linked to another influence-peddling case. His close friend Bernard Goldfine, a New England textile manufacturer, had been questioned about problems he had been having with the Federal Trade Commission and the Securities and Exchange Commission. During the course of the investigation, conducted by the House Legislative Oversight Committee, the examiners had come across hotel bills paid for by Goldfine for the entertainment of Adams. They covered a number of years. Spurred on by this intelligence, they dug deeper and quickly determined that Adams had made calls from the White House for his friend Goldfine, beginning in 1954, to a variety of government agencies.

Paralleling this revelation was the fact that Goldfine had made a series of gifts to Adams over the years adding up to several thousand dollars, the jewel of which was a vicuña coat. During the summer of 1958 the vicuña coat came to symbolize the same thing for Eisenhower that the mink coat had for Truman.

Adams did not make matters easier when he appeared before the committee on June 17 and admitted his actions had been "imprudent." All his attempts to explain, and place everything in context, came to nothing in the face of such an admission. From Nixon's point of view, from this moment on, Adams' chief imprudence was in not immediately resigning from Eisenhower's staff.

Ike pulled back from asking for Adams' resignation. Whatever tone and direction the White House had during the first six years he had been President are directly attributable to Adams' dedication and willingness to dispose of the day to day detail which bored and overwhelmed the nation's leading amateur golfer. Nixon, however, saw Adams' continued association with the White House as a burden to the Republican Party which he shortly expected to lead into a Presidential campaign.

While Sherman Adams spent the summer attempting to anticipate from which direction the death blow was to come, Nixon quietly pressed his point of view. Adams must go! He was joined in this cry by conservative Republicans who identified Adams with the Dewey-liberal Eastern wing of the party.

The blow came in September when Adams reluctantly decided to take a fishing trip to Miramichi River in New Brunswick with Jerry Persons and their wives. "I departed from Washington with some misgivings," he remarked later. After several days he received a telephone call from Gerry Morgan, from the White House, suggesting that he come back to Washington because Nixon and Meade Alcorn, the Chairman of the National Committee, wanted to talk to him. Adams knew what this meant.

When he arrived in Washington he discovered Ike was suddenly away vacationing in Newport. Faced with no alternative, cut off from the only man who might save him, he went to his meeting with Nixon. There he was soberly told the facts of life. Large contributors to the party's treasury had informed the National Committee they would not donate to the fall campaign unless he resigned. Nixon wanted him to know that although Ike had been disturbed by these reports, he had not told Nixon to ask for his resignation. He was leaving that decision completely up to Adams.

Apparently too familiar with Nixon to trust his future to what he had told him, Adams left the room and called Gerry Morgan. He told him what Nixon had said and asked him to fly to Newport and speak to the President about it. When Morgan returned he confirmed that Nixon was merely the bearer of the bad news. Ike was troubled by reports of hostility toward Adams among influential Republicans. How could friendship be allowed to stand in the way of such disturbing dispatches?

After a short discussion of tactics with Hagerty and his wife, Adams flew to Newport to personally submit his resignation to Ike. "It came as no surprise to him," Adams commented without apparent resentment. After an innocuous conversation Adams handed the President his resignation. When Ike finished reading it he gave an emphatic nod of approval and then handed Adams a previously prepared "Dear Sherman" letter. The Sherman Adams affair was now over, at least as far as Richard Nixon was concerned.

The loss of Adams was a blow to Eisenhower beyond quick calculation. Sick and distracted, Ike had come increasingly to depend on Adams to handle a large share of his responsibility for running the country. At almost the same time John Foster Dulles was being dragged down by his fatal encounter with cancer. Ike tried desperately to maintain an image of competence and independence, but his reliance on Adams was only too apparent after the Assistant President flew back to retirement in New Hampshire.

Even before the dust of the Adams controversy had settled, Eisenhower was embroiled in a major international controversy. The Chinese Communists were making aggressive gestures in the direction of Chiang Kaishek's island kingdom on Formosa. Two tiny islands, Quemoy and Matsu, lying three miles off the Chinese mainland, were still in the hands of the Nationalist troops. Mao's propaganda machine began to issue statements declaring that the situation was no longer tolerable. He massed troops on the coast opposite the two islands. Night and day artillery assaults were launched against the small Kuomintang garrisons.

Dulles began to issue position papers stating that America would never abandon not only Formosa, but Quemoy and Matsu. World War III seemed about to erupt over these two previously unheard-of islands, whose acreage was so small they did not even appear as dots on most maps of the world.

On September 11 Ike made a radio and television address to the nation in which he said the United States must fight rather than face the possibility that the islands would fall to aggression. He barred "appeasement."

Nixon joined in full voice to support any action the President might take to hold back the Red Chinese horde. As the Seventh Fleet, which had been placed on guard in the Formosa Straits by Truman, was alerted for any possibility, he warned of Chinese deceitfulness and of the inability to reach agreements with such soulless atheists.

British Prime Minister Harold MacMillan instantly let the world know that his country had no commitment to the United States in this crisis. It was apparent he would not soon forget the Suez betrayal.

Democratic National Chairman Paul Butler, always capable of walking a narrow line, said the Democrats would back the President if he ordered the islands defended, despite their disagreement with his stand. Nixon, however, had no reservations. Perhaps the time had finally come to deal Red China the death blow.

On September 27 the *Times* reported that 80 per cent of the mail received by the State Department since Eisenhower had revealed his determination to fight for the two offshore islands opposed his stand. This created a momentary crisis of confidence, since not a hint of this reaction had come through official channels. Nixon defended the Administration in the manner he knew best. He launched an attack, accusing a State Department "subordinate" of trying to "sabotage" the Eisenhower-Dulles policy by disclosing the adverse mail count. Had the mail favored Ike's stance, such a leak might reasonably have been expected to meet with his approval; however, he now let friendly reporters know that his resentment against Administration critics was mounting.

The campaign season was approaching, and when it did, Nixon traditionally got edgy. As though to warn him that unfriendly eyes were watching, Sam Rayburn let it be known he did not believe Nixon would again wage a "cruel campaign." Veteran Congressman John McCormack would not venture such a tame opinion. When asked about the "new Nixon" he said it was "a myth."

In preparation for the campaign, *the old Nixon* sent a telegram to all Republican Congressional candidates urging them to attack Democratic "radicals." They were to focus on the "radical wing" of the party and stress the purity of the Republican stand on foreign policy and the venality of the radicals' stand.

On October 25 in Sioux Falls he jovially told a press conference that he wanted to make peace with Harry Truman and he would do it when they played a piano duet at the National Press Club. Three days later Truman rejected the offer.

The campaign was milk toast for Nixon. As the statistics on distance traveled and states visited in campaign after campaign clicked off, it was clear he was essentially mending fences, showing the flag in distant provinces, lending color to colorless local campaigns, and placing potential delegates to the 1960 convention in his debt. He traveled 25,000 miles and visited twenty-five states.

The most important results of the campaign took place at opposite ends of the country, in California and New York. As Paul Butler had predicted, Knowland and Knight both lost. At no risk to himself, Nixon had been relieved of a major opponent for the 1960 nomination. Nevertheless, a hint that things were not perfect for him in his home state appeared in the results. He had insisted that Pat Hillings, his Congressional protégé, get the nomination for lieutenant governor on this hybrid ticket. Hillings went down with the top of the ticket, but his margin of loss was much greater.

In New York State the Republicans had an isolated run of good luck. Averell Harriman was defeated in the governorship "Battle of the

Millionaires" by Nelson Rockefeller. And so from the brow of Averell sprang forth, full-grown, Richard Nixon's most durable opponent for the Republican Presidential nomination.

The 1958 election, drum-majored by Nixon, was a Republican disaster. Once again the Democrats won control of Congress. With all of Nixon's electioneering since 1952, the Republicans had been able to hold control of Capitol Hill for only two years, and this despite the fact that during those lean Congressional years their indescribably popular leader reigned serenely in the White House. It was a performance unmatched in political history, and the incredible thing was that the man who had contributed most to this unenviable record was the most likely Republican Presidential candidate in 1960.

The cries of outrage coming from some sections of the party—that Dick had waged a terrible campaign and had once again led the party to defeat—meant nothing. He had learned to shrug off such bleak hindsight. On Friday, November 7, before the blood shed in Tuesday's election had been allowed to run off into the sewers, Dick was made to understand that while some had been slaughtered, he had, once again, survived. Leonard Hall called and invited himself and Clifford Folger, former National Republican Finance Chairman, to dinner. That night, Hall laid it on the line. He wanted to be given the job of driving Nixon's bandwagon. "You must start now," he urged.

Before the evening was over the pact was sealed. Hall was to have the responsibility of rounding up delegates for Dick, and Folger was to assume the other key role, Finance Chairman.

Most voters find it difficult to understand how little part they play in picking the President of the United States. Here was the proof of their impotence. On November 7, 1958, two years before any individual voter would get the opportunity to have his say, the king makers in the Republican Party had narrowed *the people's* choice to Richard Nixon and whomever his Democratic opponent might be. Hall, with his ties to Tom Dewey, the liberal Eastern wing of the party, and the conservatives of the National Committee, and Folger, with his conduits to Republican gold, had, short of an act of God, chosen the next Republican nominee.

Ike told the nation this was so when, shortly before Christmas, he finally screwed up his courage to take Mamie for their first social visit to the Nixons' home.

XXI.

Nailing It Down, or *How to Get Ike Off the Pot*

It does not seem unfair to him to say that after 1950 Nixon made no move, including brushing his teeth in the morning, without weighing its effect on his Presidential possibilities. He put it bluntly more than once: "You are always on display." And like any mannequin in a store window, the image was always frozen and unrevealing. A smile pasted on his joyless face, a mouth pouring forth capsulized responses that could have come from a computer.

The one incontrovertible fact about Nixon was that his entire adult life was frittered away pursuing something which ideally should have come to a man who had spent his time more constructively. From the moment he beat Jerry Voorhis his ratio of productivity declined. All the useful work he had done in Whittier to make the wheels of society roll ended at that point. And as the possibility to advance himself grew, even the small effort at constructiveness that marked his first days in Congress came to an end. Simply put, Nixon wanted to be President and nothing else was going to be allowed to stand in the way of that, even the possibility that he might otherwise lead a useful life.

Presidential candidates are traditionally delinquent in minding the store. If they are in Congress they spend months away from Washington touring the hustings for the approval of the small group of men who are in a position to give them the nomination. If they are governors, their faces become well known in every state but their own. Since the men who select the nominees of both parties, and, as a result, exercise the significant power in the process of selecting the probable President, are interested in vastly different things from the average voter, the shrewd candidates often appear to behave counter-productively.

They furtively poke holes in tax laws already so sievelike that they seldom produce enough revenue to run the country. They defend scoundrels who

241

would be improved by jail. They pretend to see merit in chaotic behavior of anti-social individuals or groups. In short, they reach out for any hint of advantage in the race for convention support, and willingly pay the price demanded for such dark services.

The price was never too high for Nixon. There is no concrete evidence in the record of his political life that he ever hesitated to act meanly when acting decently would have lost him the support of a member of the National Committee. Nixon plowed only one field after entering national politics. It was the weedy field of political advantage, and in this field he sowed carefully, cultivated diligently and reaped amply.

The results were predictable. He never won the affection of the majority of his countrymen. In fact, he never attained any sort of voter popularity. Once or twice he was able to scare them into voting against his opponent, but most frequently, his inability to attract general enthusiasm and yet remain in public life was astonishing.

The main reason he was able to ignore his lack of popular support was that he always had the backing of the Republican king makers. By 1959 he had no other purpose in life but to please them. However, Ike had to be dealt with. The aging President relished the idea that he was in a position to veto any potential nominee. He was not going to be forced into supporting Nixon as he had been in 1956.

To Nixon's horror, Ike's "close advisors" began spreading the word that there would be no Eisenhower candidate, but rather a group of candidates who would be acceptable to him. Nixon would most probably be one of the men on that list, but, Ike wanted every prospective candidate to know, he was not *committed* to him. This time Dick was going to have to work for his approval, instead of muscling it out of him.

Another fear was that Nelson Rockefeller might somehow nose him out at the wire. He was closely aligned with the party's liberal wing, and, as a result, had a power base. He had spent years in government service since the 1930s when he had gone to work in Latin America for F.D.R. Ike had picked him as Under Secretary of the new Department of Health, Education and Welfare. However, Ike would have to openly declare himself for Rockefeller in order to get the New York governor's campaign off the ground.

During the early months of 1959 Nixon attempted to fill, what was for him, a consummately difficult role—the role of a confident, irresistible candidate. The job of convincing Republican leaders they should nominate him had to take place the year before the convention. Most of them would be making up their minds far enough in advance so that they could reserve a good seat on the winning bandwagon.

Nixon had to stage something big to catch their eye at this propitious moment. He determined that he would make a trip to the Soviet Union to speak to Khrushchev. The more he thought about it, the more likely it became to him that nothing but good could rebound to him. As he conceived of the trip, the benefits to America were not likely to be as substantial. He described it as being "primarily ceremonial in character."

As he made his plans they were not flawed by any conceit that he might shape the course of history. "I fully realized that as Vice President I would be in no position to negotiate any issues with the Premier of the Soviet Union." Furthermore, "What I did in the Soviet Union would not in itself ensure peace, deter Communist aggression or remove any one of the trouble spots in the world."

Well, then, why go? The answer to that question, as in the case of any major act Nixon committed during those years, can be found only in the realm of politics. Think of all the luscious possibilities. Once again, as in Caracas, something might happen which would marshal public opinion to his side just at the moment that wise old Republican heads all over the country were trying to decide whether he had a chance on Election Day. And if the worst happened, and everything went smoothly, he would benefit from the image of a more mature Richard Nixon dealing effectively with our intransigent enemies. From a political point of view it was foolproof.

One would think he would have brought the matter up with Ike and made arrangements for such an expedition through his office, using the good services of the State Department. However, he chose a different route. He went to Abbott Washburn, Deputy Director of the United States Information Agency, which was then conducting a cultural exchange program between the two countries. "The Spirit of Geneva" had briefly thawed relations between Moscow and Washington during 1955, and this program to send ballet dancers westward and movie stars east was the chief manifestation of that zephyr breeze. Nixon apparently conceived of himself as a symbol as potentially effective in the Cold War as a Hollywood starlet.

Once the trip had been proposed to Washburn, Nixon explained, it was then "presented to and approved by his chief, George Allen, head of the USIA; Chris Herter, then Under Secretary of State (Adams had delivered on his promise); Foster Dulles and the President." One would have imagined that the Vice President of the United States would have reversed the order, first gaining the approval of the only man who had a greater status than himself. He was once again presenting Ike with a near *fait accompli,* apparently sure in his own mind that this was the most effective way to handle the old gentleman.

Washburn had suggested that a good reason for going to the Soviet Union would be to open the U.S. Exhibition on July 24 in Sokolniki Park in

Moscow. The main purpose was to get Nixon into Russia under one pretext or another, and the fact that Frol Kozlov, the Soviet Deputy Premier, had visited a similar exhibition in New York the previous January seemed to offer sufficient rationale.

Nixon had chosen a bad time for his political adventurism. Our relations with Moscow had cooled since Geneva. The suppression of the 1956 Hungarian Revolt by Soviet tanks had caused many Americans to raise their guard. Khrushchev was truculently denouncing imperialist warmongers, and conflict over the divided city of Berlin was again causing a crisis atmosphere.

As the end of his second term in office approached, Ike was determined to make one last great effort to bring the two former wartime allies into a more peaceful posture. Unknown to Nixon, secret negotiations had been going on which had resulted in a commitment from Khrushchev to visit the United States. Ike was to return the visit before retiring. Visions of summit conferences were dancing through Ike's head as Dick walked into his office to discuss his proposed journey to Moscow.

Since he had no knowledge of Ike's plans, Nixon was able to think, My visit would also afford an opportunity for high-level talks with Khrushchev in which I could make clear the United States' position on world issues. . . .

He was soon to find out that the Soviet Premier considered him "a slick and dishonest manipulator of words," but no one would accuse him of being so slow-witted that he did not understand, before he set out on his odyssey, that Khrushchev thought of him in the grimmest terms. He was clearly the wrong man to send into such a potentially combustible situation at such a time. Once again Ike was being forced into a position by a Nixon blinded by ambition.

As Ike sat behind his desk listening to Dick describe the hidden values of his proposed trip the idea never occurred to him that he should confide the news about the impeding exchange of visits between himself and Khrushchev. There was clearly some information which could with greater safety be shared with the Communist premier than with Richard Nixon.

The trip was planned for mid-summer. However, plugger that he was, as soon as he got the green light Dick began boning up on Russian history, culture, language and anything else anyone who had visited the Communist lair might be willing to tell him. Averell Harriman, Hubert Humphrey, Bill Hearst, Bob Considine, Walter Lippmann, Turner Catledge, all were cross-examined for any bit of advice that might be useful. "The most memorable briefing I received," he confided, "came from John Foster Dulles, the man I had sought out for advice throughout my career. . . ."

Dulles was dying. As the arrangements for Nixon's trip proceeded, Dulles was moved into Walter Reed Hospital, where he spent his last days. Nixon had tremendous respect for the Secretary of State. He said, "I believe the verdict of history will be that John Foster Dulles was one of the truly great men of our time." He visited him several times during this last illness, always sure that "I wanted his advice before asking for an appointment." He was sure Dulles would prefer it that way.

All the respect he had for Dulles, however, did not deter him from pursuing his own course when the pain-wracked statesman made any suggestion which went counter to his purpose. "He had always taken a dim view of so-called 'personal diplomacy' where the Communist leaders were concerned. He knew that more often than not these meetings were used by the Communists, not to settle differences but to exploit them and to gain propaganda advantage. . . ."

Dulles was telling him that his proposed trip was probably fruitless and might expose the United States to a harmful propaganda assault. Dulles was too well informed to wonder why this consideration did not change Nixon's thinking.

He visited Dulles on May 20, four days before his death. The Secretary's body was wasted. He was propped up with pillows in a chair and was sucking on ice cubes to dull the burning in his throat. His pessimism about the trip was never more apparent. "Show him [Khrushchev] that we are not taken in at all by the mock innocence of Soviet leaders," he advised the attentive Vice President. He spoke harshly of concrete proof we had of Soviet subversive activities around the world. "He should be told that until he puts a stop to such activities, his call for reducing of tensions and for peaceful coexistence will have a completely false and hollow ring."

On the same day Nixon had Herb Klein fly in from San Diego, where he was working as an editor on the *Union,* to take over his press relations. In 1952, 1954, 1956 and 1958, he was detached from his newspaper job in June until the November election, when he would return to impartial journalism. This time he was being called to duty more than a year before the traditional time. The message was clear. Nixon viewed the Soviet junket as part of the campaign. He needed his first-line troops in there with him.

A month after Dulles' death Ike finally got around to disclosing the still secret plans for Khrushchev to visit the United States. It was on the eve of Dick's departure, July 22, and Ike worried that Dick might suddenly find himself in a discussion with Khrushchev of a trip about which he knew nothing. Apparently Ike did not trust Nixon to react with predictable correctness. The fear that his last chance at improving relations with the Russians might be torpedoed by some Nixon blunder drove him to confide in his possible successor.

At a press conference he later described what had taken place at that meeting. "I told him, and I said 'So that you will not be astonished or surprised and feel let down by your government, should they [statements about Krushchev's trip] be opened up by the other side, you are not, yourself, and of course will not open this subject [sic].' "

In *Six Crises* Ike's instructions carry a different message. "He authorized me to discuss the trip privately with the Soviet Premier."

There was in Ike's relationship with Dick something of the father who had no trust in his son, who had been disappointed by him too many times for him to take a less defensive stance. As the reporters pressed him to discover why Nixon was going to the Soviet Union, Ike responded that the Vice President "is not a part of the diplomatic processes and machinery of this government."

But, incredibly, the Vice President was being sent on a diplomatic mission to our most implacable enemy at a time when tensions between the two countries were at a new high.

Seventy American newspapermen accompanied this widely ballyhooed trip. The country was alerted to what might happen when Richard Nixon went abroad. That the thought of Caracas was not far from his mind was apparent as soon as he landed at Vnukova Airport in Moscow on July 23. "Subconsciously," he said, "it reminded me of the rather ominous unfriendliness that I had experienced so consciously on our arrival at the airport at Caracas. . . . When we arrived at the U.S. embassy residence, I felt the same sense of relief upon reaching a bit of American soil in a foreign land that I had experienced when we had finally reached the sanctuary of the American embassy in Caracas fourteen months before."

Nixon was always a tense person. Touched suddenly on the arm he would often jump as though struck a blow. This steel-coil tension required the relaxation of sleep. Yet, it was precisely when he needed his rest most that he was least capable of obtaining it. He tended to make a virtue out of this problem. It allowed him to "keep on his toes," not to let up until some crisis in his life had been passed. In reality, it was a major contributor to his sudden bursts of hyper-emotionalism, the episodes of crying, the unexpected shouting, the hopeless bouts of depression.

The nights in Moscow were no different. "I turned in early that night in anticipation of the next day's schedule," he said reasonably. ". . . But as usual before any major crisis, I found I was too keyed up to sleep except intermittently. Finally, at 5:30 A.M., I gave up trying and decided to go out for a walk again. . . ."

Later that morning he went to the Kremlin. His introverted nature, the tension which always plagued him at such moments, and the lack of sleep conspired to make him appear at his worst in Khrushchev's eyes. "I was on edge with suspense as I entered Khrushchev's office shortly after 10:00. . . . I could sense that he was in a testy mood. He kept looking me up and down from head to toe. . . ."

Khrushchev immediately launched into a harangue, punctuated by table pounding, about the Captive Nations Week resolution passed by Congress earlier in the month. It called for people to rededicate themselves and pray for the liberation of "enslaved peoples" behind the Iron Curtain. Ike had issued the proclamation five days before Dick left for Moscow. Khrushchev bellowed that it was a "provocation." He demanded to know how Ike could have issued such a document and still have expected that his Vice President would receive a good reception in the Soviet Union.

Nixon felt Khrushchev was being insincere. He had taken the offensive on this matter, but if it had not been the Captive Nations Resolution, "he would have found some other excuse for doing so."

It was hardly a promising start for the diplomatic aspects of the mission, but it was not going to get any better. However, from Nixon's political point of view, it was promising. Dick decided not to answer Khrushchev in kind. They were in the Premier's office. There was nothing to gain by wasting his shots in this private setting.

Khrushchev finished off with what appeared to be genuine anger. " 'This resolution stinks!' he shouted, hammering the table. Then he spelled out what he meant in some earthy four-letter words, so beyond the pale of diplomacy that Troyanovsky, his interpreter, blushed bright red and hesitated before finally translating his words."

In the car with American Ambassador Llewellyn Thompson on the way to Sokolniki Park, Nixon discussed the Khrushchev diatribe. He told Thompson he was unsure of how to handle his volatile host. Thompson advised caution. The most prudent approach was to turn aside rudeness with politeness. "He said that Khrushchev's purpose was to goad me into some rash and impulsive statements," Nixon recalled, "and that I should avoid falling into his trap."

Never has an ambassador's advice been so completely rejected. No sooner had they gotten to the exhibition grounds than Nixon became aware of the fact that "a hundred newsmen gathered around us." It was no longer possible to listen in silence. Within moments they were projected into a setting that did not allow a man of Nixon's temperament to exercise the normal restraints of diplomacy. They were ushered onto a stage, a model color television studio, where, Nixon remarked, there were "literally millions of potential viewers and listeners watching every action and listening to every word we were saying."

Although at first reluctant to speak, Khrushchev again began to denounce the Captive Nations Resolution, wrapping his arms around a nearby worker and declaiming, "Does this man look like a slave laborer?" It was high camp.

Nixon claimed to be uncertain even up to this point about whether he would answer Khrushchev in kind. "Was he trying to goad me into giving him an excuse to break off the current Geneva negotiations?" Surely with a fear of that sort in mind, he would have held his temper. Answering in what he later described as an attempt "to change the subject," he said, "You must not be afraid of ideas. After all, you don't know everything. . . ."

Nixon drains the moment of its heat. However, Herb Klein, who was hanging on every word, saw the action somewhat differently. In 1971 he told me, "It was then that Mr. Nixon *poked him in the chest* and said, 'You don't know everything.' "

Khrushchev was furious. "If I don't know everything, you don't know anything about Communism—except fear."

The tension in Nixon was clearly building. "I knew that he had scored heavily and I felt it was imperative that I find an opportunity to strike back so that the record could be set straight publicly."

Why was it so imperative? Did Nixon honestly feel that if he *set the record straight* it would make the slightest difference in the course of Soviet-American relations? Clearly those relations were controlled by greater forces than Nixonian rhetoric. Was it, perhaps, personal vanity, at best, that was urging him to set the record straight *publicly*?

By the time they reached a model American home and made their way to the kitchen, Nixon was ready to lash out. It was here that what he described as the "Sokolniki Summit" took place. They began to discuss the relative merits of washing machines. From that innocuous starting point they moved to the material luxuries enjoyed by American workers. Khrushchev responded to this vision of the capitalist paradise by saying, "If an American citizen does not have dollars he has the right to . . . sleep on the pavement at night." It was a somewhat simplistic view of the welfare society, but distance and ideology tend to create such distortions.

Nixon interrupted him. "In our Senate we would call you a filibusterer. You do all the talking and you do not let anyone else talk. I want to make one point." He then went on to praise the freedom of choice that American consumers had. He claimed that was their "spice of life."

With all the months of preparation, with all the coaching from Dulles, the answer he finally gave the world's leading Communist could have been given off the top of his head. Under pressure he had reverted to type, a simple, shallow response, so stale it would have been indigestible had it been fed to the guests at a NAM luncheon.

The oratory continued to escalate. Khrushchev turned the topic back to washing machines. After a long speech Nixon asked, "Isn't it better to be talking about the relative merits of our washing machines than the relative strength of our rockets?"

Nixon described Khrushchev as suddenly giving "the appearance of turning angry and jamming his thumb into my chest." Funny the way he remembered Khrushchev jamming his finger into his chest but forgot doing the same to his host a few minutes earlier.

Khrushchev denounced American generals for rocket-rattling. Nixon had now forgotten Thompson's words of caution, the bitter taste of Ike's wariness at trusting him had disappeared. He was now just a tired, angry, militant Quaker-Fundamentalist, whose Irish blood and fear of losing a political advantage were dictating his response. "I knew that now was the time to strike back." Why? "Otherwise I would leave the impression *to the press* and through them to the world that I, the second-highest official of the United States, and the government I represented, were dealing with Khrushchev from a position of weakness."

He began to speak of military strength. Khrushchev tried to turn the subject aside. Nixon was now unrelenting. "I hope the Prime Minister understands all the implications of what I have just said." He launched into an analysis Clausewitz-style of what happens when potential military rivals face each other across a conference table. "Now we were going at it toe-to-toe," he said. "To some, it may have looked as though we had both lost our tempers." He was right, that's what it looked like. However, he did not want anyone to get the wrong idea. "But the exact opposite was true. I had full and complete control of my temper and was aware of it. I knew the value of keeping cool in a crisis."

Khrushchev was not as ready to claim coolness. "He accused me of issuing an ultimatum," Nixon remembered. "He vehemently denied that the Soviet Union ever used dictation, and he warned me not to threaten him. 'It sounds to me like a threat,' he declared, poking his finger at me. 'We, too, are giants. You want to threaten—we will answer threats with threats.' "

It looked like Nixon was about to start World War III all by himself.

The eight hours they spent together that day did not end their confrontation. Four days later he was Khrushchev's guest at his summer home twenty miles outside Moscow. Nixon's belligerence was never more apparent. "In this discussion," he said, "the rules were different, as far as I was concerned. This was a private conversation. I could answer him and counterattack, point by point, and I proceeded to do so. It was cold steel between us all afternoon."

He had such a narrow view of his role in American life. He thought of himself as a private individual having a discussion with someone he had always wanted to get at. The idea that there might be larger things at stake than his personal pleasure at being able to "counterattack" never seemed to have intruded on his thinking.

Toward the end of his ten-day stay in the Soviet Union he was given the opportunity to make a thirty-minute speech to the entire Soviet Union. Once again tension built. "For the two nights before the broadcast, I did not go to bed at all, using the time to write my final draft."

Why was he so preoccupied with the speech. He had known about it before he left the United States. The speech could have been prepared in advance, as had been many of the other speeches he made during the trip. But clearly he *was* disturbed. "One basic decision I had to make was whether to aim my speech primarily at the Russian people or at the American people, for I realized," he said candidly, "that this speech would be heard by the Russian people but also read in the press by the American people. *With the 1960 Presidential election not far off, a tough blasting speech would be politically expedient for me. . . ."* (Italics added.)

At this grand moment he was tormented by the idea that he might miss an opportunity to advance himself by artfully aiming a few arrows in the direction of the American voter. The trip to the Soviet Union was a political bonanza for him. He never regretted that he had the shrewdness to realize how crucially helpful it would be to his fortunes.

On August 3, two days before Dick returned, Hagerty announced that Khrushchev would shortly visit the United States. So intent was Ike on not being upstaged by his second-in-command that he wanted everyone to know that the credit for making the arrangements was solely his.

Ike might still be standoffish, but that increasingly appeared an irrelevant pose. The Vice President was too obviously overjoyed with his prospects. He chose his spots carefully, but wherever he went the reception was warm. Appearing at the American Legion Convention in Minneapolis on August 25, he reaffirmed the policy of self-determination for Eastern European nations, and projected the image of a much more authoritative spokesman on this subject now that he had quarreled with Khrushchev.

By December 26 Rockefeller was demoralized. So thoroughly had Nixon impressed the king makers of the Republican Party, and so firmly were they committed to him at this early date, that it was little more than a ceremonial announcement when the governor of New York explained he was withdrawing from the campaign. Nelson Rockefeller could have more easily started a party of his own than wrest the Republican nomination from the grasp of the Whittier wonder.

XXII.

Richard the Statesman

Eisenhower's reluctance to turn his job over to Nixon in 1960 is recorded by Sherman Adams, who commented, "Those closest to him believed Eisenhower might have even considered running for a third term if there had been no Constitutional prohibition against it." He got the impression that Ike "was leaving the Presidency with some reluctance and that he would miss it."

His heart attack, his ileitis, his stroke, his relatively poor health and advanced age did not prevent him from wanting to go on. As Nixon each day stepped more prominently onto center stage, Ike's aversion to seeing his policies and programs given over into his hands increased. Dick understood from the beginning that Ike was his strongest asset. However, he quickly discovered that the general was not willing to lead his charge.

"He felt it was important for me to establish my own identity as the new leader of the party," Nixon described Ike's reaction to his request for campaign aid. "He also expressed the conviction that his great influence with the American people was due in substantial part to his image of being President of all the people, and not just a partisan as Truman had been."

So Dick was going to have to go it alone. Ike just could not work up the necessary enthusiasm. He did not seem at all convinced this obsessive young political runner could lead the country.

And Nixon returned his lack of esteem. The hero-worship that had characterized his first emotions for the general had long since cooled. Although always careful to praise Eisenhower when the occasion called for formal endorsement, he was less enthusiastic when the question did not refer directly to him. When asked, during the 1960 campaign, which President came closest to meeting his test for the type of man who was good for the country, Nixon never mentioned Eisenhower. He liked the job Woodrow Wilson had done in his first term. "I would say in the twentieth century

Theodore Roosevelt is the fellow I would pick out as one who met the challenges of his time the way I would like to see the Republican Party meeting its national and international responsibilities."

It was a snub of some proportions to his boss and the one President in the twentieth century he knew best. With a certain barely repressed bitterness he remarked after the election that Ike "was far more complex and devious than most people realized. . . ."

Still, for a man who admitted he had gotten ahead "not because I was smarter but because I worked longer and harder than some of my more gifted colleagues," he had to be grateful for the long distance this amiable man had allowed him to run in his proximity. As he pointed out, he did not enjoy "the back-slapping, baby-kissing, exhibitionist activities expected of the average candidate . . ." yet he had somehow managed to outdistance all those friendly fellows. The most important reason for such an improbable success in recent years was the skill he had exhibited in exploiting the magic of Eisenhower's charisma, even when the President would have preferred to cast the glow of that magic in a different direction.

There were so few occasions on which he could personally generate any enthusiasm for his cause that it was essential to perfume the air with essence of Ike. In July, 1959 he had been able to score what he called "a decisive break" on his own when he met Khrushchev. "Until that meeting," he finally admitted candidly, "polls indicated my support was no greater nationwide than that of the Republican Party. After my return from the Soviet Union, my personal standing rose the critical five to six points above Republican strength in general—a margin I had to maintain if I were to have a chance to win in 1960."

Until Nixon's self-serving trip to the U.S.S.R. John F. Kennedy had been leading him by a substantial margin in the Gallup Poll—61 to 39. Kennedy had been charging like a confident cavalryman since he was narrowly squeezed out of the Democratic Vice Presidential nomination by Estes Kefauver in 1956. His smashing Senatorial reelection victory in Massachusetts in 1958, while Nixon was haplessly leading the Republicans to defeat, made him the front runner in the Democratic sweepstakes, and caused the skewed effect in the Gallup curve. After Khrushchev, the gap had narrowed in favor of Kennedy, 52-48, which tends to prove that a shrewd, unpopular politician, who knows which buttons to press at the right time, can get a big bang for his buck.

The fact that Nixon planned the effect carefully is beyond question. He admitted it openly. His big job was to "persuade five to six million Democrats to leave their own candidate and vote Republican. I recognized that I could accomplish this only as President Eisenhower had—by acting and speaking not just as a Republican partisan but as a representative of all the people. My trips to Caracas and Moscow had provided an opportunity for me to *appear* in this role."

Appearances are often deceiving, but since Dick was aiming at deception, his purposes were served.

By late January, 1960, the campaign team was assembled. It was led by Len Hall, Cliff Folger, Bob Finch, Herb Klein, Fred Scribner, Jim Shepley, Fred Seaton and Claude Robinson. They were disturbed only by the thought that the lack of a contest in the Republican primaries, while Kennedy, Stevenson, Humphrey, Symington and Johnson were competing for the Democratic nomination, might cause the voters to lose interest in their hero. There was some hope that Rockefeller, who was beginning to sound as though he might once again be a candidate, would inject some life into the campaign. However, when he unaccountably decided not to contest the New Hampshire primary, where he had considerable strength, even that straw man had been blown away. In *Nixon Agoinistes* Garry Wills quotes Father Cronin as recalling, "He [Nixon] went into a deep depression early in the nineteen sixties. As soon as it was clear that Rockefeller would not be a rival. . . ."

In March another cloud suddenly appeared on Nixon's horizon. Arthur Burns, the former chairman of the President's Council of Economic Advisers, visited his Capitol office, the bearer of bad news. His reading of the economic indicators led him to conclude that for the third time under Eisenhower's leadership the country was about to slip into a recession.

Burns strongly urged that Nixon convince the President to loosen controls on credit and "increase spending for national security," so as to avoid a slump which, he predicted, would hit bottom around Election Day.

That struck Nixon as being particularly bad timing. He headed for Ike's office. The President listened patiently and then invited in other economic experts. Several of them did not share Burns' pessimism, which only tends to prove the truth of Shaw's comment that if all the economists in the world were laid end to end they would still not reach a conclusion.

Unfortunately for Nixon, Ike decided once again to go with his most conservative advisors. Apparently Ike found Dick's advice freighted with self-interest, and decided the country's welfare lay in another direction. Nixon was displaying a bad case of the jitters. As the Vice President commented later, "In supporting Burns' point of view, I must admit that I was more sensitive politically than some of the others around the Cabinet table." Ike had spent a lifetime detecting the buck fever of overanxious subordinates and he decided to try to calm Dick's fears (which in this case merely seemed to confirm the truth that the man who expresses his fear loudly while others are serenely unflapped may be the one who is seeing things clearly). Although they did not detect it, the most serious of the Eisenhower recessions was well under way.

The prospects for the Republicans took another bad turn in early May. Ike was preparing to negotiate at a Summit Conference in Paris with Khrushchev when the Soviet Premier announced a U-2 had been shot down over Russia. Ike's attempt to pass off the intrusion into Soviet air space as an accidental overflight of a weather plane was quickly exposed by Khrushchev, who revealed the pilot had been captured and confessed he was spying in a photo-reconnaissance aircraft. After a raging denunciation of imperialist spies, Khrushchev withdrew from the Summit and Ike's last attempt at a peaceful understanding in his time failed. Why he had allowed such a potentially disastrous flight to take place only days before a conference he had worked years to bring about has never been satisfactorily explained. As Nixon ruefully pointed out, "The 'peace issue' was tarnished."

One of the more significant events of this campaign was Nixon's trip to New York to dine with Nelson Rockefeller in his apartment, on July 22, three days before the Chicago convention. He offered the Vice Presidential nomination to the New York governor, saying that "if he were to run for Vice President, the chances of the ticket's winning would be increased." Rocky replied he just felt he "could not put his heart into the campaign," closing the door on an alliance which probably would have spelled victory for the Republican ticket. Nixon cannot be blamed for finding it hard to forgive his indecisive rival.

On Wednesday, July 27, Nixon was nominated by acclamation, and the obsession which had been growing for the last eight years was realized. Despite the certainty of his selection, he had spent his hours at the convention in unceasing labor for a prize he already possessed. During the 1952 convention, when Ike's nomination was far from certain, the general had made it a habit of going to bed at a remarkably early hour, usually before ten. But Dick's nerves would not countenance such equanimity in the face of peril. He observed that as he approached the podium to accept the nomination he was almost overcome with "the fatigue I had felt as a result of three days with almost no sleep. . . ."

There was a strangeness about Richard Nixon's attitude toward sleep. It was almost as if he considered it his enemy. Invariably when discussing a crisis in his life, he would pause to recount how little sleep he received while preparing himself to face his test. There is such a blank unwillingness to recognize the function of sleep in refreshing and preparing the body for a high level of efficient action, and, at the same time, such an adolescent braggadocio in his recounting of the records he set without rest, that a shadow is cast on his maturity. Granted that busy men may begrudge the

—*UPI*

Four Presidents: At Nixon's inauguration as Vice President in 1953. Herbert Hoover behind a glum Harry Truman; Eisenhower partly concealed by Nixon; Henry Cabot Lodge in the upper left corner; John Foster Dulles, upper right

Arriving in Syracuse during the last week of the 1960 Presidential campaign, candidate Nixon demonstrates his thick skin

Picking up a reluctant ally in Albany, October 28, 1968

President Nixon with Ike's son, John, reporting that the general had suffered another in what was to be a final series of heart attacks in 1969

—Wide World

With Chiang Kai-shek and Madame Chiang in Taipei, November 9, 1953

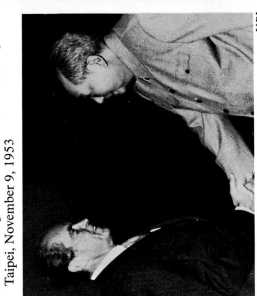

—UPI

With Chairman Mao Tse-tung in Peking, February 21, 1972

SOME DICTATORS
DICK KNOWS...

—UPI

General Francisco Franco greets the President and Pat, October 2, 1970

—UPI

General Rafael Trujillo embracing his friend in Ciudad Trujillo, 1955

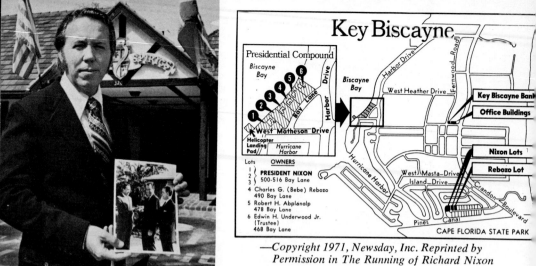

Key Biscayne

Presidential Compound

Biscayne Bay

Bay Lane
West Matheson Drive
Helicopter Landing Pad
Hurricane Harbor

Lots   OWNERS

1 } **PRESIDENT NIXON**
2 } 500-516 Bay Lane
3 }
4   Charles G. (Bebe) Rebozo
    490 Bay Lane
5   Robert H. Abplanalp
    478 Bay Lane
6   Edwin H. Underwood Jr.
    (Trustee)
    468 Bay Lane

Biscayne Bay
Harbor Drive
West Heather Drive
Fernwood Road
Key Biscayne Bank
Office Buildings
Nixon Lots
Rebozo Lot
West Masta Drive
Island Drive
Crandon Boulevard
Hurricane Harbor
Pines Canal
CAPE FLORIDA STATE PARK

Donald Berg, president of Cape Florida Development Company, holding
publicity photo for which Nixon and Rebozo posed in 1967. In another
Key Biscayne moment (bottom right) during the 1968 campaign, the candidate and his closest friend prepare to shove off for a carefree vacation at
Grand Cay

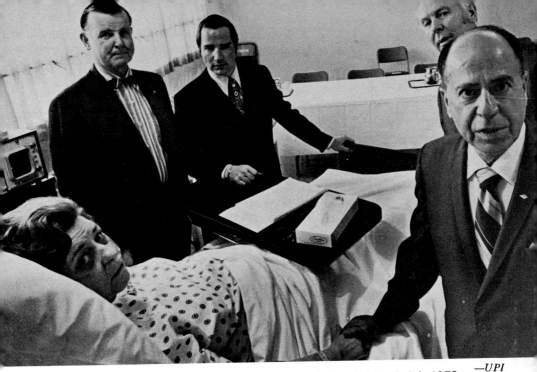

—UPI

Dr. Radetsky reassuringly holding Dita Beard's hand, March 26, 1972, just before the arrival of the Senate Judiciary Committee to question her on her ITT memo

Herb Klein, telling the author why his old friend has been misunderstood by the press through the years, August, 1971

—Leonard Lurie

Nixon and Kissinger thinking about their visit with Mao, on the plane to China, February 20, 1972

ITT, largely in the telephone business, has shown its genuine interest in diversification by purchasing the bond issue for this golf course almost directly behind the President's property on Key Biscayne

—Leonard Lurie

hours spent away from their desk, but to deny the function of sleep is to deny one's vulnerability as a man and is a step in the direction of unreality.

His acceptance speech was noted for his pledge to visit every state, something no candidate had ever proposed to do. It was almost as if he determined that his past marathon efforts to cover territory during campaigns in which he had a smaller stake had now to be surpassed.

The basic campaign strategy, if Nixon had had his way, would have been to maintain the pose of a reformed man, ready to rise to the challenges of greater responsibility. It was summarized in Herblock's famous cartoon, which led Nixon to cancel his subscription to the Washington *Post*. It showed Nixon mudslinging in the gutter. The caption had him saying: "I would act differently if I were in the top job."

By 1960 Nixon was a political machine more than a politician. His speeches were robot-like, usually the product of a master speech which had been simplified to the point of tedium and was ambiguous enough so that most people could hear it without taking offense. Father Cronin felt that the constant tinkering made each draft worse. "He keeps simplifying, simplifying. He can't leave things alone."

Nixon was now the model of circumspection, risking as little as possible against his Catholic opponent, whom he claimed to like, while hoping the Kennedy negatives would cause the ripest plum of all to drop into his outstretched palm.

Ike torpedoed the grand strategy at his August 24 press conference. A reporter asked him, "What major decisions of your Administration has the Vice President participated in?" His flip response, "If you give me a week, I might think of one."

A more damaging remark was not made during the remainder of the campaign by the most rabid Kennedy partisan. From August 24 on, Ike's moment of candor, which can most easily be accounted for by an irresistible urge to finally reveal the truth, was a predictable theme at every Nixon press conference. It was a public demonstration of the sadism Nixon had long suffered in private.

Kennedy's stratagem to smoke out a Nixon who was reluctant to close in combat depended on his constant cries that the Vice President was "afraid" to debate him on national television. Nixon vacillated. So much depended on this decision. Hall claimed that the harried Vice President constantly changed his mind and regretted his final decision. So anxious was Dick to choose correctly about whether or not to debate Kennedy that he left no stone unturned in his search for counsel.

Murray Chotiner, working out his time in the obscurity of an LA law practice, was asked for his opinion.

"I was against the debates with Kennedy," Chotiner remembered, "for exactly the same reasons I wanted him to debate Voorhis. He was giving away points to the lesser well-known man."

He urged Nixon not to make the same mistake with Kennedy that Voorhis had made with him. Besides, Nixon was going to be defending the Eisenhower record, a position that, even putting merit aside, Chotiner considered inherently disadvantageous.

Suspecting Murray was right, Nixon nevertheless agreed to four debates. By mid-August the pressure for them had become overwhelming. Each day he hesitated to take up Kennedy's challenge saw some of his support erode. The concept appealed to Americans, who were used to the idea that two opponents should face each other on the deserted street of a Western town and settle the difference between them in one dramatic showdown.

The first joint appearance was scheduled for Monday, September 26, in Chicago. It had the largest television audience since the Checkers speech. In excess of 80 million people huddled in safety in front of the screens of their television sets as the two opponents squared off against each other. Kennedy had the first shot. He claimed that the economy was in the doldrums, the country was stagnating and its international position debilitating. He proposed to "get the country moving again."

Nixon felt he had been put on the defensive, confirming Chotiner's worst fears. He failed to comprehend that he was on the defensive because he had a bad position, and that an effective performance by the Eisenhower Administration would have made him invulnerable to attack, at least on these issues. He chose instead to blame his bad press notices on the way he looked that night. He remarked that "I had never seen him [Kennedy] look more fit." As for himself, he had a "five o'clock shadow" although he had just shaved and "I knew that appearance may at times count more than substance." He knew things had gone wrong because "I had looked pale and tired." He was sure of his premonition that he had done poorly when Hannah called from California to ask Rose Mary Woods if Richard was "feeling all right."

Panic set in. "It was, then, essential that we make a comeback and the time and place to start was October 7 in Washington when we were to have the second debate." He began to drink malted milk shakes with every meal in an endeavor to build up his weight. His staff imported a makeup expert who was on an artistic level, in his field, with Michelangelo. No more simple face powder for a man who so badly wanted to be President.

The advice he received from the men whose opinion he valued most was to come out fighting. "Don't pay any attention to the critics who talk about a new Nixon and an old Nixon," he quotes one of them as saying.

Since the first debate was being increasingly referred to in the press as a "decisive" Kennedy victory, he felt there was nothing to lose. "I have seen so-called public relations experts," he said bitterly, "ruin many a candidate by trying to make him over into an 'image' of something he can never be."

In the interlude between debates he began to refer to Harry Truman as a "gallant warrior" and nostalgically allude to the "fighting campaign" he put up in 1948.

The advice from his combative friends suited his disposition, for one of the things Richard Milhous Nixon could never be was even-handed and relaxed. With some satisfaction, he remarked after the second debate that "It was a hard-hitting, sharp contest from beginning to end." Intent on measuring the effect of his new old approach, he called Murray in from the Coast.

Years later Chotiner reminisced about the chance that had been lost in 1960. "After the second debate he asked me to come see him. Dick plays the devil's advocate all the time. That's his way of picking your brain, finding out what all the arguments are before he makes up his mind. At that point I was in favor of a fifth debate. I thought he was coming on."

However, Murray's advice was not being taken as consistently as it once had been. Working against it was Nixon's basic yearning for privacy. He was inherently a shy and inhibited person, whose nature was being violated each time he forced himself into public exhibition. A speech before a huge audience, in which the mass was faceless, was bad enough. Still, it could be handled with a minimum amount of torment, especially during the earlier days when things were going his way and he was as much in control himself as he was ever to be. By 1960 the defenses he had erected to protect himself during such uncomfortable moments of public exposure had been worn down. They were to more noticeably erode with the passage of years. He could not welcome the possibility of having the handsome, confident Massachusetts Senator probe in the dark expanses of his mind for a moment longer than absolutely necessary. Although the pressure for a fifth debate continued until the end of the campaign, and Nixon was credited with doing well in the second, third and fourth debates, he rejected the idea of another confrontation.

The last of the four debates may have swung the psychological balance against continuing the fight. Nixon had been hoping to score best in this session. At his insistence, it was to be devoted completely to foreign affairs, the area in which he felt strongest after his outstanding "successes" in Caracas and Moscow.

As the date for the debate approached he became uneasy. Kennedy was increasingly focusing on Fidel Castro and "the situation in Cuba ... [which] continues to deteriorate." He blamed the Republicans for allowing Communism to exist "eight jet minutes from the coast of Florida."

Basically Nixon agreed with Kennedy's militant posture. "I had long been urging a stronger policy, within Administration councils, against Castro, " he said in *Six Crises*. Furthermore, his proposal had finally been accepted by Eisenhower during the early months of 1960, about six months before Kennedy began to advocate action against Castro. "The CIA was given instructions," Nixon continued, "to provide arms, ammunition and training for Cubans who had fled the Castro regime and were now in exile in the United States and various Latin American countries."

Nixon was faced with a terrible dilemma. "It was a program, however, that I could say not one word about. The operation was covert." He would have preferred to blast Kennedy with the truth and reap his reward in votes, but, "I was in the position of a fighter with one hand tied behind his back. . . . I could not even hint at its existence, much less spell it out."

Nixon's anguish rose a notch when on the day before the final debate, October 20, as he was trying to marshal himself for the last great effort, Kennedy released a new Cuban position paper to the press which upped the ante he was willing to pay in the fight against Fidel. He advocated direct U.S. intervention in Cuba, calling for aid to the rebels, who "have had virtually no support from our government."

Nixon was flabbergasted. "I could hardly believe my eyes." Unwilling to concede the genuineness of Kennedy's sentiments, the quality of which he proved in his commitment to the Bay of Pigs fiasco, he attributed opportunistic motives to his opponent. Nixon decided Kennedy was taking unfair advantage of him.

He claimed to believe that Kennedy had been briefed by the CIA about the Administration's more active pro-rebel position of the last six months. "For the first and only time in the campaign, I got mad at Kennedy— personally. . . . And my rage was greater because I could do nothing about it."

As was frequently true of a Nixon statement that he "could do nothing about it," he was indicating that there was nothing "honorable" that he could do about it. "Kennedy had me at a terrible disadvantage." He was supporting a policy that had "overwhelming" public approval, a policy Nixon had long privately advocated and which was now the secret policy of the government.

"What could I do?" he asked in the tortured tone of a man who is being forced by other men into a damaging silence. His desperation led him into one of the most incredible acts of double-dealing ever confessed to by a man in public life.

There was only one thing I could do. The covert operation had to be protected at all costs. I must not even suggest by implication that the United States was rendering aid to rebel forces in and out of Cuba. In fact, *I must go to the other extreme*: I must attack the Kennedy proposal to provide such aid as wrong and irresponsible because it would violate our treaty commitments. [Italics added]

In short, in order to find some argument on which he could base an attack, he was willing to repudiate publicly the position he had been taking within the Cabinet for months. He must go "to the other extreme." Why? Because not to do so would give his opponent an advantage.

And so he stood before the television cameras and, with the apparent sincerity typical of all his pronouncements, lied, "I think that Senator Kennedy's policies and recommendations for the handling of the Castro regime are probably the most dangerously irresponsible recommendations that he's made during the course of this campaign."

Then as if to prove that there was no limit to his perfidy, he proceeded to develop a series of rationalizations in support of a Cuban position he did not support that was as cunning as it was deceptive. If Kennedy's (*and Nixon's*) recommendations about intervention were followed, "we would lose all of our friends in Latin America, we would probably be condemned in the United Nations, and we would not accomplish our objective."

On and on he went elaborately predicting that if the Kennedy(-Nixon) policy were followed Khrushchev would probably start World War III. He had sweated to convince the nation that a position he had opposed in the Cabinet with all the conviction he had been able to muster, for months, was the position all right-thinking Americans should adopt.

When the debate was over, I felt that I had made as good a case as possible for *my* point of view, but I had no illusion about the effect on the public generally. I was in the ironic position of appearing to be "softer" on Castro than Kennedy—*which was exactly the opposite of the truth*. . . . My attack was effective but with the wrong audience. [italics added]

Nixon confessed to this incredible deception with an openness that forces one to question not only his morality but his judgment. This trickery, such a well-earned trademark of Nixon's style, had never been so openly embraced.

The debates were over. The pressure of such deception was too great to go on to number five. Nevertheless, on the campaign trail, where it was not necessary to look his opponent in the eye, the fraud continued. On October 23 he told audiences in Pennsylvania and Ohio, "He [Kennedy] advocates a policy which was universally interpreted as intervention in the affairs of Cuba. Again he was wrong, and the President was right."

The remaining part of the campaign was waged at a killing pace. During the last seventy-two hours before Election Day Nixon slept less than five hours. In a final terrible struggle with statistics, he made a mad dash for Alaska so that he could fulfill his meaningless pledge to set foot in every state. He was finally able to brag only that since the convention "I had traveled over 65,000 miles and visited all the fifty states." Bob Haldeman, his advance man that year, had filled all the auditoriums Nixon had visited.

However, he had not been able to fill the ballot boxes with the right number of votes. The Voices for Nixon Chorus, often one thousand strong, the 1500 teen-aged Nixonettes who turned out to greet their hero at airports, even Ike's last-minute attempt to speak out for Dick—nothing helped.

As the early results came into the Ambassador Hotel in Los Angeles, Nixon could not stand the pressure. He hopped into a car with Don Hughes, Jack Sherwood and John DiBetta of the LA Police Department, and headed south for the Mexican border. While people all over the country were casting their votes, he was in Tijuana, trying to forget it all.

Hours later he returned to the Ambassador in time to hear the television networks put on one of their more dismal performances. Before the polls had even closed on the West Coast, NBC was announcing the odds favoring a Kennedy victory had been computerized at 7 to 1. Within a short while NBC raised the odds to 15 to 1. Within the hour, 10:30 P.M. (Eastern time), precisely at the point where the results were showing Nixon closing in on Kennedy, NBC announced the odds in favor of a Kennedy victory were now 250 to 1. Both ABC and CBS predicted a smashing Kennedy victory while the polls were open and the psychological impact of that prediction on those who like to go with the winner was likely to be reat. Nixon had every right to claim foul at this point, and this episode became one of the foundations for his enduring complaint against the way the news media treated him.

By four o'clock in the morning California time Kennedy's popular vote advantage was down to 600,000 out of over fifty million votes counted, and CBS was hedging its predictions in a manner which would have been appropriate half a day earlier, "Kennedy *apparently* has won."

Nixon had earlier deposited Pat and the girls in a fifth floor suite and now decided to turn in. He had dropped off to sleep remembering the story about Charles Evans Hughes "in a similar but reverse situation in 1916." As he closed his eyes he fantasized, "Perhaps in the morning, I thought, someone might awaken me with a report that the miracle had come to pass."

Instead he was jolted awake by Julie two hours later. She had used a Secret Service man to locate her father. She was filled with tearful teen-age questions, "What are we going to do? Where are we going to live? What kind of a job are you going to be able to get? Where are we going to school?"

He tried to reassure her, then ordered breakfast for the two of them and began a post-mortem. Julie was convinced people had voted against him "because of religion. . . . That was what they were saying on television last night."

Nixon genuinely believed this was true. Discerning that Kennedy lost Protestant votes in states he never could have won, and won Republican Catholic votes in states where they represented his margin of victory, he was always convinced the religious issue worked against him. Nevertheless, he was speaking to his impressionable young daughter. "I recalled that she and I had helped Father John Cronin, one of my best and closest friends, celebrate his twenty-fifth year in the priesthood. . . . And then there were Earl Mazo and Ralph de Toledano, my biographers, who had visited in our home on many occasions and, with their families, had been so close to all of us."

Some of his best friends were Catholics. (He did not seem to be aware of the fact that Toledano was Jewish.) Julie finally said, "I think I understand, Daddy." Then, showing the resilience of youth, she added, "Well, maybe we didn't win the election, but we won in the hearts of the people." She was a good daughter, and her lovely sentiment, oh that it could be true, cut through Richard's paper-thin reserve.

"I had seen many people in tears the night before as they heard the returns, but for the first time I was confronted with the same problem. I told Julie my hay fever was bothering me as I wiped my eyes with a hand-kerchief. "

Within a few minutes Bebe Rebozo, who had flown in from Key Biscayne, Jack Drown and Ray Arbuthnot had entered the apartment to comfort him, but the healing power of their friendship was inadequate to the occasion. The final results had been too tantalizingly close. Out of a popular vote of 68,800,000 Kennedy's margin had been a scant 113,000. The electoral vote, 303 to 219, was deceptive. Actually a shift of approximately 4,000 votes in Illinois, which he lost when the Democratic votes needed materialized from Mayor Daley's late-reporting Cook County wards, and 9,000 others, in a handful of closely divided states, would have made Nixon President in 1960.

Hannah had spent the night at the Ambassador with Donald. Evelyn Dorn, who had watched her friend closely, said that when the worst was confirmed, while "everyone else was in tears . . . Hannah was calm. She just said a prayer when she heard the bad news. She was a very strong woman."

Donald, on the other hand, thought he had done his brother in again. During the campaign it had been revealed he had received a loan from the Hughes Tool Company while attempting to avoid bankruptcy. Some were unkind enough to attribute to Nixon's influence the granting of the loan. As

Dick, Pat, Julie and Tricia started to leave the hotel the next morning, Donald intercepted them and sorrowfully told Dick, "I hope I haven't been responsible for your losing the election." Richard reassured him.

There was a lifetime to spend assigning the proper measure of blame to each villain. As for now, Nixon would spend the next few weeks in the sun, relaxing in the glow of Bebe's hospitality and learning the pleasures of being a rich private citizen on Elmer Bobst's luxurious yacht, *Elisa V.* But as the days in the sun passed, his restlessness grew and it became apparent to him that life held a special torment for men who lose big. As he bitterly remarked at the time, "I have never had much sympathy for the point of view 'It isn't whether you win or lose that counts, but how you play the game.' "

XXIII.

Nix on Nixon

Pat had cried bitterly on election night while standing at Dick's side as he made his tentative concession speech to Kennedy. The experience had been degrading. She was forced to bare her grief before millions. As soon as she detected that the Miami sun had healed some of Dick's more superficial wounds, she laid it on the line. Under no circumstances did she ever want him to think of running for office again. He was not the man for that kind of work. It took too much out of him. He had no time to spend with his family. Even when he was with her she felt alone. When he was campaigning they often spent their nights in different suites. It was time for the girls to stop crying at airports as they saw their parents off.

Dick was in no mood to argue. His soul had been lacerated. Pat had every right to protest. When you lose, everyone complains. In the months that passed since his defeat, and before he officially left the office of Vice President in late January, 1961, he had already noticed a falling off of friends. "And what hurt the worst," he remarked, was to see that those for whom he "had done the most were often the first to desert." There was a cruelty about politics that was never more apparent than in those weeks immediately after a politician's greatest defeat.

And so he nodded his head as Pat had her say. It was academic anyway. Who would ever want him to run for office again? At Pat's insistence he sat down and wrote out a pledge, similar to the one written in the mid-1950s, never again to seek public office. Pat came away from that Runnymede convinced that a new life, more suited to her ambitions, was opening up for them.

But even as he was submitting Dick was scheming out the possibilities of undertaking a campaign certain desperate men had half-jokingly proposed to him. The California Republican Party had been shattered by Knowland's defeat in 1958. The upcoming race for the governorship in 1962 was not reuniting the various combatants. There was no logical candidate to oppose bumbling Democrat Pat Brown, with the glaring exception of California's own Richard Nixon.

When they returned from vacation in February, 1961, Dick found a letter from his friend Whittaker Chambers. It began on a melancholy note that suggested he was once again contemplating suicide. "It seems possible that we may not meet again—I mean at all. So forgive me if I say here a few things which, otherwise, I should not presume to say."

Nixon chose to end his autobiography with this letter from his friend, who had been by that time dead for several months. Chambers had faith in Dick's future, even if he had none in his own. After telling him that someday he would be President, "you have been cruelly checked," he offered the last advice he was ever to give him.

> Some tell me that there are reasons why you should not presently run for Governor of California. Others tell me that you would almost certainly carry the State. I simply do not know the facts. But if it is at all feasible, I, for what it is worth, strongly urge you to consider this.

The letter had an enormous impact on Nixon's still raw nerves. Although he received offers from law firms all over the country, he finally decided to accept one from Adams, Duque & Hazeltine of Los Angeles, at the very eye of the Republican storm.

Jack Dreyfus had urged him to come to New York "because of the greater opportunities for high income available there." However, "acquiring money and property, as an end in itself, has no appeal," Nixon confided. Herb Klein described the basis for Nixon's decision as being founded in self-sacrifice. "There were a lot of pressures on him from all sides. He was trying to keep the party together in California."

Still, there was that nagging feeling he had been lured back to California by the thought a victory in the governorship race would place him squarely back in the running for the Republican Presidential nomination in 1964.

Chotiner was happy to have him back. It meant they could see more of each other. However, he came down squarely on Pat's side on the question of Dick's running for governor. "I told him not to run. He had nothing to gain. Pat Brown was thought by most people to be a poor governor. If he beat him everyone would say, 'Look who he beat. Anyone would have won against Brown.' But if he lost, he was through."

It was always the practical note in Chotiner's counsel that charmed Nixon.

There was none of the nonsense about *service* or *duty* that weighed down the advice of other men. It was, *do this because it will be good for you,* or *don't do that because there is nothing in it for you.*

"I told him to take a job as president of a university," Chotiner told me contemplatively. "In fact, I had the university all picked out. It was Stanford. The man who was heading Stanford then would become president emeritus and then after a few years when Dick was ready to move on, the other man could have his old job back."

He rubbed his heavy jowls momentarily as he confirmed the wisdom of his recommendation. "In the meanwhile, Dick would not have to struggle with all those hard problems that the governor of California has. He would be able to accept speaking engagements anywhere and speak about anything that would show him in a good light."

All with one purpose in mind, another shot at the Presidency. In preparation for that Dick wrote his book, which President Kennedy suggested to him as an exercise that would tend "to elevate him in popular esteem to the respected status of an 'intellectual.' " Al Moscow, his ghost writer, made that elevation easier.

In his first year out of office he experienced a financial bonanza. He was able to boast that "My income tax alone this year will be twice as great as my salary as Vice President last year."

But money was not the only fuel that made the Nixon machine run. People like himself, he philosophized at the end of 1961, who have known the "challenge and tension" of victory and defeat, "can never become adjusted to a more leisurely and orderly pace. They have drunk too deeply of the stuff which really makes life exciting and worth living to be satisfied with the froth."

Quickly tired of the frothiness of making money, Nixon committed himself to making the race for the governorship. He announced his decision at a dinner party, and Earl Mazo reports that when Pat heard the words tumble from his mouth she "chewed him out" right on the spot. One would expect that a lawyer would regard his word, pledged in writing, a little less lightly.

The campaign was painful. Pat Brown tried to pose as a slightly overweight Jack Kennedy, while Nixon tried to impersonate Dwight Eisenhower. Californians clearly disliked both of them and it was simply a matter of which one aroused less animus.

Dick was his usual indefatigable self, racing around the state as if he were in a marathon, sleeping as little as possible, and giving new Nixon speeches. He tried to buttress the illusion of honesty by alluding to the fact that as a man who had suffered a terrible defeat, he had at last come through the fire that purifies the formerly sinful. But the old catch-phrases, "Let me answer in this way" and a myriad of other shopworn debater's techniques were still there to remind the injured of their injurer.

Brown found his task made easier because Nixon had highlighted a point of vulnerability. In *Six Crises,* published as the campaign began to heat up, Nixon had referred to the loan Donald had received from the Hughes Tool Company. Although he had assured his brother that the issue had not been responsible for his Presidential defeat, as Donald feared, the assurance was based on his feeling that "The only place the charge meant anything was here in California." Since it was officially announced, ten days after CBS's computer had given California to Kennedy, that the absentee ballots had placed California in Nixon's camp by 35,000 votes, Nixon felt justified in believing the loan exposé had not damaged his already lost cause.

However, in 1962 the race was being run exclusively in California, and even if Pat Brown were willing to ignore the loan, his campaign managers were not. Day after day the issue was floated over the battlefield. The loan was for $205,000. Why, Brown partisans wanted to know, did Howard Hughes decide a Whittier businessman, on the verge of going out of business, deserved a share of his money? Was it logical to think that the country's tenth largest government contractor was unimpressed by the fact that the man to whom he was contributing so heftily was the brother of the Vice President of the United States?

In a face-to-face debate with Brown, Nixon attempted to brazen it out. He said he had been hearing a lot of charges that he had used influence to get his brother a loan. Then waving his finger at Brown, he challenged him to present, before the television audience, any evidence to prove misconduct on his part. He did not deny that the loan had been made, but tried to leave the impression that it had resulted from nothing more than a rich man's fancy.

The full dimensions of the sub rosa aspects of this twisted deal did not emerge until January 23, 1972, when the New York *Times* came "into possession" of Department of Justice files of a study made by Attorney General Robert F. Kennedy during the spring and summer of 1961.

The FBI investigation revealed that by late 1956 Donald's chain of restaurants, Nixon, Inc., was losing $5,600 a week. The question of who approached whom in an endeavor to rescue Nixon, Inc., has not yet been established. What the study did reveal was that in December, 1956, after Dick had been reelected Vice President, a $165,000 loan was made to F. Donald Nixon.

The invisible millionaire Howard Hughes had had the money transferred to Frank J. Waters, then an attorney for Hughes Tool, and it was Waters who funneled the money into Donald's pocket. Several months later Hughes sent $40,000 more to Donald via the same circuitous route.

The $205,000 loan was secured by a vacant Whittier lot owned by Hannah Nixon. The estimated market value of the lot was $52,000. The books of Nixon, Inc., showed the debt as being owed to Hannah. Meanwhile the Hughes Tool Company carried the loan on its books as being made to Mr. Waters.

Shortly after the second loan was made, Nixon, Inc. went into bankruptcy. Hannah now turned over all her rights to the lot to Phillip Reiner, an accountant associated with Mr. Waters' law partner.

According to the *Times,* "Mr. Reiner has said that the mortgage was assigned to him to hold as a trustee although he had not put up the money for the loan."

Something caused Reiner to feel uneasy over his role in this Florentine intrigue. Perhaps it was the probing of the FBI during the summer of 1961. In any case, in January, 1962, he hired the renowned criminal lawyer Melvin Belli and filed a damage suit against Howard Hughes and the Hughes Tool Company.

Reiner maintained that he "had been made to appear as the lender of the money so that any inquiry would lead to him and stop, shielding Mr. Hughes and the tool company." He alleged that he "had been deceived in the role he played." He went on to claim that Hughes had "intentionally and fraudulently concealed" from him the true nature of their dealing with the Nixon family."

Hughes settled out of court in June, 1962, paying Reiner $150,000, but extracting a pledge from him and Belli that they were not to discuss what had happened.

Robert Kennedy gave serious thought to indicting the Nixons under statutes governing political contributions. He also considered the possibility of charging Hughes with bribery. The *Times'* story records, "Income tax consequences were examined for the Nixon family and none were found worth considering."

Nixon was not to be tried or convicted in a court of law. Rather, he was tried in the California court of public opinion, and it was there that the terrible verdict was rendered.

On the night of November 7, 1962, Nixon holed up in Suite 724 of the Beverly Hills Hotel in Los Angeles, to once again experience the masochistic thrill of losing before the eyes of millions. The old crowd had gathered round, praying that this time it would come out all right.

The newsmen were in the ground floor press room, sensing a kill. As the early morning hours slipped by and Brown's lead held at 300,000 they began to demand that Herb Klein get a concession statement from Nixon. The memory of how Nixon held off conceding to Kennedy until after ten the morning after the election was still fresh in their minds and they told Klein they did not look forward with pleasure to another such vigil. They were particularly agitated because, unlike 1960, the results were not close. Nixon was losing California by almost three times the margin by which he had lost the entire United States.

Upstairs Nixon sat in catatonic immobility. Although his whiskers had sprouted out a black mask over the lower portion of his drawn face, his necktie was still neatly squared under his chin. He stared at the television scene of the press room downstairs for minutes on end, as Chotiner hovered above him trying to detect where their strategy had gone wrong. It would have been better if they had pushed harder on the Communist issue. This statesmen crap was what had lost the ball game.

Finch and Haldeman (who had been the official campaign manager, since not quite enough time had passed to give Chotiner the title he deserved) wandered around trying to invent some plausible patter that would comfort Nixon. Jack Drown and Ray Arbuthnot joined Pat Hillings to lament their hero's death. Pat Nixon was in an adjoining room sobbing uncontrollably.

Finally at 10 A.M. the next morning Klein entered Room 724 in a mood unusual for him—he was taking a stand, instead of merely waiting for orders. A statement would have to be issued to the impatient reporters. They were beginning to look ridiculous. "You've got to go down."

"Screw them!" Nixon said, as he ripped his eyes away from the television screen. He told Klein to write out a statement and take it down to the snapping jackals of the capitalist press.

Klein went about his business in his usual unruffled fashion, but as he scribbled out the standard phrases he noticed the scene out of the corner of his eye. "One man who was pretty emotional began to cry on his shoulder and that upset him some. And a few other very old friends came in and said, 'You can't let the press bluff you out of this.' "

Klein hurried to get the unpleasant duty over with. A few minutes later he was downstairs calmly reading off Nixon's valedictory as a public man, as though he were a clerk reading the closing stock market prices.

Upstairs Nixon watched with venomous disbelief. How was it possible for him to lose to someone like Brown? The room was abuzz with agony. As Klein droned, "He wants to congratulate Governor Brown . . . wish him well . . . ," the collective anguish rose to a higher pitch. Dick shouldn't take this lying down. Those bastards downstairs should hear what he thinks of the way they messed him up with their prejudiced reporting.

Suddenly his body uncoiled and he was on his feet headed for the door. Those who were still coherent thought he was using the cover of Klein's news conference to make his escape. Instead, rumpled and unwashed, his black

Irish temper barely under control, he stomped down to the ground floor, burst onto the platform and broke into what Klein was saying in mid-sentence.

What was Klein's reaction? "Just one of surprise. I was surprised he was there. That's all the reaction I had."

It may have begun that simply, but the substance of what Nixon said during the next fifteen minutes was so extraordinary and his delivery so bizarre that many people instantly developed a new perception about him. It was as if *the real Nixon* had suddenly emerged. In a whining voice he struck out against his tormentors, not the people who voted against him, but *the press*, ". . . now that all the members of the press are so delighted that I have lost, I'd like to make a statement of my own."

He spoke in a tone that was alternately petty and mean, but which he had unsuccessfully calibrated to project detachment. "I believe Governor Brown has a heart even though he believes I do not. I believe he is a good American even though he feels I am not. . . . I am proud of the fact that I defended my opponent's patriotism.

"You gentlemen didn't report it . . . I want that—for once—gentlemen—I would appreciate if you would write what I say."

He frequently interjected a nervous titter, which he had apparently intended to sound casual. For fifteen minutes he let it all come out, as he used to do with his brother Donald after putting up with his nonsense silently for months on end. Often incoherently he lashed out at his enemies: ". . . one last thing. At the outset, I said a couple of things with regard to the press that I noticed some of you looked a little irritated about. . . . As I leave the press, all I can say is this: For sixteen years, ever since the Hiss case you've had a lot of fun—a lot of fun that you've had an opportunity to attack me. . . ."

In the frenetic emotionality of the moment, he had blocked on the date of the Hiss case. It had actually been only fourteen years since that fateful August 3, 1948. He had gone back sixteen years to the Voorhis campaign. All these years he had publicly been supporting the fiction that his enemies in the press had developed their distaste for him during the Hiss affair, and then only because of their pro-Communist sympathies. But in this moment when the guard was down, his subconscious delivered a secret. He really understood that people had started disliking him from the moment he entered politics, and that their distaste stemmed not from their subversive attitudes but from the nature of his behavior.

Perspiring freely, he tried to pull himself together. "The last play. I leave you gentlemen now and you will now write it. You will interpret it. That's your right. But as I leave you I want you to know—just think how much you're going to be missing. You won't have Nixon to kick around anymore, because, gentlemen, this is my last press conference and it will be one in which I have welcomed the opportunity to test wits with you. . . ."

Again the nervous giggle as he took a deep breath. Klein remembered thinking at this point, "I wished he wasn't there." The press has the responsibility to report all the news, he continued, ". . . and, second, recognize that they have a right and a responsibility, if they're against a candidate, give him the shaft, but also recognize if they give him the shaft put one lonely reporter on the campaign who will report what the candidate says now and then."

It seemed like the proper moment for him to turn to the Secret Servicemen and order, "Okay, boys, throw the bums out."

Instead, he spun on his heels and fled the room, leaving reporters who had known him for years, aghast. As one strove to excuse his bad form by referring to his overwrought state of mind and exhausted body, the thought kept intruding that this whining, petty man with a violent temper, who had shown such a snivelling nature in defeat, had aimed to be President of the United States.

Loyal Murray Chotiner was upstairs. His one-way gauge on Richard Nixon was again rising.

   I had no idea he was going to do it. But I thought it was the right thing
   for him to do. Let's face it. He was through. He thought he was finished
   in politics and he was right. Why shouldn't he say what he thought. He
   got it off his chest.

As soon as Nixon finished his swan song, Murray bolted out of the room. "I caught up with him at the car outside. He told me to get in with him. He didn't know whether he had done the right thing. He was upset, depressed. I told him I thought he did the right thing."

For the first time since he had known Nixon, Murray's advice had about it an element of the impractical. The press conference had certainly given his candidate an opportunity to blow off steam, but it labelled him, viewing it in its most generous light, as a poor loser, and that was not the proper image for Chotiner candidates.

In its next issue *Time* Magazine editorialized: "Barring a miracle, Nixon's political career has ended."

XXIV.

Pat Throws Away Her Cloth Coat

After the California disaster Nixon suffered as few men are privileged to, publicly and unrelentingly. There was no pride in his loss as there had been in 1960—no opportunity to torture figures into proving that if only one half a vote in every election district in the country had changed he would have been the victor.

It was too much to expect that he would be able to continue living in California, the scene of too many indignities. Even as a boy he had wanted to escape it. He described, in the last sentence of *Six Crises,* how he "used to lie in bed in Yorba Linda, California, and dream of traveling to far-off places when he heard the train whistle in the night. . . ." With a gloating Pat Brown standing over his prostrate body, the sound of the whistle was too compelling to resist.

Elmer Bobst, who was head of Warner-Lambert Pharmaceuticals, in addition to being Nixon's favorite yacht captain, acted as go-between in the negotiations to find him a job in New York. He came up with a senior partnership in the firm of Mudge, Rose, Guthrie and Alexander.

Although it would have been difficult to predict it, this was the move that made it possible for Nixon to rekindle his political hopes in the years to come. Ensconced at Mudge *et al* was future Attorney General John Mitchell, the man who was to lead Nixon's successful campaign in 1968 and spearhead his drive in '72, and Len Garment, the young lawyer from Brooklyn whose contributions as organizer, house intellect and morale rebuilder were invaluable in the final selling job. But in 1963 he was not seeking a new campaign organization, but balm. For Nixon had reached the bottom in national politics, which for a man of his disposition was the bottom of the universe.

If he had not committed himself to the California race, there seems little reason to doubt that he would have been the logical choice for the

Republican Presidential nomination in 1964. But he required a crisis atmosphere in his life, a situation in which he could compete, a race he could run. The reasons he gave for making such an obviously foolish attempt were weak and unconvincing. Chotiner knew what should have been done, *and so did he*. And now, having shoved all of his sizable pile of chips into the center of the table in a badly judged attempt to bluff the strong hand out, he found he had lost the bankroll he had so carefully accumulated.

Earl Mazo and Stephan Hess, in their 1968 contribution to campaign literature entitled *Nixon, A Political Portrait*, report that "Nixon confided to a few intimates that he aimed sooner or later to get into a big city law practice." New York had been the magnet from the beginning. He was looking for a challenge, something to lend color to what was essentially a colorless personal view of life, something that would drive thoughts of defeat from his mind.

In an interview with Robert J. Donovan of the Los Angeles *Times* in the mid-1960s, he revealed some of the near-maniacal attitudes he brought with him to Fun City.

> New York is *very cold* and *very ruthless* and very exciting, and, therefore, an interesting place to live. It has many great disadvantages but also many advantages. The main thing, *it is a place where you can't slow down*—a fast track. Any person tends to vegetate unless he is moving on a fast track. New York is a very challenging place to live. You have to bone up to *keep alive* in the competition here. [Italics added]

There is the sense of motion in what he says, but motion without meaning. He ran now not to win but to show. He joined the most important men's clubs, the Metropolitan and the Links. He ate at 21 and the Waldorf. His daughters went to the prestigious Finch and Smith colleges. And he bought a cooperative apartment in the same building as Nelson Rockefeller. Set at the southeast corner of Central Park, the white brick tower faced west into the spectacular sunsets over Manhattan's skyline. His apartment was on the fifth floor, above contact with the street, but close enough so that the windows always had to be closed against the noise of all-night traffic along Fifth Avenue.

The area is a mecca for the super-rich. It is doubtful that anyone living within a ten block radius of his apartment earned under $25,000 annually and the median income was probably closer to $100,000. The major embassies cluster there and a sizable number of New York's most opulent restaurants are within walking distance.

Nixon claims to have relished the anonymity of New York life. New Yorkers are so used to seeing celebrities, especially in this nesting area, that he could walk the streets without any fear of having his reveries disturbed by the curious.

Witnesses have described coming upon him moving swiftly along East 60th Street, alone, dressed in a coat too unfashionably long for the mid-1960s, a hat that looked as if it had been worn by a stockbroker at the height of the Depression smashed down over his forehead, and lips which were in constant motion as though in spirited conversation.

His work was far from what it would have been if he had landed a job with Sullivan and Cromwell in 1937 and ended up writing briefs for senior partner John Foster Dulles. His great aptitude for digging into dry accounts of precedent, and compiling vital minutiae was wasted in his new job in the financial district. His legal talent was not the issue when Mudge *et al* had decided to make their bid. It was clearly his name they were hiring, and it was his name they exploited. The drudges in the law library had the pleasure of doing the work he so much enjoyed, while Nixon was trotted out when the occasion arose to impress the impressionable.

Rose Mary Woods was in charge of the staff. Except for her, it had been difficult for Nixon to hold onto office help. He was too harsh and unappreciative a task-master. In the last week of the 1956 campaign, his entire office staff, with the exception of Miss Woods, had mutinied and handed in their resignation. And he had sparked a similar blow-up toward the end of the 1960 campaign when he rebuked his overworked staff for not pursuing his ambitions with the same fierce devotion he displayed.

The job at Mudge *et al* was not as demanding. Besides, Pat was a more or less steady per diem helper. She told a television audience in September, 1971, of the joy she felt during those days of typing letters and taking shorthand in Dick's outer office. Her only problem was "ducking behind the door" when a client came in. She was embarrassed at the thought that anyone might find her doing the only job she had ever really wanted to do.

He spent his leisure hours watching professional sports on television. He was hooked on football, but settled for basketball, golf, or baseball, during the off-season. Charles "Bebe" Rebozo was now his closest personal friend. The *nouveau riche* Floridian, who made his first big money by lending small sums to poor people at perilously high interest rates, made him feel at ease as no one else did. He seemed to be one of the few people who offered friendship but wanted no favors from Nixon in return.

In New York Nixon formed no lasting friendships. It was impossible for him to feel comfortable with men who had inherited their wealth and would pass it on to their children multiplied with little effort of their own. Men like neighbor Rockefeller, who not only had all the money in the world but felt at ease in any company, were held in awe. His friend Earl Mazo described him as ". . . shy and taciturn. He broods, abhors backslapping and gives the appearance of being a friendless 'loner,' a too-smooth and humorless perfectionist." Such a man could never drop his guard and, although they occupied the same building for years, he and Rockefeller scarcely knew what each other's apartments looked like. It was a relationship of many complexities, few of which were affirmative.

With the possible exception of the years he spent in the Navy, these years in New York after he lost the 1962 election saw the greatest change in the adult Richard Nixon. He turned fifty. His hairline began to recede at the temples and thin at the widow's peak. The youthful look he had retained into middle age was replaced by an anemic pallor, the trademark of aging bankers.

After a while, the challenge of moneymaking palled. It seemed improbable the last hurrah had been heard in 1962. Politics was Nixon's preoccupation and going on was not a matter of question but of necessity. All those pledges he had signed, copies of which Pat made him carry around in his wallet, could not steel him sufficiently to resist the urge to approach the starting line once again. He shared this characteristic with Stassen, the one Republican he probably disliked most. Driven by a uniquely sadistic devil—now an object of patronizing curiosity, Nixon embraced the tedious ritual of repetitious speeches delivered before dull gatherings. They were generally the most lifeless he had ever made. The two issues in his political career, the Communist threat of internal subversion and Democratic corruption were passé.

By 1963, during the golden age of Kennedy's Camelot, neither issue had its old potency. Catholic Kennedy, who had always been careful to maintain a posture of neutral friendliness toward Joe McCarthy, was immune to Redbaiting. Kennedy's Administration had been largely free of scandal. Finally, using simple credit expansion devices, the last Eisenhower recession had been brought under control. The country experienced an uninterrupted upward movement in economic activity while Kennedy was in office.

Nixon found little to snipe at in the domestic sphere. In foreign affairs the two saw America's role in identical terms. Kennedy's bumbled effort in the Bay of Pigs might have offered Nixon an opportunity to score some political points; however, he had helped initiate this gunboat diplomacy during the last months of the Eisenhower reign and was in no position to take advantage of the fiasco that resulted.

In Vietnam the situation was even less promising. Kennedy and Nixon saw eye to eye on the need to escalate the war. The imperfect peace that had existed between 1956 and 1960 was slowly giving way to active guerrilla warfare. Nixon wanted the United States to take a more direct part in the budding war.

Kennedy made his first commitments in this direction in the spring of 1961 when he sent 400 Special Forces troops and 100 military advisors to South Vietnam to join those men stationed there by Eisenhower. The moves were unpublicized. However, had Nixon heard of them, there is every reason to believe he would have applauded vigorously. Although Kennedy managed to resist hawkish pressure to send American combat troops to Vietnam, he actively pursued a policy that increased American participation all across the board. Henry Cabot Lodge, Nixon's 1960 running mate, was Kennedy's instrument in this matter.

The United States had become so deeply involved in South Vietnam that when the decision was made that President Ngo Dinh Diem had to be deposed, Lodge and the CIA were actively enlisted in removing him from office. His assassination on November 1, 1963, according to the Pentagon Papers, took place as they turned their heads politely aside.

Three weeks later Lee Harvey Oswald assassinated President Kennedy in Dallas. For Nixon the loss was dramatic and personal. He had admired and feared Kennedy since they both entered Congress in the freshman class of 1947. They had engaged in their first public debate as Congressmen that year when they traveled to Pittsburgh to disagree over the merits of the Taft-Hartley law. The rise in their careers had, in many respects, followed a parallel curve so that there was almost a mystique of co-development about them. More than any man in the country, Nixon could say, *There but for the grace of God, go I.* Had he been elected in 1960 there seems no reason to think that by November 22, 1963, Oswald would have wanted any less to kill *him.*

If Nixon had taken that day in Dallas as a departure point and allowed his interest in politics to subside, everyone would have understood. Instead, there was an intensification of his political activity. Obviously the New York track was not fast enough.

XXV.

Dependable Dick

"There is no doubt that Goldwater had the nomination wrapped up two years before the convention," said Murray Chotiner, explaining the realities of Richard Nixon's predicament. "Otherwise Dick would have wanted to run again in 1964."

When Nixon lost in California Goldwater recognized his moment had come. Without hesitating he put Taft's Southern stratagem of 1952 into operation and within a few weeks had enough commitments from Southern segregationists and Midwestern conservatives to tuck the nomination safely in his pocket. Despite this, he was shrewd enough to continue the nomination charade up until the final moment of the convention during the summer of 1964. Goldwater had learned this lesson well from his philosophical master. He was also in debt to Nixon, who had always cultivated the Southern fields with great care.

The only man who seemed capable of heading Goldwater off was Rockefeller, then serving his second term as governor of New York. However, Rockefeller, faced with likely defeat, was displaying more than his usual ambivalence about taking the final plunge.

Henry Cabot Lodge viewed the possibility of an uncontested Goldwater nomination as a disaster for the Republican Party. Having been so influential in convincing Ike to run in 1952, he was outraged at the thought that the party Eisenhower had remolded in his middle-of-the-road image was about to be captured by a pre-McKinley Know-Nothing. Before the primaries began, Lodge asked Lyndon Johnson, who was enjoying the Republican spectacle immensely, to relieve him as ambassador to Saigon and allow him to return to the Republican wars. In a manner most courageous, because it was so obviously predestined to failure, Lodge denounced Goldwater's radical rightism and declared he was willing to place his career in the Republican Party on the line in order to stop him.

Nixon seemed to perk up. Somehow the blast from Saigon had stirred hope that there was a chance to recover some ground. Lodge's supporters had entered the ambassador's name in the March 10 New Hampshire primary. He defeated Goldwater and Nixon came in fourth. There was just enough encouragement for Nixon to go fishing in troubled waters. On April 1, 1964, a plane landed at Saigon airport and out stepped Richard Nixon. The reporters pressed him to reveal the purpose of his unusual flight. After all, it was not every day of the year that a New York lawyer visited this embattled part of the world.

Nixon brushed aside such queries with a tight smile and a wave of his hand. But he was perfectly willing to discuss the escalating Vietnam conflict. He praised Defense Secretary Robert D. McNamara's conduct of the war. "We should stick to this," he declared. "There should be one voice—not this continued situation of going uphill one day and down the next."

This merely confirmed Nixon's longstanding leadership in the field of Vietnamese military adventurism. One reporter, apparently suspecting that Nixon might be split off from the Democratic administration if the political aspect of the problem could be presented to him, asked if he expected the war to become an issue in the Presidential race. "I hope it doesn't," he responded sincerely. "It will only become an issue if the policy has weaknesses worthy of criticism, if it is plagued with inconsistency, improvisation and uncertainty. That has been the case in the past."

And then as if to remove any doubts about the nature of his commitment, he added, "There is no substitute for victory in South Vietnam."

He and Lodge then met, and the purpose of his trip was clear. They spoke of Goldwater and Rockefeller and then changed the subject and spoke about Rockefeller and Goldwater. Nothing Nixon told Lodge could convince him that opposition to Goldwater was useless. Nothing Lodge told Nixon could convince him to join him in a fight for principle.

The next day Nixon flew to Bangkok, Thailand, a nation under sufficient control that a press conference might be held with some confidence it would not end in the explosion of a terrorist bomb. Displaying a statesmanlike attitude, he hacked out new ground for the most militant of his countrymen. "I would not rule out action in North Vietnam if that were what was necessary to win in South Vietnam." No prominent American politician had as yet proposed so radical an expansion of the war. Over a year was to pass before Lyndon Johnson, even with such bi-partisan support, could work up his nerve to contemplate following Nixon's advice.

Nixon told the perspiring newsmen he opposed North-South peace negotiations. "I can't visualize the North sitting down with the South and agreeing to anything that would not lead to increased Communist domination," he explained with utter conviction.

Inevitably, the questions turned to politics. He immediately revealed that he still hoped lightning would strike. Carefully explaining he was not a *candidate* for the nomination, he added, smiling modestly, that he would, however, "do whatever the party wishes me to do." He was just a good soldier in the ranks, prepared, once again, to make the supreme sacrifice if it would be universally helpful to the party. And then he added cryptically, just as he was about to signal an end to the conference, "I will indicate when there is change."

On returning home he tried to heat up the expectations of those dissatisfied with the front runner by making his availability abundantly clear. "My interest in the party nomination is only if the convention could not agree on another candidate."

As the weeks passed, however, Nixon was forced to accommodate himself to reality. On May 2, after a string of poor showings in the primaries, Goldwater swept the Texas balloting. Lodge, recognizing the futility of challenging him in this predominantly conservative state, had not entered the primary. Goldwater amassed in excess of 90,000 votes, while the almost complete count showed Nixon with 4,154 votes. What may have discouraged Nixon most was that his old South Pacific buddy, Harold Stassen, received 4,525 votes at a comparable moment in the count.

Nixon publicly revealed his sense of resignation during this week when he said that "the real ball game" was being won by Goldwater because of the delegate strength he was amassing. "So great is the Goldwater strength in local and state Republican organizations that he has gone on collecting delegates despite his setbacks."

Most Americans may have been unaware that Goldwater had wrapped up the nomination, but Nixon had come this way too often not to understand the signs. He now fell into step behind the Arizona Senator, the first American of direct Jewish ancestry to be nominated for the Presidency of the United States. In the final analysis Nixon realized the value of the nomination was questionable. Johnson, still benefitting from the spill-over of sympathy which had engulfed him after Kennedy's assassination, looked unbeatable.

Goldwater swept the convention and when he got up to deliver his acceptance speech his confidence knew no bounds. Unlike Nixon, who was primarily concerned with politics, Goldwater was an ideologue, primarily concerned with issues. Whereas Nixon's intent was always to be careful, Goldwater was reckless in his desire to proselytize for the cause. Given that conviction and his unbridled confidence, it is not remarkable to find him committing a monumental political blunder as soon as the nomination was safely in hand. His acceptance speech set the tone of his entire campaign, and condemned him to a defeat of horrendous proportions.

With the glint of a prophet in his eyes, he stared unflinchingly into the television camera and declared that "extremism in defense of liberty is no vice," and then, as if to show the other side of the coin, "moderation in the pursuit of justice is no virtue."

Although a generous reader might conclude in the dispassionate climate brought on by distance and dimmed ardor that Goldwater did not mean he intended to set up concentration camps, many a viewer who sat at home thought he heard a clear and distressing call to vigilanteeism. The use of the word "extremism" was particularly unfortunate, for it tied in altogether too neatly in the popular mind with the knowledge that some of Goldwater's money and support came from extremists, specifically, the John Birch Society.

The outcry was instant and ruinous. It was apparent, even at that early date, that he was bound to lose. Most major figures in the party's liberal wing publicly denounced him. The New York contingent was notable for its unanimity—Rockefeller and the state Senators, Jacob Javits and Kenneth B. Keating, abandoned the ticket.

Rockefeller later explained, "Senator Goldwater had advocated making Social Security voluntary, withdrawal from the United Nations, giving control of the use of nuclear weapons to field commanders, leaving the problems of civil rights to the states . . . selling T.V.A., and the immediate termination of farm price supports."

That catalogue of sins was more than enough to convince Rockefeller to take extensive vacations during the heat of this hapless campaign.

In the face of the clear knowledge that Goldwater was taking the party down the road to another defeat, it is remarkable to consider the role Nixon determined to assume. Instead of cutting his personal losses by staying as far away from the debacle as possible, he wrapped himself in the bloody flag and prepared to go down with the sinking Goldwater. His behavior looked suicidal. He campaigned as he had not in years, criss-crossing the country to the point of exhaustion, one of the few prominent Republicans to offer the moribund Goldwater aid.

In retrospect it appears that Nixon had, along with most politicians, concluded Goldwater was a sure loser. However, unlike many Republican leaders, who were repelled by Goldwater's opinions and style, Nixon saw an advantage in party regularity above personal preference.

In an endeavor to get Goldwater past the difficulties he had heaped up for himself, Nixon served as his straight man. He wrote a letter on August 4 to the bewildered nominee, suggesting that "it would clear the air once and for all" if he would issue a clarifying statement on extremism. Indicating he welcomed the opportunity to carry on a public dialogue with such a distinguished American as Richard Nixon, Goldwater released his most prominent supporter's letter with his answer. It was services of this sort Nixon rendered Goldwater, while *Republicans* like Nelson Rockefeller and George Romney were dogging him.

As if to make his position absolutely clear, on August 9 Nixon appeared on Senator Keating's weekly television program in New York. Without ruffling the apostate Keating's feathers, he smilingly told him that he intended "to do everything I can" in behalf of the Goldwater ticket. It did seem odd, in the face of the Republican stampede to desert the immediate vicinity surrounding Goldwater, to see the most astute of all Republicans weld himself to an irretrievably lost cause.

Chotiner explained it in terms of the dove and the saint. "He supported Goldwater in 1964 all the way because he felt that once the party picked the man, he had to support him."

Elements of such a philosophy undoubtedly adhered to Nixon's calculated enthusiasm. He bore no personal affection for the Arizona Senator, and on the surface only party loyalty could have warranted his huge investment of time and effort. In reality, however, he was investing in an old favorite cause, the advancement of Richard Nixon.

Even tragedy was made to work for that cause. On September 9, while Nixon was touring Iowa with Goldwater, Checkers died. One who remembered presented the bereaved with Checkers II. But Dick gave the dog away, perhaps out of respect for the memory of the newly departed, or out of fear that another scandal might somehow rend the heavens.

On the first Tuesday after the first Monday in November another funeral was held, this time for the ambitions of Barry Goldwater. He was buried with the greatest margin of votes ever to divide two major party candidates, 16,000,000. It was the worst Republican defeat since the F.D.R. sweep in 1936. Even the Republican stalwarts of that year, Maine and Vermont, cast their electoral votes for Lyndon Johnson.

Nixon has repeatedly said the worst time in a man's life comes not as he prepares for a crisis, or even while he is in the midst of it. The perilous moment comes afterwards, when a man's defenses are down and he is once again vulnerable to mistakes. By 1964 Nixon had conditioned himself never to let down, and that year some of the most important events took place the day after election, when Goldwater was sleeping it off and Rockefeller was on vacation in Spain. Nixon chose this moment, when the battle appeared to be over, to strike his most effective blows. *Newsweek* magazine quoted him as saying:

This is what's going to happen. It will take a couple of months for the dust to settle. Then Barry will be dropped like a hot potato. Rockefeller, Lodge and Cliff Case have had it, too. The party will never forgive them for dragging their feet.

There seemed no compassion for the cold destiny he predicted for Barry. In fact, his tone was detached, conveying not the slightest sympathy for a man who had suffered a calamity similar in nature, if not in scope, to his own.

One did not have to look far in search of the reason for such callousness. Goldwater was, like himself, a defeated Presidential candidate. When the time came to pick the 1968 nominee, Goldwater would still have to be taken into account. It was necessary in this moment *after* the crisis to keep his guard up and remember that as tempting as it was to be sympathetic, it was more important to eliminate a potential rival.

His treatment of Nelson Rockefeller, an undefeated, and therefore more serious threat, was direct, vicious and permanently effective. On November 5, while absentee ballots were still being counted in Arizona, which finally placed Goldwater's home state in his column by only a handful of votes, Nixon called a press conference, to exercise his prerogatives as Republican elder statesman.

Nixon's purpose was to read Rockefeller out of the party. "Anyone who sits on the sidelines in a struggle," he said, cannot assume a role of leadership afterward. At another point he criticized the "constant sniping from the rear" and snapped, "Mr. Rockefeller has had his pound of flesh."

His friend Earl Mazo, writing the story in the *Times* the next day, included Nixon's comment that "there was so much antipathy against Rockefeller among Republicans around the country that he could no longer be regarded as a party leader outside of New York State."

Rocky had suffered severe setbacks in his faltering drive toward the White House. His second marriage to a much younger woman, whose relationship with Rockefeller led her to divorce her first husband, left much of bluenosed Republican America permanently estranged. But this was the coup de grace. It established in the minds of all decent, hard-working Republican voters that Rocky was not only a dirty old man, but, even worse, a man who thought for himself.

Rockefeller, who had probably been entertaining some hope of picking up the broken pieces of the party after the right-wing disaster, felt the blade slip neatly between his ribs, and cried out in mortal exasperation from Madrid, labelling Nixon's statement "neither factual nor constructive." He spoke of the need for unity. "Mr. Nixon's latest maneuver is hardly calculated to advance this effort," he insisted. Then in an effort to discredit him with a reference to an episode Nixon was trying to live down, he concluded, "This kind of peevish post-election utterance has unfortunately become typical of Mr. Nixon."

The next day, after consulting with Dick, Ike issued a statement. He said that the party's poor showing was the result of a "false image of Republicanism." He wanted that image brought into better focus so that Americans could understand the party was not "primarily for the rich and the privileged." The ties between the Eisenhowers and Nixons were beginning to grow with the first budding of a romance between Ike's grandson David and Nixon's youngest daughter, Julie. Never one to waste a card, Dick had nursed his relations with the aging general. While others were dropping away, Nixon phoned regularly and genuflected even more vigorously than he had in the White House. He was, after all, dependable, perenially ready to serve those who might be of service to him.

It was, therefore, not surprising when he drove off to Wantagh, Long Island, on a cold December 30, to the Bide-a-Wee Home Association. There he attended a solemn ceremony in the pet cemetery as a headstone was erected which read, "Checkers, 1952-64." Even in death one who had been of service could count on dependable Dick.

XXVI.

A Run for the Roses

"I have no intention of entering politics on an elective basis," Nixon said after the Goldwater defeat, which some men took as his way of saying things looked promising.

During December, 1964, he wielded his clout within the disorganized party. He and his chief asset, Eisenhower, called the still shellshocked Goldwater to a meeting in a New York hotel and told him the facts of life. Dean Burch, the Senator's personal choice for National Chairman, had to go. The entire staff of the National Committee must join him in exile. Dick understood the pivotal nature of the National Committee in his career too well to allow it to remain in rival hands.

Not only did Goldwater agree to deliver Burch's head, but he also went along with Nixon's choice of Ray Bliss, of Ohio, as the new National Chairman. Within a few weeks after the Republican Party hit bottom, Nixon had moved in and audaciously selected the key man in the upcoming drive for the 1968 nomination. Choliner explained the reality of the situation: "After Goldwater's defeat, it was clear that Dick was going to be the party nominee in 1968. He had more brownie points than anyone."

Nixon was now in a delicate position. There was no other obvious candidate on the horizon, but a prematurely open drive for power could work against him by making him the natural target for all the other potential candidates. More significantly, it would focus national attention on his every act, increasing the possibility that any minor mistake, which might otherwise be ignored, would be blown up out of all proportion. His challenge was directly parallel to the one he had faced on the eve of his skillfully executed drive for the Vice Presidential nomination in 1952. He was going to have to pursue the nomination without seeming to do so.

There were pitfalls on all sides. It was the year in which Johnson had decided to send American combat troops to fight in Vietnam. It was also the year that black men decided to burn down and loot black homes and businesses in the Watts district of Los Angeles, and the sympathetic reaction of some liberal white Americans toward the rioters was something new that Nixon had to learn to deal with. Had he followed his own natural instincts, he would have blasted out against the coddling of lawbreakers. However, he had chosen to maintain a low profile, and so remained largely silent on this burning issue.

There was only one other politician in the country who shared the spotlight with Nixon that year. He was John V. Lindsay, who was in a remarkable number of ways a taller and more narcissistic version of Richard Nixon. The liberal, Republican-to-be-Democrat, who often voted conservatively in Congress, was making a bid to become mayor of New York. He walked the city streets, peering into garbage cans, often shedding his jacket in egalitarian fashion while chatting with workingmen along the docks. Since there were no other important contests that year, Lindsay's ten months of campaigning kept his picture on front pages, with the result that by the end of 1965 he had been magically transformed into a well-known national figure.

Lindsay's election as Republican mayor of Democratic New York in November, 1965, seemed to present the Republicans with a genuine alternative to Nixon in 1968. He appeared to be a knight in shining armor, who, although essentially a middle-of-the-road politician, had shown a beguiling gift for attracting Democratic voters on the left wing of that party.

Lindsay's political base was Manhattan's silk stocking district, the 17th Congressional District, a polygot area encompassing the blacks and Puerto Ricans of the Lower East Side and the rich radical chic from Greenwich Village to east midtown. Lindsay had managed, since the late 1940s, to placate the often diverse views of these disparate groups by a combination of sleight-of-hand and handsome smile.

Nixon's distaste for Lindsay developed naturally out of their conflicting positions, and rivalry, within the Republican Party. However, its more enduring aspect came from firsthand knowledge of the man. For Nixon was one of Lindsay's constituents and had watched with increasing anger as Lindsay spent the seven weeks before assuming office on January 1, 1966, negotiating a union contract with Michael Quill, and then fumbled the city into its first subway strike five minutes after taking office.

Never one for anything more violent than a Gaelic exchange of barroom insults, Quill was terrified at the position into which the white knight was forcing him. All he wanted was $35 million for his workers, which was a sum so short of their needs that he had no idea how he was going to sell them this sell-out. Instead the mayor refused to go above $25 million, and did his negotiations in public, not decorously in private as had Robert Wagner, Jr., a man who knew how to preserve the dignity of a *labor boss* who was willing to compromise the interests of his men.

Furthermore, "Lindsly," as Quill persisted in calling him, was threatening—and in fact sent him to—jail, where he suffered a heart attack from which he died within a few weeks. When the final settlement came, the package was expanded by the two-week strike into a $72 million tab for the city.

Lindsay immediately went on television, even while Quill was in the coma that preceded his death, and claimed he had scored a tremendous victory by giving the workers seventy-two million when they would have been willing to settle for thirty-five.

From the picture window of his Central Park apartment, Nixon missed none of this. He watched Lindsay take a city which had been operated on a relatively efficient, if not inspired manner, by a shy but effective Wagner and a professional, capable civil service, and convert it into an outstanding example of urban decay.

In short, Nixon quickly learned not to take Lindsay seriously.

Freed of any worrisome thought of rivals, Nixon might have used this period to rest and build the image of a statesman which is so easy to merchandise on thirty-second television commercials. But this was not his way.

There was something outrageously incongruous about his behavior during 1965 and 1966. He had finally achieved some sort of status. A Wall Street lawyer, with sumptuous offices at 20 Broad Street, he was now the seniormost partner in the newly named firm of Nixon, Mudge, Rose, Guthrie, Alexander & Mitchell. His income was in excess of $200,000 a year, received from tax deferred earnings on *Six Crises*, and largely public relations retainers from Pepsi-Cola, Mutual of New York, Studebaker-Packard, The Irving Trust, and Warner-Lambert, among others. Yet he spent the months before the 1965 off-year elections speaking to any group that would hear him, often to audiences of only 30 or 40 people, and eating cottage cheese and pineapple lunches in diners and small-town kitchens across America. Not for himself, you understand, but for all those good Republicans who were running for alderman and justice of the peace.

His effort drew little notice in the national press, but he *was* earning the gratitude of men who might some day be in a position to return the favor. His expenses, as in the old days of the fund scandal, were being paid in part by a group of personal and business friends who undoubtedly saw some benefit to themselves growing out of this form of generosity.

By 1966 his role as spokesman for the party, which did not seem like such an asset at that high point in Johnson's popularity, was clearly established. With the exception of Lindsay, who was having his troubles in an erupting New York, the rising men in the party were all engaged in election campaigns. Rockefeller in New York, Romney in Michigan and Ronald Reagan in California confined their activity to state boundaries and made a studied effort to eschew national issues. The field was open to Nixon.

In early 1966 a group of about twenty-five Nixon partisans, mostly based in Wall Street circles, decided they would bankroll a year-long Nixon campaign tour. Their purported reason for this maneuver was to help Republican candidates. Peter Flanigan of Dillon Read, whom Theodore White identified in 1969 as the "inspiring spirit" of this "Congress '66" cabal, described them: "We didn't know who the proper Congressmen to support were in Missouri and California. We didn't know how to spend money and we wanted to help elect Republicans; so we put the money in the hands of a man who knew where it should go." In 1971 Flanigan was described by one of "the old Nixon gang," whom he helped elbow out of the picture, as "a fast buck guy who doesn't know a damn thing about politics and has nothing more than a financial interest in Dick."

There seems little doubt that what brought this group of "inspired" amateurs together was less a spirit of mystical communion with faceless Republicans out there in the continental void, than the reviving hopes that Nixon might once again be a Presidential candidate. Three of them were Nixon's young law associates, Len Garment, John Sears and Tom Evans. Hobart Lewis, Executive Editor of the *Reader's Digest*, Richard Amberg, publisher of the St. Louis *Globe-Democrat*, Maurice Stans and John Lodge were all old Nixon friends. Clearly, Nixon was assembling the skeletal structure of a campaign apparatus.

The Republican Congressional Campaign Committee, uncharacteristically building up a rival power group within the party, donated $30,000 to Nixon's efforts. Miss Helen Clay Frick signed two dozen checks, each for one thousand dollars, which she turned over to Nixon to use on the tour to distribute to Congressional candidates as he saw fit. This had the effect among fund-starved candidates of making Nixon a man to be wooed.

The influence of rich men's money in Nixon's corner was shockingly illustrated during his drive for the Presidency in 1968. Miss Frick apparently saw nothing disreputable about putting $24,000 in Dick Nixon's hand for what was essentially his own personal use. Bankers, oilmen, and real estate speculators rushed to throw their cash at his feet, and he saw nothing ungraceful in his act of stooping to pick it up.

An additional $60,000 was raised by Flanigan from Wall Street sources, which made a good deal more possible. Traveling with Patrick Buchanan, a young newspaperman on leave from Amberg's *Globe-Democrat*, and William Safire, 37, recruited from his 1960 campaign as a public relations officer, Nixon raced through 30,000 miles in eighty-two Congressional districts.

As election day neared, the meetings of the cabal at the Metropolitan Club became more festive. Dissatisfaction with Lyndon Johnson was growing. Campuses country-wide had been exploding during the spring and protest at the escalating military effort in Vietnam was intensifying. It was clear there would be a resurgence of Republican strength in Congress. After the low point of Republican hopes reached in the 1964 Goldwater wipe-out, there was really no place to go but up. The major effort now became to identify Nixon with that rise in Republican fortunes.

Luck, as was so often the case in his checkered career, smiled on Nixon during the first week in November. President Johnson had just returned from a trip to Vietnam and had issued a statement aimed at presenting his policy in the best possible light. Nixon prepared an answer, in his role as leader of the opposition. When Johnson read Nixon's response in the papers the next morning, he called a press conference to denounce the one man in the Republican Party he had reason to know was most in agreement with his military policy in Vietnam.

In a blast against Nixon, whom he referred to as "a chronic campaigner," he drew attention to what had, to that point, been a largely ignored campaign effort by Nixon. Rather than satisfy himself with defending his Vietnam policy, he launched a personal attack at Nixon. "He never did really recognize what was going on when he had an official position in the government," he said, the contempt in his voice barely under control.

Nixon could not have been happier. He demanded and received time on all the major networks to answer Johnson. This answer, a classic instance of saying nothing in statesmanlike tones, two days before the election, allowed Nixon to claim credit for the strong showing made by many Republicans. "It's a sweep, I tell you, it's a sweep," he told everyone who came within range.

It was far from that. The Democrats still controlled the House and the Senate. But, there were forty-seven new Republicans in the House and three new Senators, which lent some truth to his claim. Furthermore, some candidates with whom he was closely associated did well. Robert Finch, running for lieutenant governor of California on the same ticket with Ronald Reagan, received 1,200,000 votes while Reagan garnered 993,739. Nixon tried to emphasize the good news for his friend Finch, while overlooking the fact that four years earlier he had lost to the same Pat Brown by 296,758.

That seemed to have been Nixon's chief defense against his former sins, the memory of his enemies. He had been around so long by 1966 that the contradictory statements, the diametrically opposite positions taken on numerous issues, the insidious remarks about noble men, the audacious smears, the incredible posturing had all somehow faded. The Nixon his ad men wanted elected was the man they created and carried around in their portfolios. The Nixon who wanted to be the thirty-seventh President of the United States, unfortunately, was molded by the betrayals of two decades and the self-inflicted character wounds of all overly ambitious men.

XXVII.

The Winner, but Not Yet Champ

Hannah's death in 1967 brought about another display of Richard Nixon's obtuseness. He chose his favorite evangelist, Billy Graham, to deliver the graveside eulogy for his Quaker mother. Acts of this sort, by a man who might rule the most powerful country in the world, were permissible, he seemed to say. Who in the Republican Party could challenge such a man?

For a while it looked like it might be George Romney. Romney had followed the traditional path trod by those interested in becoming President. He had succeeded in winning one job after another, and doing well in each new assignment. His business career, crowned with a spectacular turnabout in the financial situation of the American Motors Company after he became its president, was proof, in the American tradition, that he knew how to get things done. When he turned to politics in 1962, his efforts were once again successful. First elected as governor of Michigan in that year by 80,573, he was reelected every two years by larger vote counts until 1966, when he rolled up an impressive margin of 527,047.

What made Romney a particularly threatening candidate to Nixon was his alliance with Nelson Rockefeller, who was at another low point in his enthusiasm for seeking the Presidency. However, he was willing to play the roll of king maker. Two weeks after Rockefeller and Romney had been reelected in 1966 they joined forces at the Dorado Beach Hotel in Puerto Rico, cheered by the latest polls that showed Romney leading President Johnson by 54 to 46 percent.

Romney maintained this edge in the polls for the next six months, while Nixon let him burn himself out in the early part of the race. Dick went about his business quietly, hoping the full glare of publicity would soon show Romney's clay feet. It was essentially the strategy of a confident man. And Nixon had every reason to be confident. The Taft-Goldwater elements in the

GOP which, short of a miracle like Eisenhower, dominated the party, were now turning to him. The fact that Rockefeller openly committed himself to Romney was the kiss of death for the earnest Mormon, as far as Barry's friends were concerned. They were looking for a stick with which to beat their bleeding-heart, turncoat enemies within the party, and Richard Nixon was the kind of seasoned lumber that perfectly fitted their requirements.

Nixon decided he would spend six months in 1967 as far from the scene as possible, while Romney had the dubious honor of trying to answer all those nasty questions at daily press conferences about the increasingly unpopular Vietnam war. Hobart Lewis offered the services of the *Reader's Digest*. It would sponsor a world tour for Dick, and print his articles about famine in Biafra and disease in East Pakistan. While Romney swung at the low fast balls, Dick would be in the shade of the dugout, waiting for the inevitable call to come later in the game.

Before he left, Nixon took part in another one of his controversial land deals with Bebe Rebozo. *Newsday* printed a biting editorial on October 14, 1971, after a six month's investigation by a team of Pulitzer Prize-winning reporters, in which the impropriety of these deals was assessed.

> We are suggesting . . . that the President has shown a lack of sensitivity, responsibility and care in the choice of a friend. All eyes focus on a President. His symbolic role is no less important than his executive one. He should set the moral tone of the nation by all of his actions, private and public. Let's face it: The deals made by Bebe Rebozo and the Smathers gang have tarnished the presidency.

One of the transactions *Newsday* discussed involved a man named Donald Berg. He had been a gold prospector in Alaska, had worked in a Fairbanks saloon and gambling house, and finally drifted south promoting a string of bowling alleys, on his way to the Elysian land-speculating fields of Florida. When I visited Key Biscayne in April, 1972, for research on this book, Berg was one of the few residents on the opulent island willing to speak to anyone asking questions about Rebozo or Nixon.

Berg's major effort went into breathing life into a subdivision called Cape Florida Development on Key Biscayne, just south of Miami, an area largely controlled by Rebozo's Key Biscayne Bank. The subdivision was about 4,500 feet from Nixon's Florida White House, which in February, 1967, was still owned by Dick's close friend of many years Democrat George Smathers.

On February 18, Nixon came to Florida for the wedding of "swinging" Governor Claude Kirk. Berg, who was spending every waking hour in promoting the sale of his expensive lots, had been working on Rebozo to set up a publicity photo with Nixon.

"Our subdivision was fairly dormant up to that time," Berg told *Newsday*, with an openness which stemmed from his understanding nothing but good could come from the widest possible dissemination of the news that he not only associated with Klondike five-card stud specialists, but also had business dealings with the President of the United States. "The island had been through a couple of hurricanes. . . . I believe he [Nixon] had just gotten into town the day before. . . . I think I talked to Bebe and suggested, you know, that when Mr. Nixon came in I'd appreciate it if he came by the office. I had a photographer from the island. I've still got the negative. . . . It was made into an eight-by-ten glossy."

Berg was apparently a man who didn't mind giving away prints, but knew negatives had to be kept in a safe place. The picture of Nixon shaking hands with Berg, with Bebe smilingly standing to one side, appeared in papers all over the country. "All of a sudden people knew where Key Biscayne was," Berg delightedly confessed. "He exposed the product like soap on TV."

In consideration for this service, Nixon was allowed to buy two lots in Berg's development, for which he had been dickering for several months through Rebozo, at a discount that came to $20,000. Francisco Saralegui, Cape Florida's vice president, said he would have been even more generous with Nixon if he had had his way. "He was a public figure. To be honest," Saralegui said, in an attempt to point a moral, "you have to take the publicity value into account. If it had been me, I wouldn't have charged him anything."

Bebe was also allowed to purchase the lot adjoining Dick's, at the same discount, a favor extended to no other sun-lover. Nixon recorded the purchase of the first lot on April 4, 1967 in the Dade County clerk's office. However, the sale of the second lot remained unrecorded for over four years. The tax bills for the first lot were sent by the county to a California law firm headed by one of Nixon's major campaign fundraisers, Herbert W. Kalmbach. However, the county sent tax bills for the unregistered lot to Berg's Cape Florida Development Company, since, on the record, it appeared to be the owner. Berg has subsequently maintained that he merely forwarded those bills to Kalmbach.*

Time magazine, March 27, 1972, revealed how beneficial it is to be a friend of Richard Nixon. Kalmbach had quit his insurance job in 1960 to work for Nixon's election. After the 1962 debacle, Nixon sent a note to some of his California campaign workers: "If you need a job, get in touch with Herb, and he will fix something up for you." Kalmbach became vice president of Macco Corporation, a land-development company. In 1968, he was one of Nixon's chief fundraisers. His home base was the Lincoln Club in conservative Orange County, near San Diego. The millionaire members of that club still boast that, without their money-raising efforts, Nixon would not be President. Just prior to Nixon's election, Kalmbach organized a new law firm,

Why did such a careful man as Richard Nixon allow this valuable piece of *his* property to remain in the name of Cape Florida Development Company? He was risking the possibility that their bankruptcy might sweep away his investment. He has also refused to explain why his tax bills were not sent to him.

The fact that he had the time to spend pursuing financial advantage is an indication of the confidence he now felt. A caucus of his new cabal in the Waldorf Towers on January 7, 1967 had convinced him that the nomination was probably his. At the meeting were Bob Finch, Peter Flanigan, William Safire and, representing the new braintrust from his law firm, thirty-six-year-old Tom Evans. They went over the delegate count for the convention, which was still over a year and a half away. They concluded he had, at that moment, reasonable expectations of 603 votes, enough to assure nomination.

Aside from Romney, Nixon felt his chief competition came from personable Charles Percy, the new Senator from Illinois, who had shown his vote-getting appeal by defeating redoubtable Paul Douglas. As far as Rockefeller was concerned, Nixon gave him no chance for the nomination. Conceit and fear mingled in this appraisal, for in reality, Rockefeller, had he been willing to make a determined drive, had the money, experience and personality to give him a real fight.

But Rockefeller was not willing to make the effort at that point. To show his support for Romney, he not only supplied him with speechwriters and money, but he encouraged Leonard Hall to accept the management of his campaign. Clifford Folger, from the desk of his Washington bank, took charge of Romney's finances. The Eastern Establishment's choice was immediately apparent, and it was equally clear that, without an Eisenhower, the liberal wing of the party was not likely to have its way this time.

But Romney's campaign really came apart as a result of a statement he made on a Detroit taped television program, the Lou Gordon Telephone-in Show, on August 31, 1967. Up to that point he had managed to retain his lead among Republican aspirants, in the Gallup and Harris polls, although, as Nixon predicted, constant exposure had worn away some of his support.

Gordon, the program's moderator, was pressing him about his vacillating position on Vietnam. He asked the tired governor, "Isn't your position a bit inconsistent with what it was, and what do you propose we do now?"

Kalmbach, DeMarco, Knapp & Chillingworth. He was so sure of his place in the scheme of things, and the success of his new venture, that he rejected Nixon's offer to become Under Secretary of Commerce. Instead, within months after Nixon's election, money circles on the West Coast referred to Kalmbach as "the President's lawyer." In four years Kalmbach, *et al*, mushroomed from a four-man fledgling fellowship, handling the business of a few local clients, to an operation using the services of twenty-two lawyers. Among the thirty new clients, representing some of the nation's largest firms, is the Marriott Hotel chain, whose airline catering service is now headed by Donald Nixon.

Romney displayed the handsome smile, calculated to be at least fifty percent of any answer he gave, and said, "Well, you know when I came back from Vietnam, I just had the greatest brainwashing that anybody can get when you go over to Vietnam. Not only by the generals, but also by the diplomatic corps over there, and they do a very thorough job. And since returning from Vietnam, I've got into the history of Vietnam, all the way back into World War II and before. And, as a result, I have changed my mind."

Five days later, when the tape was actually shown, the news media seized on that one remark as proof positive that George Romney did not have too considerable a brain to wash. Undoubtedly the judgment was unfair, but it took the wind out of Romney's sail. He pressed on somewhat irresolutely, under prodding from an unhappy Rockefeller, who saw Nixon's uncontested victory as the clear result of Romney's withdrawal.

The issue was finally decided just before the New Hampshire primary in 1968. Romney, ever faithful to duty, although the polls indicated all hope was gone, was campaigning in the New Hampshire shows. Nixon eyed him tensely from New York, after finally announcing his own candidacy. This was to be a critical test. Was Romney making any progress in his attempt to recoup his earlier popularity? Were even bedrock organization Republicans weary of Nixon?

There was some reason to worry. Although Nixon had always been a favorite of the party regulars who came out to cast their votes, New Hampshire was noted for its unpredictability on primary day. Furthermore, Rockefeller had many confederates in that state and he was putting a good deal of effort into Romney's campaign.

Nixon was nervous. The pressure kept building, as it always did, but he was not as young as he had been. Coping with tension was becoming a greater problem. Reaching out for a known quantity, he dispatched Chotiner to the battlefront.

"I went up to New Hampshire shortly before the primary," Chotiner told me proudly. "I was there at the same time as Romney. I attended one of his press conferences. I just wanted to get the feel of the state. I wandered around Manchester. I'd drive into a gas station and get a couple of gallons, then go to a couple of more getting two or three gallons each time, and feeling people out. I ate more donuts and drank more coffee than I ever did before in my life. Then I came back to New York and told Dick that he had nothing to worry about."

From other equally reliable sources, Romney received the same message and, on February 28, just before the primary, announced that he was withdrawing from the race. When Rockefeller, now under renewed pressure to contest the nomination, subsequently told a mid-March press conference he would only accept the nomination if it was handed to him on a platter, the fight was over. It was Richard Nixon, by default, by superior scheming, and by habit.

For by this time Nixon was the man that the Republicans ran for President. They did it every once in a while and would probably consider doing it until he became senile or the Constitutional limit on his occupation of the office was reached.

The problem now became one of walking that perilously narrow line between opposing philosophies. How could he manage to avoid taking a stand on divisive issues that would alienate large sections of the electorate? The main one to be studiously avoided was the Vietnam war. The country was too sharply divided. No matter which position he took, people were bound to be outraged. Complicating the matter further was the fact that he personally remained a hawk, convinced of the correctness of Johnson's policy of escalation, and determined that if he won in November, he should not become the first President to lose a war.

But how to avoid letting the doves know that. Many of them were talking of voting for him. Leonard Bernstein told a Madison Square Garden rally for Eugene McCarthy that if Hubert Humphrey won the Democratic nomination, he would vote for Nixon. He then explained what passed for his reasoning. Nixon, he said, would make things so bad that there would be a revolution, and then at least the air would be cleared. That there was a small number of people in the audience of 20,000 who applauded his madcap remarks is a measure of the fact that if Nixon did nothing to disturb the tenuous equilibrium of that quixotic group, he had every reason to believe their votes would be cast in his column on Election Day.

The January Tet offensive by the Viet Cong had been a turning point in public support for the war. Although the Communists had been repulsed on every front and had not managed to capture a single city they had attacked, the impression somehow gained currency that Tet had been a victory for the forces of Ho Chi Minh. How much of this can be attributed to wish fulfillment, on the part of men who were not outraged by the sight of middle-aged Americans walking down Fifth Avenue in the publicity capital of the country waving Viet Cong flags, is difficult to determine. What is not difficult to determine is the fact that support for the war ebbed from Tet on.

Some Americans were so tired of this apparently endless war that other realities began to be viewed in terms of fantasy. So that when Eugene McCarthy challenged Lyndon Johnson in the New Hampshire primary, spending millions of dollars in an active campaign while Johnson said nothing to encourage his supporters in that state, and Johnson nevertheless defeated the Wisconsin Senator, McCarthy's supporters proceeded to label his defeat a victory. On the basis of this misrepresentation, and ten million dollars which his rich friends contributed during the next five months, he was able to make the Vietnam war the central issue in the 1968 campaign.

So overwhelmed was Johnson by the outraged press reaction to his Vietnam policy that he took the occasion of a nationally televised speech on that subject on Sunday night, March 31, to announce that he would not seek reelection. Although he had been elected in 1964 by the largest margin ever achieved in a Presidential contest, and would probably have won in November, 1968, had he allowed himself to be renominated, the previous three years had so robbed him of the will to go on that facing more hostility seemed sheer masochism. In his 1971 memoirs, *The Vantage Point: Perspectives of the Presidency, 1963-1969*, Johnson spoke of his fear of "disability" because of his 1955 heart attack. "I frankly did not believe in 1968 that I could survive another four years of the long hours and unremitting tensions I had just gone through."

The assassination of Martin Luther King, Jr. a few days after Johnson's unexpected announcement, and the subsequent assassination of Robert Kennedy in Los Angeles in June, made Johnson's decision to seek the serenity of his Texas ranch seem even more reasonable.

Pessimism over the condition of the country and its destiny gripped the public. Although unemployment was practically non-existent, the remaining pockets, expecially among unskilled adolescents who had dropped out of school, were highlighted in the media. Instead of pointing with pride to the fact that more people were employed than ever before in the history of the world, the press belabored Johnson for not finding work for the handful of Americans no President had ever successfully engaged in useful effort.

Progress toward equality for minority members, accelerated under Johnson's Administration to a point unimagined by reformers in the previous generation, was viewed by militants, who had access to the press, as too little and too late. Revolution was viewed soberly by many influential people as the logical next stage in the development of a truly democratic society. Men whose preachings could lead nowhere but to the fascism of anarchy were praised on some university campuses as progressive philosophers.

And all this, fundamentally because of the Vietnam war. Johnson was responsible for escalating the war, for taking American boys and sending them to their death in Asia; therefore, nothing he did could stand the test.

Even the rioting that took place in Miami, as Nixon was being nominated, which resulted in the death of four black men, was laid at Johnson's door. And the rioting that took place in Chicago when the Democrats met to nominate Hubert Humphrey clearly was not the fault of the kids who were involved in it, according to these ideologues, but rather a normal result of justified criticism of the war, which could not be confined to the protest areas designated by Mayor Daley's police.

That Richard Nixon managed to win the nomination and conduct a successful campaign without taking a stand on this burning issue is amazing and a measure of the anti-Johnson-Humphrey hostility that existed in the radical recesses of the Democratic party. After the fiasco of the Chicago convention, Nixon led Humphrey in the polls by an astronomical margin.

Nixon's strategy to hold onto that lead was predicated on avoiding any sort of revelation about his Vietnam stance. He combined this with a deft refocusing of issues, so that it would not be necessary for him to comment on Vietnam, or constantly appear to avoid the subject. They key issue was not to be the war, but rather *Crime*. The main effort was to make the biggest possible impact with that issue in the fear-ridden cities of the North, while wooing the traditionally conservative Democratic South, where his political savvy told him the margin for his victory would be found.

Ralph De Toledano tells the story of how he inadvertently acted the catalyst in the reaction that made possible the selection of Spiro Agnew as Vice President—a story that reveals the importance of the "Southern Strategy" in Nixon's mind. Toledano claims that immediately after Nixon was nominated, he was talking to Melvin Laird, soon to be Nixon's Secretary of Defense. Since the question of who would be the Vice Presidential nominee was the only important one left to the convention, Toledano brought the matter up. "It's going to be Chucky-boy," Laird responded.

Toledano was not surprised, since he was one of Nixon's more devoted political admirers, and this seemed a characteristically shrewd Nixon maneuver. Charles Percy was liberal and handsome, Toledano thought. He would disarm the Northern liberals who otherwise might be reluctant to work for Nixon. Toledano passed his intelligence on to the numerous friends who crossed his path, assuming that since Laird had been willing to tell him, a newspaper man, about it, the deal was set. Within two or three hours the world would know what he knew.

To Toledano's chagrin, he suddenly found himself paged by Strom Thurmond. Thurmond, a former Democrat, and arch-segregationist who had run for President against Harry Truman in 1948 because he was too sympathetic to blacks, was now solidly on the Nixon bandwagon.

Ushered into Thurmond's presence, Toledano was shocked to find him furious. "Ralph," he began, his self-control slipping, "I hear Laird says it's going to be *Chucky-boy*. Now, before I go to Dick, I want to hear that story from your own lips."

As soon as Toledano had completed his account, Strom stormed out of the room. When he returned he informed Toledano that Chucky-boy was out and Spiro was in. How had he brought that off, Toledano inquired. "I told Dick that if he went through with it I was going to get up on the floor of the convention and denounce him, and blow up the god-damn party."

The surprise of the convention occurred as a result of Thurmond's enduring clout. John V. Lindsay, super-Republican-liberal, rose to his feet when Nixon's stage manager pointed his finger and delivered a glowing nomination speech for Spiro Agnew, Thurmond's protégé, who had already earned the hatred of civil rights advocates by his tough handling of the spring Baltimore riots.

Once the ticket was fired up, Nixon put his winning strategy into effect. For the last time he was going to use Ike, at that moment close to death. As soon as he had locked up the nomination, Dick urged Republicans to "win this one for Ike." His speeches always attempted to evoke the magic of the hero of Normandy: "I had a good teacher. I am proud to have been part of an administration that ended one war and kept us out of others."

John Mitchell was put in charge of the campaign apparatus, with headquarters on Park Avenue, halfway between Nixon's Central Park apartment and his Broad Street office. In early summer Herb Klein came back to handle the press. However, reflecting the dawn of a new day, where he had previously traveled at Nixon's side in every campaign going back to the early 1950s, he was now given the grandiose title of "Manager of Communications," told he was in charge of formulating policy and left to watch the news tickers in national headquarters.

The only other member of the old Nixon gang who was allowed to play a part in the campaign was Chotiner. He was attached to Mitchell's staff in New York and given the Western territory as his area of responsibility. As one member of the old gang put it, "Murray is strictly a technician. He's a genius. He really is." There was awe in his voice as he spoke of Chotiner. "I've watched him in campaign after campaign, and he really knows politics and how to run a campaign, and how to stay in the background while he does it."

Even in times of plenty geniuses are not always available. For the first time since 1956 Nixon's resident genius was officially back on board. One of his own dicta, time heals all wounds, was proving true. There was scarcely an eyebrow raised when Chotiner was seen walking the carpeted suites of the Park Avenue headquarters.

However, youthful Joe McGinniss was as shocked as if he had seen a ghost rise from the dead, and he scarcely had the presence of mind to turn on his tape recorder. He speaks of the terrible moment in *The Selling of the President 1968*:

And now Murray Chotiner—*Murray Chotiner*—showed up at Fuller and Smith and Ross wanting a five-minute commercial made of an endorsement Dwight Eisenhower had given in July. A film of the endorsement was shown in the screening room. Murray Chotiner sat with his lids hanging low over his eyes. Dwight Eisenhower was wearing pajamas and lying in bed and they had put a microphone around his neck. He was a very sick man.

"No," Harry Treleaven said. "That's one thing I'm not going to do. I'm not going to make a commercial out of that."

"If you can't get five, how about at least a one-minute?" Murray Chotiner said.

"No, I'm not going to make any commercial at all."

Toward the end of the campaign the artists from Madison Avenue came up with a more tasteful presentation. David Eisenhower, sitting next to his wife-to-be, Julie Nixon, was allowed to read his grandfather's endorsement. Although this took the scene away from the death bed, there was a sense that they had sent a boy to do a man's work.

The major problem to settle was how to treat the Vietnam issue during the last three months before the election. It had been a minor miracle that Nixon had been allowed to side-slip taking a position up to this point. However, such luck could not be depended on to continue. The advertising wizards were consulted. Proposals were drawn up which would achieve maximum appeal; not maximum sense, or maximum promise for the country.

H.R. Haldeman, who as chief of staff was now taking a more central position among Nixon's advisors, felt Dick must take no chances. He must be everyone's friend, smile a lot, and project the image of *the New Nixon.* No matter that the "new Nixon" was a gimmick from the previous decade. People had short memories. Haldeman was joined in this advice by Mitchell, Chotiner and all the other men around Nixon shrewd enough to understand the basically cautious nature of their champion.

In every previous campaign Nixon had run around the country as though perpetual motion were the key to success. But this time the emphasis would be on television. This kind of campaign was expensive, but it was exactly suited to Republican pocketbooks. An analysis of reports eventually filed by all national candidates, made by Dr. Herbert E. Alexander, of Princeton, permits only one conclusion. Nixon set out to buy the election, and his affluent friends made it all possible.

Richard Nixon spent $35 million to win. No other candidate in history had even approached that sum. He spent $24.9 million between the end of the Miami convention and Election Day, which more than equalled the total spent by both candidates in 1964. The money came rolling in. W. Clement Stone, a Chicago insurance executive, officially reported donating $154,000; however, there are indications his actual contributions may have reached $500,000. Max Fisher, Detroit industrialist, came through with $103,000 after pouring almost as much down George Romney's rat hole. Henry Salvatori, a Los Angeles oil explorer, who always enjoyed giving money to Nixon, gave him $83,000, when the homosexual scandal in Ronald Reagan's staff caused him to seek a more decorous outlet for his generosity.

But there were even larger donors. The Mellon family, whose banking accumulations in Pittsburgh had always played a role in Republican financing, came through with $279,000, while the Sun Oil family of J. Howard Pew opened their Philadelphia purse to the tune of $208,000. There were ten contributors who knew exactly what they wanted when they separately contributed approximately $50,000: They wanted to be ambassadors, a job that apparently always had a price tag on it. They were all appointed to major embassies around the world, led by IBM's Arthur K. Watson, whose $54,875 took him to Paris, where his propensity for stuffing money into the cleavages of airline hostesses while inebriated qualified him in early 1972 for notice in Jack Anderson's column.

Being thrifty by nature, Nixon spent his money with care. The Federal Communication Commission reveals that $12.6 million was spent on television and radio, with the bulk of it going into the visual media. Great emphasis was placed on spot commercials, which had the advantage of allowing a simple, unexplained statement of position seem an adequate presentation of a point of view. There is a built-in acceptance of such *commercials* in American society that has allowed men to sell soaps that pollute the environment, pass off inferior cars as luxury transport, and, in this case, empty promises as solid leadership worthy of a majority endorsement.

His spot commercial on Vietnam, which appeared widely around the country, illustrated this bogus approach:

> Never has so much military, economic, and diplomatic power been used as ineffectively as in Vietnam. And if after all of this time and all of this sacrifice and all of this support there is still no end in sight, then I say the time has come for the American people to turn to new leadership—not tied to the policies and mistakes of the past. I pledge to you: We will have an honorable end to the war in Vietnam.

Among the things the spot ignored was the fact that the "new leadership" Nixon was offering was directly "tied to the policies and mistakes of the past." In fact, a case could be made for the contention that Hubert Humphrey, who was pledging to end the war if *he* was elected, had opposed our taking part in Vietnam affairs during the 1950s while Nixon was insisting in Ike's councils that at all costs we must not let that Asian domino fall.

In retrospect it is also clear that Nixon was being less than honest with his prospective supporters across the nation. He had not made a simple pledge to end the war, which was what the doves wanted, and thought he was pledging. The word "honorable" subtly altered every intention he had about military withdrawal. As he subsequently revealed, after taking the Presidential oath, he had no intention of presiding over an American "defeat." He intended to withdraw from Vietnam only after a "victory."

What he was really pledging was that the "ineffectively" used American military economic and diplomatic power would be used more effectively. Since he had supported the dropping of the atomic bomb in Vietnam at the time of Dienbienphu in 1954, such a vaguely worded promise should have raised more questions in the minds of the television viewers than it answered.

He fleshed out this *pledge* with an even more cryptic series of remarks that he made in formal speeches delivered before mass audiences. He had a "secret plan" to end the war. He would reveal what this "secret plan" was as soon as he was elected.

Fittingly enough, Nixon himself provided the fullest explanation of why his "secret plan" approach was entirely fraudulent. During the 1952 campaign and before Ike came out with his melodramatic "I will go to Korea" speech, Adlai Stevenson had suggested *he* had a plan to bring the Korean War to a successful conclusion. He would, however, make no further reference to it until after the election for fear of giving the North Koreans vital military information. Nixon had blasted the Illinois governor immediately:

> Mr. Stevenson is putting out bait for voters and working a cruel hoax on the men fighting and dying in Korea . . . if he continues to leave the impression in the public mind that he has some magic formula which could bring the Korean War to an end on an *honorable* [italics added] basis. . . . if he has had such a plan, he should have disclosed it to the Joint Chiefs of Staff. . . . Certainly he cannot contend that the Joint Chiefs would give his plan to the Communists. . . . The time for ending the Korean War should not be selected on the basis of the effect it may have on an election.

"Secret plan" was no new game for Nixon when he played it in 1968. He knew he was engaged in a risky political maneuver. However, the course of public opinion was swinging so violently away from support of the war that anything sounding like repudiation of Johnson could pass as repudiation of the war.

Congressman Donald W. Riegle, Republican of Michigan, disclosed on May 30, 1971, that Nixon had gone much further in private to reassure the doves in his own party. Riegle told of a meeting in Nixon's New York apartment on June 22, 1968 which was attended by anti-Vietnam Republican Congressmen. At the end of an hour and a half of generalized references to secret plans to end the war, the skeptical Congressmen prepared to leave. Nixon took Riegle aside. "Don," he said with blinking eyes and great intensity, "if we're elected, we'll end this war in six months." That's how long it took Ike to end the Korean War.

Riegle was surprised by the unsolicited vow. "I did not expect him to make that statement," he said almost three years later as he expressed his bitter disillusionment over the war's continued ferocity. However, Nixon's purpose had been served. He had immobilized criticism in his own party from men like California Congressman Paul McCloskey, who claimed Henry Kissinger told him Nixon had a plan to end the war within sixty days after he took office.

Nixon had gotten a second chance at the Presidency, and he was absolutely determined to make the most of it. At the height of the campaign he gave an insight into his attitude toward his way of life:

> Anybody in politics must have great competitive instinct. He must want to win. He must not like to lose, but above anything else, he must have the ability to come back, to keep fighting more and more strongly when it seems that the odds are greatest. That's the world of sports. That's the world of politics. I guess you could say that's life itself.

It was almost as if it had all been for nothing. As though he was still the callow young man who had vacantly faced down Jerry Voorhis. Surprisingly, he had learned nothing. At fifty-five, after being Vice President for eight years, after taking part in two campaigns for the Presidency, he was capable of making it all sound as if he was engaged in a sporting event, perhaps the World Series of politics.

Nixon had set his heart on being President, had devoted himself to his ambition with consummate guile, and luck had dealt him the right cards.

What a sense of relief he must have had when the results came in and he realized that the Humphrey drive of the last few weeks of the campaign was going to fall short. The horror of those days must have been almost unbearable, as rumors circulated that Johnson was going to call a bombing halt to help Humphrey, and Nixon relived the nightmare of being overtaken by Kennedy. Kennedy was always in Nixon's mind as Humphrey repeatedly challenged him to television debates and he manuevered to avoid so potentially searing a confrontation.

That the final results only gave him 43.4 percent of the vote as against Humphrey's 42.7 percent, making him a minority President, with a smaller percentage of the vote than he had won in 1960, seemed to make no impression on him. George Wallace had siphoned off 13.5 percent of the traditionally Democratic votes, making Nixon's victory possible. Although Hannah would not have agreed, as Richard had often pointed out, it was not the *way* you played the game, but whether you won or lost.

He had won, and the question that suddenly confronted him was, what now?

XXVIII.

Bebe-Baby and the Boys

When Richard Nixon stepped across the threshold of the White House a transformation took place, at least in the public man.

For one thing, he immediately began sporting gold cuff links emblazoned with the Presidential eagle. Then he moved to disassociate himself from the ripe aroma arising from Bebe Rebozo's Florida land deals. Although he held on to Berg's Cape Florida Development lots, he prepared to rid himself of his largest single investment, 185,891 shares in Fisher Island, Inc., a land speculation scheme that involved Rebozo, Smathers and a number of other wheeler-dealers tied in with them.

Fisher Island, named for Carl G. Fisher, the 1920s developer of Miami, is a 213 acre parcel just off its southern tip. It is separated from the mainland by a channel dug in 1904 during Theodore Roosevelt's Administration, and it is today unoccupied, except for two oil storage tanks and an old private estate. In order to convert the island from a thick mass of Australian pine into the semi-tropical paradise its owners envision, it is essential the island be reconnected with the mainland by a causeway. The cost of the link is so prohibitive that the only hope its owners have of realizing profit on their venture is to obtain government financing.

The president and treasurer of Fisher Island, Inc., in fact its founding spirit, is that unassuming helpmate to future Presidents, Bebe Rebozo. Only Rebozo knows the complete list of his fellow investors, and his well-known discretion has never allowed him to divulge their names.

In an extensive investigation of the deal by *Newsday*, which involved four hundred interviews and the scrutiny of twenty thousand documents, it was ascertained that Rebozo, with money provided by Hoke T. Maroon, a Miami banker and Smathers backer, started acquiring property for the group in the late 1950s. Eventually Fisher Island, Inc., owned 90 percent of the island.

On Bebe's advice Dick bought into the speculation in 1962, when his thoughts of public office were at an all-time low. He continued making purchases until 1968. By that time he had almost 10 percent of the two million outstanding shares—most purchased at $1 a share.

Just before he took office, Ronald Ziegler, the President-elect's youthful press secretary, said that Nixon had no intention of divesting himself of his Fisher Island holdings, and, in fact, was not even going to put them in a blind trust, as so many recent Presidents had done with their investments when they assumed office. Ziegler said Nixon could see no way that his actions as President could affect the island's land values. Such lack of foresight was not a promising omen.

However, in February, a few weeks after he was inaugurated, it was announced that the President was indeed disposing of his holdings.

It was in this act of divestment that some of the seamier aspects of the symbiotic relationship between politics and land speculation were exposed. Why Nixon decided to sell has never been explained. However, Hoke Maroon, the corporation's largest single stockholder, apparently insisted that Nixon's shares must be bought back. Rebozo's first proposal was that *he* be allowed to purchase the President's share, but Maroon objected, contending it would appear that the Medici of Key Biscayne was merely fronting for his friend.

Newsday quotes Maroon as telling his friends: "I wanted Nixon out. How can you pull a political deal when the President of the United States is your partner? Everyone in the world is looking over your shoulder."

Maroon was the key man negotiating the deal with Nixon. The company's first offer was $1 a share, or approximately what Nixon had paid and a fair offer, since the causeway had not been built and the corporation had not made a penny for its investors, while costing them money as annual tax assessments were levied. The offer infuriated Nixon and Rebozo. They insisted that $3 would be a price more to their liking.

However, since the corporation had no funds in its treasury with which to pay the President, the burden not only of paying him the original price for his investment, but a 200 percent profit, seemed too much for the remaining stockholders to bear.

The dickering went on, with Nixon showing a Scrooge-like willingness to use his position to milk his former business associates. In a discussion with Nixon about the proper price, Maroon prefaced his protest with: "But, Dick—" only to be cut off by an angry Nixon, who coldly interjected: "Don't you dare call me 'Dick.' I am the President of the United States. When you speak to me you call me 'Mr. President.' "

Mr. President was after the best price, and although this required some horse-trading, he obviously knew how to stand on his dignity. They settled on

$2 a share, the highest price ever paid for the stock. Simultaneous sales made to other individuals went for $1 a share. A West Palm Beach stockholder in the Fisher Island bubble told *Newsday*, "I wish I could sell mine for $2 a share. This thing has been so discouraging to me over the years. It's all been requests for additional funds."

The problem now facing the Fisher Island combine was how to raise the money to pay Nixon off. There was still no money in the treasury. Bebe could attest to that. The 185,891 shares of Nixon's stock, presuming that it could be resold immediately to anyone but Bebe, would only raise half of the $371,782 the corporation was planning to pay him.

At this point their machinations began to seriously compromise the President. A new corporation, based in Orlando, suddenly appeared on the scene as the Nixon sale was being arranged. Its name was Condev, and it was so new at this point, according to its vice president, Joseph Gardner, that it had not yet been incorporated. Gardner was a prominent construction man in mid-Florida and a friend of George Smathers.

According to Gardner, Condev was brought into existence for two purposes. Its major objective was to buy Fisher Island. It was also planning to form a joint venture with Major Realty Corporation for the construction of an industrial park in Orlando. The newest member of Major Realty Corporation's board of directors was George Smathers.

The go-between acting for Condev was William Rebozo, Bebe's nephew. William suggested that Bebe's Fisher Island, Inc., grant Condev an option to purchase the island. Since an option is a thing of value, William proposed to deposit $350,000 of unincorporated Condev's money in the corporation's treasury account as a sign of good intentions. William's cut was a substantial broker's fee from Fisher Island, Inc.

After several months Condev decided to cancel the deal. Apparently Gardner and his board of directors, none of whom had to be listed since the firm was unincorporated, finally realized what everyone had always known, that the causeway connecting the island to the mainland was not going to be built for some time. At this point Condev forfeited its $350,000 deposit.

Who put up the money that made Nixon rich? Perhaps George Smathers and Bebe Rebozo will someday help answer that question. One thing is certain. Condev led a shadowy existence. Soon after it deposited its bundle on the steps of the White House, Gardner announced its proposed venture with Major Realty had been cancelled. The only thing this hapless corporation had managed to do, although some of the shrewdest businessmen in Florida were behind it, was to pay Fisher Island, Inc., $350,000 for an option, which was never exercised, which money coincidentally almost matched the amount Fisher paid Nixon for his stock.

Although Nixon moved to cut himself off from Rebozo's Fisher Island scheme, he did not cut himself off from Bebe. In mid-1971 Herb Klein told me, with no sign of jealousy, that his old friend's "closest personal friend would be Bebe Rebozo. It goes back a long time to when he was a Senator. They enjoy doing things and relaxing together. They've been friends since that time. . . . the one he probably likes to spend more time with, just to kick things around with on a boat or something, is Bebe."

The friendship had a strangely low-keyed beginning and has continued that way ever since. By mid-1951 Nixon was utterly exhausted. He had been running without stop since 1946 and was burning himself out with overuse. He had been drained by the Hiss-Chambers affair, which had been kept going largely by massive infusions of Nixon nerve. Following close on the heels of that extravaganza was the consuming fight with Helen Gahagan Douglas and those first furious months in the Senate, as he tried to steady himself for the drive that would win him a spot on the 1952 ticket.

As the first Senate vacation approached he discussed the possibility of some diversion with his old House associate, Claude Pepper's replacement in the Senate, George Smathers. Plugging Florida was part of Smathers' job, and Dick's resistence to a sales pitch was low. Smathers put him in touch with W. Sloan McCrea, a Florida banker often associated with Smathers' business deals and a stockholder in Fisher Island, Inc., and Bebe Rebozo, whose friendship with Smathers dated back to their high school days.

These two, Smathers assured Nixon, would be happy to act as his guides and companions, and make themselves useful in a hundred different ways. McCrea was away on business when Nixon arrived, and so Bebe became his sole companion. From the beginning Pat and the children played a peripheral role in their relationship.

Bebe described their first meeting some time later. Nixon, apparently not quite sure *what* one did on a vacation, arrived laden with a substantial amount of paper work. There were no sparks of instant comradeship struck between the two. Dick remained taciturn, almost belligerently silent. What Bebe did not know was that this was no reflection on him but rather typical Nixon social behavior. Brother Donald has related that one reason Dick does not mind spending time with his Whittier family is because they know he does not like his introspective silences disturbed.

Bebe went through the motions. He took his guest deep-sea fishing, but found that most of the time Nixon sat quietly in a corner doing his Senatorial homework. Nixon scarcely indicated he knew Bebe was around, hardly speaking a word during the days they spent together. Rebozo said he was positive the vacation had been a bust. He claims to have been shocked several days later to have received Nixon's warm letter of appreciation. From such an acorn did their mighty friendship grow.

In the years that followed Nixon spent an accumulation of months vacationing as Bebe's houseguest at Key Biscayne or at the nearby Villas, usually in a suite rented by Smathers. The two frequented the English Pub on the Key, where for a $20 fee they became members of the Pewter Vessel Drinking Society. As recently as 1971 their engraved pewter beer mugs still hung side by side on the pub wall. The flavor of their friendship comes through in the following story which appeared in *Newsday*:

> Another business associate of both Nixon and Rebozo remembered when Rebozo and a few partners owned a Coral Gables motel, called the Gables Court. He said Rebozo had been suspicious that he was getting a short count from the motel manager on the number of nightly rentals. Another one of the partners was driving past the motel late one night and reported to his associates that he had seen Rebozo and Nixon counting cars in the parking lot.

As the ties grew closer, Bebe could be expected to fly anywhere at a moment's notice to comfort his friend. On election night in 1960 he was on hand at the Ambassador Hotel to soften the blow. But his area of involvement with Nixon apparently does not include politics. [Rebozo was a registered Democrat until after Nixon's election in 1968.] It has simply been business and pleasure.

Rebozo's main function in Nixon's life seems to be to allow this introverted man to get off by himself, where he will not have to turn on the mechanical smile and chop out those wooden gestures that are supposed to signal friendly recognition. The pattern was established early and has only altered slightly. Nixon arrives at Key Biscayne, and within a short time they are out on Bebe's small houseboat, usually by themselves. Occasionally one or two friends are invited.

A man who knows them both is quoted by *Newsday* as saying, "Bebe and the President can sit together for hours and say practically nothing to each other. And that's fine with the President. He likes it that way."

If Rebozo is a court jester, he is not made from the usual mold. It is hard to imagine Nixon taking to a comedian. Rebozo seems more neatly to fit the role of a valet who unaccountably pays his own way. He cooks, fusses around the boat, stays out of the way and defends Nixon's prolonged silences from intrusion. Rebozo has explained to his friends that Nixon "needs time to think in private."

Another story is told of this aspect of their relationship by a mutual business associate. One of their business partners was invited to join them for a three-hour jaunt on Bebe's houseboat up the Inland Waterway to Palm

Beach. The three boarded the boat and after exchanging greetings, Nixon sat down at the cabin table and "lapsed into silence." Bebe became as silent as his friend.

Apparently sensing he was not fulfilling his function as a light-hearted boating companion, the businessman tried to get the conversation started. But as soon as he began to speak, Rebozo cut him off with a firm, "Ssshhh!" In a shocked whisper Rebozo added, "He's meditating." That was the last word spoken on the trip.

Stories abound of this retreat into silence. One of Nixon's associates tells of the time Nixon was Vice President and he and his wife were invited to Rebozo's Key Biscayne house. When they arrived they saw Nixon sitting in a corner, so lost in thought that although they called out a warm hello, he never returned their greeting, or in any way indicated he realized they were present in the same room during their entire visit.

After seventeen years of accepting Bebe's hospitality Nixon finally decided to buy a place of his own on Key Biscayne. No one was too shocked when he purchased George Smathers' stucco ranch house at 500 Bay Lane. Even less surprising was the fact that Dick's next door neighbor was Rebozo.

Smathers had never lived in the one-story waterfront building. He purchased it in 1967 for $110,000 and had used it primarily as a rental unit for Nixon. On December 20, 1968, the President-elect bought the house from Smathers for $125,000.

On the other side of the Nixon house, going away from Bebe's ranch, was a stucco house owned by Manuel Arca, Jr., a Cuban refugee. Soon after Nixon bought 500 Bay Lane, he decided his privacy was still incomplete. Bebe, acting on Nixon's behalf, as he did in all relations the President was forced to have with local residents, approached the Arcas and suggested they could demonstrate their patriotism by moving out of the neighborhood. Arca had lived there since 1958 but concluded that, since "the President of the United States wanted it, what else could I do?"

After a minimum of negotiating Arca sold his home for $127,600, although he felt the five-bedroom, five-bathroom house was worth $145,000.

With a certain amount of dispatch, the Key Biscayne "Presidential Compound" was being assembled. Next in line, adjacent to Bebe's house, was 478 Bay Lane, the home of Perry and Lucy O'Neal, since 1964. "We loved the island," Mrs. O'Neal said as she explained why they finally sold. "We decided to sell because they [the Secret Service] were deviling us to death." The deviling took the form of not being allowed to have full access to their own property without signing in and out, and having the Secret Service men "take the chairs right off my porch and sit on them because they'd have a dandy view."

Bebe made the opening approach, but until the sale was completed the O'Neals did not know the identity of the buyer, although they apparently believed it was the President. The only announcement that had been made concerning the purchaser was that the house was being bought by "an interest representing the President."

It was at the end, on February 4, 1969, when the purchaser was forced to reveal himself at the signing, that the O'Neals discovered their home had not been bought by Nixon, but by his other close friend Robert Abplanalp. The price was $150,000. Two days later it was announced Abplanalp had leased the house to the Secret Service. The agreement, to last approximately eight years, and cover all maintenance and increases in taxes, would bring Abplanalp about $142,500, almost the price he paid for the house. Mrs. O'Neal revealed sourly that the government had never offered to make the same arrangement with her.

Robert Abplanalp deserved a Presidential favor. He had become, in recent years, one of Nixon's closest friends. What this meant for the head of Precision Valve, the biggest manufacturer of the increasingly used aerosol canister, is the same thing it meant for the President of the Key Biscayne Bank—quiet, unobtrusive, obedient service.

Abplanalp owns an island in the Bahamas called the Grand Cay. He is its only resident and has built a house on a bluff overhanging a lagoon from native stone quarried on the island. The house is centered around a large glassed-in living room. Two bedrooms abut the living room. Each has its own bathroom. The floors are tile and the furnishings are rattan. This was where Nixon spent a good deal of his time when the White House press secretary announced he had gone to Florida for a few days. Of the eighty days Nixon was reported by the White House to have spent in Florida between January, 1969 and December, 1971, approximately half that time was spent on Grand Cay, either alone with Bebe, or with Bebe and Abplanalp. Pat only visited the island once.

In order to make his vacation transportation more convenient, the government built a helicopter landing site in the bay, immediately adjacent to the former Arca property. This was done at a cost of $342,000, although there was a helipad, formerly used by Nixon, 1,000 feet from the Presidential compound. Apparently Nixon needed more privacy for his comings and goings than was provided at the existing facility.

Real estate was much on Nixon's mind during his first year as President. In 1969 he purchased a five-acre estate called Casa Pacifica in San Clemente, California, for $340,000. It is on the Pacific coast, between Los Angeles and San Diego. He takes his longer vacations there, since the greater privacy afforded by this fourteen room Spanish-style villa suits him even better than Key Biscayne's. There is every indication he is more relaxed there than in any other setting. Surrounded by palm, cypress and eucalyptus, he often stretches out to relax on a patio adjoining the house, primly attired in a sports jacket.

In an endeavor to build his image as a mellowing man, he allowed ABC's television cameras in 1971 to photograph him and Pat strolling along the 350-foot beachfront hand in hand. The waves splashed to within several feet of them as they approached the camera. Suddenly a more energetic wave rushed up the beach. Showing his coordination had not improved with the passage of time, Nixon stood there staring at the on-rushing wave as the salt water washed over his black dress shoes. Then, unable to turn his embarrassment aside with a graceful or humorous gesture, the President of the United States, First Lady in tow, whirled about and trudged grimly away from the camera, while water spurted from his insteps.

Although San Clemente is three thousand miles from Key Biscayne, Bebe had not become a stranger. When the message arrived at his desk in the Key Biscayne Bank, he was ready to fly across the continent to his friend's side. He became a fixture at San Clemente and on yacht trips down the Potomac. When pressures became overwhelming, the President and Bebe took off for a ride through the Southern California countryside, to the consternation of the Secret Service.

As for the rest of the old Nixon gang, they are mostly gone, replaced by a less tarnished, more serviceable group. Chief among them is Harry Robbins Haldeman, 45, whose role in the White House can most closely be compared to that of Sherman Adams, during the Eisenhower years. Haldeman protects Nixon's privacy with what appears to be almost too much vigor. "Even John Mitchell comes through me," he told a *Look* magazine reporter proudly.

Haldeman was permanently mesmerized by the image of Nixon as the anti-Communist crusader, which he absorbed during the Hiss-Chambers era. By 1956 he was hanging around Nixon headquarters. Between elections he worked for the J. Walter Thompson advertising agency. When he came to the White House in 1969 he brought with him other Thompson alumni—now press secretary Ronald Ziegler, appointments secretary Dwight Chapin, and his own aides, Lawrence Higby and Bruce Kehrli. Haldeman has been described by a White House colleague as "by far the second most important man in government." He himself declines to accept that evaluation. "All the power in the White House is in one man. I don't think there are seconds or thirds or fourths." Very Adamsesque.

In this appraisal, Haldeman reveals his superior understanding of the relationship that men around Nixon have to him. They are his servants, his loyal retainers, who can be replaced without any sense of emotional loss, because no emotional commitment has been made. In fact, they seem chosen to act as a buffer against many of the old gang who have some call on his loyalty.

Ralph De Toledano, who by late 1971 had not been able to penetrate the wall Haldeman had erected around the Oval office for many months, was particularly bitter when speaking to me about the leader of Nixon's so-called German Mafia. "Bob Haldeman is the kingpin there. He's keeping everybody out. And he's deliberately keeping 'the old gang' out. . . . the people who stood by him during the whole 'secret fund' episode, they're not there."

There was something pathetic in Toledano's voice as he spoke about his fall from grace. There was no hint of the possibility that his old friend Dick might have given instructions he did not want to be bothered. His story reflects the bitterness of some of the old gang toward the Lord Chamberlain of the White House:

> The first thing he did when he [Haldeman] moved into the job was to buy himself a movie camera. Sound and film. Very expensive. And he's been filming everything. And, he's going to sell this movie, all this footage, when he gets out, and make a million dollars.

After saying that "Nixon just thinks he's taking home movies," an outraged Toledano described an incident in the filming of what he described as "the greatest documentary in the world."

> And he has interfered with things. Remember when Princess Anne and Prince Charles were here. They were going to have this party and they had a rock group there. They were rehearsing on the White House lawn in the afternoon. Nixon sent word down, he was meeting with the National Security Council and he couldn't hear himself think, to turn down the amplifiers. Some aide came down and turned down the amplifiers and Haldeman was recording all this behind a bush. He leaped out and said, "Who turned that down?" [The aid responded,] "The President wants it down." And he said, "*Bleep* the President!"

Toledano was bitter about his treatment, but also about other men who had done their best for Nixon through the years. Murray Chotiner, whom he felt had been the victim of anti-Semitism, came in for a strong expression of affection and admiration. To illustrate Chotiner's utter loyalty to Nixon, Toledano referred to Nixon's one attempt to pay off an old debt, which might easily have caused him some embarrassment.

Shortly after the inauguration Nixon decided to appoint Chotiner to the White House staff with the rather amorphous title of General Counsel. Toledano had been partying with Chotiner that day. "Murray keeps everything between him and Dick so much to himself that even though we had been drinking all day at his place, he didn't mention a thing about this until I accidentally heard the announcement on the radio."

Chotiner moved into the White House, where he survived for nine months. He told me about what must have been a painful episode without any sign of the pain. "We sort of all decided together that it was not the right spot for me. I was too closely associated in people's minds with politics and it was a bad idea to have politics associated in people's minds with the White House. At the same time, I felt I was not doing much. It was getting to be routine. I could see myself settling into a rut. I've never liked that. At the same time, I felt I had to make more money. I have certain obligations. No one showed me the door and handed me my hat."

The rationalization involved in Chotiner's statement was extensive. Why it should take nine months for Nixon to realize that Murray was "too closely associated in people's minds with politics" is hard to understand. At the same time it seems difficult to believe it took nine months for Chotiner to remember he had obligations requiring him to make more money. In an endeavor to strengthen his claim of near-voluntary exile, he pointed to a framed letter from Nixon that hung on the walw near his office desk. Toledano also referred to the same kind of letter received from Nixon recalling "our years of friendship," which he had framed and hung on his office wall.

Shortly after World War II Toledano was one of the brilliant liberal leaders-in-training at the Ethical Culture Society in New York. It had seemed obvious he had tremendous potential. When he tied himself to Joe McCarthy and Nixon the potential seemed to be channeled into the fulfilling of other men's ambitions. Why had he gone down that self-destructive path?

After a moment of somber reflection he responded:

In my case it was a series of factors. First of all, I genuinely admired him. As a man, as a *political* man, and as a man who knew the score; knew how things worked: the whole business of Washington, the maneuverings—it was fascinating. And I admired him, the way he operated. At the same time, we have gotten involved with him, and the more he was attacked, the more we defended him, the more we fought for him.

In my case, my whole journalistic career was tied up with Nixon, to the extent that I had to justify my own position. And then, you know, let's face it, there is something very attractive about being near the seat of power.

To the observation that Nixon's friendship with Chotiner seemed *pro forma,* a mere working relationship, Toledano grimly responded, "That's the only relationship you do have with Nixon . . . there are very few of the human juices in Nixon. You like him. You admire him. But not because you feel that he loves you. . . . I mean, I always knew that in a showdown, if my friendship with Nixon were embarrassing to him, that he'd just let me go."

But why then should anyone want to stay with this distant man, sad in face, and sad in his heart—especially when the best they had to hope for was a framed letter for their office wall.

XXIX.

On How to Press the Wrong Buttons and Still Light Up the Sky

Lyndon Johnson took Richard Nixon on a tour of the White House shortly before inauguration, and Ike's ghost once again rose to embarrass him. He had to confess to the man Ike had always preferred to himself that there were parts of the national mansion he had not seen until that moment.

Almost as if in a fit of revenge, the oath of office having been taken, Nixon ordered a crew of wreckers moved into the Oval Room to destroy any trace of his predecessor. Furniture, portraits, book shelves, rocking chairs, even utilitarian news tickers, television sets and a console of telephones were consigned to oblivion. The rug was stripped from the floor and the paint from the walls; this was the symbolic announcement of a new day.

But what was the new day to be like? Nixon's vision of it was not too far from that of Herbert Hoover, the man who had tried to help him many times during his stormy career. Basically a puritan, Nixon abhorred welfare and could muster nothing but contempt for those who had to resort to it. When two of his Milhous relatives revealed they were on the welfare rolls in California, the President's frosty reception of the news signaled a feeling that went beyond the ties of kinship.

Inherently a fearful man, he was verbally committed to holding firm against the "forces of crime." Yet, despite his emphasis on law and order in the campaign, his basically weak approach to the exercise of power kept him from proposing any meaningful program that would reduce its impact. Amazingly, the statistics on violent crime increased at an average rate of more than 10 percent for each of the first three years he was President. Yet, he sat immobilized on Bebe's houseboat, apparently capable of doing nothing more than issue a directive that the name Mafia should no longer be used to identify a national criminal organization, attempt to appoint conservative Supreme Court justices, who someday might be persuaded to allow

317

Ronald Reagan to resume use of the San Quentin gas chamber, and retain J. Edgar Hoover as head of the FBI long enough so that he could become the oldest employee ever to have drawn a paycheck from the federal government.

It was in the field of economics that he was so damagingly betrayed by his conservative philosophy. It was in this area that he completely misunderstood what he was looking at, and yet, moved most decisively. As a result, this was the area in which he did the greatest harm.

In order to understand the magnitude of his mistakes it is necessary to assess the condition of the country when he took office.

The last Eisenhower recession had been dealt with promptly by Kennedy. A liberal dose of Keynesian credit expansion quickly lowered the number of unemployed and raised the pace of economic activity. When Johnson took over at the end of 1963, he found the economy in good running order. Inflation was almost non-existent, as it had been through Kennedy's foreshortened term, and as it was to be until the middle of 1965.

Unfortunately Johnson carried through on a tax lowering effort begun by Kennedy, which Johnson later came to regret, and which formed the basis for much of the economic difficulty of the next seven years. As Kennedy originally envisioned the tax bill passed after his death in 1964, it was to be divided into two parts. The reform section of the bill was to eliminate long standing tax loopholes, which allowed the rich to evade their fair share of the burden of running the government.* In addition, there was to be an equitable lowering of tax rates. This would benefit the economy, so its advocates argued, by driving away any lingering effects of the economic sluggishness inherited from Eisenhower.

However, long before the so-called reform bill made its tortuous way through Congress, the need to stimulate the economy had disappeared. Furthermore, the power of the super-rich had been mobilized, so that the reform aspects of the legislation had been completely removed from the bill. The major result was to drastically lower taxes on the small percentage of people in the highest income bracket. If anything, it was more inequitable

* *Time* magazine reported, January 11, 1963, that while there was still officially a 90 percent tax bracket, no one paid the Internal Revenue Bureau more than approximately 35 percent of their gross income. At the same time, there were special privilege clauses in the law which allowed a handful of men in the country, who had annual incomes in excess of $2 million, to avoid paying one penny in income taxes. *Fortune* magazine put the whole matter in perspective when it published its April, 1968 report on American millionaires. Its November, 1957, study had uncovered 155 individuals with a net worth in excess of $50 million. By 1968, with the cut-off point doubled, there were 153 people with a net worth of over $100 million. The country then contained in excess of ten thousand millionaires, many of them receiving their largely untaxed incomes from money paid by the state and local governments to cover the interest on their debts, which were accumulated because of an unfairly low tax rate on the rich.

than the previous 350-page-plus, hodgepodge Internal Revenue Act.

The full inflationary effect of that tax reduction for individuals and corporations was first felt in 1965. At that time factory production was at close to capacity. Real annual growth was at 6.3 percent. This contrasted with an average annual growth during the last five years of the Eisenhower Administration of 2.3 percent, while production had been at approximately 65 percent of capacity.

Unemployment had declined from 6.7 percent under Ike's benevolent hand, to 4.5 percent, which, in practical terms, meant close to full employment. Throughout the Kennedy Administration and continuing into the first two years of Johnson's regime, wholesale prices remained almost unchanged and consumer prices rose at the unimpressive rate of 1.2 percent a year.

However, the beginning of the bombing of North Vietnam, and the escalation of our effort in that interminable war, came precisely at the point where the economy was working at full capacity. It automatically meant that some industrial facilities, and a part of the labor force, were going to be diverted to greater military production.

Production for civilian needs had to suffer. The suffering might only be negative in its effects; plants that should have been built to turn out the goods demanded by the increasingly affluent consumers could not be built as rapidly as required. However, the end results were the same. There were, by the middle of 1965, too many dollars in the hands of consumers and too little industrial capacity available to satisfy their demands. This is the classical formula for inflation. The remedy, given the fact that Johnson wanted to continue the war, should have been to raise income taxes progressively, in that way removing purchasing power from potential competitors in the marketplace. That would have had the additional benefit of allowing us to begin paying off some of the staggering national debt.

Politically, that was an absurd suggestion. Congress had just spent two years stitching together the rag that was now our new corporate and income tax laws. It was inconceivable that large numbers of legislators would be able to work up enough enthusiasm to revise the revisions over which they had so recently labored. As a result, precisely when our leaders should have been clamping down on the economy, they were allowing approximately $14 billion in tax cuts to be placed in the hands of consumers and businessmen. It was like spraying liquid oxygen on a hot flame.

While in office Johnson never had the courage to confess his error, although in his memoirs he spoke of the 1964 tax law as the major domestic blunder of his Administration. He tried to contain the resulting inflationary pressure by "jawboning" with businessmen and union leaders who, sensing the advantageous position they were in, were trying to make a better thing out of the good thing they had been enjoying since Ike left office.

A master at persuasion, he had some success. By 1968 the *real* gross national product had increased by 50 percent over what it had been in 1960. Spendable take home pay had grown for the average family by more than 30 percent. Unemployment, when Nixon took office, was at the near record low of 3.3 percent. The country had never experienced such widespread, sustained prosperity. However, the annual rate of inflation was at 2.5 percent, substantially more than it had been from 1961-1965. Although this was not by any means a run-away inflation, it had become a worrisome political issue.

Nixon had spent a good deal of energy during the campaign frightening voters with stories about the deleterious nature of the inflation the country was experiencing, and the incredibly pressing need to do something about it. Although he had lived through, in fact, voted for, the post-World War II skyrocket Taft-inflation, and should have realized the gentle nature of the inflation 1968 America was experiencing, there is every indication he was serious about these expressions of fear. The stock market sensed he was about to press the panic button, and during the period after he was elected, but before he took office, his friends with the large portfolios showed their confidence in his judgment by driving down the market indexes. Unfortunately, their fears were justified.

Almost as soon as he took office, he announced he was taking steps to curb inflation. At his first press conference on January 27, 1969, he said, "The primary responsibility for controlling inflation rests with the national Administration and its handling of fiscal and monetary affairs."

It did not have the Nixonian ring of a paragraph submitted by an expert but reworked by "the great simplifier" to reflect his style. It raised the fear that although committed to act he had no strong interest in what he was about to do. For a country yearning for knowledgable leadership, this conjured up a fearsome spectre.

There are many devices available to a President who is determined to cool down the economy. His choice of which one he will use always depends on his personal economic philosophy. It also depends on his perspicacity. In this instance Nixon was betrayed by both.

The idea of asking for a tax increase, fully justified by his need for funds with which to pay for a war he completely endorsed, was politically abhorrent to him. Which is another way of saying he could not bring himself to make such an unpopular move. The fact that it would have been a responsible position to take in no way made it appealing. Instead he endorsed the Congressional move to raise income tax exemptions, signing these inflationary provisions into law at the beginning of 1970. He did this despite the fact that his bland first Secretary of the Treasury, David Kennedy, had told the Advertising Council in Washington months earlier that the country was facing "a runaway inflation."

Nixon decided to taper off on the money supply. With less money in circulation, the pressure on the economy would ease. This was a perfectly reasonable approach to take. However, money could be removed from circulation in many different ways. Since he did not want to approach the taxpayer directly, he chose to tighten the money supply within the confines of the banking industry. This seemed to make good sense, since bankers are alert to the problems caused by excessive inflation. Provided the approach was right, they could be expected to cooperate in a silence which approached conspiracy.

Three devices can be employed to manipulate the amount of money circulated through the economy by banks. They approached the problem from different angles. Only one was used.

He could have prevailed on the Federal Reserve System, soon to be headed by his friend and appointee Arthur Frank Burns, to raise the reserve ratio. This would have increased the percentage of its deposits each bank would have had to keep in its vaults, and in so doing, effectively limited the amount of money available for mortgages, or for loans to businessmen. With that simple technique the economy would have slowed down instantly, and could have been controlled at will by an upward or downward adjustment of the reserve ratio as the need arose. The Open Market Committee could have also been utilized to sell government bonds, thereby drying up cash in the hands of potential inflators.

The third technique, and the one he chose, was to allow interest rates to rise on the theory that the number of people who would be willing to borrow money at 8 1/2 percent was bound to be fewer than the number willing to borrow it at 6 percent. There was a certain truth to this. However, it was not as sure a remedy as the raising of the reserve ratio or the operation of the Open Market Committee. There are always a great number of people who are so convinced their next investment will make them millionaires that an exorbitant interest rate does not discourage them. All it does is make it less likely they will be able to repay their creditors and stay solvent.

Expressing his determination to lick "inflation" by cutting down on the number of bank loans, Nixon gave the green light to the rise in interest rates, but guaranteed the failure of his approach by doing nothing to limit the amount of loans his banking friends could make. The only thing he accomplished was to increase the cost of borrowing money, making bankers richer while everyone else was getting poorer. This proved to be the trigger mechanism for a fantastic increase in genuine inflation. Men who were now borrowing money at 8 1/2 percent, or more, found that the only way to repay their loans was to raise prices. Workers, who had contented themselves with modest 3 1/2 percent average salary increases during the years of Democratic prosperity, now demanded much higher wage increases with which to meet the steeply rising prices.

In short, the annual rise in the cost of living index, which had been at a modest 2 1/2 percent when Nixon was maintaining that it was excessive, quickly raced up to 5 percent by the end of his first year in office. Before another twelve months had passed, it was at the frightening rate of 6 percent. He had pressed the button for inflation to go down and instead it had shot up.

At the same time unemployment, which had been at 3.3 percent of the total work force when he took office, was gyrating in the first months of 1972 in the neighborhood of 6 percent. The Dow-Jones Industrial stock market average, which had been at 950 at the beginning of 1969, had fallen to 631.16 on May 26, 1970, less than a year and a half after he took over. America simultaneously had inflation and recession, something no other President had ever been able to accomplish.

Having achieved this dubious honor, the question most often asked was, could Nixon do anything to right the precariously tipped economy. The signs that he was prepared to move decisively were nowhere to be seen. In fact, he seemed determined to act as if the nothing he was doing was just exactly what had to be done.

Nine months after he took office, as the indicators zoomed toward the economic stratosphere, he announced "we are winning the fight against inflation." On a nationwide radio talk on October 17, 1969, he said: "We are not going to change our game plan at the end of the first quarter of the game, particularly at a time that we feel we are ahead."

There was reflected in this unmerited optimism the con man who had always been Richard Nixon. However, as President, misrepresentation could mean catastrophe. That he understood the dimensions of the problem is beyond doubt. Arthur Burns had been trumpeting the bad news for months. Although Burns was a minority of one in pushing for more active Administration intervention in the processes of the free market, his opinion normally was enough to convince Nixon. The brilliant economist, who had remained loyal to Nixon through the dark years after 1960, became head of the Federal Reserve System in January, 1970. He quickly eased the tight money policy that had been driving up interest rates, choking off financial activity and deepening the recession. However, he told Nixon that the FRS could not reverse the course of the economy all by itself. It required Nixon's active participation. That was the one thing he was most reluctant to offer.

Instead he gave increasing attention to George Shultz's conservative opinions. Shultz, soon to become the most influential Nixon advisor on domestic matters, was an academic economist who had been appointed Secretary of Labor in the first Nixon cabinet on Burns' recommendation. He was made virtual economic czar in June, 1970, when he was put in charge of the new Office of Management and Budget, an agency whose already immense powers had been vastly expanded.

Burns was advocating a modified form of wage and price controls based on voluntary compliance. He wanted the President to appoint a board that would review proposed wage and price increases. When it felt such increases were out of line with increased productivity, or a threat to price stability, Burns wanted the board to have the authority to blast out against the greedy culprits. It was, however, to have none of the enforcement powers available to the controllers of World War II and the Korean War eras.

Shultz, on the other hand, felt the advice his patron had been giving until recently should be the nation's guide. The economy should be left unfettered. No doubt there were problems, but the natural forces that automatically worked for stability in a free economy would soon reassert themselves—that is, provided some New Deal quacks were not allowed to tamper with the delicate mechanism that was primitive capitalism.

Nixon was stretched between two distant economic poles and the space between them seemed to be widening. He knew Burns was usually right in recognizing when the economy had been held down too long. Almost invariably when he spoke of 1960 he blamed his loss on the fact that Ike had refused to heed Burns' advice, which Nixon had endorsed, to loosen credit and money before Election Day. He never tired of reciting unemployment statistics for the month before Election Day, which showed a rise of over 400,000. A man of such foresight, whose loyalty had not wavered even after California-1962, could not be casually ignored.

But Shultz was preaching a course of action that coincided with Nixon's own conservative political syle. It also matched his life style. After all, what Burns was urging would require him to become an activist. To an introvert like Nixon, that was always a painful prospect. How much more comfortable to hide behind the facade of the White House and pretend he was merely acting out the role of careful custodian of cautious capitalism. He had found a way to violate Truman's old dogma that the buck passing stops at the President's desk. He was passing the buck to the ghost of Adam Smith, who seemed to materialize daily in George Shultz's mimeograph room in time to crank the handle for the latest optimistic press releases.

Burns' advice on how to curb inflation was by no means the only possible avenue of attack. Economists are notorious for taking opposing positions, especially in relatively early stages of potential crises before the outlines of the problem are clear. They have wonderfully inventive minds, and Burns' simple suggestion had by no means exhausted their bag of tricks.

For example, Nixon could have used the government's overwhelming fiscal power to force a lowering of bank interest rates, thereby revitalizing the key construction industry. At the same time, lower interest rates, which stimulated business activity, could have been balanced by a rise in the progressive income tax. This would dry up some of the exorbitant income being received by the super-rich, while conveying to the nation the Administration's determination to act responsibly. It was just such medicine the country needed and exactly the type of treatment Dr. Nixon was most reluctant to prescribe.

Instead he acted as if the only alternative to doing nothing was to accept Burns' advice about getting labor and management to agree on voluntary compliance with suggestions from a powerless wage and price board. On June 17, 1970, he again misstated the alternatives available to him in a television address to the nation.

> Now, I realize that there are some people who get satisfaction out of seeing an individual businessman or labor leader called on the carpet and browbeaten by government officials. But we cannot protect the value of the dollar by passing the buck. That sort of grandstanding distracts attention from the real cause of inflation and it can be a dangerous misuse of the power of government.

If he acted, as Burns was insisting, then it would be a "dangerous misuse of the power of government." The only alternative, he seemed to be suggesting, was not to act. This was simplistic nonsense. A casual discussion with any economist unaffiliated with the Nixon establishment would have produced several dozen standard suggestions for dealing with the nation's economic dilemma.

But all he could hear from behind the Berlin Wall constructed by his White House staff was Burns, who had been responsible for convincing him in 1969 to tighten up the money supply and raise interest rates, or Shultz, with whom Burns now temporarily disagreed. They were presenting him with a narrow view of the possible remedies, and he did not have the perspective in his wholly political background to challenge their essentially conservative economic views.

During the first two years of his administration he maintained his doctrinaire sit-tight position, hoping against hope that Shultz's contention that the economy was about to regain its balance would momentarily prove justified. But time was running out. Meaningful upturns in the economy take months. If conditions were going to improve substantially by Election Day 1972, he was going to have to start pressing some of the proper buttons.

As 1970 drew to an end, the news continued to be terrifyingly bad. The 1957-1959 dollar, which had dropped in value by the time Johnson left office to 81.1 cents, had continued to plummet under the glazed stare of a paralyzed Nixon to approximately 72 cents in 1971 and below the mid-60's in 1972. It came as a severe shock to his most conservative friends to realize the value of the dollar could decline under anyone but Franklin D. Roosevelt.

In an attempt to give the illusion he was doing something significant, Nixon made a surprising announcement on December 14, 1970. Democrat John Connally, Lyndon Johnson's close friend from Texas, was to be the new Secretary of the Treasury, replacing the competent but colorless Republican banker David Kennedy.

The news had a certain dramatic impact. It captured the headlines. Some men were stunned by the thought that Nixon had managed to persuade one of the leading Democrats to join his dull cabinet. However, the major effect was political while the area of national difficulty was economic.

Connally knew nothing about economics. He was essentially a political warhorse who could be depended upon to deliver several hundred vaguely plausible words per minute on any subject. Balance of payments, rediscount rate, incomes policy—all these were terms almost as strange to him as any foreign tongue. But with his stump speaker's egotism he was as willing to discourse on them as he was to defend the oil depletion allowance. His immediate response to critics who claimed he knew nothing about economics was "I can add."

Nixon had made a move which promised absolutely no improvement. In general economic philosophy, Connally was perhaps even more darkly conservative than Burns and Shultz. He had worked for Texas oil and banking interests for over twenty years. Nixon was merely displaying his tendency to try to change the subject with a loud noise, a tendency that would get out of hand in the next year as the increasing desperateness of his situation made him thrash around for some act of prestidigitation with which to distract the public.

By the beginning of 1971, Nixon realized time had run out. While Shultz, with a show of obstinacy which often separates the winners from the losers, was broadcasting on all wave lengths "steady as she goes," unemployment edged above the 6 percent mark. The media, already unhappy with Nixon's Vietnam policy, and by now permanently spooked by Nixon the man, was depicting American economic difficulties as being several shades worse than they actually were.

Arthur Burns had already reversed the tight money policy. For a while monetary supply was increasing at an annual rate of 10 percent, normally enough to shake the country out of a mild recession. However the remedial steps had been too long in coming. It was going to be more difficult to recover from the effects of this economic illness than it would have been if the right dose of monetary medicinals had been applied earlier.

In addition, the direction in which the economy moves often depends on nothing more tangible than the confidence people have in themselves and their leader. In large areas of the country there was very little confidence in Richard Milhous Nixon. Nowhere was this more apparent than in the high echelons of the business community. Economist Pierre Rinfret, who had been close enough to Nixon to be included as one of his advisors at Mission Bay, California, in the major strategy session after he was nominated in 1968, held the torch aloft for the readers of the *Wall Street Journal.* By July 3, 1969, Rinfret was so disenchanted with Nixon that he issued a memorandum to his clients entitled "We Accuse" in which he dramatically broke with the man he had worked so hard to elect. "We accuse this Administration of incompetence," he began angrily. "We accuse the Administration of totally miscalculating the need for advance economic planning before it got into office and for being totally unprepared once it did. It went into office with slogans and little else."

By the beginning of 1971 Nixon had abandoned any thought that he might fulfill the age-old Republican promise to balance the budget. Half-hearted attempts at this in the first two years of his Administration had resulted in slowing down the economy, while the budget became increasingly unbalanced. On January 29, 1971, he submitted a budget to Congress for 1972 which he admitted would be $11.6 billion out of balance. In view of the fact that the country had just passed through a year in which the deficit had reached over $20 billion, and things looked no better for the present year, his estimate seemed concocted with a large dose of wishful thinking. The eventual deficit was $40 billion, the largest since World War II. However, he had conceded there would be a sizable deficit, and thereby signaled the beginning of the end of his patience with Shultzism.

As the spring and summer of 1971 wore on, and it became clear Burns' manipulation of the powers of the Federal Reserve was only making a minimal impact on the problem, Nixon searched desperately for some way out of his dilemma. What he appeared to want was a slogan; something snappy like "prosperity is just around the corner."

The releases by the Bureau of Labor Statistics dealing with the cost of living index had begun to be viewed by Nixon as a monthly crisis point. If the advance word was that the sheet was bad, efforts would be made to time some *other* important announcement for simultaneous release so that the front pages of the nation's newspapers would not be dominated by forecasts of gloom and doom.

On the other hand, even the slightest leveling off in the rise of wholesale prices, or the momentary hesitation in the steep rise in the rate of inflation, was enough to rouse the J. Walter Thompson contingent in the White House to extravagant claims of success, which did honor to their previous efforts on behalf of their beer, detergent and cigarette clients. It was the era of Dick-the-supersalesman.

Finally in April, 1971, Nixon ordered an end to monthly briefings by career technicians at the BLS. It was also announced that there would be a shakeup at the BLS so that top civil service professionals would be replaced by political appointees. Senator William Proxmire, Chairman of the House-Senate Joint Economic Committee, predicted that "After November 1, when the Bureau of Labor Statistics provides an analysis of the latest economic figures, it will be what the Administration wants the public to believe about the figures, not what objective economic experts believe they signify."

As the saying goes, statistics don't lie, but liars can use statistics. Senator Proxmire was pointing out that after November, during the entire Presidential election year, the statistics would be in the hands of "analysts whose conclusions would be subordinated to the political interests of the Administration."

By mid-summer Nixon had endured the heat for as long as he could. The decline in his standings in the polls were the statistics that really interested him. The Harris poll indicated 70 percent of the people thought he was managing the economy poorly.

However, numbers of any sort, no matter from which direction they came, were causing him sleepless nights. Then came one final deluge of bad economic news. The balance of payments, reflecting our trade relationship with other nations, had shown an alarming increase in the imbalance between the amount of goods and services we exported to them and the much greater amount they were selling to us.

The American dollar, which had until recently been the most solid of currencies, was now under siege by speculators around the world. They were betting it would have to be devalued. The greenback was suddenly the weakest major national currency, with much of the money Burns' FRS was pumping into the economy making a bee-line for West Germany and Japan.

During the first weeks of August the final straw floated gently down toward the camel's back. Railroad workers won an inflationary 42 percent pay increase which was to be apportioned out over the following 42 months. Nixon's attempt to depict this as a major victory for the modified attempt at jawboning, in which he was finally allowing himself to participate, had fallen flat. Steelworkers won a similar increase amounting to 30 percent over three years. In the week of August 15, with what appeared to be inspired haste, the steel manufacturers raised prices by 8 percent.

The following day Pierre Rinfret sent a telegram to his clients advising them to boost their prices immediately, since the steel settlement "locks in inflation." He further urged them to give their unions what they wanted and then raise prices to produce the desired profit margin. "There is no point in taking the heat," he said in a tone approaching self-pity, "if the government won't stand behind you."

General Motors, which understood this sort of business behavior without any advice from Rinfret, announced a 3.9 percent price increase, which amounted to an average of $176 on each 1972 Chevillac.

Burns, now confiding his fears to all who would listen, jolted the Joint Economic Committee of Congress when he said "inflation is proceeding at both an unacceptable and a dangerous rate."

Nixon panicked. All those Democrats and labor leaders had been crying for wage and price controls, well he'd give them controls. It did not matter that he had repeatedly rejected such action in the past. Only recently he had said, "I will not take this nation down the road of wage and price controls, however politically expedient they may seem." It did not matter that he had been maintaining his "game plan" was working. It was time to face grim reality, and the grimmest part of his personal reality was that his chances for reelection in 1972 were growing slimmer with each passing day. In the face of that, George Platt Shultz could be completely right and still be wrong.

A barrel of powder and a spark could produce a blinding flash and a deafening noise. Set off at the right time, this might distract the voters long enough to get him past November, 1972. If enough people were not confused by the first detonation, he could press another button which would result in a still louder noise.

Nixon had his pastepot and scissor on the table. He was snipping a little off the bottom of a memo from Burns and the corner of a brief from Shultz. After he banged it all into place he would give the simplified version to Connally, who would announce it to the public, smile and make it all sound vaguely plausible. With a little luck the sky might yet light up "winner."

XXX.

Meany vs the Champ, in a Fight to the Finish

On Sunday night, August 15, 1971, with only a few hours' advance warning, Nixon addressed the nation. He began tensely, occasionally tripping over words. He was calling for a freeze of wages and prices in order to stop the terrible effects of inflation. The freeze, he proclaimed, would last for three months, and was the keystone of his New Economic Policy.

There was a striking similarity to Lenin's New Economic Plan in the early 1920s, when the Communist dictator, faced with a bankrupt economy, announced a brief return to capitalism. Nixon had become capitalism's Nepman in reverse and he could not help signaling this fact with his choice of a title for his New Economic Policy.

The speech was laced with homilies about the value of the dollar and the need for universal sacrifice. However, the details were largely missing. The next day at noon John Connally came into his own. The White House announced he would meet with the press to discuss the details of what the President had in mind.

This was clearly the President's responsibility, and this was clearly the occasion for a Presidential news conference. However, Nixon had shown his distaste for this kind of give and take. It was time for someone else to carry the load. What better load carrier was there than Connally. The fact that he had only recently been won over to Burns' modified incomes policy approach, and that he had been in Texas on vacation when Nixon's nerves snapped did not disconcert Connally. He was to be the torchbearer, a well lit role. There were satisfactions in that fact.

With a remarkably rapid delivery that passed over the inconsistencies and contradictions so swiftly that they scarcely elicited a hostile question from the dazzled newsmen, Connally informed the world of Richard Nixon's version of fair and equitable government controls over wages and prices.

First and foremost, since the question had been raised overnight, the President had not omitted mention of controls over profits, dividends and interest by accident. In this fair and equitable system, there were to *be* no such controls. Did that mean that the only people whose income would be frozen were workers? Well, yes. He did not want to put it just that bluntly, but when you came down to knuckle against skin, that was what it was all about. Did that seem fair? Well, given an opportunity to perform a patriotic service for the nation, Connally and the President were sure that American workers would do their duty. But, what about American bankers and manufacturers? The variety of double-talk that smothered such objections took Connally safely through the conference, but augured badly for the future.

The President had received power to freeze wages and prices from Congress under the Economic Stabilization Act of 1970. He had objected to the idea of the bill when it had been proposed and had worked against its passage. Since its passage his denunciations had not ceased and he frequently maintained he would never use its anti-free enterprise provisions.

George Meany, the seventy-seven-year-old leader of the AFL-CIO, immediately denounced the one-sidedness of the President's proposal. He now became the rallying point for the opposition. "I think everything he has tried to do is a failure. He didn't give us jobs. He didn't cool off the economy or halt inflation. He is still the handmaiden of big business as he always has been. I don't think there has been any change in that."

Taking a deep breath, he momentarily clamped down on his ever-present cigar and then continued contemptuously, "I think that he is still the same old Nixon who feels that the only way to have a prosperous America is to keep the big corporations fat and prosperous."

His voice shaking with anger he said, "I can't buy anything on the economy from President Nixon or Arthur Burns, because they have failed completely."

Meany's voice was almost the only influential opposition heard to the NEP through August and part of September. The polls indicated a remarkably favorable reaction from all sections of the population. People were so unhappy with the erosion of their salaries that they welcomed any move that gave the appearance of doing something to stem it.

The horror was that Nixon, concerned as usual with political outcomes, had devised a solution whose only promise for success lay in its ability to victimize the working people of America. In this it was no different than any solution proposed by conservative business-oriented economists. The regressive tax laws passed during the previous twenty years across the nation have borne witness to that sad fact.

He was going to freeze wages and prices. However, only one of those two economic factors was capable of being frozen by voluntary methods. Wages, which are paid by bosses, can easily be frozen. What boss would bypass this opportunity to appear a patriot by withholding pay raises to his workers. Employers' cooperation was guaranteed when Connally revealed the owners of business could merely add the withheld wage increases to their ledgers as additional profits.

The freeze of prices was not nearly as susceptible to control. Unlike wages, there was no large body of strategically placed enforcers. The fact that prices had been "frozen" at the highest level they had hit at any time during the previous month was not enough of a concession to jolly along most businessmen. With no price board checking compliance and levying penalties against violators, as there had been during the two previous times the nation had tried its hand at controls, compliance was bound to be evaded.

The cost of living figures for the month of August, half-in and half-out of the freeze, were inconclusive. They went up with the same monotonous regularity they had shown before the President's proclamation. However, it was difficult to say what part of that rise had occurred before August 15. The technicians at the BLS, serving their last hours in their jobs, seemed reluctant to draw any conclusions which might further alienate their boss.

However, the figures for September, released on October 22, were unmistakably negative. Prices paid by consumers rose two-tenths of 1 percent. Although that was a smaller rise than the average during the previous six months, it was clear that even under the impact of first-flush enthusiasm for Nixon's attempt to cool down the economy, the entrepreneurs of America had not been able to resist their all-too-human impulses.

Paul W. McCracken, chairman of the President's Council of Economic Advisers, announced, on the eve of his resignation, there would be an investigation. He spoke of "possible violations" of the freeze. He listed several items, women's and girls' apparel, footwear, orange juice, beef and margarine, that would be investigated. The job would be done by some undefined process by the much overburdened Internal Revenue Service. When they would report, what would be done if they discovered violations, all this and much more remained as vague as Nixon's promise to do something about inflation.

The cruelty of his deception was apparent when a study was made of his other economic proposals of August 15. At that time he not only *froze* wages and prices, while exempting profits and interest rates, but he also announced tax windfalls for corporations. The excise tax on automobiles was to be rescinded. Furthermore, Detroit automakers were to be given an additional special favor. Nixon imposed a 10 percent levy on all foreign cars being imported into the country.

Both moves had an inflationary impact. The 10 percent increase in the price of imported automobiles was not going to dissuade many people from purchasing the cheaper imports. It was simply going to make it more expensive for them to do it. It also threatened retaliation and a raising of tariff barriers similar to those of the 1920s which helped start the Great Depression.

Every attempt to introduce an element of justice into Nixon's economic measures, by calling for balanced sacrifice by American businessmen, was greeted with an incomprehensible look of disdain by Connally. And Connally's was the only one on display, as for months on end Nixon remained unavailable for questioning on any part of his New Economic Policy.

When he announced his Phase II plans on September 16, which would take the economy beyond the date the initial freeze was to end on November 14, he explained he wanted control of wages and prices only "in major industries." Overlooked in this decision was the fact that the most outrageous increases in the cost of living during his two and a half years in office had come about in the service industries. Doctor and dentist fees, entertainment, restaurant tabs, repair services of any sort, even dry cleaning, had been the truly inflating factors. He made no provision for that 53 percent of the economy. As for the rest, it was once again to be voluntary, which meant that wages were to continue in the deep freeze while price rises were to be winked at.

The next day, when Nixon should have followed up his speech to the nation with a press conference, John Connally once again got into his fielder's uniform.

By this time an understanding of the inequities in Nixon's conservative vision of wage and price controls had spread beyond George Meany. The polls indicated a majority of American workers now believed the President's plan was not in their interest. Connally was besieged with questions about controls over excess profits. While manager Nixon watched his star fielder perform over the White House television set, Connally delivered himself of the opinion that there was "no such thing as excess profits."

His contention was that average profit margins had not been high during the previous few months, therefore those who called for controls over excess profits were either ignorant of the facts or enemies of the profit system.

Ignored so thoroughly that one hesitated to attribute it to anything but a lack of honesty was the fact that an excess profits tax would only be levied on *excess* profits. If a firm did not make any *excess* profits, it would not be taxed under the provisions of a new bill with such a specific name and purpose.

(GM announced in February, 1972, that 1971 had turned out to be a record-breaker for profits, and the second best sales year in its corporate history. Chrysler announced on April 17 profits for the first three months of 1972 were three times what they had been for the same period in 1971. Simultaneously, Ford reported that its first quarter had been the most profitable ever. By early May, the stock market was making an assault on the all-time Dow-Jones high, as corporations, many of whom were doing lower volumes of business, were issuing extraordinary profit reports.)

The truth was that Nixon never for a moment considered holding down profits as he had decided to hold down wages. The question was a heated topic of conversation only among workers. Nixon had said he was against it, and that had ended any tendency by his conservative advisors to even raise the subject.

To realize how badly Nixon had handled the American economy one had only to refer to the aims he set for his New Economic Policy. Soon after his television explanation of what Phase II would be like, the Cost of Living Council, which was the shepherd organization headed by Connally, sitting over the new Pay Board and Price Commission, announced the President's goal. It was to reduce the annual rate of increase in consumer prices from 6 percent to approximately 3 percent by the end of 1972.

What an incredibly modest goal. When Nixon had come into office the rate was at 2 1/2 percent. He had been so unhappy with that figure he had started the string of actions which touched off the inflation he was now theatrically trying to curb. Circumstances had so altered his ambitions that he now viewed a rate of inflation at or above what it had been when he took office as a desirable goal, if only he could achieve it.

It was to be gained at the expense of those members of society least able to afford it, the salaried worker who was being told to sacrifice without a murmur, or be labeled unpatriotic. Others far better able to afford a contribution were being exempted from anything resembling an inconvenience. However, the real imbalance in the economy was caused by the special treatment this privileged group had received since Eisenhower first began to sharply reduce their share of federal taxes. At the same time, local and state governments were raising sales taxes and inventing other ingenious forms of regressive taxes with which to burden the poorer 90 percent of society.

Nothing Nixon was doing held out much promise for redressing this balance.

However, even if Nixon's modest goal was to be achieved, it should never be forgotten that it was accomplished by penalizing only one group in society, the same group his high interest rates had earlier victimized. What he was attempting to do was redistribute wealth, but, unlike Franklin Roosevelt, this time, under his unenlightened leadership, the rich were to be made richer. The middle class drones, who were dependent on salary checks, were once again to understand that their function was to work hard to pay for the mistakes of their leader.

George Meany indicated he understood what lay behind Nixon's actions when he rhetorically asked the House Banking and Currency Committee on October 4, "What lies down the road, new panicky moves, new stunts, new surprises, new television programs starring the President?"

It did not take the aging labor leader long to find out. Meany had become progressively more vocal in his opposition. What grated most was the fact that Nixon's Phase II guidelines had wiped out the pay raises many Federation unions had negotiated months, even years, before the freeze. To him this represented a perfect example of the resilience of Nixon's Taft-Hartley bias.

One of the most inviolate rights businessmen claim is the sanctity of contracts. Yet, suddenly these contractual raises, which had been won only after labor agreed to forego its demands in other areas, were being denied by a business-oriented national Administration. Meany was convinced Nixon would never be capable of intervening against any legal contract arrived at between two business conglomerates. Furthermore, it had become clear to him the freeze on prices was a farce. The consumer price index figures for the month of October were released in mid-November, and there had been another rise of .2 percent. But prices were not supposed to rise at all. During the three months of Phase I *wages* had not risen one nickel throughout the country. In fact, there had been some movement downward, since there was no floor under which wages would not be allowed to fall.

Complicating the issue even further was the action taken by the fifteen-member Pay Board in the case of the newly negotiated coal miners agreement. The owners and miners had agreed earlier to a three-year contract which clearly violated the Phase II guidelines adopted by the Pay Board on November 15. Once having reached this agreement, which was predicated on the owners' understanding that there would be a substantial raise in the price of coal to pay for the new contract, the agreement was submitted to the Pay Board for its approval.

There was no possible way for the Board to approve the new pact. The Board's guidelines had limited raises to 5.5 percent annually. The miners were scheduled to get three times that figure in the first year. However, the miners had marshalled substantial support for their economic demands. Arch Moore, the governor of West Virginia, had acted as mediator in hammering out the contract. He had personally pleaded their case before the Board. The mine owners, envisioning their usual more-than-adequate price increase to cover the wage increase, were palpitating in anticipation of raising the living standard of their workers. Finally, the miners had been on strike for weeks to gain their objectives, and many of them had stayed out after the agreement had been reached while the Pay Board deliberated.

On November 19 the Board announced it had approved the miners' wage increase. The vote had been 10 to 3, with labor and management representatives unanimous for the increase, while the public members had cast three votes against and two abstentions.

The five public members had then issued a bitter denunciation of the majority action. "We found that the contract provides for an estimated increase in average hourly compensation of 16.8 percent during the first year, which is more than three times the amount contemplated. . . . It is highly improbable that the rate of inflation will be reduced sufficiently to meet the goal of the stabilization effort if increases of this magnitude are permitted."

It was clear to Meany that the miners had wrung the *inflationary* raise out of the Pay Board by means of political and economic muscle. The miners had driven home to him the old lesson of the bargaining table; low wages are the lot of the weak. It looked as if Meany had won. On November 18 he gathered together his flock in annual convention at Bal Harbour, Florida. It was to be an anti-Nixon rally, at which the brethren would be mobilized to demand justice of the New Economic Policy, or fight to scrap it.

At its Thursday, November 18, session the convention had voted to instruct the five labor members on the Pay Board to refrain from voting on most matters. They were to remain on the Board, but only vote when their ballots were needed to insure a decision favorable to labor. This position was to be maintained until "the validity of contracts" was recognized by the Board.

In his opening speech to the convention George Meany, pounding the lectern with his plumber's fist, described the Board as a "stacked deck." His cheering audience was then told, according to the *Times*: "If the President doesn't like the terms we lay down here, let him kick us off." His fighting speech was greeted tumultuously. When the shouts finally died down, he sarcastically told the delegates to "wear your tuxedos tomorrow," because the President was coming to address them.

Once again, the occasional bold, inappropriate stroke. Meany was about to find out the surprise Nixon had in store for *him*.

Nixon had never addressed the AFL-CIO convention. He was choosing this low point in his relations with labor to "beard the lion in its den," as the Republican press gleefully described his maneuver. The signs that his New Economic Policy was a failure were growing steadily clearer and it was not too soon to find a scapegoat. What better place to find it than at a labor convention where there were few Republicans to alienate.

The White House press mills immediately described Nixon's planned visit as a "courageous" attempt to reach the rank and file through a forceful presentation to their leaders. It was clear Nixon had weighed the move for its political impact and decided he had more to win than lose. The worst that could happen would be a tempestuous display of bad manners by the delegates that would redound to his credit among the vast numbers of uncommitted "decent Americans" who believed the office of President should be treated with respect.

Nixon was introduced to the delegates on Friday, November 19, by Meany, and received a subdued, hostile, but polite round of applause. He immediately began flim-flamming. "I have brought with me a prepared text . . . .I am not going to read that text to you today." Instead, he said, he was going to speak their language . . . "You like it straight from the shoulder."

(Nixon's method of putting a speech together was well known. He actually disliked reading formal speeches. Important ones were reduced to essentials and largely committed to memory, with room enough left for well rehearsed *improvisations.* Although he preferred this technique—believing it struck the listener as sincere—it served him poorly. Invariably such speeches are pitted with slips and errors in judgment. However, until recently his advisors were unable to alter his approach.)

He almost immediately raised the spectre of why he had come. He mentioned newspaper speculation and the objections of his "advisors." "Putting it quite bluntly, one of them said, 'Why are you going?' They said, 'You know a majority of those that are going to be at this great convention are against you politically.' "

Then came one of his grand non-sequiturs. "I'll tell you why I came here: [Raise your hand if you really think he is going to tell.] Because while some of you may be against me politically and some of you may be against my party I know from the experience over the past three years that when the chips are down organized labor's for America and that's why I'm here before this [great] convention today."

He went on to claim inflation had been caused solely by the Vietnam war. There had been 539,000 Americans in Vietnam when he took office. "By January of next year we will have brought home 400,000." In addition, the winding down of the war had caused 2,200,000 Americans to be "let out of defense plants and out of the armed services over the past three years."

His statistics were correct, but he was ignoring their significance. Unemployment had gone up by millions since he took office, but this had not resulted in the usual deflation such events almost invariably cause. Instead, his high interest policy had mushroomed inflation, while his tight money policy had restricted industry's ability to build plants and create new jobs for returning veterans and dispossessed defense workers. The country was in the midst of a recession. Only 75 percent of its industrial capacity was being utilized, the lowest rate since the Eisenhower years. The labor leaders sitting in the auditorium knew this better than anyone and they listened to Nixon try to shift the burden of blame in gloomy disbelief.

He cleared his throat nervously and then quickly said, "Now I understand there's been some disagreement about whether that freeze worked." There was some moaning in the audience. "It was a remarkable success," he claimed as derisive laughter rose from his listeners.

Never one to respond well to personal criticism, Nixon let his temper flare. He plunged on. "I have noted that President Meany's had some things to say about Phase Two. As a matter of fact it's a little hard not to note what he's had to say."

Apparently he had come to labor's house to belabor its leader. No longer in perfect control, he rushed on. He wanted to quote from Meany's speech of the previous day. He claimed that Meany had said, " 'If the President of the United States doesn't want our membership on the Pay Board on our terms, he knows what he can do.' " Looking out at the audience grimly and speaking with conviction, he said, "Well you know President Meany is correct. I know exactly what I can do and I'm going to do it."

The threat was clear. Recognizing he had lost his audience completely, he could not restrain his impulse to distort to his own advantage. "And, my friends," he said unctuously, "whatever some of you may think, a great majority of the American people and a majority of union members want to stop the rise in the cost of living and that's what we're going to do."

The only inference to draw was that labor *leaders* wanted the cost of living to go up. There was something so incongruous about such a conclusion that once again his honesty or his reasoning powers had to be called in question.

When he finished there were a polite few seconds of applause. Meany shook hands with him and then turned to gavel the delegates back to order. As soon as Nixon had left, in recognition of the extraordinary acting display to which they had just been treated, Meany said the convention "will now proceed with Act Two." There was an outburst of laughter and cheering.

Although Nixon had been planning to stay in Florida, and Rebozo was waiting on the helipad at Key Biscayne to whisk him off to Abplanalp's retreat at Grand Cay, Nixon abruptly changed plans and headed back to Washington. His press secretary explained the President "just decided to go back." He was now going to join Mrs. Nixon at a performance that night of the Khmer dancers from Cambodia.

Almost immediately after Nixon's Bal Harbour fiasco CBS radio revealed the transcript of his remarks had been altered. He had committed two errors, neither one of which was ever to go on historical record. He had referred to

Spiro Agnew, but had identified him as President Agnew. More interestingly he evoked his father's memory in an attempt, as usual, to exploit it. He referred to the fact that his father was a laborer to indicate his respect for labor, and concluded, "I respected my father until the day *I* died." That used to be called a Freudian slip.

The next morning an additional excuse was given for his change of plans. It was not that he had been wounded by his cold reception. He simply wanted to organize the Republicans for an all-out fight against the Democrats' idea of financing Presidential campaigns out of public funds. Such an attempt to decrease the influence of the super-rich on politics was clearly a blow to the Republican way of life. At this point in time the International Telephone and Telegraph Corporation's $400,000 pledge to Nixon's campaign was not yet public knowledge, and, therefore, Nixon's disinterest in petty contributions from the citizenry seemed puzzling to some.

But whatever the official reason, it was clear Nixon had suffered another cut so cruel that all he could do was turn and flee back to the security of that imposing white building on Pennsylvania Avenue. The next morning he went even further into seclusion, helicoptering to Camp David, an area in the Maryland mountains so remote the prying eyes of tourists would never find it.

This was the shattered reaction of a man who preferred to avoid decision making, who had taken on an old man, apparently a soft touch, and had been forced to run for cover. Once again, Connally stepped into the breach. Tuning up his lilting voice, he sang out that the old man had been *arrogant, boorish, and discourteous.* He prefaced his evaluation with a show of pretentious modesty, "In my humble opinion. . . ."

Meany responded tartly, "I have the impression the President did not come here to make a speech. He came here to contrive a situation under which he could claim that he had been unfairly treated."

The battle of Bal Harbour was over. By March 23, 1972, as the BLS announced the largest one-month rise in the cost of living since the previous June, Meany led four of the five labor representatives in resigning from the Pay Board. Frank E. Fitzsimmons, President of the Teamsters Union, refused to follow Meany's example. As surrogate for James Hoffa, whom Nixon had allowed to be released from jail a few weeks earlier, he would have appeared ungrateful had he taken any other course.

Noting that the cost of food had taken its sharpest one-month increase since 1958, Meany labeled price control a "farce." While prices rose, "uncontrolled," the Pay Board was doing an effective job in "squeezing the workers' pay check."

Nixon went before the cameras. "Yesterday, George Meany walked off the job," he said, as though this finally explained why he was not getting the inflation he had induced under control.

Meany had been the victor in many such brawls, but Nixon was still the champ. If the old man of labor stayed healthy long enough, however, it was possible that, with his help, a new champ was going to be crowned.

XXXI.

How Dick Won the War

Nixon became a hermit in the White House. He avoided members of the press, the only way he had discovered to avoid revealing his distaste for them. In 1969 he had approximately six press conferences, roughly the same number he endured in 1970 and 1971. By contrast, Ike met Washington newsmen on a more or less weekly basis, when he was not on vacation or ill and in recovery bay.

When Ike died in 1969 he left his former Vice President with at least two legacies: His grandson David, who, whatever his talents, was someday likely to be seriously considered by some king maker as a reasonable enough facsimile of his grandfather to merit the Republican Presidential nomination. David married Nixon's youngest, Julie, and so sealed an alliance Richard had been trying unsuccessfully to make for twenty years.

The second, and equally durable, was a conviction that nothing the general had done was good enough to be imitated by his lieutenant (j.g.). Nixon's humiliation had been too complete, had gone on for too long, and had ended on too casual and expedient a note to make any thought of Eisenhower more than a painful recollection. Considerations of justice aside, one could understand the attitude that caused Richard Nixon to speak Dwight Eisenhower's name on ceremonial occasions, and nevermore.

Theodore White interviewed Nixon on his second day in office and reported on this phenomenon in *The Making of the President 1968*. He found the new President's resolve firm on two points. "He had already made one prior decision about the National Security Council before inauguration. . . . It would be different from Eisenhower's Security Council. . . . He, as President Nixon, would not have his options limited . . . he wanted no consensus brought to him."

Ike had been a team player, often deferring to department heads he thought were more competent in their own fields. Dick would not make that mistake.

White also found him determined to ignore Ike's method of relating to his Cabinet. Nixon's "Cabinet would meet once a month; it had been called together too often in Eisenhower's time, and members had been bored by discussions not relevant to their departments."

Of course those *bored* government leaders had been kept in close touch with their chief and events in other departments, which might have given them a clearer view of the whole picture. But that had been Ike's way and therefore automatically subject to question. Besides, Ike enjoyed the company of his Cabinet. Dick enjoyed Bebe's company, and the Cuban-born banker was not destined to serve in that official capacity. Nixon knew few of the men who were going to fetch and carry in the Cabinet, and that was the way he wanted to keep it.

Stewart Alsop quotes a White House aide's description of Nixon's "inwardness." "None of us is really close to him. He's like a polite but distant hermit—he emerges every once in a while from his cave, blinks in the light, and then goes back again."

He was also going to reverse Ike's method of dealing with press conferences. Ike, busted syntax and all, enjoyed grappling with contentious newsmen, but Dick had no intention of exposing himself in that most perilous of all journalistic snakepits.

Through all the years he had been running to be President the press had had to be dealt with. It was a conduit to power. One became President by manipulating the press, by keeping your name on the front pages, by forcing those hostile editors to give space to your statements and activities. But once having grasped the orb and sceptre there was no problem in catching their eye. What a great relief he must have felt to realize there was no longer need to seek out all those pushy, inquisitive men who took professional pride in asking embarrassing questions. Furthermore, he had seldom held a press conference which went smoothly, in which there was not at least one *faux pas*. He chose to attribute his generally poor results to maliciousness on the part of an antagonistic press, but in reality, it was usually the reflection of a clumsy performance by a man who never felt comfortable in public.

He had suffered through twenty-five years of what must have seemed to him like indecent exposure, often crimsoning after finishing a filibustering, quadruply-qualified answer, while waiting for the next attempt by some vicious news hawk to degrade him. It was no longer necessary to endure such insolence. He could now go sit quietly in a corner while Haldeman and Ziegler protected him from any invasion of his privacy. What a strange truth he had come to. It had been necessary to arrive at the center of the world's attention to finally escape notice.

There was another reason to retire from view. He had been elected on spurious pledges. He was going to reduce crime, end inflation and get American boys out of Vietnam. Implicitly his "end the war" pledge was meant to be redeemed immediately after inauguration. There is no doubt that had he told the voters in 1968 it would take him at least four years to lower the number of American troops in Vietnam to what it had been under Lyndon Johnson in 1965, a good number of them would have seen more merit in Humphrey. And had he developed a taste for speaking the complete truth, and candidly admitted he had no intention of removing all Americans from South Vietnam before the end of his four years in office, he might never have had those four years.

Soon after taking office he revealed what his "secret plan" had been all along. He would never allow American troops to leave South Vietnam in defeat. An American President had never been accused of losing a war and he was not about to be accorded that distinction in the history books. However, he was going to "wind down" the war. The number of troops would be reduced until at some future date (unspecified), after certain conditions were met (only vaguely defined), our combat role in Southeast Asia would be at an end. However, he did not intend to hand over that area to the Communists. He intended to "Vietnamize" the war. By means of a series of steps, encouraged by our monetary support and the sure knowledge that we were leaving, the government of General Thieu was to understand survival depended on self-reliance.

Daniel Ellsberg, in an article printed in *The New York Review of Books* of March 11, 1971, several months before he became a *cause célèbre* with the publication of the Pentagon Papers, suggested that survival of the Thieu government was not one of Nixon's absolute requirements. In an early display of his compulsion to tell all, Ellsberg described conversations with Henry Kissinger, briefly Ellsberg's boss.

> During 1968 Henry Kissinger frequently said in private talks that the appropriate goal of U.S. policy was a "decent interval"—two to three years—between the withdrawal of U.S. troops and a Communist takeover in Vietnam.

Ellsberg felt that once Kissinger moved into the White House with Nixon it became "evident" that the *decent interval* could not begin until after the 1972 elections.

The conclusion that Nixon had decided to abandon the anti-Communists of South Vietnam to their enemies does not depend on Ellsberg's word. The internal evidence is even more convincing. His speeches about de-escalating the war were followed by substantial troop withdrawals. The pace was rapid enough so that by the beginning of 1972 few Americans were losing their lives in combat, but slow enough so that the Thieu government would not collapse. It was a promising strategy which might work if only the Viet Cong would cooperate and not launch another Tet-type offensive before Nixon had an opportunity to put his best face before the electorate, which for the first time would contain eighteen-year-old draftees. The North Vietnamese invasion in strength of South Vietnam during the second week in April indicated how perilous had been his calculation. The beefing up of the naval and air commitment, the increase of marines and the maintenance of troop levels in Thailand, even while he trumpeted the news of each withdrawal of South Vietnam based infantrymen, indicated how illusory were his promises to end the war.

How did this square with the previous positions he had taken on Communist aggression? In 1951 he had said of the fighting then going on, "The only way we can end the war in Korea is to win it on the battlefield. . . . The Administration policy [which he supported] adds up to this: They will continue the war as it is until the Communists somehow, sometime in the future, see the light and quit."

If he was being consistent, a weakness of which he had no reason to be accused, then perhaps he was working for a Korean-type settlement. Eighteen years after the end of the Korean War the United States still had over ten thousand men stationed in Korea. Nixon's most optimistic projections envisioned no less than thirty-five thousand Americans in Vietnam by Election Day 1972. There is every indication that on questions of military preparedness and armed might to deal with what he viewed as the ever-present danger of barely contained "aggressive world Communism," his views had remained constant through the years.

In his 1950 Senatorial campaign he had come out in favor of "fighting Quakerism," and explained, "It is not easy for me to take this position. It happens that I am a Quaker; all my training has been against displays of strength and recourse to arms. But I have learned through hard experience that, where you are confronted with a ruthless, dictatorial force that will stop at nothing to destroy you, it is necessary to defend yourself by building your own strength."

Again in 1954: "I say this: The United States is the leader of the free world, and the free world cannot afford in Asia a further retreat to the Communists."

At a press conference on June 1, 1971, when he had withdrawn 50 percent of the American troops who had been in Vietnam when he took office, he made it clear his philosophy had not changed:

Well, my views with regard to war are well-known. I grew up in a tradition where we consider all wars immoral. My mother, my grand-mother—on my mother's side—were Quakers, as I often pointed out to this press corps, and very strongly disapproved of my entering World War II.

As far as Vietnam is concerned, like all wars it involves activities that certainly would be subject to criticism if we were considering it solely in a vacuum. But when we consider the consequence of not acting. I think we can see why we have done what we have. To allow a takeover of South Vietnam by the Communist aggressors would not only result in the loss of freedom for 17 million people in South Vietnam, it would greatly increase the danger of that kind of aggression and also the danger of a large war in the Pacific and in the world.

Clear enough?

Years after he had promised to end the war men were still dying in Vietnam, but now without the sense of purpose that had comforted many of the early casualties. A great majority of the people wanted the war to end, which would normally have been reason enough for him to want to end it, but somehow, he could not let go.

On April 30, 1970, while Kissinger was holding secret talks in Paris with the North Vietnamese to end the war, Nixon ordered American troops to spearhead a drive into Cambodia. They were to clear out Viet Cong staging areas in such exotically named locations as Parrot's Beak and Fish Hook, and they were to locate the elaborate underground headquarters of the Communist forces.

The fact that all this was done with the agreement of the Cambodian government meant little to Nixon's growing number of domestic enemies. The Cambodians had been gritting their teeth for years at the sight of North Vietnamese occupying border areas of their country and using them as sanctuaries from which they could safely launch attacks against South Vietnam. Nixon's critics also ignored the fact that for the two weeks before the invasion the Communist trespassers in Cambodia had been in the midst of an offensive to capture Phnom Penh, the Cambodian capital, and topple one of the dominoes which had been a little farther back in line.

To the critics of Nixon's war policy, the American thrust into Cambodia was a direct escalation of the war he had pledged to de-escalate. It was just another example of his perfidiousness, proof, if proof were needed, that Americans could not depend on Nixon's word.

Stung by the criticism, he rushed to explain. He wanted to assure everyone all American operations in Cambodia would cease within sixty days. It had all been done to hasten the war's end, and it was resulting in wonderful benefits. He recited a list of rifles, hand guns, different calibres of ammunition and other varieties of ordnance whose capture he felt had surely dealt a deathblow to our Communist enemy.

However, the credibility gap between the American people and their President, which had closed so dramatically with the termination of Johnson's Administration, once again yawned. American war correspondents, by now the most unfettered news gatherers in the history of man's inhumanity to man, were blowing down Nixon's house of cards with each dispatch they filed. The underground network, which unimpeachable CIA intelligence had pinpointed, was not there when American troops arrived. Carefully following new CIA directions, the nerve center of Communist activities in Cambodia was again approached with ferocious intentions and equally frustrating results. And so on for several weeks, as the elusive underground city proved never to be where the updated intelligence reports had it.

Although the Lon Nol government seemed to have been saved by our intervention and the casualty statistics did not match a normal week-end listing of those killed in stateside automobile accidents, Nixon had exhausted the patience of a large number of Americans. Dissatisfaction with his Vietnam policy paralleled the growing dissatisfaction with his mismanagement of the economy. His ratings in the polls were at an all-time low, which, perhaps, explained why the list of potential Democratic Presidential candidates grew with each passing week.

Withdrawal from Cambodia one week before the June 30, 1970 deadline and continued lowering of the total number of Americans in Vietnam cooled down the war issue in time for the 1970 elections. The Senate repeal on June 24 and July 10 of the Gulf of Tonkin resolution, which had been used by Johnson to justify escalation of the war, further pacified the anti-war critics. The war, consequently, played a relatively small role in that Congressional election. The results were nevertheless dismal from the Republican point of view: Congress remained firmly in the hands of the Democrats.

By February Nixon was ready to attempt another military coup which he hoped would strengthen the Thieu government. There was to be a repeat of the Cambodian operation, only this time the country invaded would be Laos, and the invaders would not include Americans. It was to be a South Vietnamese operation. True, Americans would fly the sophisticated bombers which would chew up the reinforcements being rushed down the Ho Chi Minh Trail to the battle zone, but no public reference would be made to that. Until some inquisitive newsmen began to notice Phantom jets flying into the combat zone, our involvement was clandestine.

In an attempt to avoid the charge heard at the time of the Cambodian campaign, that an expansion of the war was being undertaken without Congressional consent, word of the impending military operations circulated in Washington and around the world for more than a week before the troops finally moved. First one date and then another was advertised. Astonishingly, the Oval Room strategists were quoted as being uncertain whether the invasion would come at this point or that point and at this or that time. Never had an enemy in the history of warfare been so accurately appraised of the plans of his adversary as Minh's troops were in February, 1971.

The assaults made by the South Vietnamese were predictably repulsed after a short advance into Laos; they had only managed temporarily to cut three of the four main branches of the North Vietnamese supply route to the south. Nixon was quickly on television to explain why these retreats were in reality victories, but the hasty pullback of our allies raised fears that Vietnamization was not working and America might have to shore up the Saigon government indefinitely.

Through it all Nixon maintained he was merely attempting to end American participation in the war as skillfully as possible. The temporary increase in American activity, the sallies into enemy territory, all this was being done to further the cause of peace.

On March 8 Nixon decided to get his views before the world in an interview with C. L. Sulzberger, foreign affairs expert for the *Times*. Sulzberger subsequently wrote, "He spoke easily, sitting relaxed in an armchair and more or less thinking aloud as he began to recapitulate his aims, methods and hopes." Although the ground rules of the interview apparently did not originally include the right to publish its contents, Nixon quickly felt himself sufficiently comfortable, and in control, to grant Sulzberger's request to take notes and make his views public.

He wanted everyone to know the Vietnam war was ending. "In fact," he added gratuitously, and with an innocence that made Wilson's hopes for the peace after World War I seem reasonable, "I seriously doubt if we will ever have another war. This is probably the very last one."

However, lest this unexpected streak of idealism disorient his admirers too much, he quickly added, "I'd like to see us not end the Vietnamese war foolishly and find ourselves all alone in the world."

To this note of realism he now added a not-unaccustomed Nixonian dose of political realpolitik. "I could have chosen that course my very first day in office. But I want the American people to be able to be led by me, or by my successor, along a course that allows us to do what is needed to help keep the peace of this world. . . . We must not forget our alliances or our interests. Other nations must know that the United States has both the capability and the will to defend these allies and protect these interests."

That seemed once again to confirm the Nixon postulate that America must play an active policing role in the military controversies which break out with such regularity around the world. If true, it meant long years of American participation in South Vietnam in one role or another.

But Nixon clearly felt he and Henry Kissinger had worked out a strategy which would reconcile the apparent conflict in his position. In almost a gay mood he responded to Sulzberger's question about the probable level of American troops in South Vietnam by mid-1972: "Well, you know I can't disclose the withdrawal figures. But let me say this: Those who think Vietnam is going to be a good political issue next year are making a grave miscalculation."

He grinned broadly at the thought of how he was outmaneuvering his opponents. Knowledge of Henry Kissinger's secret negotiations in Paris, which at that point had been going on for a year and a half, may have added to his confidence about neutralizing the political impact of the war issue:

> Now I am not applying our policy there for political reasons but for reasons of national security. Nevertheless, those who are counting on Vietnam as a political issue in this country next year are going to have the rug jerked from under them. [*He gave the rug a jerk on the night of January 25, 1972, when he told a nationwide television audience about Kissinger's "thirty months" of fruitless secret diplomacy.*] Certainly the way the Laotian battle is going is helping our withdrawal program. And I can tell you that if I were running as a political candidate, I wouldn't select as an issue something that is likely to become a nonissue.

His greatest concern, as usual, was with political strategy. Technician that he was, this was an opportunity to dispense advice, albeit to his political enemies. The slightly hysterical, barely submerged note of fear, masked by an aggressive display of distended feathers and puffed cheeks, was characteristically Nixonian.

He crossed his legs and smiled from his armchair at the White House photographer, then concluded in a jumble of words strung together with great difficulty.

> We are not bent on conquest or on threatening others. But we do have a nuclear umbrella that can protect others, above all the states to which we are allied or in which we have great national interest. This is the *moral* [italics added] force behind our position.

He was under intense pressure. One is tempted to say he was facing another crisis. Four days earlier he had told a press conference of his plans in a manner which seemed contrary to what he was telling Sulzberger. "As long as there are American POWs—and there are 1,600 Americans in North

Vietnam jails under very difficult circumstances at the present time—as long as there are American POWs in North Vietnam, we will have to maintain a residual force in South Vietnam."

He was well aware of the fact that the French had great difficulty in gaining the release of their soldiers captured by the Vietminh before the surrender of Dienbienphu. In fact, they never did achieve a satisfactory explanation of what had happened to large numbers of them. In view of that, it appeared as if he were setting up a condition for withdrawing American troops that could not be met.

At the same conference he had warned that his response to enemy missile attacks on our planes flying over Laos would "not be tit for tat." He was not a tit-for-tat man.

Through the chaos of conflicting pronouncements emerged the outlines of a policy much in line with what Ellsberg had predicted. The troops were to be withdrawn, but only to a given level before the end of 1972. In order to protect them, Nixon was willing to stage sorties with which to caution the North Vietnamese and keep the yapping dogs away from his heels.

Henry Kissinger, who had fled Nazi Germany at fifteen, and become a full professor at Harvard while specializing in the study of political power, was blamed for much of the substance of Nixon's decisons. Few seemed willing to credit Nixon with the ability to mold what was proving to be a relatively subtle foreign policy. Subdued, hard-working Kissinger, who liked to be photographed in public escorting beautiful women, was often identified, along with H. R. Haldeman and George Shultz, as "the second most important man in the government." He shared Haldeman's reluctance to accept that title. He explained, "The trouble is that so many people, so many students simply don't understand my job, which is one of presenting various options to the President, of presenting all the halfway reasonable points of view which exist."

He was willing to concede his role went a little beyond the clerical duties he had described: "It would be preposterous to say that somebody in my position is not asked which course he prefers. Of course I have convictions, and when the President asks me what I think, and he often does, I tell him."

At this point, Kissinger held the curtain aside for a moment and Nixon in the White House could be clearly glimpsed. "And then the last thing that usually happens is that he withdraws for a day or two with all the papers and then makes his decison."

The Laos invasion triggered clamor against the war. On April 24, 1971 a Washington rally attracted 175,000 protestors and received the support of eleven Senators and forty Representatives. The following week less responsible smaller groups rampages through Washington disrupting Senate deliberations from the overhanging galleries of the chamber. They sat in Congressmen's offices and stages guerrilla theater in the corridors of the House and Senate office buildings. Thousands were arrested on May 4 and 5 when they attempted to block the capitol's rush-hour traffic.

A Gallup poll published about that time revealed 69 percent of the sample interviewees did not believe what Nixon was telling them about the war. A similar poll taken in February, 1967, showed 65 percent of those interviewed had similar misgivings about Johnson's pronouncements. Apparently Nixon's credibility gap was already wider than Johnson's. Perhaps it was because he had been working at creating it for a longer time.

By the spring of 1971 Nixon had become as much a prisoner of the White House as Johnson had been. During the last two years of his Administration Johnson had not felt safe in public, and, as a result, made few public appearances. Memories of Kennedy's fate were too vivid.

Nixon had watched helplessly during the first two years of his Administration, as much the same constrictions enveloped his own movements. A man in his position did not have to be paranoid to suspect some deranged owner of one of the millions of high-powered rifles in the country was lining him up in a telescopic sight. It had been months since he had appeared before a large audience, and handshaking trips through anonymous crowds, a relatively familiar method of campaigning for him in the past, were no longer attempted.

On May 29, he ventured into the open at West Point. It was considered so safe that when South Vietnam's Vice President, General Ky, visited the United States it was the only place he was allowed to appear before any large number of people. In a speech made to 3,700 cadets, the Quaker-born Nixon praised the military virtues. "The emotional anti-militarism and moral upheaval of our times will test you severely," he warned the young soldiers. "It is no secret that the discipline, integrity, patriotism and self-sacrifice, which are the very lifeblood of an effective armed force and which the Corps represents, can no longer be taken for granted in the army in which you will serve."

There was regret in his voice. Something had gone out of American life. Respect for law and order, respect for the flag, respect for the teacher, respect for the policeman, and, in addition (he was adding a new one to the list), respect for the *military ethic.*

"The symptoms of trouble are plain enough—from drug abuse to insubordination—[but] I believe, in perspective," he tried to inject a not of hope "that the military ethic remains strong in the hearts of America's fighting men. Your special task will be to reaffirm it, and to give it new life and meaning for the difficult times ahead."

The West Point speech represented Nixon's most enduring adult conviction about the way to solve international disputes. He was a confirmed militarist, who had throughout his career opted for military solutions.

He had wanted to fight for Formosa during Truman's Administration. He had favored MacArthur's plan to conquer North Korea and bomb China during the Korean War. He was the loudest defender of Dulles' "liberation" policy toward the satellite nations of Eastern Europe, a sure-fire lead-in to World War III. He had proposed dropping the H-bomb on Ho Chi Minh in 1954, been in favor of American defense of Quemoy and Matsu in 1960, helped create the plans for the Bay of Pigs invasion, and applauded every escalation of American forces in Vietnam combat.

His bombing of Hanoi and Haiphong on April 16, 1972, and the mining and blockading of all North Vietnam harbors on May 8, something Lyndon Johnson had never been able to bring himself to do even at the height of his determination to win, confirmed that Nixon's approach to conflict had not changed.

His militaristic attitudes showed clearly in an article he wrote for the December, 1965 *Reader's Digest:* "The tide has finally begun to turn in the war of Vietnam. It is my conclusion after three trips to Asia in the last eighteen months. . . . The South Vietnamese, with our help, have a good chance of victory. What has made the difference is the impact of American air strikes in North Vietnam and our commitment of ground troops in South Vietnam. . . . A real victory . . . will take two years or more of the hardest kind of fighting. It will require stepped-up air and land attacks."

The only thing that worked against a more aggressive military role for American forces during his period as Commander-in-Chief, prior to the spring, 1972, North Vietnam invasion of the South, was his political conclusion that it would make him unpopular. He entered office with the determination to make a power play for victory. However, he understood he had a limited amount of time to go all out. As the time for his reelection bid approached that time ran out. He now put forth a policy that went completely against what he thought was right. The quality of the man was so second rate that he moved away from a twenty-five-year stand, to which he was intellectually and emotionally tied, so that he could remain on the popular side of this issue. Super-hawk was finally content to act like super-dove.

What a terrible time to be President. Some wiseacres were always comparing him to Calvin Coolidge, the great unsmiler. If only he had lived in Coolidge's time when there were no great economic problems, no wars to settle. Instead, he was doing his best to minimize American participation in the war, and no one was bothering to give him credit for his efforts.

If only the press were on his side. They were capable of selling any outlandish proposition. The media that had made heroes out of gangsters, luminaries out of Hollywood personalities, such a media was capable of convincing America he had won a great victory in Southeast Asia, if only it would. Spiro had spoiled it all for him. What did it matter that he had spoken the truth from *both* their hearts, it had cost him the support of all but the most die-hard Republican publishers.

Something had to be done. By Election Day, 1972, a majority of American voters had to believe he had won the war and delivered on his promise to create "a generation of peace." Kissinger was working on it. Graham was praying on it. There was reason for confidence.

XXXII.

Snowballs Hit Below the Farm Belt

By March, 1971, Nixon realized he had been backed into a corner. His inability to deliver on his end-the-war pledge, his inept handling of the economy and general lackluster performance as head of state had placed him at a low point in public esteem. On March 1 he made an effort to reverse his political fortunes, and the disastrous results of the attempt told him that stern measures were necessary.

Heading a limited objective mission, Nixon led the White House cadre out to Des Moines, Iowa, on what he hoped would be a good-image exposure in friendly Republicanland. Taking no chances, White House aide John Ehrlichman, as second-most-important-man-in-the-country in domestic matters, had laid out an unambitious schedule which was programmed to last a scant four and a half hours.

The largest block of time was devoted to a speech before a joint session of the Iowa legislature, many of whose members could boast of having a picture with the President shaking their hand hanging on the wall of their office.

Nixon knew he was in trouble in the Midwest. Farmers, who had always seen their best days under Democratic Presidents and rewarded their benefactors by voting Republican, were hurting badly. They had expected a great deal from Nixon, forgetting his support of Ezra Taft Benson's low subsidy bias during Eisenhower's Administration. Instead they had fared about as they usually did under Republican penny-wise-dollar-foolish agricultural policies.

Inflation, which had skyrocketed under Nixon's bungling direction of the economy, had affected the farmer even more drastically than the general population. A two-row corn picker which had sold in 1966 for $3,600 was going for something over $5,000 as Nixon helicoptered down for his visit with the Iowa lawmakers. Furthermore, there had been a calamitous corn blight during the 1970 growing season and many farmers had experienced the misery of no crops to gather at harvest time.

Nixon had decided the blight would hit again in 1971 and as a result had instructed the Agriculture Department to encourage more planting. This was accomplished by the simple expedient of reducing the amount of money the government paid farmers for letting their land lie fallow. Since the farmer was not going to be paid to keep his fields out of production, his only viable alternative was to buy machinery and seed needed to cultivate the surplus acreage which had previously been profitably set aside.

Therefore, as Nixon made his way into the legislative chamber, the residents of this buckle state on the farm belt were largely impoverished by a blighted crop and deeper in debt than they had been since the days of Ezra Taft Benson.

Nixon's last visit to Des Moines had been on September 14, 1968, when as an all-things-to-all-men Presidential candidate he had issued a statement from a cornfield denouncing the low cost-price parity ratio of 74 percent, calling it "dismal" and "intolerable in my book." He drove a picker-sheller while his agricultural statement was analyzed by skeptical farmers, who were trying to convince themselves he was the best thing that had happened to them since the invention of DDT.

By November, 1970, the parity ratio had sunk to 67 percent. The Midwestern farmers showed their displeasure with Nixon by replacing eight Republican Congressmen and five GOP governors with Democrats in that month's elections.

As Nixon mounted the Iowa rostrum, parity support prices were at the not much more satisfying rate of 70 percent. His speech, observed attentively by soft-spoken Secretary of Agriculture Clifford M. Hardin, was meant to mute the trumpets of criticism.

Nixon told these parliamentarians, many of whom earned their living as farmers, that he intended to end their problems by getting rid of the Department of Agriculture. No sign of disagreement crossed Hardin's placid face. Nixon smoothly said he intended to distribute the department's functions to four separate super-departments. He tried to explain why this would benefit the farmer, hurrying his listeners over a thinly covered patch of logical quicksand. Today there was "only one" Cabinet secretary defending the farmer's point of view. "Under my proposed reorganization, four Cabinet secretaries—half of the Cabinet—will be speaking up for the farmer when his diverse interests are at stake."

It was merely new packaging. Nixon was looking for something that would catch the woebegone farmer's eye and give him a vision of greener pastures, at least until after the 1972 election.

This was characteristic of his approach to any serious problem. First there would be an exhaustive study of the problem, which would take months longer than it should have. He would listen to every point of view, often playing devil's advocate in a manner that seemed calculated to ventilate the alternatives, but which most often merely had the effect of needlessly prolonging vacuous discussion.

As Nixon finished his speech and walked out into the cold winter air, he had hopes his proposed reshuffling of agricultural agencies would be enough of a palliative to quiet his farm belt critics. After all, it would take time to see if his proposed reorganization would work. Fair men would not sabotage his efforts with carping criticism. Patriots would all join hands and hope that the new super-agency's more efficient processing of photocopy, computer-written answers to farmer's complaints would bring about prosperity.

Once outside he was forced to face the illusiveness of his hopes. There were 1,000 demonstrators in the plaza in front of the legislative building. They were in an ugly mood. There were boos and catcalls. The signs told the story: *17 cents a pound hogs; $1.25 pork chops—why? Impeach Nixon. Hog prices are too low. Nixon plan hurts retirees. . . . We want HIGHER Social Security benefits. End the war now.*

Suddenly a volley of snowballs, and at least one baseball-sized rock, were thrown at Nixon. His reaction, given with a chuckle, "snowballs are fun." He did not say what rocks were.

Later in the day, safely back at the White House, he made a reference to the fact that a bomb had exploded under the Senate chamber in the Capitol Building. "Violent people," he said grimly, would not succeed in closing public buildings or keeping the President at home. "They would like to keep the President in Washington rather than come out in the country. Well, it won't work."

But the point was that it *was* working. The farmers were angry enough to make snowball throwing seem the thing to do. Blacks were convinced his expressions of support for the neighborhood school and against forced busing was merely a symptom of racial antagonism. And the quality of his Supreme Court nominees was so low that no one was shocked when four of the eight he proposed were found so lacking in stature that they never survived the scrutiny of their judges.

If the President of the United States was not totally safe in Iowa, where *would* he be safe? Nixon's answer seemed to be that better times were just beyond the horizon. As soon as crops were harvested in the autumn, and farmers once again had the money to pay their creditors, he would again be welcome in Iowa.

Miscalculation piled on miscalculation. The return of the blight, which

Nixon had so confidently awaited, never materialized. Instead the growing season in the Midwest was phenomenal. As the summer wore on and this became more evident to the agronomists in the Department of Agriculture, panic set in.

Farmers are susceptible to a vicious law of economics, referred to as The Paradox of Values. Simply stated, it says when farmers market exactly the amount of produce needed by the consumer they get their best price. But when they attempt to market only a small amount more than consumers need, the price they receive declines precipitously. This is not true of other consumer goods, where the excess production can be stored until demand for it recurs. This paradox had been the source of a great deal of farmer misery under the pre-New Deal unregulated free enterprise farm system. When the regulators miscalculate, as they did so seriously in the spring of 1971, The Paradox of Values is there to remind them of the terrible forces with which they have tampered.

By September, as the corn feed crop began to inundate rail depots and glut storage facilities, prices headed sharply down. A bushel of corn which cost an Iowa farmer $1.08 to grow was bringing him 95 cents. A year earlier, when there was insufficient corn to take care of the demands of buyers, the price had been $1.50 a bushel.

What was Nixon to do? No doubt the government had saved some money in the spring by cutting back on acreage allotment payments, but since it was now costing so much more than it had saved, perhaps the best thing to do was to loosen the acreage allotment purse strings. Four months before the usual date for the annual announcement, the Department of Agriculture revealed it was more than doubling the amount of acreage to be taken out of production in 1972. It was going to cost the government an additional $700 million, but an election was worth it.

Apparently aware of this almost unavoidable consequence of his ruinous agricultural policy, Nixon started the last year of his first term with a rapid series of public relations maneuvers which was his substitute for meaningful action.

On November 12, little more than eight months after he had unveiled his monumental reorganization plan for the Department of Agriculture, he announced his decision to abandon it. It was apparent farmers had not bought his merger promotion. Farm papers throughout the Midwest denounced him for proposing a scheme they felt was aimed at further reducing farmers' influence in government.

Nixon grabbed his alternative plan off the drawing board—the one labelled "Find a Scapegoat." In a gathering before Washington newsmen, which was notable for its surface cordiality, Nixon announced Clifford Hardin was resigning.

Hardin, a mild-mannered gentleman, now joined a lengthening list of Nixon Cabinet discards. Almost half his original Cabinet had not managed to last out the first three years of the Nixon era. Gone were David Kennedy, Treasury; Walter Hickel, Interior; Robert Finch, Health, Education and Welfare; George Shultz, Labor; and what's-his-name gone with the entire Post Office Department. George Romney was barely hanging on with a death grip by his grinning teeth. At the beginning of 1972 Maurice Stans resigned as Secretary of Commerce to take over what was apparently thought to be a more important job, chairman of the fund-raising committee for Nixon's reelection campaign.

Earl L. Butz was to take Hardin's place. He had shown Nixon he was qualified to help the farmers when he had been one of Benson's Assistant Secretaries from 1954 to 1957. At the ceremonial occasion when Nixon announced he was sending Butz's appointment to the Senate for approval, the aloof Butz showed his quality as a man when he turned to the embarrassed Hardin, while Nixon smiled approval, and said accusingly, "The price of corn is too low, Mr. Secretary—below the cost level." A short turn in the opposite direction would have brought his eyes to rest on the man whose responsibility for that ludicrously pitiful fact was more direct.

Since Butz was highly unpopular with farmers, his selection by Nixon seemed inept. In reality many of Nixon's selectees had been of less than mediocre calibre. Few outstanding men were ever willing to work for him. He was no Kennedy, whose blinding presence and resort to the lofty rhetoric of idealism often drew men of superior talent to his side.

His confirmation hearings before the Senate brought out that Butz served on the board of directors of three giant agribusinesses, companies which produced farm supplies or processed farm products—companies whose objectives were often in conflict with those of the family farmer. His critics, McGovern, Humphrey and Fred Harris, of Oklahoma, depicted him as "an agent of the corporation conglomerates that were destroying family farms and driving farmers off the land." He was confirmed by a vote of 51 to 44, only after a Senatorial row which suggested the Democrats thought Nixon had provided them with another issue. Butz seemed unconcerned and hinted at the reason for his equanimity when he described himself as a "political animal." He had unsuccessfully sought the Republican nomination for governor of Indiana in 1967. The day his appointment to Agriculture was confirmed, December 2, he announced the government's support price for

1972 corn was being raised, a move which lent support to his boast of political savvy. It also set off a chain reaction in the following months which led to an inflationary rise in the supermarket price of beef and pork.

Whether Nixon was aware of it or not, he and Eisenhower had been pursuing a farm policy whose major practical result had to be the reduction of the number of farm families in America. Ike wanted to get the government out of the farm business. He justified such shortsightedness by references to earlier American virtues, self-sufficiency, independence, pride. He seemed unable to understand that these undeniable virtues were not germane to the Midwestern farmer who had outright ownership of little more than the pants he wore.

By the beginning of 1972 only about 9 million Americans lived on farms. This was down from approximately 30 million in the 1930's, when the total population was almost half the size. Rural Iowa bankers were predicting that, if conditions did not improve, 25 percent of their customers would be forced to esert their farms before the end of the year. In his 1968 acceptance speech, Nixon had said, "I see a day when life in rural America attracts people to the country, rather than driving them away." As President, everything he did had xactly the opposite result.

The beneficiaries of this human erosion were not the American consumers. They had witnessed an extraordinary rise in prices simultaneous with the growth of the factory farm. There seemed very few beneficiaries, indeed, and most of them were friends of Richard Nixon.

As increasing numbers of farmers were dispossessed from the land and made their way to the cities, where unemployment was so high Nixon had given orders that the Bureau of Labor Statistics was no longer to issue monthly figures on *that* calamity, the prospects for Nixon's reelection diminished. Perhaps George Wallace would rescue him again. But short of that, his prospects looked dimmer than those of any incumbent who had sought reelection since Herbert Hoover exhibited that particular variety of bad judgment.

XXXIII.

Tricia Plus Chinese Checkers Equals Two Brownie Points

A massive publicity campaign was mounted. Three new public relations men were put on the White House staff during the week of April 29, 1971, raising the number of that crucial cadre to twenty-two, not counting their secretaries and office staff. They burnt barrels of midnight oil. There was work to be done.

Nixon's face became standard as a magazine cover in unexpected places. *McCall's* and other women's journals suddenly ran stories playing up his human qualities. He posed for pictures with Pat walking along the beach at San Clemente. He appeared on the "Today" show, held interviews with New York *Times* and London *Daily Telegraph* correspondents; he even had his third press conference of the year that week.

Finally Rose Mary Woods was trotted out to speak of her boss. On WABC-TV she described him gently. "I think basically he is shy, and like a lot of shy people he appears not to be warm."

Miss Woods had worked for Nixon for over two decades. During that time she had never displayed the slightest desire to go before the television cameras. Whatever her opinions of her boss, they had, till this moment, been allowed to remain her private property. However, Nixon was in trouble, and at a time like this even private sentiment had to be exploited.

What more sentimental event is there than a wedding, and Nixon had the good fortune at this dark moment in his destiny to marry off his oldest daughter, Tricia, to Edward Finch Cox. He did it with an explosion of publicity which brought smiles to the faces of America's caterers. Nixon defenders point out that Lyndon Johnson had done the same for his oldest daughter, Lynda Bird, in a White House ceremony, and held a reception for his youngest, Luci Baines, at the White House after a church ceremony.

359

There is justice in the comparison, but in Johnson's case the element of exploitation seemed relatively minimal: He had apparently gone a long way in the direction of deciding not to run for reelection when nuptial-time arrived. The celebrations for his young birds seemed nothing more than a proud Texas father, his pockets stuffed with greenbacks, trying to rent the largest, swankiest hall in town for his "darlins."

With Nixon, every move seemed calculated to confirm that he considered this a marriage for his daughter and an opportunity for himself.

For a man of his political temperament his situation was desperate—extraordinary measures were called for. In view of what was shortly to come, his adventures in Nixonmony were merely a warm-up.

Had the elections been held in June, 1971, Nixon's chances would have been perilously slim. Since charm was never his strong suit, shock was to be his main technique in reversing this calamitous state of affairs. Shock immobilizes your opposition, and if skillfully applied, the opposition would remain numb until the day after election.

Tricia's marriage, however, allowed him to start his shock treatment on a reassuringly, although synthetically, human note. *Women's Wear Daily* played its usual role in wedding-dress espionage. Those interested in an advance view of the bride's dress waited impatiently while the fashion super-spies tried to ferret out the blueprint. The New York *Times,* always interested in exclusives, obtained the recipe for the multi-storied wedding cake and caused an overnight crisis in the White House kitchen when their chefs baked a duplicate only to have it dissolve before their startled eyes. Such priceless publicity. Had Haldeman and his cadre of Madison Avenue veterans worked up the advertising campaign themselves, they could not have hoped for better results.

It was time to move Dick stage-center. Two days before the wedding he chatted informally with newsmen, the first time that had happened in months. There was no talk of inflation or the war; it was all about his little girl. Yet the conversation struck a poignant note: "I was out making a political speech the day she was born." He was reaching for something that would symbolize the nature of their relationship, and campaigning quickly sprang to mind. "I wasn't around much while she grew up," he continued. "For the rest of the time, up to the present time, it seems I've always been saying goodbye . . . goodbye to her at airports."

What he said was sad, but he said it so calmly, so glibly, that it seemed to impress his public relations staff as the closest approximation of paternal happiness they might expect from him. Two days later, June 12, they found time, shortly before the outdoor wedding, for Nixon to take a stroll in the Rose Garden surrounded by journalists swept up by the joy of the occasion.

They crowded around him, smiling broadly and asking questions about Tricia.

He tried to parry them. He spoke of the threatening weather. It had been Tricia's idea to hold the ceremony outdoors and rain was falling sporadically. What sort of girl was she, a reporter wanted to know.? He smiled enigmatically. "She's jealous of her privacy," he said quietly. "I would not be *able to, nobody will be able to, analyze her character.*"

Why, that was what people always said about him, wasn't it? It must be another case of the apple not falling far from the tree. He smiled broadly and said he had to get back inside, since things were just about to get started.

The guest list was a roll call of the people who had been important in Nixon's life. Bebe Robozo flew up from Key Biscayne and Robert Abplanalp flew down from Bronxville. There was the old California bunch, the Raymond Arbuthnots and Jack Drowns. Elmer Bobst was not forgotten, nor was Los Angeles fundraiser Henry Salvatori. But Murray Chotiner did not make the list, and his replacement, Len Garment, was similarly snubbed.

Show biz was represented by Red Skelton, Ethel Waters, Art Linkletter, Freeman Gosden and Mrs. Bob Hope, the closely related world of the theatrical pulpit by Billy Graham and Dr. Norman Vincent Peale. The Smathers family had sent son Bruce, a former Tricia beau. Arthur Burns and George Shultz eyed each other from folding chairs at opposite sides of the aisle. Brothers Donald and Edward represented the gathering of the clan. Three of Pat Ryan's nephews also listened as Reverend Edward G. Latch, the House of Representatives chaplin, read off the service written by Tricia, with heavy borrowings from Methodist and Catholic ceremonials.

Through it all the television cameras carried the festivities to every corner of the country. Only for the briefest moment, as the couple were exchanging vows, was the gaze of the unblinking lens averted. As Nixon walked back to the White House, Pat resting on his arm, he gave the cameramen the three-ring sign of the satisfied beer drinker.

Although it had been uncertain up until the last moment, Nixon was apparently so pleased with the way things had gone that he allowed one of the marginal events to be re-inserted into the script. At the reception, the television cameras were allowed to view the first five steps taken by Tricia and her father in the ritual dance that betokens a new relationship. Then the members of the Cabinet mercifully moved in with their ladies to obliterate the sight of their stiffly correct, precariously balanced chief.

The reviews the following day warmed the hearts of the future J. Walter Thompson board of directors. There had been a breakthrough. But it was a tough act to follow. Dick was out of daughters.

Within hours the drawing board was covered with safe projects that would allow Nixon to be aired out a bit. The first stop came ten days later in Atlantic City, when he appeared before the American Medical Association, one of the professional branches of the Republican Party. Just how safe an appearance it was is indicated by Nixon's reference to the fact that he was the fourth President to address the AMA (the others had all been Republicans: William McKinley in 1897, Calvin Coolidge in 1927 and Dwight Eisenhower in 1959). Nixon assured himself of a warm reception when he referred to Edward M. Kennedy's liberal health insurance plan as "nationalized compulsory health insurance" which "would tear apart" the present health system.

With the ring of applause still in his ears, he began a tour of Republican Indiana. Iowa was going to be allowed to cool down for a while.

At noon on June 24 a helicopter came out of the blue and set him down on the parking lot of the Jennings County High School in Vernon, a town of 500 in the southeastern corner of the state. He had been invited by the high school chapter of The Indiana Junior Historical Society. The kids had compiled a history of the Milhous family and were erecting a plaque which read:

> Hannah Milhous Nixon; mother of President Richard M. Nixon, was born on a farm four and a half miles southeast to which her grand-parents came in 1854. Hannah's parents moved to California when she was 12 years old.

So shocked were the citizens of Vernon to see the President in their midst that the North Vernon *Plain Dealer* felt compelled to put out a special red, white and blue edition calling the visit "the biggest thing that has happened to Jennings since Morgan's Raiders tried unsuccessfully to breach the Union defenses around Vernon back in the Civil War days."

That was a long time between special editions, but the editors revealed they had not allowed themselves to grow rusty. "You can also say that there is a lot of political manner to a visit of this nature and the fact that President Nixon is coming to Jennings is sure-fire evidence that he has every intention of running for reelection in 1972. . . ."

In the courthouse square Nixon told the crowd of 700 he was going to say "what I think my mother would want me to say."

Then with hands chopping the air he intoned, "She would want me to say to this group: Keep your religious faith. She would say that religious faith has sustained her through some very difficult times. Finally, she would want me to say to you that we in this country should dedicate ourselves to the cause of peace." First Tricia, then Hannah. In a crisis family is always called on to help out.

He then spent twenty minutes shaking hands with the crowd, while Secret Service agents scanned the smiling faces for a crashing Weatherman.

The next day he was in Chicago for another rally. He addressed the combined conventions of the National Retired Teachers Association and the American Association of Retired Persons. His message was one of reform. "I do not believe that Medicare and Medicaid funds should go to substandard nursing homes in this country and subsidize them." There was a suggestion in what he was saying that his political opponents felt Medicare funds should be spent to maintain substandard nursing homes. Of course he did not quite *say* that, but that was the essence of the Nixon style. Accusation by indirection and implication.

He told them he planned to call a White House conference to determine how nursing homes could be upgraded. Then he departed from his prepared text to reminisce about the last time he had seen his mother. At 82 she was near death and under heavy sedation. Richard had flown out from New York, where he was practicing law, to visit her. "Just as I was ready to leave to go back to New York I said to her, 'Now, mother, don't you give up.' Her eyes flashed and she leaned up in bed and said, 'Don't *you* give up.' "

Regarding his audience earnestly, he added, "I didn't give up. That is why I am here today."

Before the day was over he had flown back to Washington and then helicoptered to the Presidential retreat at Camp David. Here the circle was completed as he was greeted by the honeymooners, Tricia and Ed. The newlyweds had dropped out of sight after the bridal bouquet had been thrown, and resurfaced now for the first time heartened by the sight of the President's glowing, grateful face.

The humanizing ploy had worked. The press and public had enjoyed the wedding. (One young TV viewer told the President, "You danced good.") He'd made their day in Vernon. And the elderly had applauded quietly from their seats. The momentum had to be kept up. It was time for a dramatic announcement, something that would prove to the easily-convinced that he was decisive and innovative. By the time the election campaign got underway there should be no one who would be able to call him a do-nothing President.

And so the final planning for the most electrifying event of the Nixon years took place, an event that guaranteed no historian would ever rank him below John Tyler on his list of important Presidents. He was on the verge of announcing he would make a trip to mainland China before May, 1972, tantamount to recognizing the Communist Chinese government.

Nixon had built his career on the proposition that patriots should never recognize Mao's China. He had endlessly proclaimed that Americans must

look forward to the day when Chiang Kai-shek and his Formosan government would recapture the mainland from those barbarous, atheistic Reds.

In 1960, when first seeking the Presidency, he had declared, "I can
think of nothing more detrimental to freedom or peace than the recognition
of Communist China."

Showing that defeat had not changed his mind, he told Kennedy, at a
meeting in the Key Biscayne Hotel on November 14, 1960, that he must resist
all advice to recognize Mao.

During the entire period between that intimate moment in the Florida sun,
when Kennedy made an adroit effort to unruffle his rival's feathers, and
1967, there was no slightest indication Nixon had relented.

In October, 1967, as part of his drive to give himself a statesmanlike image
for the 1968 campaign, he wrote an article for the prestigious quarterly
Foreign Affairs. In it he suggested his mind was opening to a new idea. The
article, entitled "Asia After Vietnam," reasonably but vaguely postulated
that "any American policy toward Asia must come urgently to grips with the
reality of China."

There was a hint in that of a developing streak of détenism. He went
further: "Taking the long view, we simply cannot afford to leave China [He
had already ceased to call it *Red* China or *Communist* China] forever outside
the family of nations, there to nurture its fantasies, cherish its hates and
threaten its neighbors."

Clearly this was a call for the inclusion of China in the United Nations. But
it was amorphous enough to offer him several paths of retreat should any of
his old friends, who had not noticed the shift of public opinion on this
question, raise any sort of clamor.

The possibility of protest was remote. Nixon was not the leader in this
movement to "come urgently to grips with the reality of China." He had also
been careful to mount an obscure rostrum before a distinguished but infi-
nitesimal audience when he chose to float this trial balloon in the *Foreign
Affairs* quarterly. Some alert researcher for the John Birch Society might
come across it in his ceaseless quest for subversives in the intellectual
community, but he was hardly likely to attribute to his hero the venomous
intent of those fuzzy-minded eggheads.

Herb Klein's final judgment was that "The China initiative was pretty well
spelled out in a paper he wrote for *Foreign Policy* in 1967." But Nixon
homilies in that paper, such as, "The world cannot be safe until China
changes," left too much to the imagination to allow Klein's partisan in-
terpretation to end the discussion of what Nixon really had on his mind.

However, six months after the election, on July 21, 1969, President Nixon
did indeed take action which indicated a profound change in his point of

view. The White House announced henceforth Americans traveling abroad would be allowed to bring $100 worth of Chinese goods back into the country. Furthermore, United States scholars, students, scientists, physicians and newsmen were going to be allowed to travel to mainland China. Fidel Castro's Cuba remained out of bounds.

Aside from mysterious conversations which had been taking place between Washington and Peking representatives in Warsaw for several years, these were the only gestures of tractability the American government had made toward Mao since General Wedemeyer tried to act as a Chinese mediator in the late 1940s.

The State Department, although well on its way to being subordinated to Henry Kissinger, was allowed to point out that the moves were unilateral in nature and there was no expectation of reciprocity from Peking. However, the signal was clear. If the Chinese Communists were willing to put aside the banalities of the Cultural Revolution long enough to consider a possible rapprochement, Nixon wanted them to know he was not a prisoner of old ideas.

As the decline in his popularity became more precipitous, Nixon's interest in striking a new note in Chinese-American relations intensified. There was also the practical matter of trying to reach some sort of accommodation with Mao before he had so sharply reduced our forces in Vietnam that they no longer provided him with any bargaining position in Asia.

The Chinese Communists gave him reason to hope for a change in their anti-American position when they invited the U.S. Ping-Pong team to visit Peking in April, 1971. The smiles that resulted from that trip seemed to make many formerly preposterous ideas seem reasonable.

On April 16,1971 the President had an important statement to make to the American Society of Newspaper Editors in Washington. Almost wistfully he said he hoped to visit China someday, although he was not sure it could happen while he was in office. But that certainly suggested he hoped it *might*.

At a news conference on April 29 he again expressed that hope. There is no more public place than a press conference for the President to express a wish which will fly to the ends of the world.

By this time Nixon and Kissinger had determined an attempt would be made to arrange a state visit to mainland China. "Informed officials," who preferred to remain anonymous, indicated to *Time* magazine reporters that Rumania's President, Nicolae Ceauşescu, became the intermediary who arranged the next step in the visit. He had received Nixon warmly more than a year earlier in Rumania, when Nixon became the first President to set foot in a satellite country. The visit had gone so well that Ceauşescu became the logical man to make the contact with his other friends, the Communist Chinese.

Whatever the details, on July 1 Kissinger left Washington purportedly headed for a tour of Vietnam, but actually clutching an olive branch for Mao. After extensive conversations with President Nguyen Van Thieu, during which he told him nothing of his true reason for being in Asia, he left Saigon on July 5, apparently intent on taking the slow, tourist route back home.

He paused in New Delhi to placate the Indians, because of the vital stop he had to make next in Pakistan. The two impoverished countries, driven by Malthusian imperatives as much as anything else, were on the verge of war which formally broke out on December 3. The Kissinger-Nixon decision to come down on the side of the Pakistan dictatorship, which was commiting genocide in East Bengal and was being supported by the People's Republic of China, precisely at the moment when it had become apparent that the Bangladesh were on the verge of winning their independence, was a glaring example of neo-brinksmanship at its worst. At the beginning of the fourteen-day war we had been friendly with both sides. Within that two-week period Nixon's blunders created a situation where we were despised by both sides. Columnist Jack Anderson's revelation of the minutes of secret conferences chaired by Kissinger at which, in Dr. Strangelove fashion, he spoke of "tilting" our support toward Pakistan in the form of aircraft transshipped covertly through Jordan, was still several months in the distance. On July 8, when he arrived in Rawalpindi, Kissinger's eyes were focused on the less critical problem of Sino-American public relations.

At this point the plot thickened. After a 90-minute visit with soon to be deposed President Yahya Khan, word was passed that Kissinger was going to the mountain resort of Nathia Gali for a well-deserved holiday. The next day the Pakistan government announced Kissinger had been forced to extend his stay in the mountains because of a "slight indisposition." His stomach was upset, so the story went. Correspondents freshened their copy with references to "Delhi belly."

Actually Kissinger had not gone to the mountains. Instead he was taken to Rawalpindi airport, placed aboard a Pakistan Boeing 707, with three aides, and flown to Peking. They landed at an airfield outside the city at noon on July 9, and were driven to a villa on a small lake outside Peking where they were served lunch. At four that afternoon Chou En-lai entered the room and the man John Foster Dulles had refused to shake hands with at Geneva in 1954 had his hand vigorously and warmly grasped by one of the second-most-important-men in the American government. The session lasted eight hours, and the following day, after a tour of the Forbidden City, a second session of equal length was held.

Sixty-four hours after he left Pakistan, Kissinger surfaced again. Despite Nixon's jaundiced view of the cynicism of newspapermen, they never more clearly displayed their innocence. There was Henry Kissinger—described by one of his many girlfriends as resembling a prosperous Bronx delicatessen owner—despite the ravaging effects of a supposed dysentery, five pounds heavier than when they had last seen him.

Perhaps, after all, it *was* cynicism that misled them. The media had grown used to picturing Kissinger as the "swinger" of the Nixon entourage. Eager to seize on one of the men around Nixon they might humanize for their readership, newsmen had settled on the unlikely figure of Kissinger. Separated from his wife, Kissinger spent those infrequent moments away from his desk in the presence of a series of lovely women. This had been enough to virtually brand him as the Nixon version of Casanova. Obviously such an individual could only be a pale version of the original, if it were going to be possible for Nixon to endure him. However, the canons of journalism require that each Administration have its swinger, and in this puritan paradise hardworking Henry would have to do.

Had Kissinger been taken by the Moslem rulers of Pakistan to some garden of joy in the mountains, there to experience the pleasures reserved for the powerful? The press fantasized. When he left Pakistan with such a happy look on his face, and made straight for that Elysium of European society, Paris, their fantasies seemed to take on more weight. A twenty-four-hour extension of his stay in Paris, officially described as being for social reasons, put the finishing touches on converting his supposed diplomatic trip into a round-the-world orgy.

Kissinger arrived at the Western White House on July 13 and spent the next three days in conference with the President. Secretary of State Rogers (it had by this time become necessary to give his full title so as to identify the official nature of his position) was included in picture-taking ceremonies which showed all three of them smiling broadly.

On Thursday, July 15, the reason for their happiness became apparent. Early in the day Ronald Ziegler indicated the President had an important announcement to make. There was no indication of its nature, merely that everyone would want to listen as he addressed the nation.

That evening Nixon and Kissinger motored into Los Angeles from San Clemente. They went to the Burbank studio where "Laugh-in" normally was televised, and with absolute deadpan the President took ninety seconds to announce a complete reversal in American foreign policy. The substance of the message was read off simultaneously in Peking.

Premier Chou En-lai and Dr. Henry Kissinger, President Nixon's Assistant for National Security Affairs, held talks in Peking from July 9 to 11, 1971. Knowing of President Nixon's expressed desire to visit the People's Republic of China, Premier Chou En-lai on behalf of the government of the People's Republic of China has extended an invitation to President Nixon to visit China at an appropriate date before May, 1972. President Nixon has accepted the invitation with pleasure. The meeting between the leaders of China and the United States is to seek the normalization of relations between the two countries and also to exchange views on questions of concern to the two sides.

He said he was undertaking this "journey for peace" because he felt the cause of peace required the participation of the 750 million people of China. At the same time he made what must be considered one of the emptiest gestures of all time toward Chiang Kai-shek on Fortress Formosa.

Our action in seeking a new relationship with the People's Republic of China will not be at the expense of our old friends.

The phrase "old friends" sounded as if it were meant to be "former friends." He suddenly seemed to be playing a game of Chinese checkers, where one was allowed to jump forward, backward or sideways, even over one's own men, and still be within the rules of the game.

The reaction was instantaneous and everything Nixon must have expected. On the whole, Americans were pleased. Partly because they are always pleased with what their President says he will do, at least when he first proclaims his intentions. Many were happy because the China policy of five successive Presidents had never seemed to promise anything more than a perpetually hostile stalemate, and had often seemed to promise nothing less than atomic war.

Democratic Senate Majority Leader Mike Mansfield was "flabbergasted, delighted and happy." He went on to say, "I am looking forward to a new day." Almost as enthusiastic was Nixon's former opponent, the once-again *Senator* Hubert Humphrey, who commended the President for "this important diplomatic initiative."

Clearly, Nixon's traditional enemies were overjoyed with his new line. Equally clearly, his traditional friends were not nearly so entranced. Sensing a dangerous aberration, they hesitated at first to speak up, but before the end of the week, their angry response recalled their manner of dealing with other obvious traitors.

William Loeb, publisher of the Manchester, New Hampshire, *Union Leader*, wrote of a recent dinner at the White House in which he and his wife "found the Nixons to be fine people. But the first consideration is not personal friendship. This newspaper considers President Nixon's proposal to visit Communist China and the change in policy toward Red China to be immoral, indecent, insane and fraught with danger for the survival of the United States."

He had never said anything worse about Alger Hiss.

New York's conservative Senator James Buckley, the more restrained of the brothers, said, "A rush to embrace China without counting the cost to the United States has created too high expectations here." William, the altogether unlikely leader of popular conservatism in America north of the Mason-Dixon Line, more colorfully remarked, "F.D.R. would have hesitated to go to Berlin to wine and dine with Adolf Hitler—but we are about to do that, and all the liberals who can't stand the Greek colonels are jumping for joy."

California conservative Walt Hintzen did not draw such a delicate historical comparison. He merely labelled Nixon's decision to become the first President to visit China as "obscene."

What seemed to be bothering the largest number of his right-wing supporters was the thought that the Nationalists' days as rulers of Formosa were numbered. So much of their energy and thought had gone into the preservation of that remnant of the old China. Was all that to be wiped out now simply because Nixon was anxious to make a popular move? And all that brave talk of the two million Kuomintang refugees on Formosa liberating the 750,000,000 mainland Chinese, was that all to be forgotten?

Former Congressman Walter Judd, whom Ike had considered as his running mate in 1952 instead of Nixon, said, "It's a smashing blow to the hopes of millions of oppressed people in Asia who are yearning for freedom."

Senator John Tower of Texas, and Strom Thurmond, joined in with a reverberating, "Amen."

George Meany, one of Nixon's strongest foreign policy supporters, commented, "His trip to China is another charade. I don't think there is anything that we can gain. . . . I think this was just a great publicity stunt."

Through the rest of July the unanswered question remained, to what did Kissinger have to agree in order to wrangle the invitation for Nixon? The initiative had come from Nixon. He had sent Kissinger hat in hand. What price was he being forced to pay?

On August 2 Secretary Rogers provided part of the answer. He announced the United States would "support action in the General Assembly this fall calling for seating the People's Republic of China."

He went on to insist we were in no way softening our opposition to the Communist bloc move to expel Nationalist China from the United Nations.

There was in this new American position so much sanctimonious hypocrisy that it immediately became apparent the Nationalist delegation's position had been irreparably damaged. Its days in the United Nations were clearly numbered.

Through all this Nixon remained incommunicado.

Peking did not modify its position and continued to insist it would never sit in a United Nations which included Nationalist Formosa, but Nixon's representatives spoke as if they could envision no problem. Rogers simply stated, "We think that they are now interested in becoming a member of the United Nations."

He was endorsing a "Two China" policy. Both governments, which were reluctant to share space on the same globe, were to share adjoining seats in the General Assembly. In 1960 Nixon had told President-elect Kennedy at Key Biscayne what he thought of such a plan.

> The issue wasn't whether Red China had one vote in the Assembly, or even the veto power. What was really at stake was that admitting Red China to the United Nations would be a mockery of the provision of the Charter which limits its membership to "peace-loving nations." And what was most disturbing was that it would give respectability to the Communist regime which would immensely increase its power and prestige in Asia, and probably irreparably weaken the non-Communist governments in that area.

Kennedy had been leaning in the direction of adopting that compromise position. Nixon's unrelenting opposition at the meeting must have played a role in making him hang back from such a step. Now, years later, after a good deal of mischief had occurred because of the continued split between the two world powers, Nixon was rushing at top speed to end all enmity before election day.

Having gained as much advantage as he could from the original terse statement about the trip to Peking, Nixon proceeded to construct an escape hatch in case things did not go as smoothly as he had previously indicated. On Sunday, October 24, he delivered a radio address. The occasion was the new three-day weekend Veterans' Day celebration. After alluding to the Vietnam war as "the least understood war in our history," he cautioned the nation for the first time. "We go [to China] with no false hopes, and we intend to leave behind us in America no unrealistic expectations."

This realistic appraisal came in the midst of the final debate on the twenty-year-old argument about admission of Communist China to the United Nations. The debate had been going badly against our stated position. The majority of the delegates did not endorse our belief that the People's Republic of China would accept a seat in the world body as long as Nationalist China was a member. As a result, in violation of its philosophy of being an organization open to all, the majority was moving toward expelling

Formosa and giving its seat on the Security Council to mainland China.

So emotional had the debate become, and so disorganized were Chiang's defenders by Nixon's proposed visit to Mao, that the U.N. was about to expel a member for the first time. Twenty-four hours after Nixon's Veteran's Day speech the issue came to a head. On the key vote, to consider the expulsion of Nationalist China an "important question," which would require a two-thirds vote to carry, the American resolution lost by a vote of 59-55. By democratic vote one of the most important issues ever to come before the United Nations was declared to be an *unimportant question.* Then by a vote of 76-35 the decision was made "to expell forthwith the representatives of Chiang Kai-shek from the place which they unlawfully occupy at the United Nations and in all the organizations affiliated to it."

The chief delegate of Tanzania was so overwhelmed with joy he jumped to his feet and led his fellow delegates in a victory jig at the front of the General Assembly. George Bush, American chief delegate, remarked wistfully, "It's hard to believe that a few hours ago we didn't think we had anything to worry about."

Some of the delegates explained it had been difficult to take seriously Bush's exhortations to preserve Taipei's seat when Nixon had chosen this moment to send Kissinger back to Peking to make the final arrangements for his trip. The flood of publicity about how hungry Henry was wolfing down *Wor Shu Up* at the Peking Palace washed away any hope Bush might have had to preserve a remnant of our former policy.

Nixon seemed content to explore the *terra incognita* on which he had set foot, but clearly his hopes for what he would find had diminished. On November 9, after Dr. Kissinger's return, he once again cautioned the American people not to expect anything "dramatic" from his visit.

Spiro Agnew took a different tack to reach the same conclusion. He tried to make Kissinger's effort appear casual, almost comic. He told a fundraising dinner of rich, skeptical Republicans that one of the main results of Kissinger's absence from Washington had been to throw his many girlfriends into despondency. "The flag out in front of the Y.W.C.A. was flying at half mast," he joked soberly.

John Stewart Service, the former State Department official whose career had been ruined by McCarthy's charges of Communist sympathies during the 1950s, added to Nixon's note of caution. Although obviously pleased with Nixon's decision to make his trip to Peking, Service, after spending six weeks talking to the leaders of China, told reporters on November 11, "I don't think he's going to find a great deal of give and take."

The warning flags were up. A man truly interested in reconciliation might have become discouraged. But Nixon was truly interested, among other things, in the domestic political advantage he might achieve. The long series of preparatory conferences with our allies from France, Britain, West Germany, Japan and Canada in December, 1971 and January, 1972 kept his name on the front page. The pictures of stately ceremonials in which he was the central honored representative of United States power projected a continuous positive image of him through the dreary winter which marked the first months of his fourth year in office.

The Chinese had allowed him to select the dates that he would be their guest. He had chosen to arrive exactly two weeks before the New Hampshire primary. The four days he spent in Peking in "free-wheeling" discussions with Chou En-lai and Mao Tse-tung, and his subsequent visit to Shanghai and Hangchow allowed him to dominate the American news media up until the eve of the New England balloting. It was a unique way to campaign, but Congressman Paul McCloskey, who had been sloshing through the snows of New Hampshire for months in an attempt to stage an upset defeat of Nixon in this first primary, was willing to testify to how effective it was in burying whatever slim hopes he had.*

The pursuit of victory had taken him to Peking on February 21. His slow air boat to China took several days longer than it had to, and had the immediate effect of obliterating the chorus of criticism which daily appeared in certain journals.

His arrival at Peking Airport was delayed so that it could be viewed in prime evening television time in the United States, via a satellite transmitter which had been placed in orbit specifically to convey Nixon's image into every American living room.

That nothing was accomplished which could not have been accomplished, and indeed probably was accomplished, by Henry Kissinger in the role of Presidential emissary is underscored by the blandness of the final communique and the banality of Nixon's public remarks.

Escorted to the Great Wall, after 150,000 citizens of Peking had been roused out at 4:30 A.M. to chip and sweep the ice from his path, he gazed at the stone dragon that curled through the Loess mountains to the horizon. He appraised the miracle wrought by so many anonymous hands and relieved himself of the poetry which pounded through his brain. "I think that you would have to conclude that this is a great wall."

*Liberal McCloskey received 20 percent of the vote, and conservative John Ashbrook garnered 10 percent. Despite the fact that three of every ten Republicans voted against Nixon, McCloskey announced on March 10 that he was dropping out of the race because "the harsh reality of the situation is that you cannot run a credible Presidential campaign without substantial sums of money." That was a harsh reality supporters of democracy were going to have to face. In a partial attempt to deal with the problem, Senators Mike Mansfield and George Aiken introduced a Constitutional amendment on March 13 calling for a single national Primary Day to efficiently and mercifully select party nominees.

Escorted by a weary Chou through an exhibition of export merchandise in Shanghai on the last day of his visit, he peered through a magnifying glass at a microscopic seed of ivory on which was engraved Mao Tse-tung's "Ode to the Plum Blossom," and with a sigh of admiration informed the world of something it had never suspected: "Art is my weakness."

The joint communiqué was widely viewed as containing major concessions by Nixon toward the Communist regime, which were in no way reciprocated by the President's scrupulously proper hosts. Accepting Mao's premise of twenty-three years that there is "but one China and that Taiwan is part of China," Nixon went on to promise that "ultimately" the United States would withdraw its 8,000 troops, who had been symbolic protectors of the island. There was no mention made of Nixon's previous pledge to defend Formosa against "Communist aggression."

While the press of the world commented on Nixon's diplomatic defeat, Pat chatted with members of the reportorial staff on the plane winging back across the Pacific. Displaying a lack of comprehension of the meaning of what she had been experiencing, she revealed that she had been entranced with Chou En-lai. "He's a real charmer," she enthused girlishly. "He has a delightful sense of humor. We had some fun moments."

Always quick to claim victory where there had been defeat, Nixon delayed his return to Washington for nine hours, grounding his plane in Alaska until enough time had elapsed so that *Air Force I* would touch down in the nation's capital again in prime evening viewing time. The five thousand anti-Communist government officials and their families who turned out obediently applauded (much in the fashion that the five thousand party faithful greeted Chou when he returned to Peking airport after seeing the Nixons off), apparently motivated by their hopes that the President had done enough to safeguard their jobs for another four years.

Nixon's reversal of policy is undoubtedly for the good in the long run, as he now maintains. Any move toward peaceful conversation holds more promise than belligerent stiffnecked stalking. Chou En-lai's more moderate faction inside the Communist government was probably strengthened by Nixon's gesture of accommodation. The disappearance from view of hysterical chorusing Chinese waving Chairman Mao's handbook and chanting his vacuities was an immediate dividend for the New Nixon orthodoxy.

But what does this say about the years of relentless Nixon opposition to such a move? He had growled and clawed against a conciliatory approach, creating a fearful atmosphere which held off peaceful gestures for two decades. Might the bloody course of the Korean War have been altered if Nixon had gotten control of his Chinese Communist phobia twenty years before he did? Questions of that sort arise at frequent intervals when considering the twenty-three years of Richard Nixon's enormous impact on American foreign policy.

Although he only wanted to be President, the positions he took to get there destroyed the careers and reputations of many men and women and froze American policy into a rigid mold, which he would allow to thaw only after his main ambition had been achieved. Was the realization of that ambition worth all the misery it caused? Perhaps Henry Kissinger provided an insight into the way Nixon might answer that question if he could ever muster the strength to be frank.

> I believe in the tragic element of history. I believe there is the tragedy of a man who works very hard and never gets what he wants. And then I believe there is the even more bitter tragedy of a man who finally gets what he wants and finds out that he doesn't want it.

Nixon still seems a long step away from that confrontation with reality. Although Tricia's wedding and the new rapport with the Chinese Communists seem unrelated, they are symptoms of the same mental process. Richard Nixon still wants to be President, although he may, with Kissinger's help, be glimpsing the tragic shallowness of such an aspiration, when it is divorced from compassion and any sign of selflessness.

In the meanwhile he plots out a course that will once again take him to victory in the Presidential sweepstakes. Every advantage that can be gained from shock or sentiment will be seized. He is still the Richard Nixon who in 1960 could comment without flinching, "I believe that I spent too much time in the last campaign on substance and too little time on appearance: I paid too much attention to what I was going to say and too little to how I would look."

One of the tragedies of his life is that he is not likely to make that mistake again.

XXXIV.

Again No Personal Gains

However, the applause had scarcely died down after his China trip, when one of Nixon's closest associates dispelled the euphoria which had gripped the White House staff.

As leap-year February drew to a close, *Washington Post* columnist Jack Anderson reported the details of the romance between the Nixon Administration and the $7 billion conglomerate, International Telephone and Telegraph. The disclosure was made during the Senate hearings on the confirmation of Assistant Attorney General Richard Kleindienst to succeed John Mitchell. Anderson charged that Kleindienst and Mitchell had secretly made possible a settlement favorable to ITT in an anti-trust suit which was worth billions to ITT, in exchange for a $400,000 donation to the proposed August 21, San Diego Republican convention.

Anderson did not accuse Kleindienst or Mitchell of "personally" accepting money from ITT. The charge was much more serious. It involved institutional bribery of a nature, and on a magnitude never before seen in Washington. No longer were the bribes to individuals in the form of mink or vicuna coats. Furthermore, it quickly became apparent that President Nixon was directly involved, and was, in fact, the chief beneficiary.

Anderson published a memo dated June 25, 1971, stamped "Personal and Confidential" from boisterous Dita Beard, ITT Washington lobbyist, to William R. Merriam, head of ITT's Washington office. The memo dealt with her efforts to get John Mitchell, then Attorney General, to mobilize Nixon and those in the White House "on the higher level only" to bring pressure to bear against Richard McLaren, head of the Justice Department's Antitrust Division. McLaren was intent on divesting the conglomerate of its newly acquired control over the Hartford Fire Insurance Company, a move that would have been financially disadvantageous to ITT.

The memo was utterly frank and concluded with the discreet suggestion, apparently ignored, *"Please destroy this, huh?"*

The subject of Mrs. Beard's memo, clearly labelled so at the top, was the "San Diego Convention." Apparently some rumors had spread that ITT was subsidizing the Republican gathering and Mrs. Beard was fearful that this truth, if it became too widely known, would destroy her agreement with the *higher levels* of the Nixon Administration. She was urging caution. "If it gets too much publicity you can believe our negotiation with Justice will wind up shot down. *Mitchell is definitely helping us* [italics added], but cannot let it be known."

She had begun on a note of panic. "I'm so sorry that we got that call from the White House [asking, she later told Senators, about the size of the ITT donation to the Nixon campaign]. I thought you and I had agreed very thoroughly that under no circumstances would anyone in this office discuss with anyone our participation in the Convention, including me. Other than permitting John Mitchell, Ed Reinecke [Republican Lieutenant Governor of California], Bob Haldeman and Nixon (besides Wilson, of course [San Diego Republican Congressman]) *no one* has known from whom that 400 thousand committment [sic] had come."

She went on to enthuse about the benefits the $400,000 would produce for ITT. "I am convinced . . . that our noble committment has gone a long way toward our negotiations on the mergers eventually coming out as Hal [Harold D. Geneen, president of ITT] wants them. Certainly the President has told Mitchell to see that things are worked out fairly. It is still only McLaren's mickey-mouse we are suffering."

McLaren was dispatched with Florentine finesse. After Anderson printed the Beard memo, McLaren told the Senate Judiciary Committee that although he felt he could win his anti-trust case in the Supreme Court, he was led to abandon the effort after a good deal of pressure had been brought to bear on him.

The pressure had to be considerable, because in a forty-eight-page memo dated February 24, 1971, four months before he agreed to a settlement favorable to ITT, he had urged that court action was "essential . . . win or lose."

Describing the reasons for his determination to prosecute ITT, McLaren wrote that the merger plan of the conglomerate "involves a major acquisition by ITT whose history in the last decade makes it the most acquisitive corporation in the nation's history. Indeed, ITT is the archetypical example of the diversified corporation which has grown almost entirely by acquisition. It has swallowed some 101 companies. . . ."

In February it looked as if nothing could dull McLaren's determination to pursue his vision of a more truly competetive free enterprise system.

I recommend most strongly that we appeal this case to the Supreme Court. At my confirmation hearing, and since then, I have taken the position that the Antitrust Division must move vigorously to hold the trend toward economic concentration which has resulted from the wave of conglomerate mergers that have taken place in the last decade.

I have felt that this wave carried with it the same dangers for the economy at large as other types of mergers—a tendency to concentrate great economic power in the hands of a few. . . .

McLaren was about to see how effectively that economic power could be used. Apparently without McLaren's knowledge, six months before he wrote his forthright memo, his boss, John Mitchell, had been approached by ITT's Harold Geneen. Mitchell described the meeting, whose existence he had previously denied to newspapermen, to the probing Senate Judiciary Committee.

Geneen had come to him on August 4, 1970, to have "an entirely theoretical discussion" about mergers. Although the Justice Department was at that time processing only four anti-trust suits, three of which were against ITT, Geneen was only allowed to spend his thirty-five minutes with the most inaccessible man in Washington pleading against McLaren's policy of attacking mere "bigness."

Of course, it could be no other way. As Mitchell pointed out, if a discussion had taken place on the pending ITT cases, he would have been guilty of a conflict of interest, since his former law firm had once represented an ITT subsidiary. Therefore, Mitchell maintained, he had taken time out of a busy day to discuss "philosophy" with one of the country's previously unheralded economic philosophers.

While McLaren rushed to prepare his case against ITT the men on the higher level of government were concerning themselves with other matters. Mitchell was increasingly involved with the political aspects of Nixon's career. He had already begun to concentrate on the arrangements for Nixon's reelection campaign, which were soon to force him to submit his resignation as Attorney General.

The major effort of the White House staff now seemed to be to change McLaren's mind. On April 29, less than three months after McLaren had written his uncompromising memo, Mitchell arranged for two meetings in his office with ITT's merger expert, board member Felix G. Rohatyn. The meeting, Mitchell told the Judiciary Committee, had nothing to do with ITT. It concerned the merger of a New York brokerage firm which had attracted Rohatyn's interest. Present at that meeting was Peter M. Flanigan, White House aide, whose former law firm had ITT as one of its largest clients.

Immediately after the meeting Rohatyn was escorted downstairs in the same building to deliver his "presentation" to McLaren in an effort to persuade him to settle the three ITT cases. Mitchell apparently wanted Senators Edward Kennedy and John Tunney, who were questioning him closely, to accept his assertion that all of this was the merest coincidence.

A further coincidence was the fact that Peter Flanigan was then charged with the responsibility to find an "impartial" analyst who could make an "independent" study to see whether it was true, as ITT claimed, that it would suffer "hardship" and the stock market would suffer a harmful "ripple effect," if it were forced to divest itself of several of its subsidiaries.

The only man Flanigan could reach from his White House desk immediately outside Nixon's office was Richard J. Ramsden, a thirty-four-year-old Wall Street investment analyst, who had worked for Dillon, Read when Flanigan had been a partner of that Wall Street firm. Ramsden's money management firm, Brokaw, Schaenen, Clancy & Company, made a good deal of its profit from business dealings with ITT. Ramsden told the Senate investigators April 17 he was given his instructions by Flanigan and ordered to deliver his "independent" report to Flanigan.

To "help" him with the study Flanigan supplied one document, prepared by ITT, which Ramsden said was "in the nature of an advocate report." He told the Senators that Flanigan had not identified the source of the document. It was weeks after he had handed Flanigan his report that he discovered from the Senators ITT's authorship of the guideline document.

Although he drew no "hard" conclusions about the possibility of divestiture, he told the Senators that his report questioned "whether there would be any significant ripple effect" if ITT was forced to give up control of its contested acquisitions. Although he charged the government for only two days of superficial work, his *report* became the pivotal document on which McLaren was to base his eventual reversal. For some strange reason, having perhaps to do with the habit of some accountants to keep two sets of books, Ramsden was paid for his days of labor by the Commerce Department.

Almost immediately after Ramsden delivered his opinion Ed Reinecke, California's lieutenant governor, came east to visit with Mitchell. In May he confided in Mitchell that ITT had made a commitment to sponsor the Republican convention. When confronted with Reinecke's statement, Mitchell denied hearing any such thing during the visit, which he said he remembered being devoted only to Reinecke's plea for more aerospace industry in California, a unique subject to be raising with the Attorney General. He further explained that any remark Reinecke might have made about the Republican convention arrangements would make no impression on him, since he had "no interest in it."

The Senate hearings held the attention of the nation for weeks, winding their way through a labyrinth of contradictory statements. Kleindienst compromised himself immediately when he assured key Senators of the committee in a private meeting that he had absolutely no role in negotiating the ITT settlement, a statement he was rash enough to repeat before a public session of the committee, just before he was forced to "refresh" his memory and admit he had taken part in such sessions.

As the committee probed, the extent of big business dealings with the White House became more shockingly bizarre. ITT's Merriam ordered a crew of demolition experts into Dita Beard's office to shred every document in sight because, he told the astounded Senators, "there might be a lot of others in there like that [Beard memo]."

Anderson subsequently published the contents of another such memo. It revealed that ITT, with substantial holdings in Chile, was attempting to get the White House and the CIA to join it in an attempt to stage a coup in that South American country to prevent the 1970 election of its Marxist President, Salvador Allende.

Constantly challenging the image of corporate intelligence, and the credulity of a patient American public, were the antics of Dita Beard. With the publication of the memo by Anderson she disappeared from sight, only to show up days later in a Denver osteopathic hospital with a "heart attack." Her doctor, Victor L. Liszka, simultaneously being investigated by the Justice Department for alleged criminal activity involving Medicaid overcharges, told the Senators that she often behaved in a "distorted and irrational" manner. He publicly violated a basic canon of the doctor-patient relationship, in an apparent effort to convince the world that his patient's word could not be trusted. He admitted discussing the matter with the Justice Department before appearing at the committee session.

His strange behavior was matched by hers. When the committee's curious Senators could no longer restrain themselves and journeyed out to Denver on March 26 to conduct the hearings at her bedside, she alternately admitted and denied all, and then suffered a pain in her chest, according to her doctor, which resulted in the termination of her testimony. Her release from the hospital the following week raised some eyebrows, but, alas, the world is filled with skeptics.

The opinion of these skeptics was reinforced two weeks later when it was announced by the U.S. Attorney for Denver, James L. Treese, that the Justice Department was thinking of indicting another of Dita Beard's heart specialists, Dr. L. M. Radetsky. Dr. Radetsky had monitored the electrocardiograph machine at Mrs. Beard's bedside as she testified. As the Senators began to elicit some damaging responses, it had been Dr. Radetsky who told the shaken lawmakers that his patient had suffered a relapse and ordered the session terminated. He declared that the Senators would not be able to question her for at least six months; or, put another way, until after the election.

When informed of Dr. Radetsky's trouble with the Justice Department on April 11, Senator Kennedy complained bitterly. He said the members of the Judiciary Committee had looked to Dr. Radetsky for advice about Mrs. Beard's condition. He asserted that they should have been warned by the Justice Department of the possibility of criminal action against him.

Within the week two eminent heart specialists hired by the committee to examine Mrs. Beard reported that they were unable to detect any sign of an abnormal heart condition. Although they had conducted a series of independent tests, they reached the same conclusion.

The trail-covering operation became a major activity of several members of the White House staff. Almost immediately after he brought himself to accept the White House view on the ITT merger settlement, McLaren found himself tapped for a promotion to the federal judiciary. When the story broke, McLaren's knee-jerk reaction was to defend everyone's motives, but as the details of each participant's conflicting testimony began to fill in the outline of the Beard memo, he imposed a moritorium on any further comment.

Peter Flanigan, who was available for intimate conferences with the lobbyist of any suitably large American corporation, was forbidden by Nixon to honor the request of the United States Senate to enlighten it with an explanation of his role in achieving ITT's desires. When he finally testified on April 20, the limitations Nixon had set down as a condition for giving approval for such an appearance were so narrow that his few reluctant answers were unilluminating.

What had become clear, despite the most strenuous efforts to obfuscate the issue, was that the White House had become involved in negotiating an illegal political contribution from a corporation, which the corporation was making in return for a favorable settlement in a legal matter of paramount concern to its fortunes.

Grant, Harding, Truman and Eisenhower knew nothing about the scandals in their Administration until they read about them in the newspapers. The scandal in the Nixon Administration was of a different and more sobering nature. It is the first one that has taken place within the White House. Nixon is the first President directly implicated in charges that money could buy, on the highest level, White House favors.

Appearing before a press conference on March 24, the President tried to explain his attitude toward the involvement of White House aides in "dealing with law enforcement matters." He defended Flanigan and commented, "What is improper is for a Presidential aide to use influence for personal gain. . . ."

Echoes of the 1952 fund scandal seemed to be heard in his voice. Once again he seemed incapable of discerning any personal gain that did not result in a direct exchange of money which was immediately converted into some private corporal pleasure. He claimed to be unable to detect the personal advantage to Flanigan, Mitchell, Kleindienst, McLaren and himself.

It had become clear that the moral level which had allowed Nixon to blink his way through the Checkers speech had not perceptibly risen.

XXXV.

Nearing the Finish Line

Even after his 1960 loss, when he had made another renunciation of politics in writing to Pat, she knew he was incapable of keeping his word. "Knowing him," she said without anger in 1971, "I was positive he would get back in."

Nixon was in the race until the end. He had been side-tracked for a moment but a purpose molded so singlemindedly for two decades was not likely to be changed while there was still strength left. And so the grind of training went on, past the point where there seemed any reason to continue.

Many of those who watched him endlessly circle the track were unwilling to accept the testimony of their own eyes. They established the myth that Richard Nixon was too complex for us to understand; that what appeared to be he was really just the surface of a mystery. Earl Mazo said in 1959, "For all his prominence and the millions of words that have been written and spoken about him, surprisingly little is known about Richard Milhous Nixon."

As recently as 1971 the much more critical Robert Novak and Rowland Evans supported the myth when they wrote, "We tried to understand Nixon," but, "the more we talked to people, the more he seemed to be fading away from us."

Men who have known him well, in that symbiotic relationship that passes for friendship, often prefer to believe his austere veneer, his lack of human commitment and inability to communicate on any level but the political, is merely the outward aspect of an internally intricate mechanism whose workings are beyond their comprehension.

It seems likely that this is as far from the truth as one can get. Richard Nixon has been plumbed and probed as few men are. A multitudinous number of interviews have been recorded with him, Pat, his mother, his children and people who have known him back to the crib. His countrymen have often seen him on television as he took his stealthiest steps, where formerly men possessed by his ambition have had the comfort of the shadows.

We know much less about men who have been equally in the limelight, but about whom lack of information is never claimed. Lyndon Johnson quickly comes to mind. But even someone as well documented by public relations handouts as John F. Kennedy has left an enormous void in terms of his innermost life.

This is an aspect of the lives of public men. They practice to deceive, since success depends on a paradox. They must keep the high opinion of their peers for advancement, but they often must privately compromise with the devil.

It is not that information is lacking about Richard Nixon. It is that we recognize in our nation's leader a defensive, skittish person, fearful of human contact, who is capable of exhibitions of monumental insincerity and we are reluctant to place on him the final negative evaluation his nature merits. It is almost as if by doing so we would be casting a reflection on ourselves, our democratic form of government and our beautiful, vital country. After all, Nixon may have yearned for power, but we gave it to him.

So let it finally be said. He is just what he appears to be, a sad, lonely, morally bankrupt man, who trusts no one, knows that pain comes from all directions and would rather be somewhere else. We meet such people everyday, but not in the White House.

Why should he have ever wanted to be there? The answer lies partly in Toledano's observation that there is a magnetism about power. Even weak men want to be near it, to experience the sensation of potency it gives them. The illusion that the symbols of power, once they are won, will convert their weakness into invincibility forces many frail men into torturing themselves beyond reason. All for the empty reassurance of a cheering crowd. All because of an inability to function without tension toward more meaningful human goals.

In Nixon's case the torment has always been close to the surface. The tears that Toledano saw after the Vice President returned from visiting with Ike were tears visible to all men when Dick's need to commit some foul act was brought together with the knowledge of shame bred into him by Hannah and Frank.

The basic tragedy of Richard Nixon's public life has been the fact that he has never allowed his knowledge of right and wrong to keep him from doing wrong. He has always been so anxious to win that he has concerned himself with the appearance of truth, while always being ready to omit, exaggerate and lie when self-interest was to be served.

After 1969 the rituals and honors of his office hid this Richard Nixon from view. The press release image was softer, more thoughtful. There was an illusion that he was a different man. But it took no more than a too-clever appearance before the Bal Harbour leaders of the labor movement to reveal the emperor without his clothes. Once again he appeared ready to skin-out Jerry Voorhis, or run with Joe McCarthy if there was a clear enough margin of profit.

As election 1972 approached the incendiary Nixon emerged from behind the Georgian facade of the White House. He was mustering his energies for the final lunge toward the finish line. Having led most of the way would be meaningless if he did not, in this last great race, finish first. The final glittering prize, reelection, the indisputable proof that people thought he deserved to be President, would have to be won. It would determine whether he would be listed with John Tyler, Millard Fillmore, Franklin Pierce, or men like Theodore Roosevelt, Woodrow Wilson, yes even, perhaps, Dwight David Eisenhower.

There was involved in this the vanity as well as the loneliness of the long distance runner. That flawed motive which drives hollow men on helped Nixon rid himself of moral restraints as the challenge of the ballot box approached. With what appeared to be deliberate intent, but what was in reality by now a reflex action, he reverted to an earlier, youthful style, a style muted during the 1968 campaign, and which had not won for him since 1950. Apparently anticipating a much more difficult race than he had run in 1968, Nixon began to smear his opponents.

The first sign of it came on February 7 when his crew-cut trainer, H. R. Haldeman, took a position in the center of the track, with his stopwatch poised to clock his runner, who was just then turning into the final lap.

Haldeman made one of his infrequent appearances in public on the NBC "Today" show. Questioned gently by Barbara Walters, as they sat in easy chairs in front of a log-burning fireplace, he praised Nixon's thirty months of secret Vietnam negotiations in Paris. He completely ignored the fact that Nixon had chosen to start his campaign for reelection by destroying the secret channels of communication which had been established between Washington and Hanoi. It was a cheap price to pay in exchange for a quick spurt against his opponents.

Acting as if Nixon's newly spliced together, eight-point, conglomerate peace plan was likely to receive a better reception than his earlier fourteen, or ten, or five-point plans, Haldeman proceeded to berate the Democrats for voicing "the kind of criticism that can get in the way" of an affirmative answer from the North Vietnamese. Once he betrayed a willingness to accept that preposterous possibility, his subsequent leaps of imagination were not too startling.

Speaking with an intensity only an ad agency man on the make could muster, he said that before Nixon had revealed his super-plan to end the war, "you could say that his critics—people who were opposing what he was doing—were unconsciously echoing the line that the enemy wanted echoed."

Was he really going to say what it sounded like he was going to say? As his skin glistened under the hot television lights, he continued with great deliberation, "Now, after this explanation—after the whole activity is on the record and is known—the only conclusion you can draw is that the critics now are consciously aiding and abetting the enemy of the United States."

In words worthy of the old Nixon, Haldeman was accusing the Democrats of treason. Just to make sure that he was not misunderstood, Miss Walters asked whether he thought Senate critics were helping the enemy. Haldeman replied without hesitation, "In this particular posture, I think they are consciously aiding and abetting the enemy."

The statement was so extreme that for a while it seemed that Haldeman, who was known to be an unrelenting zealot, was merely letting some personal vitriol bubble to the surface. Such partisan, unfair charges had not been made since 1966 when Nixon began the year by denouncing Johnson for not escalating the war fast enough and ended it by accusing him of escalating incorrectly.

The Democrats were in a rage. Charges flew of McCarthyism and political demagoguery.

Two days later Nixon obliterated any thought that Haldeman had been speaking spontaneously without White House approval. In a radio address that morning he unctuously assured his opponents that he welcomed criticism and did not question their sincerity or patriotism. However, he said that their criticism should be of the nature that would contribute to, rather than deter, the search for an *"honorable* peace." [Italics added.]

He wanted to remind his opponents: "we have only one President at a time, [and] only the President can negotiate an end to the war." It was a less direct way of saying substantially what Haldeman had said so bluntly. While denying he was attacking the patriotism of his opponents, he was accusing them of aiding the enemy.

Disguising his partisanship under a frock of sanctimony, Nixon claimed that in the 1968 campaign he had, in a passion of nobility, refused to criticize Johnson's peace initiatives. This was a blatant distrotion of what he had actually done in that campaign. He had spent the better part of 1968 trying his best *not* to have to commit himself on the Vietnam war. He had deliberately attempted to side-slip the necessity of taking a stand on an issue where he was in basic agreement with Johnson, although he knew that a majority of the electorate did not agree with either of them.

NEARING THE FINISH LINE   387

Despite his oft-repeated claim that he was intent on leaving the Vietnam war out of the campaign because he did not want to interfere with the President's conduct of the war, he had managed to profit substantially from the war issue. As the campaign neared an end, his constant references to his "secret plan" to end the war proved the most effective criticism he could have leveled against his Democratic opponent.

The next day, February 10, at his first press conference in months, Nixon sharpened the tone of his criticisms. He claimed that if his opponents continued to state their objections to his position they might prolong the war by encouraging the enemy to postpone serious negotiations.

Blinking his eyes, he said, "The responsibility for the enemy's failure to negotiate may have to be borne by those who encourage the enemy to wait until after the election."

In short, it was not to be Nixon who failed to end the war in the four years he had been President. With a daring that was spectacular he was blaming the Democrats for his failure to honor his 1968 pledge.

In a barely-concealed attempt to silence criticism with the implication of treason he coolly advised his opponents to change their ways. "They apparently have determined that they wish to take another course of action. I disagree with the course of action. I would strongly urge at this point that all candidates for the Presidency . . . review their public statements and really consider whether they believe that they are going to help the cause of peace or hurt it, whether they are going to encourage the enemy to negotiate or encourage him to continue the war."

As Haldeman watched from a nearby couch, his stopwatch mind calculating the effect of each word, Nixon concluded, "You will have to let the people judge as to which is right."

In what had obviously been a carefully planned orchestration of Nixon's campaign against the patriotism of his opponents, Attorney General Mitchell, almost simultaneously addressing a group of Republicans in Washington, praised three Democrats, Humphrey, Jackson and Mansfield, none of whom at that time seemed likely to be Nixon's opponent in November, asserting that they at least were not "doing or saying anything to undercut the President's negotiating position." At this point Mitchell was two days shy of resigning as Attorney General in order to take on what Nixon considered a more important job, chairman of his reelection committee.

This was the same Mitchell who had witlessly cautioned the American public in 1969 never to believe anything said by him or his leader. "Watch what we do," he owlishly cajoled, "instead of what we say."

Mitchell was followed within hours by Secretary of Defense Melvin R. Laird, who told the Civic Clubs of San Diego that "Responsible men will not encourage the enemy to hold out in anticipation of a more generous settlement. Responsible men will recognize that we can have only one President at a time."

Sharing the California spotlight with him was Communications Director Herbert G. Klein. He told the Orange County Lincoln Club that Senator Muskie had "undermined prospects of a negotiated settlement in Vietnam."

Nixon has cast the shadow of a barracks emperor on the Presidency. Like those malevolent Romans, he was determined at all costs to seize and hold power. "Victory," as Chotiner put it, "is all that matters."

Some theorists claim Nixon is the quintessence of what our democratic system can be expected to produce in the way of a leader. Our politicians are encouraged, by the need to gain repeated endorsements from a superficially-informed electorate, to become charlatans, to blur their true character and to present an appealing, although often false, picture of who they are.

William Knowland suggested how close Nixon came to this pattern when he commented about him years ago, "I do not consider a Pepsodent smile, a ready quip, and an actor's perfection with lines, nor an ability to avoid issues, as qualifications for high office."

There is no myth implicit in what Knowland said. He did not throw up his hands and say, "I'll never understand that man." Instead he presented a vision of an empty man, quipping, grinning, reciting lines, in short the Nixon who during the last twenty years has bemused and astounded the decent.

In *Six Crises* Nixon is seen through his own eyes, and, although the posturing is often outrageous, there are surprisingly few myths about himself which he allows to stand. He pictured himself as being alternately calculating and belligerently semi-hysterical. Everything he described was in the form of a psychological emergency. He viewed most of these six episodes as moments in which he would survive or perish. They were not simply incidents, no matter how important, in a life filled with high and low points. They were crises in which the question in his mind was could he hold himself together or would he fall apart.

As he grew older and his responsibilities increased, his ability to handle them diminished. And so a wall was constructed about him, with sentinels at each gate, with orders to let no one pass. At the front gate Haldeman, at the back gate Klein, posting picket in front of "the quiet room" where Nixon now took afternoon naps, and guarding the Key Biscayne service entrance, Bebe Rebozo.

That concealed man, hiding behind a phalanx of praetorian mercenaries, is the product of the convention system. As such he owes his good fortune to the king makers who have controlled the five conventions at which his destiny has been determined. These men are not the delegates we watch every four years in convention city wearing the funny hats and answering the roll call when their delegation is being polled. The men responsible for Richard Nixon seldom appear in public and even less frequently run for office. They are not interested in the titles of office, but in the power conferred on them by the gratitude of those they have helped. They never present themselves to the voters for judgment about their abilities or programs. They are in the political business, and in that business men like Nixon achieve for them what they are incapable of achieving for themselves.

They saw in him, at a very early stage in his career, the qualities they valued. He had a mindless morality which allowed him to strike poses of seeming ethical substance. At the same time nothing they asked of him seemed to arouse his revulsion. He was a man capable of reasoning on a direct line and presenting a point of view in a simple, straightforward manner. But his ability to differentiate did not extend to the point where it challenged any basic premise they held. The affairs of others, their welfare, their happiness, seldom engaged him. His intelligence was consistently applied only to the sly process of self-advancement. He was anxious to do nothing, except win, which made him their perfect instrument.

His former doctor, Arnold Hutschnecker, generously concluded that, "His behavior indicates that, as President, he *may* [italics added] turn out to be . . . the controlled, adjusted personality, moving with strength through negotiations toward peace."

It was a gamble with bad odds. Having bent himself into a shape most pleasing to the king makers, Richard Nixon was hardly likely to develop, so late in life, into the well-adjusted, independent man of peace Hutschnecker tentatively suggested. He had compromised too much of himself in an endeavor to achieve the little that he had decided would be enough. Title without honor. Fame without approval. Power without purpose.

There is no doubt Eisenhower quickly came to know the nature of the man he had so casually allowed Tom Dewey to pick as his running mate in 1952. The scene of their reconciliation meeting in the mountains of Colorado after the Checkers speech, which has been immortalized on film, confirms the nature of the older man's feelings.

After the Wheeling airport reunion, the Republican National Committee decided it would be necessary to stage the reuniting of the leaders of the ticket in a sylvan setting which would convince the gullible of their enduring friendship. The two nominees were brought together at the side of a mountain stream and handed fishing poles. Then the cameras were turned on. In the first scene, the two anglers stood ankle-deep in the trout stream. Ike was expertly casting his fly line. They took one step upstream and Dick stumbled over his feet on the bed of rocks. Ike moved on.

In the second scene, Dick was watching Ike cast. As the general pulled back on his rod, Dick jumped three feet, as though he thought Ike were going to strike him.

The third scene showed Ike and Dick seated on a plank against the side of a log cabin. The sound was activated and Dick, sham intensity written on his youthful face, said that November was going to see a "victory for the party."

Ike turned patronizingly in his lumberjack shirt, and patted Dick's knee. "It will be a victory for the party and a victory for the country, *my boy*," he corrected with an acid smile on his face.

But Ike had left out the more important victory for his *boy*, the victory of Richard Nixon over his enemies. It was that victory which was then, and is now, the goal of all his efforts. Without Eisenhower the possibility of achieving that victory would have been remote. Without his bored acquiescence, without his vain, unjustified belief that as long as he was President it did not matter *who* presided over the Senate, Richard Nixon would have merely been a footnote in the history of California.

Instead raw persistence, and very little else, placed him at the head of the most powerful, justice-loving nation in the history of the world.

Henry Kissinger, while working for the cause of Nelson Rockefeller in the summer of 1968, is reputed to have remarked about his future boss, "That man is not fit to be President." That sentiment stands as the judgment of millions who have watched Richard Nixon make his way in politics. It is the judgment he sees in the eyes of many of his countrymen as he seeks their support.

There is only one more victory to achieve, and time enough to dream that with it will come contentment. Sorrow floods the mind at the realization that to win this race he will eagerly betray the last of the best that is in him.

Selected Bibliography

Adams, Sherman, *Firsthand Report; The Story of the Eisenhower Administration.* N.Y.: Harper & Brothers, 1961.

Alsop, Stewart, "Nixon on Nixon." *Saturday Evening Post,* July 12, 1958.

————, *Nixon and Rockefeller; A Double Portrait.* Garden City, N.Y.: Doubleday, 1960. (Transcript of the 1958 Nixon interview, as Alsop remembered it, in the Appendix.)

————, "The Square Majority." *The Atlantic Monthly,* February, 1972.

Ball, George W., "Nixon's Appointment in Peking: Is This Trip Necessary?" *The New York Times Magazine,* February 13, 1972.

Begeman, Jean, "Nixon: How the Press Suppressed the News." *New Republic,* October 6, 1952.

Bendiner, Robert, "All Things to All Republicans." *The Reporter,* November 4, 1954.

————, "The Chotiner Academy of Scientific Vote-Catching." *The Reporter,* September 20, 1956.

————, "The Presidential Primaries; Haphazard, Unfair and Wildly Illogical." *The New York Times Magazine,* February 27, 1972. (Brilliant Bendiner at his best.)

Block, Herbert, *Herblock's Here and Now.* N.Y.: Simon and Schuster, 1955.

Buckley, William F., and Bozell, L. Brent, *McCarthy and His Enemies.* Chicago: Henry Regnery, 1954. (Young Buckley defending the indefensible.)

Carleton, William G., "A Grass-Roots Guide to '58 and '60." *Harper's,* July, 1958.

Cater, Douglass, "Nixon for Nixon." *The Reporter,* November 13, 1958.

————, "Who Is Nixon, What Is He?" *The Reporter,* November 27, 1958.

————, "Government by Publicity." *The Reporter,* March 19, 1959.

Chambers, Whittaker, *Witness.* N.Y.: Random House, 1952. (Indispensable.)

Champion, Hale, "California's Governor Knight: Balance of Republican Power?" *The Reporter,* February 23, 1956.

Cooke, Alistair, *A Generation on Trial; U.S.A. v. Alger Hiss.* N.Y.: Alfred A. Knopf, 1950.

Costello, William, *The Facts About Nixon, An Unauthorized Biography.* N.Y.: Viking, 1960.

Coughlan, Robert, "Success Story of a Vice President." *Life,* December 14, 1953.

————, "A Debate, Pro and Con—Subject: Richard M. Nixon." *Life,* July 16, 1956.

Davis, Elmer, *But We Were Born Free.* Indianapolis and N.Y.: Bobbs-Merrill, 1952.

De Toledano, Ralph (with Victor Lasky), *Seeds of Treason.* N.Y.: Funk, 1950.

————, *Nixon.* N.Y.: Holt, 1956. (Written with the cooperation of Rose Mary Woods and the Nixon staff—an attack on Nixon's critics.)

————, *One Man Alone, Richard Nixon.* N.Y.: Funk and Wagnalls, 1969.

Donovan, Hedley, and Grunwald, Henry, "Interview with the President—Man of the Year." *Time,* January 3, 1972.

Donovan, Richard, "Birth of a Salesman." *The Reporter,* October 14, 1952.

Donovan, Robert J., *Eisenhower: The Inside Story.* N.Y.: Harper & Brothers, 1956.

Drury, Allen, *Courage and Hesitation* (Photographs by Fred Maroon). N.Y.: Doubleday & Company, 1971. (With the cooperation of the White House staff.)

Eden, Anthony, *Memoirs—The Reckoning.* Boston: Houghton Mifflin, 1965.

Ellis, Edward Robb, *A Nation in Torment—The Great American Depression.* N.Y.: Coward-McCann, 1970.

Ellsberg, Daniel, "Laos: What Nixon Is Up To." *New York Review of Books,* March 11, 1971.

Evans, Rowland, and Novak, Robert, *Nixon in the White House: The Frustration of Power.* N.Y.: Random House, 1971.

"Fighting Quaker." *Time,* August 25, 1952. (Cover story.)

Goldman, Eric F., *Rendezvous with Destiny.* N.Y.: Alfred A. Knopf, 1952.

Greene, Robert W., *et al.* "The Florida of Richard Nixon," *Newsday,* October, 1971. (Series of six articles . . . of outstanding value.)

Harrison, Selig S., "Nixon: The Old Guard's Young Pretender." *New Republic,* August 20, 1956.

Heckscher, August, "The Future of 'The Party of The Future': The Nixon Problem Is Not Yet Settled." *The Reporter,* September 20, 1956.

Hiss, Alger, *In the Court of Public Opinion.* N.Y.: Alfred A. Knopf, 1957.

Hughes, Emmet John, *The Ordeal of Power—A Political Memoir of the Eisenhower Years.* N.Y.: Atheneum, 1963.

Hutschnecker, Dr. Arnold A., "President Nixon's Former Doctor Writes About the Mental Health of Our Leaders." *Look,* July 15, 1969.

Johnson, Lyndon B., *The Vantage Point: Perspectives of the Presidency, 1963-1969.* N.Y.: Holt, Rinehart & Winston, 1971.

Jowitt, Earl (former Lord Chancellor of Great Britain), *The Strange Case of Alger Hiss.* Garden City, N.Y.: Doubleday, 1953.

Katcher, Leo (with Shannon, William V.), "The Story of Poor Richard Nixon" (Series of four articles.) New York *Post,* September 30-October 3, 1952.

Keogh, James, *This Is Nixon.* N.Y.: G.P. Putnam's Sons, 1956. (With the cooperation of Rose Mary Woods and the Nixon staff.)

————, *President Nixon and the Press.* N.Y.: Funk and Wagnalls, 1972. (Pleading of Nixon's case, finally as a member of the White House staff.)

Knebel, Fletcher, "Did Ike Really Want Nixon?" *Look.* October 30, 1956.

Kornitzer, Bela, *The Real Nixon: An Intimate Biography.* N.Y.: Rand McNally, 1960. (With the cooperation of Rose Mary Woods and the Nixon staff.)

Kraus, Sidney, ed., *The Great Debates: Background—Perspective—Effects* (including texts of the four debates). Bloomington, Indiana: Indiana University Press, 1962.

Lasky, Victor, "Why Nixon Was Nominated." *Look,* September 23, 1952.

Lurie, Leonard, *The King Makers.* N.Y.: Coward, McCann & Geoghegan, 1971. (The story of how Nixon became Ike's Vice President and a blast at the convention system.)

————, *Biography of the President: "The Man"* (Transcript of television program with Leonard Lurie and Ralph de Toledano). Maryland Center for Public Broadcasting, Baltimore, October 14, 1971.

Marine, Gene, "What's Wrong with Nixon?" *The Nation,* August 18, 1956.

Mazlish, Bruce, "Towards a Psycho-historical Inquiry: The 'Real' Richard Nixon." *Journal of Interdisciplinary History,* Vol. I, Autumn, 1970.

Mazo, Earl, *Richard Nixon: A Political and Personal Portrait.* N.Y.: Harper, 1959.

————, "Family's Comeback from Defeat: The Nixons Now." *Good Housekeeping,* March, 1962.

————, and Hess, Stephen, *Nixon, A Political Portrait.* N.Y.: Harper, 1968.

McGinnis, Joe, *The Selling of the President 1968.* N.Y.: Trident Press, 1969.

Miller, William Lee, "Religion, Politics, and the 'Great Crusade.' " *The Reporter,* July 7, 1953.

————, "The Debating Career of Richard M. Nixon." *The Reporter,* April 19, 1956.

Moos, Malcolm, *The Republicans—A History of Their Party.* N.Y.: Random House, 1956.

Morris, Richard B., *Fair Trial.* N.Y.: Alfred A. Knopf, 1952. (Account of the Hiss trials.)

Murphy, Reg, and Gulliver, Hal, *The Southern Strategy.* N.Y.: Scribner, 1971.

Nixon, Hannah M., "A Mother's Story" (as told to Flora Rheta Schreiber). *Good Housekeeping,* June, 1960. (Valuable source.)

Nixon, Patricia Ryan, "I say He's a Wonderful Guy" (as told to Joe Alex Morris). *Saturday Evening Post,* September 6, 1952.

Nixon, Richard M., *The Challenges We Face—Collection of Speeches and Papers.* N.Y.: McGraw-Hill, 1960.

————, *Six Crises.* N.Y.: Doubleday, 1962. (Indispensable, protracted exercise in self-revelation.)

————, "Why Not Negotiate in Vietnam." *Reader's Digest,* December, 1965. (At his most hawkish, shortly before assuming his low profile.)

————, "If Mob Rule Takes Hold in the United States." *U.S. News & World Report,* August 15, 1966.

————, "Asia After Vietnam." *Foreign Affairs,* October, 1967.

"Nixon Fights, Wins and Weeps." *Life,* October 6, 1952.

"Nixon's New Role." *U.S. News & World Report,* December 6, 1957.

Osborne, John, *The Nixon Watch.* N.Y.: Liveright, 1970.

————, *The Second Year of the Nixon Watch.* N.Y.: Liveright, 1971.

Panetta, Leon E., and Gall, Peter, *Bring Us Together; The Nixon Team and the Civil Rights Retreat.* Philadelphia: Lippincott, 1971.

Phillips, Cabell, "One-Man Task Force of the G.O.P." *The New York Times Magazine,* October 24, 1954.

"Quizzing Nixon." *U.S. News & World Report,* August 29, 1952.

Reuben, William A., *The Honorable Mr. Nixon.* N.Y.: Action Books, 1958.

Riggs, Robert L., "Flexible Dick Nixon." *The Progressive,* November, 1955.

Rogin, Michael, and Lottier, John, "The Inner History of Richard Milhous Nixon." *Transaction Magazine,* Rutgers University, N.J., November, 1971.

Rovere, Richard H., "Nixon: Most Likely to Succeed." *Harper's,* September, 1955.

————, "A Reporter-at-Large: The Campaign: Nixon." *The New Yorker,* October 13, 1956.

————, *The Eisenhower Years.* N.Y.: Farrar, Straus and Cudahy, 1956.

Rubin, Morris H., "The Trouble with Nixon, A Documented Report." *The Progressive,* October, 1956.

Safire, William, "Nixon's Way: A View from Within." *Washington Post,* October 3, 1971. (One of Nixon's speech writers discusses his speaking style, and makes it all very clear.)

Scammon, Richard M., and Wattenberg, Ben J., *The Real Majority.* N.Y.: Coward McCann & Geoghegan, 1970.

Schlesinger, Arthur, Jr., *Kennedy or Nixon: Does It Make Any Difference?* N.Y.: Macmillan, 1960.

Sevareid, Eric, *In One Ear.* N.Y.: Alfred A. Knopf, 1952.

———, ed. *Candidates 1960.* N.Y.: Basic Books, 1959. (Two interesting studies of Nixon from opposite viewpoints by Philip Potter and Frank Holeman.)

Shannon, William V., *The Nixon Story* (Series of six articles). New York *Post*, October 17-22, 1955.

Smith, Howard K., *White House Conversation: The President and Howard K. Smith.* Transcript, ABC Television, March 22, 1971.

Stevenson, Adlai E., *Major Campaign Speeches 1952.* N.Y.: Random House, 1953.

Sulzberger, C. L., "Interview with Richard Nixon on Foreign Policy." *New York Times*, March 10, 1971.

"The Nixon Story." *U.S. News & World Report*, May 11, 1956.

Truman, Harry S., *Memoirs.* Garden City, N.Y.: Doubleday, Vol. I, *Years of Decisions*, 1955. Vol. II, *Years of Trial and Hope*, 1956.

Voorhis, Jerry, *Confessions of a Congressman.* Garden City, N.Y.: Doubleday, 1947.

Walsh, Denny, and Flaherty, Tom, "How the Nixon Administration Blocked Justice," *Life*, March 24, 1972. (The revelations here, along with the ITT scandal, helped the Republicans decide on May 5 to move their convention to Miami.)

Walters, Barbara, "An Interview with the President." *Harper's Bazaar*, August, 1971.

Wechsler, James A., *The Age of Suspicion.* N.Y.: Random House, 1953.

Whalen, Richard J., "The Nixon-Connally Arrangement." *Harper's*, August, 1971.

White, Theodore, H., "The Gentlemen from California." *Collier's*, February 3, 1956.

———, *The Making of the President 1960.* N.Y.: Atheneum, 1961.

———, "Razor's Edge for Nixon and the GOP." *Harper's* February, 1961.

———, *The Making of the President 1964.* N.Y.: Atheneum, 1965.

———, *The Making of the President 1968.* N.Y.: Atheneum, 1969.

White, William S., "What Bill Knowland Stands For." *New Republic*, February 27, 1956.

Wills, Garry, *Nixon Agonistes.* N.Y.: Houghton Mifflin, 1970.

Wilson, Richard, "Is Nixon Fit to Be President?" *Look*, February 24, 1953.

———, "The Big Change in Richard Nixon." *Look*, September 3, 1957.

———, "Can Rockefeller Knock Off Nixon?" *Look*, April 28, 1959.

———, *Setting the Course the First Year; Major Policy Statements, Commentaries.* N.Y.: Funk, 1970.

Witcover, Jules, *The Resurrection of Richard Nixon.* N.Y.: G. P. Putnam's Sons, 1970.

Woods, Rose Mary, "Nixon's My Boss" (As told to Don Murray.) *Saturday Evening Post.* December 28, 1957.

Wren, Christopher S., "Nixon's Haldeman: Power Is Proximity." *Look*, August 24, 1971.

"You Won't Have Nixon to Kick Around Interview." *Newsweek*, November 18, 1962.

Zeligs, Dr. Meyer A., *Friendship & Fratricide—An Analysis of Whittaker Chambers and Alger Hiss.* N.Y.: Viking Press, 1967.

Newspaper files and media microfilm:

New York *Times*: for innumerable quotes and day-to-day data about Nixon's public
    activities. The *Times* is also invaluable for transcripts of press conferences and
    important speeches.
Washington *Post*: for the generous use of its facilities.

Time magazine and *Newsweek* magazine: two rich sources for material behind the
    Washington scene.
New York *Post* and *Newsday*: for their critical view which often exposes otherwise
    neglected sources.

Index